LEGAL ENCOUNTERS ON THE MEDIEVAL GLOBE

THE MEDIEVAL GLOBE

The Medieval Globe provides an interdisciplinary forum for scholars of all world areas by focusing on convergence, movement, and interdependence. Contributions to a global understanding of the medieval period (broadly defined) need not encompass the globe in any territorial sense. Rather, *TMG* advances a new theory and praxis of medieval studies by bringing into view phenomena that have been rendered practically or conceptually invisible by anachronistic boundaries, categories, and expectations. *TMG* also broadens discussion of the ways that medieval processes inform the global present and shape visions of the future.

Volume 2

LEGAL ENCOUNTERS ON THE MEDIEVAL GLOBE

Edited by
ELIZABETH LAMBOURN

ARC HUMANITIES PRESS

Library of Congress Cataloging in Publication Data
A catalog record for this book is available from the Library of Congress

ISBN 9781942401094
eISBN 9781942401117

mip-archumanities.org
Printed and bound in the United States of America

CONTENTS

LIST OF ILLUSTRATIONS

Plate

Figures

Maps

Tables

EDITOR'S INTRODUCTION TO "LEGAL ENCOUNTERS ON THE MEDIEVAL GLOBE"

ELIZABETH LAMBOURN

THE SEVEN ARTICLES gathered in this thematic issue analyze a variety of legal encounters ranging from South Asia to South and Central America, via the Horn of Africa, the Middle East, and Europe. According to its founding manifesto, connectivity is one of *The Medieval Globe*'s core foci: "the means by which peoples, things, and ideas came into contact with one another" during this era.[1] As a system of ideas embodied in people and enacted on bodies—and also as a material, textual, and sensory "thing"—law has been a primary locus and vehicle of contact across human history. Our choice of the term "encounter" further underlines the human components of these contacts: it is defined variously as "a meeting face to face" or "the fact of meeting with a person or thing."[2] Honing in on acts of encounter has encouraged our authors to reflect on the people behind and within legal systems, and on human encounters with various material expressions of law.

As a scholar of the "non-West" by training, my special aim was to ensure that work on European legal worlds would be placed alongside the varied and vibrant research on regions elsewhere on the medieval globe. (Future issues could, of course, broaden this lens still further, through contributions on legal encounters in Southeast Asia and the Far East, as well as across Austronesia, Oceania, or North America.) Of necessity, the period explored here is a "long medieval." Contributors engage with sources covering more than a millennium, from the fifth to the sixteenth centuries, and we have all written in full awareness of the complex and contested nature of periodizing categories and labels.[3] Until quite recently, for example, Americanists have not embraced the term "medieval" as a descriptor for precontact or early colonial eras.[4] For South Asia, the term has often framed by literal or metaphorical "scare quotes," and the same has been true for sub-Saharan Africa.[5]

---

1 Symes, "Introducing *The Medieval Globe*," 4.

2 *OED: Oxford English Dictionary*, 5:215, s.v. "encounter"

3 See Davis and Puett, "Periodization and 'The Medieval Globe.'"

4 This is changing rapidly: see, for example, Pauketat and Alt, *Medieval Mississippians*. The symposium "The Medieval Americas: Violence, Religion, and Cultural Exchange before Columbus" was convened at the University of Illinois on April 3, 2015: <http://www.medieval.illinois.edu/events/conferences/> [accessed October 3, 2015].

5 Again, this is changing: the symposium "Medieval Africa: The Trans-Saharan World,

The articles gathered here do not ignore this problem; indeed, Patricia Skinner's essay provides a particularly detailed survey of the term's loose chronological application in recent South Asian historiography and sets it against more common European usages. But on the whole, we have chosen not to see this as a barrier to scholarly dialogue. Nor is the need to establish points of direct contact between many regions of the globe an impediment to the exploration of synchronous histories or to meaningful dialogue among scholars across these regions. Ultimately, such comparative and methodological exchanges may lead to the elaboration of viable alternative terminologies, periodizations, and spatial imaginaries; for now, we aim to advance *The Medieval Globe*'s project of *doing* (as well as theorizing) globalized medieval studies. Hence each contribution offers a different, very individual example of this praxis, unified by our shared theme.

In keeping with this ethos of encounter, only three of our authors—Phillip Ackerman-Lieberman, Donald Davis, and Jerome Offner—might be described as legal historians, in the sense that the study of past legal systems constitutes, or at one time constituted, a primary area of their scholarly training and research. The majority of scholars writing here—myself, Susan Ramírez, Patricia Skinner, Habtamu Tegegne, and Laurel Wilson—are historians who use legal sources in our research. Some of us do so regularly; for others, this is a new engagement with legal materials and the specialist scholarship surrounding them. Contributors also range from well-established scholars to those who have only recently completed their doctorates. All answered a call for contributions that encouraged a broad interpretation of where and how the idea of legal encounter might be explored: whether at the intersection of different legal systems or within a single document, corpus, or locale; or through human representatives or practitioners of different legal systems. They were encouraged to think about legal encounters enabled by mobility, via mobile peoples' dealings with "Other" legal systems (legal extraterritoriality is a particular issue here) or in jurists' efforts to deal with forms of mobility (social, religious, economic, sexual) within their respective cultures. They were also urged to focus on places of legal encounter as well as legal encounters with, and accommodations of, novel ideas, people, or things.

In this issue, two articles center in different ways on one of the most geographically extensive and lengthy legal encounters in human history: that between European and indigenous American legal systems as a result of European exploration and colonization from the late fifteenth century onwards. Both contributions

500–1700" was held at Harvard University on February 5–6, 2015. Africa, South Asia, the Americas, and other regions are the focus of various ongoing projects sponsored by the Global Middle Ages Project (GMAP): <http://globalmiddleages.org/> [accessed October 11, 2015].

focus on the frequently cataclysmic encounters that took place in the "New World," although the questions they raise apply wherever Europeans, their laws, or their assumptions about law, have ventured. In "The Future of Aztec Law," Jerome Offner's aim is to recover "the substance and nature of a legal tradition developed in the Americas in isolation from the rest of the world and now forever lost in time."[6] Offner writes very explicitly for what he calls an "Old World" audience, presenting a historiography of Aztec jurisprudence and legal practice and outlining the special challenges posed by surviving sources. Although some of these challenges are unique, Offner's discussion addresses the perennial and pervasive problem of teasing out the interplay among established rules, jurisprudential principles, and actual behavior: the interface between law in theory and in practice. He also draws attention to the ways that premodern/indigenous sources have been shaped and contaminated by modern/imperialist categories and historical methods: a problem familiar to scholars in many fields. For example, his discussion of the graphic communication system (GCS) that mediated the Nahua language and an array of cultural practices emphasizes the extent to which the past performativity of so many medieval documents and recording technologies have been lost or overlooked. Law resided first and foremost in people, not texts, and our study of past legal sources will always be hampered by the impossibility of direct participant observation. In many ways, Offner offers a positive model for the future of the global medieval.

In "Land and Tenure in Early Colonial Peru: Individualizing the *Sapci*, 'That Which Is Common to All'," Susan Ramírez focuses very directly on the Spanish conquest and settlement of Inca Peru and the encounter between European expectations of land ownership and administration, and indigenous concepts of land and its occupation. Iberian newcomers carried ideas of permanent ownership rooted in ancient and medieval European precedents to the Inca empire's many ethnic groups, who conceived of the earth as so sacred "that it could not be possessed in perpetuity by anyone."[7] Ramirez's detailed discussion of often unpublished archival sources conveys the complexity and nuanced nature of this encounter over the course of the sixteenth century.

This issue's featured source showcases Habtamu Tegegne's study of a newly discovered legal text, "The Edict of King Gälawdéwos against the Illegal Slave Trade in Christians: Ethiopia, 1548." His recent find is an important contribution to the study of the slave trade in the Indian Ocean during this pivotal century, but his chief concern in this essay is to examine the immediate and longer term con-

6 Offner, "Future of Aztec law," 1.

7 Ramirez, "Land and Tenure in Early Colonial Peru," 34.

texts in which this document should be interpreted. Tegegne situates the edict (*fetha* in Ge'ez) within a deep history of Ethiopian law little known beyond specialist scholarship. With its layering of Coptic Christian, Islamic, and postclassical Romano-Byzantine elements, "the intricate and hybrid Ethiopian legal system exemplifies the interconnections and translation processes involved in the production of normative texts in many areas of the medieval globe, the result of cross-border communication processes and a special fruit of enduring Coptic-Ethiopian religious ties and interactions."[8] Parallel to this, Tegegne concentrates on situating the promulgation of the edict within the contemporary regional politics of the Horn of Arica, notably the decades-long war between the kingdom of Ethiopia and the neighbouring sultanate of Adal. Together with Elizabeth Lambourn and Phillip Ackerman-Lieberman's study of the reception of Chinese porcelain within the rabbinic systems of Aden's twelfth-century Jewish community (see below), Tegegne's analysis reveals the western Indian Ocean to be a place of significant and far-reaching legal encounters.

Indirect legal encounters are the topic of Patricia Skinner's contribution: "Mutilation and the Law in Early Medieval Europe and India: A Comparative Study." As its title makes explicit, this essay does not rest on evidence of contact between European and South Asian legal systems, but argues that placing them in communication with one another enriches the study of both. Skinner reminds us of Marc Bloch's assertion that comparison is "a means of better understanding one's *own* area of expertise, and exposing assumptions that a model developed in one part of the world [is] applicable, uncritically, elsewhere."[9] On one level, this is the intellectual encounter of a Europeanist with the unfamiliar sources and legal scholarship of South Asia; on another, Skinner's comparative exercise allows her to distil common aspects of the operation of law in both areas that are easily lost in narrower contexts. She observes that, in both Europe and South Asia, "written law *mattered* [...] and functioned as a symbol of rulers' authority."[10] While this may seem self-evident, all of the essays gathered here repeatedly point to the fact that laws are often promulgated or systematized at times of conflict, fragmentation, or rapid social change; this suggests that it was not so much law itself than the *making* of law, the processes of intellectual ordering and ceremonial publication, that mattered most. Law produced a physical, visual, and aural record of law making: a legal *thing*.

8 Tegegne, "Edict of King Gälawdéwos," 75.

9 Cited in Skinner, "Mutilation and the Law in Early Medieval Europe and India," 117.

10 Ibid., 120.

This point is upheld and demonstrated explicitly in Laurel Wilson's essay "Common Threads: A Reappraisal of Medieval European Sumptuary Law," an ambitious comparative analysis of the mass of seemingly inconsistent and ineffective sumptuary laws drawn up in the territories of Spain, Italy, France, and England during the thirteenth and fourteenth centuries. As Wilson cogently demonstrates, to read these laws as instrumental—as intended to effect real change—is to miss what they actively *did*. Wilson shows that the earliest bodies of sumptuary legislation reflect moments of rapid social change, in particular a multiplying urban elite or gentry that occupied an "interzone" at the juncture of older knightly classes and the upper bourgeoisie. In this context, sumptuary laws were not intended to control the wearing of specific types, colors, or qualities of clothing; rather, they affirmed traditional virtues and values, and ultimately sought to maintain the social order. The fact that they were never, or rarely, upheld and frequently repeated and reissued illustrates the core fact that "written law mattered" for its symbolic, ordering function.

The final two essays included here are Donald Davis's "Toward a History of Documents in Medieval India: The Encounter of Scholasticism and Regional Law in the *Smṛticandrikā*" and "Chinese Porcelain and the Material Taxonomies of Medieval Rabbinic Law: Encounters with Disruptive Substances in Twelfth-Century Yemen," co-authored by Phillip Ackerman-Lieberman and myself. Both turn around the organizing role of law in the face of what has been termed the "promiscuous profusion" of the real world.[11] In Davis's essay, the focus is the encounter between Dharmaśāstra, the Sanskrit textual corpus containing systematized discussions of all major legal topics, and the profusion of real world documents involved in a variety of legal processes. Taking as his starting point a key chapter on documents from the twelfth-century digest of Hindu law, the *Smṛticandrikā* (Moonlight on the Laws), Davis offers a new English translation of the Sanskrit text and, with it, a close commentary on the documentary taxonomies evinced in this source and their relationship to known documentary types. He uncovers the palpable tensions between the digest's "scholastic compulsion to be true to the commentarial tradition by not elaborating further categories of document beyond those mentioned in the accepted root-texts" and the author's own working knowledge of the abundance of documentary types that existed "'in accordance with local standards.'"[12] Working outward from this tension, Davis is keen to reinvigorate the study of South Asian documentary cultures, in particular by moving his discipline "beyond vague invocations of literacy and documentary culture in the

11 Clunas, "Trade Goods, Commodities and Collectables," 45.

12 Davis, "Toward a History of Documents in Medieval India," 169.

singular"[13] towards a more developed understanding of regionally and chronologically specific literacies, documentary functions, material patterns, and other issues. Like all of the contributors to this issue, Davis writes with the non-specialist in mind; and, like Offner and Tegegne, he offers a concise and cogent introduction to legal corpora and their study, alongside a specialist discussion of the opportunities that they represent.

The function of law in relation to "real world" objects and concerns is central to understanding the reception of new Chinese ceramic technologies among the Jewish communities of the medieval Middle East: the topic of the essay co-authored by Phillip Ackerman-Lieberman and myself. This essay brings rabbinic sources into direct dialogue with material culture through a collaboration by scholars specializing in each of these fields. It reflects part of a broader and very recent new direction within the study of Middle Eastern material culture, and one more commonly applied, experimentally, within the field of Islamic law. Recognizing that the objects of material culture were the product of legal processes as well as of craftsmanship, this strand of scholarship regards objects as sites of negotiation between the theory and the praxis of law. In this case, we focus on the encounter between material taxonomies developed within rabbinic Judaism as part of the regulation of purity (*ṭohora*) and impurity (*ṭuma*), on the one hand, and new ceramic technologies and types of object that did not fit these categories, on the other. Focusing on the earliest dated and located set of questions surrounding the taxonomic position of Chinese porcelain within this system, the article explores the implications of these questions for the history of porcelain's (ongoing) legislation within Judaism as well as the history of ceramic exchanges between China and the Middle East.

While ostensibly about legal encounters in the medieval past, this issue as a whole is also very much about encounters "in the now." Our sources have agency: they acted in the pasts that we study; they act in the world now in multiple ways; they act on us as we study them; and they act on others through the medium of scholarly publication. Most prominent among these interactions, perhaps, are the one-to-one encounters between the scholars and their legal source materials. However, encounters among academic disciplines, methods, regions, and temporalities also permeate these pages. These encounters range from purposeful cross-disciplinary collaboration, to comparative studies such as those of Skinner and Wilson, to encounters "on the page" with other bodies of scholarship testified in the footnotes of every contribution—and, of course, the plethora of verbal and written exchanges among scholars, past and present, that our acknowledgements

13 Ibid., 172.

only ever half capture. I think I can safely speak for my fellow contributors in saying that the process of producing this volume has helped all of us to articulate our own standpoints far more clearly than if we wrote safely inside our own disciplinary confines and for our usual specialist audiences. Offner, for example, explicitly marks his contribution as a place of encounter between the lost legal tradition he studies and the non-specialist readership to which he reaches out. Each of these essays constitutes an act of scholarly generosity in digesting a complex body of sources and scholarship for the benefit of new audiences.

In important ways, these essays also call attention to renewed encounters with indigenous and premodern legal systems. In Mexico, a new generation of contemporary Nahuatl speakers is returning to Aztec legal sources with new questions and frames of reference. All over the world, rabbinic texts dating back to antiquity continue to guide the behavior of observant Jews and to frame their relationships with almost every material object in the (post)modern home. In all of these encounters, the legal past is very much alive in the present. Recognizing this helps to underline the vibrant range of research being undertaken on, and from, legal sources. There is no human society that does not have law in some form, and there is a rich and growing body of scholarly work examining legal cultures around the medieval globe. Yet while some of this work is being undertaken within the discipline of legal history strictly defined, more often it is in the writing of other medieval histories that fresh questions about the nature and function of law and the creation of "legal worlds" are emerging. This makes for stimulatingly diverse interpretations of law's place in medieval studies, but it can also impede exchanges between regional specialists and among disciplinary specializations, lessening the overall impact and utility of this research. This issue of *The Medieval Globe* is accordingly designed as a space of encounter for scholars of law in all its aspects, in any context, and from diverse perspectives.

Bibliography

Clunas, Craig. "Trade Goods, Commodities and Collectables: Some Ways of Categorising Material Culture in Sung-Yuan Texts." In *Arts of the Sung and Yüan*, edited by Maxwell K. Hearn and Judith G. Smith, 45–56. New York: Metropolitan Museum of Art, 1996.

Davis, Donald R., Jr. "Toward a History of Documents in Medieval India: The Encounter of Scholasticism and Regional Law in the *Smṛticandrikā*." In *Legal Worlds and Legal Encounters*, edited by Elizabeth Lambourn, special issue, *The Medieval Globe* 2, no. 2 (2016): 167–98.

Davis, Kathleen, and Michael Puett. "Periodization and 'The Medieval Globe': "A Conversation." *The Medieval Globe* 2.1 (2016): 1–14.

Lambourn, Elizabeth, and Phillip Ackerman-Lieberman. "Encounters with Disruptive Substances: Chinese Porcelain and the Material Taxonomies of Medieval Rabbinic Law." In *Legal Worlds and Legal Encounters*, edited by Elizabeth Lambourn, special issue, *The Medieval Globe* 2, no. 2 (2016): 199–238.

Offner, Jerome A. "The Future of Aztec Law." In *Legal Worlds and Legal Encounters*, edited by Elizabeth Lambourn, special issue, *The Medieval Globe* 2, no. 2 (2016): 1–32.

The Oxford English Dictionary. 2nd ed. prepared by J. A. Simpson and E. S. C. Weiner. 20 vols. Oxford: Clarendon Press, 1989.

Pauketat, Timothy R., and Susan M. Alt, eds. *Medieval Mississippians: The Cahokian World*. Santa Fe: School for Advanced Research Press, 2015.

Ramírez, Susan Elizabeth. "Land and Tenure in Early Colonial Peru: Individualizing the *Sapci*, 'That Which Is Common to All.'" In *Legal Worlds and Legal Encounters*, edited by Elizabeth Lambourn, special issue, *The Medieval Globe* 2, no. 2 (2016): 33–71.

Skinner, Patricia. "Facial Mutilation and the Law in Early Medieval Europe and India: A Comparative Study." In *Legal Worlds and Legal Encounters*, edited by Elizabeth Lambourn, special issue, *The Medieval Globe* 2, no. 2 (2016): 115–139.

Symes, Carol, "Introducing *The Medieval Globe*." *The Medieval Globe* 1 (2014): 1–8.

Tegegne, Habtamu Mengistie. "The Edict of King Gälawdéwos against the Illegal Slave Trade in Christians: Ethiopia, 1548." In *Legal Worlds and Legal Encounters*, edited by Elizabeth Lambourn, special issue, *The Medieval Globe* 2, no. 2 (2016): 73–114.

Wilson, Laurel Ann. "Common Threads: A Reappraisal of Medieval European Sumptuary Law." In *Legal Worlds and Legal Encounters*, edited by Elizabeth Lambourn, special issue, *The Medieval Globe* 2, no. 2 (2016): 141–165.

Elizabeth Lambourn (elambourn@dmu.ac.uk) is Reader (Associate Professor) in South Asian and Indian Ocean Studies at De Montfort University in the United Kingdom, where she works on diverse aspects of mobility in the precolonial Indian Ocean world. Coming to history from a background in the study of material culture, her research is particularly focused on the identification and study of new material archives and on Indian Ocean materialities.

Abstract This introduction presents and draws together the articles and themes featured in this special issue of *The Medieval Globe*, "Legal Encounters on the Medieval Globe."

Keywords Law, legal systems, jurisprudence, global studies, medieval studies, encounter, connectivity.

THE FUTURE OF AZTEC LAW

JEROME A. OFFNER

THE YEAR 2019 will mark half a millennium from the Spanish intrusion into central Mexico. Throughout this region and beyond, the Spaniards encountered a great world civilization, enormously complex and ancient, some small portions of which a few members of their society managed to record, motivated by conventional religious, economic, political, and legal concerns, although often as well by fascination with what they encountered.[1] As the postcontact society and economy changed, more rapidly in some areas than others, asserting and ascertaining the content of precontact Aztec law became a vital concern of Spanish missionaries,[2] colonists, colonial administrators, surviving indigenous elites, and indigenous communities.[3] Although the fate of indigenous law under the new Spanish hegemony is a compelling topic in itself,[4] this article is concerned with recovering the substance and nature of a legal tradition developed in the Americas in isolation from the rest of the world and now forever lost in time. What we can know of this unique tradition, nevertheless, remains of interest to millions of contemporary Nahuatl speakers in Mexico as well as to Mesoamerican researchers and all scholars interested in comparative legal systems.

In the 1980s, I published a monograph and a series of articles on Aztec law, concentrating on the city and small empire of Texcoco, where documentation on precontact law was most plentiful. Although I was careful to communicate the dynamism, factional disputes, and change in the Texcocan system in these works,

---

1 Townsend, *The Aztecs*; Coe and Koontz, *Mexico;* and Smith, *The Aztecs*, provide broad and detailed descriptions of the civilization encountered, although there is no consensus view on many of its aspects.

2 The term "Aztec" has increasingly been replaced by the name of the hegemonic ethnic group, the Nahua (see below), in spite of the fact that there were many ethnic groups in the region (e.g., Otomi, Totonac, Tepehua, etc.), often successfully living together, although generally (but not always) under Nahua rule. The Nahuas were not themselves a unitary group; subgroups exhibited significant cultural and linguistic differences that often, in conjunction with differing economic interests, led to armed conflict. In this article, "Aztec" will generally be employed to emphasize the political and legal administration of this multiethnic situation.

3 Gibson, *The Aztecs under Spanish Rule*, remains the classic study in this respect, along with later work by García Martínez, *Los pueblos de la Sierra*.

4 E.g., Cline, *Colonial Culhuacan*; Kellogg, *Law and the Transformation of Aztec Culture*; Megged, "Between History, Memory, and Law."

I reemphasized these aspects in an article in 1993 on inter-state and intra-familial killing as vigorously pursued by the elite in Aztec societies.[5] Although Mesoamerican studies have continued to develop in the past two decades, no other investigator primarily interested in precontact Aztec law has emerged, with the exception of Carlos Brokmann Haro.[6] In almost all other instances, Aztec law continues to be mentioned only in decontextualized fragments. Meanwhile, some investigators (such as Frederic Hicks and Pedro Carrasco) have persisted in declaring what the content of Aztec law must have been as determined by their own Marxist and Polanyist ideologies, especially with regard to land tenure and political structure. Other investigators have taken an empirical approach to the available data, revealing the nuances and complexities found in reality.[7] In one of Hicks's last articles, for example, we see him working to reconcile the richness of detail regarding land tenure, as reported in sources from Tlaxcala (just outside the Basin of Mexico), with the strictures of his ideology.[8]

Perhaps the major current tendency, however, has been to mistake reports of Aztec laws,[9] whether in pictorial or alphabetic form, for the entirety of the Texcocan legal system,[10] with little consideration given to the evident but poorly understood intricacies of Aztec jurisprudence and how it varied from town to town across the empire.[11] It is, in fact, in the richness of reports of precontact indigenous behavior

---

5 See comments below on limitations on the power of Aztec rulers.

6 Haro, *La estera y la silla*. This short monograph is essentially an extended review of published work, rather than the product of original source research. Nevertheless, it follows and presents both legal and anthropological issues well while deftly contextualizing the Aztec legal system with special attention paid to the interests of Mexican readers. Some areas of agreement and a few areas of disagreement with this valuable study are mentioned below.

7 E.g., Harvey and Prem, *Explorations in Ethnohistory*; and Cline, *Colonial Culhuacan*.

8 Hicks, "Land and Succession in the Indigenous Noble Houses of Sixteenth-Century Tlaxcala."

9 Or, more specifically, what may or may not be legal rules: see below.

10 Lee, "Reexamining Nezahualcóyotl's Texcoco" and *Allure of Nezahualcoyotl*. See also Mohar Betancourt, *Códice Mapa Quinatzin.*

11 Haro understands the importance of appreciating and analyzing the Aztec legal system as more than just a list of legal rules. Nevertheless, he unaccountably believes that adherence to legal rules in precontact Mexico was so strong that "true jurisprudence" (*jurisprudenica verdardera*) could not develop: *La estera y la silla,* 13–14, 94. (The use of "true" when coupled with a modern Western understanding of a concept usually signals a lapse into ethnocentricity by a modern Western writer insisting that the cultural concepts of "the Other" should be the same as or very similar to modern Western concepts.) On the contrary, numerous reports regarding the creation and application of law in rapidly changing

that we can begin to appreciate the interplay between legal rules,[12] jurisprudential principles, and everyday conduct among the Aztecs, as well as the actual behavior within and attitude towards the legal system. At the same time, we can gain hints regarding how the various legal systems regarded plaintiffs and defendants and how legal process actually functioned. Such sources also record social discord and dysfunction, as well as cohesion; and the intersection of indigenous conceptions of law and morality.[13] Chief among these are the works of Fray Bernardino de Sahagún, a Franciscan friar who worked with indigenous informants in the sixteenth century to produce an encyclopedic account of Aztec culture.[14]

This necessarily brief article is written for specialists in Old World medieval studies and is intended to: introduce the nature of and the challenges involved in interpreting the surviving materials; highlight some interesting aspects of Aztec law and society; and suggest fresh approaches to Aztec law, given new tools available for research on Mesoamerica. The relative paucity of information compared to other vanished legal systems, especially in the areas of case law, legal process, and jurisprudence, presents many problems for students of comparative law; but perhaps specialists can also find here new avenues of research into this distinctive legal tradition, a last representative of precontact jurisprudential thought and

---

Aztec society, a few of which are cited below, make it clear that jurisprudential thought was both sophisticated and highly valued among the Aztecs. The reputation of Nezahualcoyotl, the ruler of Texcoco (1431–72), rested in considerable part on his success in redesigning and managing the legal system of Texcoco during tumultuous and divisive times. Specific instances of legal reasoning, where legal rules did not fit the facts of a precontact case, can sometimes be found carefully recorded across the contact boundary decades after the case occurred. In addition, there were many regular meetings of legal personnel in which difficult cases could have been discussed and decided both among themselves and in consultation with the rulers, e.g. Offner 1983: 56.

12 E.g. Offner, Law and Politics in Aztec Texcoco, p. 56. "Legal rules" (*leyes*) were *nahuatīlli* in Nahuatl, a noun derived from the verb *nahuatiā*, "to give orders to someone" (Karttunen, *Analytical Dictionary of Nahuatl*, 157). It is worth noting that the verb *nāhuati*, "to speak clearly," and the noun *nāhuatl*, "something that makes an agreeable sound," are distinguished from the first pair of words by a long initial vowel *ā* instead of a short *a*.

13 See Burkhart, *Slippery Earth,* for the best description of Aztec mores and morality.

14 Sahagún's account of Aztec culture includes extensive parallel passages in Nahuatl and Spanish. His efforts were directed at eliminating Aztec religious practices by better understanding them, but the enthusiasm of his informants was clearly contagious, and all manner of data was incidentally collected along with the targeted information the informants chose to share. See Klor de Alva, Nicholson, and Keber, *The Work of Bernardino de Sahagún*; and León Portilla, *Bernardino de Sahagún*. Calnek, "The Sahagún Texts," presents an early and still very useful series of observations on indigenous and Spanish biases and perspectives in Sahagún's work.

practice in what came to be called the New World. They may also find that the problems and methods surveyed here are applicable to sources produced in other areas of the medieval globe.

The Nature of the Sources on Aztec Law and Two Introductory Examples

The remnant sources of precontact Aztec law are found principally in:[15] a few dozen Spanish alphabetic texts produced by Spanish colonists and Nahuas;[16] perhaps two dozen published alphabetic texts of the Nahuas, produced in their language, Nahuatl; and several dozen published documents produced by Nahuas employing a sophisticated graphic communication system (GCS) that was far more complicated in its messaging than linear text.[17] In addition, some alphabetic

15 This article does not provide a catalogue of such sources, both because of their number and the deep contextualization of law in many sources. The numbers provided above are rough approximations made more imprecise by the difficulty in separating reports of precontact Aztec law from indigenous law as it developed in the colonial period. The major sources of Aztec law are mentioned in this article, its bibliography, and in Offner, *Law and Politics in Aztec Texcoco*. However, there are occasional mentions of indigenous law in the 161 reports from towns where Nahuatl was spoken, compiled in the *Relaciones Geográficas* series (see Cline, "The Relaciones Geográficas"; Harvey, "The Relaciones Geográficas"). *The Handbook of Middle American Indians* (vols. 12–15) and *Supplement to the Handbook* (vols. 3–5) remain the definitive guide for sorting through the many hundreds of available published sources to identify candidates possibly containing information on precontact Aztec law. In addition, colonial archival and community-owned materials, including pictorial manuscripts, are continually being brought to light with many finding their way to publication.

16 As noted above (n. 2), the Nahuas were and are a diverse group of speakers of Nahuatl, a member of the Uto-Aztecan language family. Representatives of this group are found in the North American West (e.g., Shosoni, Comanche, Hopi) and Mexico (e.g., Yaqui, Cora, Mayo, Huichol). Exactly when Nahuas arrived in Mesoamerica remains controversial: see Dakin and Wichmann, "Cacao and Chocolate." They did not enter in a single wave and the last surge of migration, after ca. 1100 CE, was very likely motivated by extended drought conditions and the perception of richer societies and more comfortable living conditions further to the south—reasons sometimes mentioned in the indigenous sources. Among the members of this last wave of migrants were the Mexica who founded Tenochtitlan and eventually its empire. The Nahuas were not the only immigrant group in the region. Texcoco was founded by groups of unknown linguistic affiliation whose later ruler, Techotlalatzin (ca. 1377–1409) was credited with declaring Nahuatl the official state language. See Offner, *Law and Politics in Aztec Texcoco*, 37.

17 Appreciation of the complexity of this graphic communication system has been enhanced recently by the groundbreaking work of Katarzyna Mikulska ("'Secret Language'"

sources were based on Nahua documents that had been originally produced using their GCS. The distinctive nature of this evidence shapes the modes of argumentation as well as what can be said or hypothesized about the Nahua legal tradition.

To illustrate the complexities of these historical materials and the methods developed to deal with them, we will consider two examples from the available sources: an early Spanish source based on indigenous pictorial manuscripts and accompanying oral performances, and a slightly later indigenous pictorial source rendered in the Nahua GCS, although with a degree of Spanish influence. This pair of examples will begin to illustrate the range of both difficulties presented and possibilities offered by the data.

The first example comes from the last pages of the *Historia de los Mexicanos por sus pinturas* (History of the Mexicans through Their Paintings).[18] This document can be dated to about 1535,[19] or within a generation of the Spanish intrusion. And, as its title implies, it is written in Spanish and based on documents prepared in the Nahua graphic communication system. The author of the document, perhaps the early and celebrated Franciscan missionary Fray Andrés de Olmos, tells us that he compiled the report from various *libros y figuras* (books and images) presented and explained to him by *viejos* (old people) who had held indigenous religious and political positions and who had therefore been present when texts and images had been used in performance.[20] Such coordination between indigenous written and oral performances was vital to the Nahua GCS, and the complexity and volume

---

and *Tejiendo destinos*), with some aspects of it being applied to non-religious documents by Offner ("Ixtlilxochitl's Ethnographic Encounter"). Although glyphs are found in considerable numbers in such important historical documents as the *Mapa Quinatzin* or *Codex Xolotl* (*Códice Xolotl*, ed. Dibble), they provide only a portion of the meaning communicated. Most of the messaging is accomplished by richly generative sets of standardized images arranged in similarly richly generative standardized methods on pages or in sculptural compositions. These compositions have usually been casually swept into the Western conception and classification of iconography. Although writing is usually taken to involve sets of signs of similar size in some form of alineation, the Nahua GCS challenges this definition. Further, these documents were only a part of an overall communication system that coordinated them with oral presentation and performance, with the ultimate meaning tailored to the composition of the audience. The deliberate multivalence of this system also facilitated geopolitical analysis, diplomacy, warfare and other forms of statecraft, as well as negotiation for rights to land, labor and tribute in both the precontact and postcontact eras. See Offner, "Exploring"; "Improving Western Historiography"; and "Ixtlilxochitl's Ethnographic Encounter."

18 *Historia de los Mexicanos por sus pinturas* (ed. García Icazbalceta), specifically 258–62.

19 Gibson and Glass, "A Census," 345.

20 *Historia de los Mexicanos por sus pinturas,* 228.

of information that could be communicated in this way was more similar to the multimedia environment of a play or a movie than to the experience of reading a linear alphabetic text, which had little hope of capturing more than a small portion of either the intended or available meanings.

The effort of understanding this alien communication system is rewarded by far greater insight into Aztec and Nahua cultures, which require a departure from persistent Western text-centric notions of the (largely illusory) advantages ascribed to linear text, such as the supposed lack of ambiguity in such texts or beliefs that such texts enjoy fixed meanings across time. For example, the Spanish descriptor *libros* (books) used to describe the objects presented to the author of the *Historia* is misleading, since common forms of written documentation in the precontact era were screenfolds, or individual pages of indigenous paper or animal skin. To confuse matters further, any Mesoamerican document, precontact or postcontact, with even a minimal amount of illustration has come to be known as a *códice* (or codex), although only a very few postcontact works actually take the form of a codex.[21] Most, if not all, indigenous written compositions were not designed to be read from end to end, but served instead as reference or source books. Furthermore, indigenous documents were not the statement or source of a fixed and set text but were instead bases for explication, explanation, justification, and elaboration of themes both visible on the page and known in the culture. The Nahua graphic communication system thus allowed both specific and non-specific messages to be conveyed, depending on the associated oral presentation of the experts communicating the content of a document. Certainly, the document's content limited the range of possible presentations, and glyphs might name particular places and people and dates might be specified, further limiting possible interpretation and presentation, but it is unlikely that any one presentation of an indigenous document was identical to another.[22]

In the context of Nahua studies, the *Historia de los Mexicanos por sus pinturas* is therefore a very early and valuable source based on, but containing only a small portion of, what was available in the (now lost or dead) indigenous sources and people from which it was derived. Yet its legal content has been little studied. It is also of particular interest because it is the recording of an ethnographic encounter between a Spanish priest and a group of indigenous experts that serves as a striking memorial of the gulf that persisted between the Spaniards and the Aztecs more than a decade after first contact. Most of the insights into Aztec culture must be obtained from inference and through indirection.

21 See Boone, "Aztec Pictorial History."

22 See Mikulska, "'Secret Language.'"

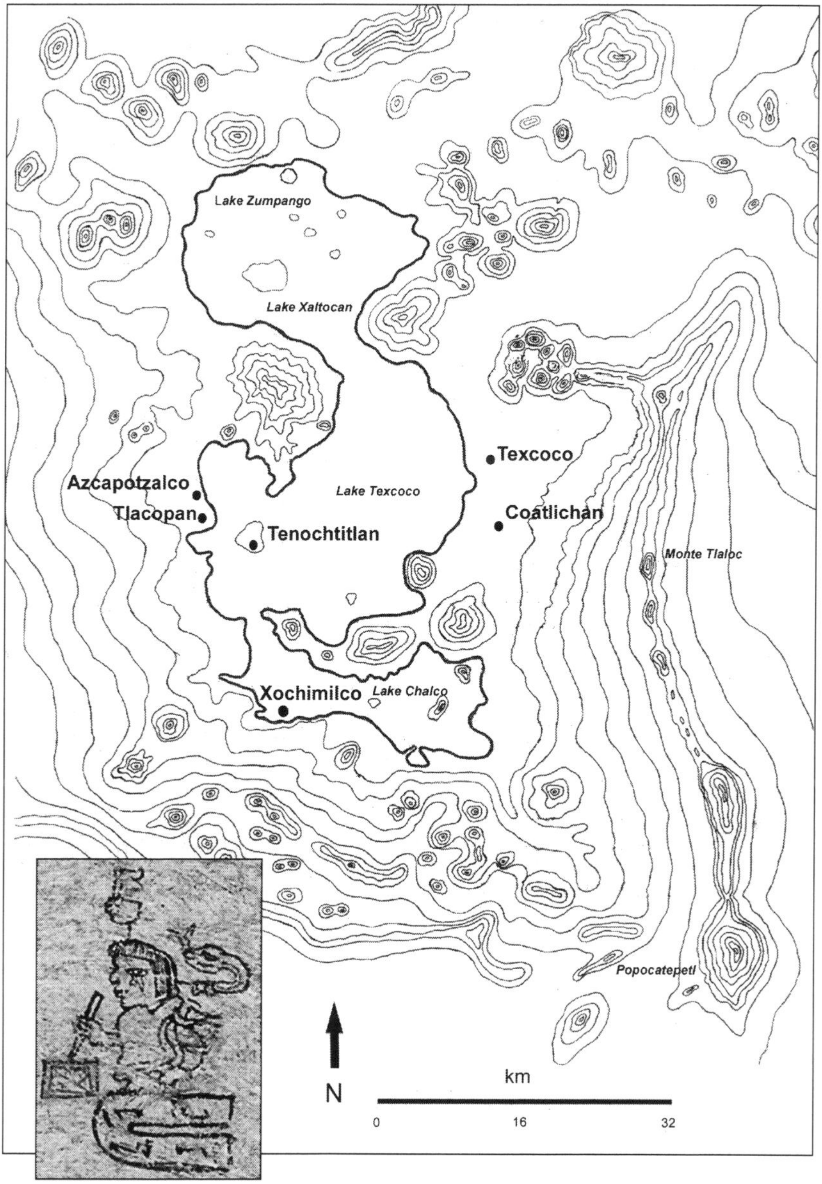

Map 1. Cities in the Basin of Mexico. The inset shows the scribe named Coatl ("Serpent"), who arrived in Texcoco with his people, the Tlailotlaque, during the reign of Quinatzin (which ended ca. 1377) and who was carefully depicted in the Codex Xolotl more than a century later, by a successor and perhaps direct descendant *(Paris, Bibliothèque nationale de France, MSS mexicain 1.1). Contour lines and city locations have been adapted with permission from Jeffrey R. Parsons,* Prehispanic Settlement Patterns in the Texcoco Region, Mexico *(Ann Arbor: University of Michigan Museum of Anthropology, 1971), 4.*

The legal materials included in this source begin with the ruling dynasty of Tenochtitlan (now part of Mexico City; see **Map 1**), which came to be the most important Aztec city well before 1519. In this section, a ruler is named, along with length of rule; for example, Acamapichtli (ca. 1376–ca. 1396)[23] is considered the founder of the Mexica ruling line in Tenochtitlan, so his reign of twenty years is noted along with what can be described as legal decisions, as well as jurisprudential considerations and their supporting rationales, as elicited from the Nahua witnesses by the Spanish author.

The first legal decision mentioned involves two women who had sex with each other. Some legal process is detailed: they were stoned at a certain place near the most powerful city of the time, Azcapotzalco, after the ruler of that city had informed and gotten agreement first from the ruler of Coatlinchan and from Acamapichtli of Tenochtitlan, which was probably the least important town of the three at that time. A second decision arose from the death of the brother of the ruler of Azcapotzalco, the powerful Tezozomoc (ca. 1371–ca. 1426). He married his brother's widow, but she went to the nearby town of Xochimilco and had sex with a man, and the same three rulers as before had ordered them to be stoned. The Spanish author then states—*dicen* (they say), referring to his informants—that it was *costumbre* (the custom) that a widow should only marry her husband's brother, thus making a distinction between law and custom. Left implied is exactly why the two were stoned—the commission of a *maldad* (wicked act/perversity) is the only offense mentioned—but since it occurred after the ruler Tezozomoc had taken her as his wife, the offense was presumably adultery, for which the penalty was often stoning. We next learn that if a woman married someone other than her husband's brother, any lands and what they contained would be taken from her. This is not conveyed so much as a legal decision but as a standard administrative procedure, clearly to preserve resources among consanguineal kin. We know that land could be attached to offices, to entities, or owned by individuals, including women, with bundles of rights and duties attached to each situation, but we are not told what types of land were involved in this case.[24] Thus, we can already see legal process and decision-making, along with administrative procedure, in operation at this time and in relation to prevailing custom, all within a multi-ethnic, if small, imperial structure centered on the city of Azcapotzalco. It is worth noting

23 The regnal dates of the first three rulers of Tenochtitlan are not precise but fall within a fairly narrow margin of error when available sources are collated and compared: see Boone, "Aztec Pictorial History," 38, 152–53. Here, I reference the indigenous dates painted in the *Codex Mendoza.*

24 Offner, *Law and Politics in Aztec Texcoco*, 93, 114, 124–39, 143–44, 146–47, 151, 167, 170–71, 205–6, 214, 217, 219, 222–23, 245, 279.

that these cases are reported as historical occurrences and not as hypothetical examples for jurisprudential contemplation, although perhaps the informants sought to engage the Spanish author in such an exercise by providing such striking examples. The friars' persistent interest in and puzzlement with regard to indigenous sexual behavior and mores must have been obvious to the Aztecs by the time of this interview.

As mentioned above, the *Historia de los Mexicanos por sus pinturas* was the product of a new and daunting ethnographic interface, involving translation not merely of Nahuatl to Spanish, hardly ten years after first contact, but also the translation and comprehension of complex pictorial documents and oral performances. It is unlikely that the indigenous experts were allowed to develop their full oral performances on particular topics,[25] and the lack of shared knowledge evidenced by the Spanish priest as he failed to engage with them productively in expected ways must have been deeply disturbing and dismaying to the experts as evidence of his appalling ignorance and lack of proper education. In addition, little evidence of systematic questioning guided by Western legal training can be detected in the testimony of the Spanish author.[26] The linked mentions of administrative procedure and custom in response to the case involving the ruler of Azcapotzalco's brother's widow illustrate the complexity of information generated by this ethnographic encounter, yet the author could only capture a fraction of this information in his alphabetic script. The incomplete descriptions of the legal cases and supporting jurisprudential thought, therefore, whether in this or in other documents, were a product of inadequate ethnographic investigation and recording rather than defects or lack of sophistication in the indigenous legal system. Further, the Spanish author had his own deeply inculcated sexual mores and, as noted above, was trying to understand those of the Nahuas. What we are seeing in this document, therefore, are notes on those aspects of the interview that proved most striking and interesting to the interviewer; they were not intended to be an adequate description of Nahua jurisprudential thought or legal practice. I would suggest that what we see here is a typical "zeroing in," by

25 We do not know how such oral performances were conducted; however, they involved specialized language and gestures including song at times. Nevertheless, the entire process would have been stunted by the lack of acculturation of the Spanish friar.

26 Alonso de Zorita (1512–88), a Spanish jurist with varied New World experience, was in Mexico from 1556 to 1566: Warren, "Introductory Survey," 73–74. This source provides the best Western-derived analytical insights into Aztec law. Although by Zorita's time legal content and procedures had changed considerably, he brings out the complexity of indigenous jurisprudential thought to a greater extent than other Spanish sources: Zorita, *Breve y sumaria relación.*

Spaniards, on legal rules as something easy to extract (that is, to decontextualize) and "understand," however flawed that resulting understanding might have been. When the *History* later turns to the cataloguing of legal rules, interpretive problems caused by the resulting simplification and decontextualization of information become even more acute. The lost performative content of Aztec law continues to be a key problem in its interpretation by the modern Western scholarly tradition of legal study.

In contrast to this initial interest in sexual behavior, the document also details three crimes involving maize, an important and sacred food crop for the Nahuas.[27] Two boys stole maize seeds that had already been planted. They were sold as slaves,[28] and the price of five *mantas* (pieces of woven cotton cloth, a medium of exchange or *tilmatli*) was given for each.[29] A more complicated case involved a woman who was observed stealing maize from a granary by a man who demanded sex from her in exchange for silence. She submitted to his demand, but he revealed her theft anyway. She then reported the whole story, and the man was given as a slave to the owner of the stolen maize while the woman went free. We are left to guess at the details of the jurisprudential reasoning in this fascinating case. In the third case, two boys each stole five ears of corn while they were forming kernels or grains. They were ordered to be garroted because stealing maize in this condition was considered worse than stealing maize that had not yet formed any kernels.

During the reign of Huitzilihuitl (ca. 1397–ca. 1417), the *History* again returns to sexual behavior, and we are told that a man from Texcoco discovered his wife with a priest in the temple only three days after she had given birth. The three rulers condemned the woman to death, but no punishment for the priest is mentioned. In another case, a man killed his wife's lover but not the wife herself, and then reconciled with her, for which both he (as murderer and usurper of the state's authority) and she (as an adulteress) were executed.[30] In the following reign of Chimalpopoca (ca. 1418–ca. 1427), we are told that a woman encountered a drunken man of whom she took sexual advantage; she was stoned, but the man was not punished. In a final return to crimes of theft, we learn that a man put another man to sleep with a spell and stole all the grain in his granary, with the help of his (the perpetrator's) wife. That couple was then executed for the crime.

---

27 Nicholson, "Religion in Pre-Hispanic Central Mexico," 401, 416–19.

28 There is still no thoroughgoing study of Aztec slavery as an economic and legal institution, leaving a significant investigational avenue open for future scholarship.

29 See Anawalt, "Costume and Control."

30 For an analysis of Aztec adultery law, see Offner, Law and Politics in Aztec Texcoco, 257–66.

We are next provided with a closing pair of what may be legal rules or jurisprudential principles that caught the author's fancy: a man could be enslaved for stealing a turkey but not a dog,[31] because it was said the dog had teeth to defend itself.[32]

After brief military, genealogical, and political interludes, the *Historia* offers a list of what are specifically said to be *leyes* (legal rules). Five involve conduct in war and military legal process. The author records that one of five captains (who were also acting as judges) "investigated the offenses and painted them" (se informaba de los delitos y los pintaba) and then shared the images with the other four captains and the ruler.[33] Here we see the capacity of the Nahua GCS to be highly specific when required and also its reliability as evidence produced in court. If all agreed that an offense had been committed, five other officials carried out capital punishment. Eighteen legal rules then deal with commercial offenses, including theft, illegal sale of property, failure to repay a loan, and dealing with and in slaves. Three (or four) legal rules involving drunkenness follow, and the list concludes with two legal rules regarding incest, two more dealing with sexual offenses, and a jurisprudential observation that the only sufficient proof for adultery was finding the guilty parties together, at which point they would be stoned publicly.

Closely related portions of this report appear in another document, *Estas son leyes que tenían los indios de la Nueva España, Anáhuac o México* (These are Laws that the Indians of New Spain, Anahuac or Mexico Had). This document can be securely dated to 1543 and attributed to a priest in Valladolid (Spain).[34] It mentions that some of the same legal rules we have just surveyed were not authentic, because they were derived from a non-authentic indigenous *libro*.[35] It then reports additional sets of legal rules that probably have a Texcocan origin.[36] Texcoco was

---

31 In indigenous testimonies, the term *gallina* (hen) refers to a turkey hen; chickens were a Spanish import.

32 Here, one can detect the possibility that the informant was deceiving the Spanish author in some of the interviews on which he drew to compose this section, perhaps facilitated by the author's interest in the more striking scenes in the pictorial source, especially those involving sex.

33 Historia de los Mexicanos por sus pinturas, ed. García Icazbalceta, 260.

34 *Estas son leyes*, ed. García Icazbalceta, 315.

35 Ibid., 310.

36 The fourfold division of the legal rules in this text matches, to some degree, the legal jurisdiction of the four Texcocan councils: Offner, "Distribution of Jurisdiction." The description of a war declaration procedure for rebellious subject rulers and towns also matches the war declaration scene in the *Mapa Quinatzin*, leaf 3 (fig. 1, col. 2, row 2) more closely than any other description except for Ixtlilxochitl's report: Offner, "Aztec Legal

the second most important Aztec city at the time of contact and was renowned for its legal expertise, beginning with the ruler Nezahualcoyotl (1431–72) and continuing under his son Nezahualpilli (1472–1515). The claim of inauthenticity, then, may have to do with comments made by the informants of the author of *Estas son leyes*, arising from rivalries between the elites of Texcoco and the more powerful Tenochtitlan, which carried over from precontact times into the Spanish colonial political and legal systems.[37] It is certain that Nahua towns could have different legal hierarchies, legal processes, legal rules, and jurisprudential thinking.[38]

At this point, it is instructive to consider the second example of an indigenous source, the *Mapa Quinatzin* (**Figure 1**) from Texcoco.[39] This document was composed in the Nahua GCS but with some Spanish influence in its composition.[40] We do not know why it was prepared. Possible purposes and uses range from indigenous court recordkeeping and legal instruction to a presentation piece intended for a Spanish audience. Further, we cannot determine how closely its presentation of legal rules and precedents followed precontact indigenous practice. We do know, however, that Toribio de Benavente Motolinía (1482–1568), an early Franciscan missionary and perhaps the most acute ethnographer of the immediate postcontact period, was able to apprehend a great many legal rules from Texcoco by consulting indigenous documents prepared with the Nahua GCS. It would, he said, take a few explanations to understand them, and these were sometimes supplemented by additional consultations with *un buen maestro* (a good master).[41] Another outstanding self-trained ethnographer from a half-century later, Fernando de Alva Cortés Ixtlilxochitl (d. 1648), tells us that Nezahualcoyotl promul-

---

Process." At least three other legal rules are closely related to the legal vignettes in the *Mapa Quinatzin*, leaf 3 and leaf 2 (the flight of a slave into the palace to obtain freedom).

37 Offner, "Dueling Rulers."

38 Here, I take issue with Jongsoo Lee, who attempts to argue that the legal system was the same in all towns: "Reexamining Nezahualcóyotl's Texcoco." This is part of a larger revisionist agenda that attempts to strip Nezahualcoyotl of any individual authorial agency, whether in jurisprudence or poetry/song: an argument founded on faulty pictorial document readings and lack of sound ethnographic and historiographic methodology.

39 The *Mapa Quinatzin* consists of three extant paper leaves, all now kept in the Bibliothèque nationale de France. The first depicts early Texcocan history; the second portrays some aspects of Texcocan political and legal structure and administration. The third (Paris, Bibliothèque nationale de France, MS Mexicain 396) describes the legal content discussed here. A high-resolution digital image can be found online at <http://gallica.bnf.fr/ark:/12148/btv1b10303825m> [accessed September 4, 2015].

40 See Lesbre, "Manumission d'esclaves"; "Mapa Quinatzin"; and "Los fuegos del Palacio Real."

41 Motolinía, *Memoriales*, 359.

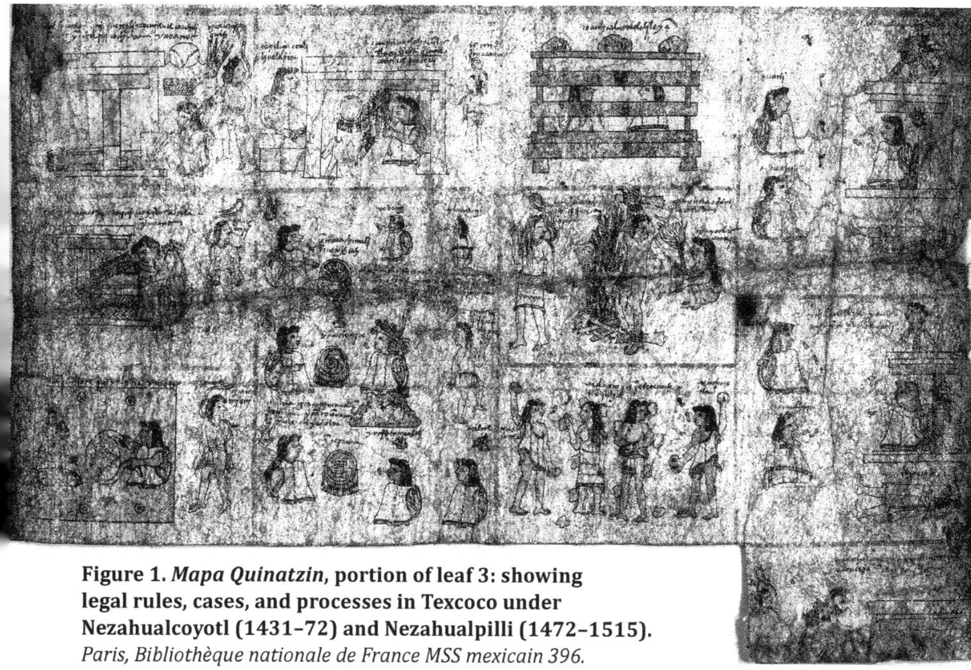

Figure 1. ***Mapa Quinatzin*****, portion of leaf 3: showing legal rules, cases, and processes in Texcoco under Nezahualcoyotl (1431–72) and Nezahualpilli (1472–1515).**
Paris, Bibliothèque nationale de France MSS mexicain 396.

gated eighty laws and that jurisdiction over these laws was divided among four councils in Texcoco.[42]

The appearance of the legal vignettes in the *Mapa Quinatzin* (see **Figures 1 and 2**), then, may or may not be similar to what Motolinía, or the author of *Estas son leyes,* used to write their compilations of legal rules. They begin after a strip at the top of the leaf, filled with historical information, including town conquests and

42 Ixtlilxochitl, *Obras historicas,* 2:101. The author was a *castizo* (three quarters European, one quarter indigenous American) and descendant of Nezahualcoyotl of Texcoco, although his family was from nearby Teotihuacan (not to be confused with the great Classic Period site of the same name). He became fascinated by the history of Texcoco by his twenties and, working closely with a variety of native informants and well as Spaniards, produced the best known explication of an indigenous pictorial document, the *Codex Xolotl,* itself the greatest surviving example of Nahua historiography. For complementary examinations of his at times astonishing linguistic, cultural, and ethnographic expertise and accomplishments, see Whittaker, "The Identities of Fernando de Alva Ixtlilxochitl"; Offner, "Ixtlilxochitl's Ethnographic Encounter." The Nahuas employed a vigesimal counting system, so twenty or "one count" of legal rules for each council would make a pleasing symmetry, although the evidence for such distribution of jurisdiction can only be partially assembled. See Offner, "Distribution of Jurisdiction."

Figure 2. ***Mapa Quinatzin*****, leaf 3, column 3: showing legal rules and penalties for adultery in Texcoco under Nezahualcoyotl (1431–72) and Nezahualpilli (1472–1515).** *Paris, Bibliothèque nationale de France MSS mexicain 396.*

a conversation (to the right) between the rulers of Texcoco and Tenochtitlan. This narrative appears to be a continuation of a prior page (perhaps leaf 2 of the map, or an entirely lost folio). Underneath this strip are four columns containing legal information. The grid organization is like no other part of the *Mapa Quinatzin* and has its closest analogues in the types of documents priests used to generate prognostications of individual lives, based on dates of birth, or the marriage prognostication pages in the *Codex Borgia*.[43] The items within each column are similar, but it is initially unclear whether the columns are to be read from top to bottom or vice versa; or from right to left, or left to right; or whether they are to be read in any set order at all.[44] Probably, as is the case with the more complicated Nahua documents, such as the Texcocan *Codex Xolotl*, or the screenfolds used for prognostication, they were to be contemplated all at once as an organized extracted fragment of an interlocking system of thought—jurisprudential in this case, from which examples could be drawn for various instructional purposes.

43 *Codex Borgia*, 58–60. A digital edition of the exquisite *Codex Borgia* (Rome, Biblioteca Apostolica Vaticana, Borg. Mess. 1) is available at <http://digital.vatlib.it/en/view/MSS_Borg.mess.1> [accessed September 5, 2015].

44 The marriage prognostication pages in the *Codex Borgia*, for example, are ordered by a sequence of numbers used for prognostication, from two to twenty-six. Twenty-five vignettes related to each of these numbers are arranged across the three pages in boustrophedon fashion, beginning with two on the lower right of page 58 and ending on the upper left of page 60. (The pages themselves are read from right to left in the screenfold). Further, the favorability of each number shown in the vignettes is generated by an underlying but not depicted indigenous divination procedure: a sort of algorithm. See Offner, "Starting from Zero."

The progression of jurisprudential instruction or analysis may be contained in the visual ordering of the page: the commonality of offenses by column has frequently been noted. The other folios of the *Mapa Quinatzin* have a general (but not thoroughgoing) top-to-bottom organization, so perhaps the top of each column is a good place to start. This approach certainly works for the third column, where adulterers are shown temporarily confined in a prison before punishments are administered. And the fourth column contains cases involving legal corruption, with a case from the reign of Nezahualcoyotl shown on top. Legal rules against theft occupy the leftmost column, and the second column lists offenses against the state. Returning to the third column, where a man and a woman are depicted in a wooden cage with stones weighing down the top to prevent their escape, we see two sets of punishments for two types of adultery just below this image. The more serious offense, where a woman's husband has been killed by her partner, is punished more severely: the adulterous man suffers a horrific death by burning as salt water is repeatedly splashed on him. The woman's punishment is a comparatively mild strangulation. The more common punishment for adultery is then depicted below: stoning for both offenders. Here the folio has unfortunately been trimmed, so we cannot see the additional scenes in this column.

What we are missing, as we attempt to understand this document, is Motolinía's "buen maestro" to tell us why the columns are arranged in this order and the rationale underlying the progression of cases in each column. But whether pre- or postcontact, this is clearly a snapshot of Texcocan jurisprudential thinking. The flexibility of the Nahua GCS ranges from the general, as in the punishment for common adultery, to the specific: the name of a corrupt judge killed during the reign of Nezahualpilli (1472–1515) is notable (col. 4, row 2). We see an emphasis on widely applicable legal rules, but, at the same time, we see specific cases that were quite possibly cited later as legal precedents.[45]

In an interesting contrast, the *Codex Mendoza* from Tenochtitlan places no emphasis on codified law or legal precedent but instead shows the scene of a judicial hearing of uncertain substance and outcome (**Figure 3**).[46] On the following page, we see the court of appeals in the ruler's palace, with the (bearded) ruler

45 See Brokmann Haro (*La estera y la silla,* 93–95) for a brief but useful discussion of the roles of precedent and custom in the Aztec legal system. Accurate assessment of the emphasis placed on each in Aztec jurisprudence requires much greater contextualization through intensive source study. See below.

46 Most of the non-alphabetic content of this manuscript (Oxford, Bodleian Library, MS. Arch. Selden. A. 1) can be found online: <http://bodley30.bodley.ox.ac.uk:8180/luna/servlet/view/all/what/MS.+Arch.+Selden.+A.+1?sort=Shelfmark%2cFolio_Page%2cRoll_%23%2cFrame_%23> [accessed September 5, 2015].

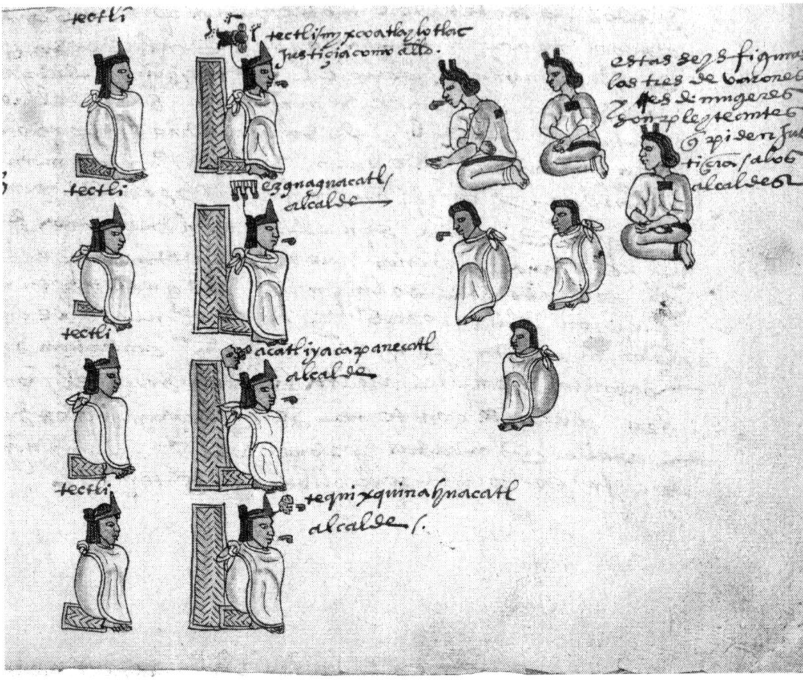

Figure 3. Three men and three women ask for justice in Tenochtitlan; four judges hold court, with judges-in-training behind them.
Codex Mendoza, fol. 68r (detail): Oxford, Bodleian Library MS. Arch. Selden. A. 1. Reproduced courtesy of the Bodleian Library, University of Oxford.

himself, Moteuczoma, the court of last appeal, near the top of the palace (**Figure 4**). The section of the *Codex Mendoza* in which these scenes appear is certainly not related to indigenous precontact modes of presentation but was instead designed as a representation of Aztec life for Spanish inspection. It is possible to propose some similarities of purpose for the *Mapa Quinatzin* and the *Codex Mendoza*. It is also possible to argue that schools of jurisprudence differed between Texcoco and Tenochtitlan, although comparatively little is known of jurisprudence and legal process in Tenochtitlan. And it may be only the choice of artists for the *Codex Mendoza* or the charge given to them by that city's surviving elite that led to their lavish attention to ethnographic details of Aztec life and only a superficial portrayal of legal process in Tenochtitlan. In any case, in the only examples we possess, each city and its elite chose to present their legal system in quite different ways. In Texcoco, it is a prominent part of the *Mapa Quinatzin*. In the *Codex Mendoza*, it is a small portion of the codex's ethnographic section, itself small in comparison to the many pages expended on military conquests and tributes due to the conquerors.

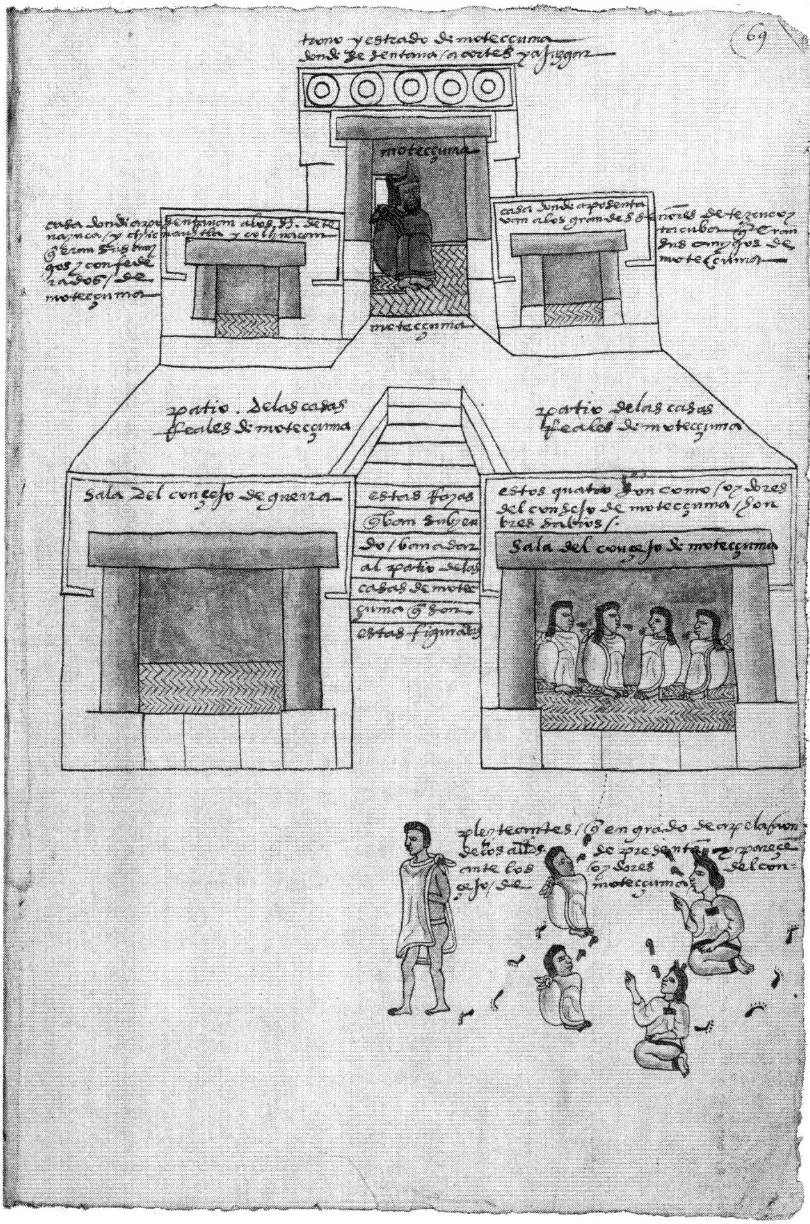

Figure 4. Litigants (at lower right) appeal decisions at the Council of Moteuczoma: decisions of the four judges could be appealed to Moteuczoma Xocoyotzin (shown seated, with beard, at the top of this drawing of his palace).
Codex Mendoza, fol. 69r: Oxford, Bodleian Library MS. Arch. Selden. A. 1. Reproduced courtesy of the Bodleian Library, University of Oxford.

Aztec Legal Rules and Legalism at Texcoco

An important matter to consider at this point is the nature of Nahua legal rules and their role in Aztec jurisprudence. As mentioned above, "legal rules" were *nahuatīlli* in Nahuatl and shared a semantic field with "orders." But were these legal rules, jurisprudential principles, or ethnographic summary observations by the Spanish? The evidence tends strongly toward the first option, and in an interesting way. I have already traced the considerable evidence for "legalism," or strict adherence to legal rules in adjudication, in the city of Texcoco.[47] After a difficult "warring states period" in the Basin of Mexico and surrounding regions that culminated in the fall of Azcapotzalco in 1428, Texcoco emerged with Tenochtitlan as leader of a new Aztec world order.[48] Nezahualcoyotl was faced with uncertain allies and subordinate rulers, as well as disloyal relatives, multiple ethnic groups in conflict, and rapidly developing imperial and economic systems that further fomented social disruption. Nezahualcoyotl and his court responded to this period of extreme divisiveness and chaos by promulgating a legal code to standardize the legal systems of diverse ethnic groups in different places. He also standardized legal administration and processes in order to limit corruption by reducing the discretionary power of judges. These measures increased the efficiency of the courts while the severe sanctions and public and participatory punishments in the code enhanced social control.[49]

The legal content of the *Mapa Quinatzin* discussed above supports the emphasis on strict application of legal rules to cases. Not only does it catalogue these rules, but it shows at least two unpleasant futures for errant judges. And in the *Historia de los Mexicanos por sus pinturas*, we see an abrupt change after the reign of Chimalpopoca, in 1427, from anecdotes of legal decisions to the formalization of legal rules, indicating that Tenochtitlan may have institutionalized a similar system.[50] Unfortunately, however, we have no certain evidence that this was the case, and judges in Tenochtitlan may have used precedent, legal rules, and jurisprudential reasoning to varying degrees as cases came before them. Of course, to some extent, the same must have been true of Texcoco, in that codified law can never encompass all that can happen among human beings. When the legal rules were insufficient to settle a case, the judges could resort to jurisprudential principles,

47 Offner, "Aztec Legal Process" and *Law and Politics*, 66–69, 71–85.

48 The Aztecs traditionally conceived of political authority as coming from three cities. Thus, Tlacopan, with ethnic and cultural similarities to the fallen Azcapotzalco, became the least important member of a ruling Aztec triple alliance along with Tenochtitlan and Texcoco.

49 Offner, *Law and Politics*, 82.

50 Haro, *La estera y la silla*, 108.

such as the principle of a reasonable man,[51] or they could rely on precedent. And so it is not surprising when we see, in *Estas son leyes*, how cases with facts not specified in the code might be handled: "For other offenses they [the judges] also made [the perpetrators] slaves, but [these decisions] were discretionary; but the above said were legal rules with which no judge could dispense, except for killing the one who committed them, so as not to make him a slave."[52]

In summary, however, it must be acknowledged that while we do have strong evidence for legalism in Texcoco, we cannot assume that this approach was used in other Aztec polities. Indeed, Texcoco's reputation for expertise in the legal process may well have arisen from its emphasis on legalism and accompanying rigor in supervising the legal process and punishing errant judges. (As we have noted, two such instances are highlighted in the *Mapa Quinatzin*). That is, its reputation was forged by the close, disciplined, and reliable relationship it maintained between legal rules and/or jurisprudential principles and their application to facts during the legal process, rather than by promulgating well-regarded legal rules. To my mind, these facts accord with an overall Nahua epistemology. Working from the totality of a system of jurisprudence instilled through careful training, supported by pictorial transmission of both legal principles and specific cases, Nahua jurists could proceed from the general to the specific, applying pertinent legal rules to cases but also judging wisely in the cases that did not fit a specific rule. We see this range of responses in the surviving indigenous pictorial materials. In the alphabetic texts, except when they report directly on pictorial sources, we see, in contrast, a sort of failed fieldwork—a narrow focus on decontextualization of individual rules, without sufficient regard to the structure and wisdom of the indigenous schools of jurisprudence that produced and wielded them. It should be remembered, then, that the reported legal rules are dismembered fragments of sophisticated schools of Nahua jurisprudence.

Other Methods for Contextualizing Aztec Law

One of the neglected tasks in the study of Aztec law is the cataloguing of all reported Aztec, Nahua, and Otomi legal rules,[53] jurisprudential principles, and related

---

51 Offner "Aztec Legal Process" and *Law and Politics*, 69–71.

52 *Estas son leyes*, ed. García Icazbalceta, 315: "Por otras cosas también hacían esclavos, mas eran arbitrarias; mas estas sobredichas eran leyes que ningún juez podía dispensar en ellas, si no era matando al que las cometía, por no hacerlo esclavo" This mention of judicial discretion is, in my opinion, further evidence of jurisprudential thought among the Nahuas.

53 The Otomi were the second most prominent ethnic group after the Nahuas, who appear to have arrived later. They spoke a tonal language from an entirely different language group.

ethnographic observations or summaries available in the sources. A related task would be to link these items to particular political systems in particular towns, begin their systematic analysis, and thus to gain additional insight into indigenous forms of jurisprudence.

Table 1. Formal Analysis of Adultery Rules in Texcoco under Nezahualcoyotl (after Offner 1983: 262).

Social class of criminal	Was adulteress's husband killed?	Type of Evidence	Sex of Criminal	Punishment
Non-*pilli* (non-noble)	No	Direct	Irrelevant	Public stoning*
		Indirect	Irrelevant	Strangulation, body dragged to a temple outside the city and thrown into a *barranca*
	Yes	Irrelevant	Female	Strangulation, body dragged to a temple outside the city and thrown into a *barranca*
			Male	Burned alive, water and salt applied during the process*
Pilli	Irrelevant	Irrelevant	Irrelevant	Strangulation, remains cremated after adornment

* The body was probably also dragged to a temple outside the city, where it was thrown into a *barranca*. Both of these legal rules are depicted on *Mapa Quinatzin*, leaf 3, column three, rows 2 and 3. Row 1 of Column 3 shows accused or guilty parties imprisoned in an open-sided jail with stones on top to prevent escape through the top. Cf. Lee 2008 who mistakes the first row as a device for crushing adulterers with a heavy stone and omits from his drawing of this scene the gloss for Row 1: "coauhcalco tetlaliloya(n)" or "cuauhcalco" "in the wooden house" "tētlālioyān" "the place where people are made to sit." This leads him to an erroneous analysis of Texcocan legal rules on adultery.

In the documentary examples provided above, we saw how the *Historia de los Mexicanos por sus pinturas* contains frames of reference composed of an ethnographic encounter and rich ethnographic details. These frames of reference are summarily stripped away, in a manner that should be instructive to us today, in the later Spanish document *Estas son leyes.* The visual impact and richness of detail of the *Mapa Quinatzin*, even without its accompanying oral presentations, has proven more resistant to Spanish or modern decontextualization. Additionally, Sahagún's works and other sources contain a myriad of references, often indirect, to precontact beliefs, customs, and actual behavior that have a clear potential to enhance understanding of the legal system and jurisprudence of Tenochtitlan.

Treating these rich data as an integrated whole, therefore—with proper allowances for political and temporal localization—will help reduce the distortion that they have suffered through their inadequate reporting in modern European texts. In 1983, I made such an effort in a study involving the legal rules against adultery, drunkenness, and theft as observed in Texcoco and surrounding towns, using a method of componential analysis.[54] Table 1 presents a summary of legal rules under Nezahualcoyotl, although it is clear from the available sources that there were different schools of jurisprudential thought regarding adultery, even within the small Texcocan empire.[55]

Legal rules, a few cases or legal decisions and jurisprudential principles, are useful first steps along the way to understanding Aztec legal systems, but they also need to be considered within their cultural and societal contexts. Some additional insight can be gained by a study of the Nahuatl language and specific terms and expressions having to do with legal matters. For example, *tēuctlatoā* meant "to hold court" and is a compound of *tēuctli*, "lord," and *tlatoā*, "speaks." The verb for judging or sentencing was *tzontequi*, composed of *tzontli*, "head of hair," and *tequi*, "to cut." Nahuatl terminology delineated four steps in the judicial process: accusation, investigation, decision and sentencing, and execution of punishment.[56] Witnesses were expected to tell the truth and "swore" on the earth goddess in a deeply embedded traditional gesture called *tlalqualiztli*, literally "earth-eating" or "the eating of earth."[57] Nevertheless, there was also a word for bribing or corrupting a judge: *tēmpachoa*, from *tēntli*, "lips/mouth," and *pachoā*, "to cover," as well as two more expressions for a judge abusing his authority by putting something under his *petlatl*, "mat," and *icpalli*, "seat" (*petlatitlan, icpaltitlan tlaaquiā*, or

54 Offner, *Law and Politics*, 255–79.

55 Ibid., 257–66.

56 Reparation was sometimes considered along with punishment: Ibid., 245–50.

57 See Olko, "Body Language in the Preconquest."

tlapachoā).[58] At present, these expressions are only dictionary entries, so another productive avenue into the future of Nahua law is to study the texts and contexts in which such words appear. For example, we know from the inquiries of Fray Bernardino de Sahagún, who relied on informants mostly from Tenochtitlan, that the law could be described as a snare: "This saying was said of one who accused one before the ruler. He was told: 'Take care, for the snare, the trap lie quivering before authority, that is, in the presence of the ruler.'"[59] Recent archival work is also turning up previously unknown legal terms deeply contextualized in Nahuatl texts. For example, *tlatecpāntzin*, a word for a decision and decree in a civil case, was recently discovered by Benjamin Johnson in a sixteenth-century manuscript.[60] The reverential suffix *-tzin* attached to the noun form, coming more than a century after the reign of Nezahualcoyotl, who reportedly issued the decree, shows that the decisions he made at that time were still held in the highest regard.

At the same time, paying attention to the social and political context of these systems is, of course, essential but extremely difficult. And the nature of these contexts has, in fact, been the subject of somewhat feckless disputation due to the intrusion of nineteenth- and twentieth-century political ideologies from Europe into Mesoamerican studies. It is one of the great ironies of Mesoamerican studies and their influence on contemporary Mexico that the concept of *lo indigeno*—what is "the indigenous"—has largely been shaped by this renewed European conquest. Indeed, a key characteristic of this middle and later twentieth-century work on the Aztecs was its reliance and insistence on intrusive Western ideologies, de-contextualization, and advocacy. In many senses, this was not a historiographic exercise at all but instead amounted to recruitment of fragments of indigenous data to fit predefined stages of Marxist or Polanyist economic formation. As a result, modern students approaching this literature must become diligent textual archaeologists, sorting through layers of odd and often distorted semantic penumbrae surrounding and obscuring such terms as *communal land tenure*, *corporate landholding*, *usufruct rights only*, and so forth.[61]

58 *Petlatl, icpalli* was in fact a Nahuatl expression meaning "authority." Brockmann Haro (*La estera y la* silla, 9) titled his book after this diphrasism in Nahuatl, which was intimately related with political and legal authority. (He misspells *petlatl* as *petatl*, however.)

59 Sahagún, *Florentine Codex*, bk. 6, 243: "Injn tlatolli, ilviloia: in aqujn ixpan moteilviaia tlatoanj, anoço in aqujn itlan nemj tlatoanj: ilviloia. Ximjmati: ca vncan neujujxtoc in tzonoaztli, in tlaxapuchtli in jxpan petlatl, icpalli: qujtoznequj: in jxpan tlatoanj."

60 Johnson, "Nezahualcoyotl and a *tlaxilacalli*," referencing Texcoco, 1581, Biblioteca nacional de antropología e historia, 3a Série de Papeles Sueltos, leg. 7, exp. 218, fol. 10r.

61 Offner, "Improving Western Historiography."

More than thirty years ago, I presented an alternative interpretation to this "first principles" approach to characterizing this civilization as a form of despotism directing an economy integrated solely by redistribution.[62] The Aztecs are more accurately characterized as a collection of serially warring and allying city states with economies integrated by market forces as well as redistribution. While centralization of power in Tenochtitlan seems to have accelerated sharply during the reign of Moteuczoma Xocoyotzin (1502–20), this process was interrupted by the Spanish intrusion. An earlier attempt at centralization of power by Tezozomoc and his successor son Maxtla of Azcapotzalco ended in the later 1420s with a successful revolution by Tenochtitlan and Texcoco, supported by powerful allies inside and outside the Basin of Mexico, and we can by no means exclude the same fate befalling Tenochtitlan absent the Spanish intrusion.

Among the data mined from sources to support and present the authoritarian view of Aztec society were sumptuary laws, particularly those that are attributed to Moteuczoma Ilhuicamina (r. 1440–69).[63] In 1980, Patricia Anawalt evaluated the evidence for sumptuary laws and concluded that "the recorded laws reflect a creed more than a reality."[64] As the leading expert on Aztec textiles, this was no casual conclusion on her part. She carefully summarized the evidence for allegedly strict control of the circulation of *tilmatli* (cloaks) in sources such as those found in Sahagún's writings and in Diego de Duran's *Historia de las Indias de Nueve España*,[65] and contrasted them with incidental reports of behavior from those same sources to show that "tilmatli circulated in Aztec society through means other than those recognized by the official sumptuary laws."[66] *Tilmatli* were also sold in the marketplace and were awarded as prizes, and could be sold by the recipient. Anawalt concludes by saying:[67]

---

62 Offner, "On the Inapplicability of 'Oriental Despotism'" and "On Carrasco's Use of Theoretical 'First Principles.'"

63 Peperstraete (*La "Chronique X,"* 143) suggests that certain conquests and perhaps the legal reforms of this ruler may instead belong to the later ruler of the same initial name, Moteuczoma Xocoyotzin. She argues that the indigenous structuring of the narrative required the rise of the empire towards its zenith under the first Moteuczoma (Ilhuicamina) and its later fall under the second Moteuczoma. Reports of reforms under the second Moteuczoma would not accord with this preferred narrative pattern.

64 Anawalt, "Costume and Control," 43.

65 Peperstraete (*La "Chronique X,"* 13–23) provides an excellent short study of Fray Diego Durán (ca. 1537–88), born in Sevilla, who spent some childhood years in Texcoco (1543–50) and entered the Dominican order in 1556.

66 Anawalt "Costume and Control," 41.

67 Ibid., 43.

> A detailed study of the chronicles makes it apparent that Aztec society was becoming increasingly dependent on luxury goods. In so doing, it abandoned the frugality of earlier days, an echo of which survived in the official severity of the sumptuary laws. No doubt the descriptions of these regulations, which come to us from the contemporary Indian informants, represent an idealized image of the military and political order in pre-Conquest Tenochtitlan.

Anawalt's insights into law as reported in the written and pictorial sources were both early and profound, but they have not been sufficiently appreciated, and her methodology has not been applied to other important areas of Aztec life. For example, these same sources could be explored for references to other items supposedly strictly regulated, such as *pulque* (an alcoholic drink derived from the *maguey* [*agave*] plant). With regard to consumption of alcohol in Aztec society, we find that its use was not in fact restricted to those over fifty-two years of age (one full count of the Aztec calendar round). For example, in a legal case cited above, wherein a woman took sexual advantage of a drunken man, the man was not punished. Anawalt's insights, however, go beyond observing the variance between legal rules, idealized conceptions, and actual behavior. Her work demonstrates how the mere presence of legal rules in the sources creates a false impression of strict social control in the eyes of modern investigators. She also exposes how the acceptance and promotion of the reported sumptuary laws by ideological proponents have created a false image of an authoritarian society.[68]

In the same way, excessive and uncritical reliance upon reports of land tenure, most often bequeathed to us by or on behalf of societies' elites, has long been a convenience of those seeking to classify civilizations according to the antique grand developmental theories originating in the nineteenth century. In 1981, I presented some of the considerable evidence for individual landholding and a market in land among the Aztecs.[69] But such landholding practices were not supposed to exist, according to various Marxist and Polanyist theoretical formulations, and so the evidence has been for the most part either ignored or subject to attempts to explain it away. Nevertheless, persistent known as well as continuously discovered data are eroding and contradicting the theoretical strictures of the past, leading to emerging ambiguity even in the works of archaeologists. In the third edition of his introductory work *The Aztecs*, Michael Smith presents the conventional view

68 For an evaluation of recent scholarship on sumptuary laws in a European context, see the article by Laurel Wilson, "Common Threads," in this issue.

69 Offner, "On the Inapplicability of 'Oriental Despotism,'" 46–48, and "On Carrasco's Use of Theoretical 'First Principles.'"

regarding land tenure: "the *tlatoani* [ruler] owned or controlled the land within his city-state."[70] A few pages earlier, however, when describing *calpolli* land held by commoners rather than nobles and usually seen as the least likely to involve individual ownership, Smith cites a passage from the work of James Lockhart and states that "rights for use of an individual plot could be sold, but the land remained under the general jurisdiction of the *calpolli* and *altepetl* (city-state)."[71] Lockhart, for his part, writes:

> A land sale, then, was openly brought before the authorities, and a feast-like ritual accompanied the transfer like any other. Indeed one way of looking at a transaction of this type is that the seller for a consideration relinquished his allocation from the *altepetl/calpolli* and permitted the authorities to reallocate it in the usual way to the buyer.[72]

Such circumlocutions reveal a struggle to negotiate equivalences and differences among modern Western conceptions of land ownership and Aztec and Nahua conceptions. They stand in contrast to an important source on land tenure which is straightforward in reporting that a commoner in need of funds to maintain his important ritual status as a "receiver" of Huitzilopochtli (the most important god of the Nahua of Tenochtitlan) "sold his land" (quinamaca itlal) or "somewhere he arranged a loan" on it ("canah netlacujlli quichioa").[73] He did this with various types of land, including *calpolli* land ("quichioa in calpollali"). The passage says nothing about permissions and feasts, only that he might lose a certain type of land on which he owed labor service *tequitl* ("ximmilli ie in ipan tequjtia"), if he did not produce that service (*tequitl*)[74] for the land. And the text names several other types of land this commoner might sell or on which he might get loans: "the enclosed land, the marshy land, the dusty land" (in chinamitl, in chiauhtlalli, in teuhtlalli). This brief passage, offered as an aside by one of Sahagún's informants, is full of evidence of the sophistication of precontact land tenure and the Aztec economy. It should also be noted that these "receivers" of Huitzilopochtli indulged in a little drunkenness, with no comment made about illegality, at the end of their period of expenditure, fasting, and service.

---

70 Smith, *The Aztecs*, 155 and 134.

71 Ibid., 135.

72 Lockhart, Nahuas after the Conquest, 154.

73 Sahagún, *Florentine Codex*, bk. 3, 9.

74 *Tequitl*, at least as described in many colonial documents, could also involve the provision of tribute in kind, although almost always related to products for domestic consumption: maize, turkeys, eggs, and so forth.

As I proposed in 1981, what is going to be required for the future of Aztec law is a more careful and exacting study of the bundle of rights and duties involving land (or involving other people, entities, and property) that existed in Aztec and Nahua societies, and evaluation of the extent to which these rights and duties were accepted, influenced actual behavior, and were enforced.[75] The anachronistic notions of "private property" or "communal land" employed in the developmental/comparative schemes of the last century and a half lead to little more than a rediscovery of the original Western discriminations built into such formulations. Meanwhile, excessive claims of state control of the economy (made by followers of Marx and Polanyi) have, in retrospect, not only stunted investigations into Aztec slavery and its implications for the role of labor in the Aztec economy, but also inhibited inquiry into Aztec commercial law. Nahuatl terminology reveals a rich set of terms for buying, selling, charging, paying, loaning, lending, and borrowing—and also the price, cost, wholesale, and retail—that originated in a complex precontact economy. Sahagún's work is full of incidental mentions of economic and commercial behavior, including the existence of canoe-borne fresh water sellers, whose very existence in an allegedly authoritarian society with a redistributive economy seems more than a bit curious. And while Western-language dictionaries of Nahuatl have existed since the sixteenth century, terse translations of indigenous words do not capture sufficient context for their emic content to be apparent, since modern dictionary users have generally operated from their culturally specific etic perspectives. This again points back to the need to study law, in context, in Nahuatl documents. Finally, the popular image of Aztec rulers as unrestrained autocrats, especially as mapped onto contemporary Mexican politics, needs changing. I have already delineated some of the power blocs and competing interests with which even powerful rulers such as Nezahualcoyotl and Moteuczoma Ilhuicamina had to struggle to maintain their power.[76]

Conclusion

In summary: whether we are discussing sumptuary laws regulating the consumption of clothing and drink, legal rules of land tenure, or Aztec labor law and commercial law, the detailed consideration of ethnographic information, adequately reported and analyzed, can render more accurate and meaningful comparison of medieval civilizations that emerge as rather more complicated than those sug-

75 Offner, "On the Inapplicability of 'Oriental Despotism,'" 46–48.

76 Offner, "Distribution of Jurisdiction and Political Power" and "Dueling Rulers and Strange Attractors."

gested by narrow, modern paradigms. And it is along this path that much of the future of Aztec Law lies. The richest source of ethnographic data for the Aztecs and Nahuas remains the work of Fray Bernardino de Sahagún. Descriptions of precontact behavior by his indigenous informants should be investigated in order to throw light on a number of basic issues: the variance among legal rules, jurisprudential principles, and everyday conduct; the actual behavior within and attitude towards the legal system among ordinary people, and vice versa; the need for additional information on legal process; reports of social discord and dysfunction, as well as cohesion; and the intersection of indigenous conceptions of law and morality.

Through this source, and a few others, we can begin to see the participants in Aztec society going about their daily lives. We need not, therefore, rely exclusively on top-down reports by relative cultural outsiders regarding the legal system. To some degree we are fortunate that the most prominent Aztec legal system, that of Texcoco, was legalistic and did give priority to the strict application of the facts of a case to the exigencies of applicable legal rules, but we can also see that these legal rules and jurisprudential principles existed because the actual behavior of people frequently conflicted with them. And as we see from Anawalt's inquiry into Aztec sumptuary laws, the appearance and prominence of legal rules in the sources create the illusion of far greater social control among the Aztecs than actually existed. What survive in the sources as legal rules are therefore important but decontextualized fragments of sophisticated systems of jurisprudential thought based on indigenous observation and contemplation of human behavior. Recovering these systems of thought will require understanding and evaluating both old and new evidence in novel ways. In other words, the future of Aztec law will more resemble ethnography than the old method of *a priori* imposition of Victorian era social evolutionary schemes, carried over into Mexico by Europeans in the twentieth century, and which declared Aztec society to be authoritarian, despotic, and limited in its humanity and range of expression. And, happily, the field of Nahua ethnography is already changing, through the contributions of contemporary Nahuatl speakers who are now exploring their own cultural history. I look forward to the future of Aztec law.

Bibliography

Primary Sources

[*Codex Borgia*]. *Códice Borgia*. Vol. 1 [facsimile]. Madrid: Sociedad Estatal Quinto Centenario, 1993.

The Codex Mendoza. Edited by Frances F. Berdan and Patricia Rieff Anawalt. Berkeley: University of California Press, 1992.

Códice Xolotl. Edited by Charles Dibble. México: UNAM/The University of Utah, 1951.

Estas son leyes que tenían los indios de la Nueva España, Anáhuac o México. In *Nueva colección de documentos para la historia de México,* edited by Joaquín García Icazbalceta, 3:308–15. Mexico: Andrade y Morales, sucesores, 1891.

Historia de los Mexicanos por sus pinturas. In *Nueva colección de documentos para la historia de México,* edited by Joaquín García Icazbalceta, 3:228–63. Mexico: Andrade y Morales, sucesores, 1891.

Mapa Quinatzin. Códice Mapa Quinatzin: justicia y derechos humanos en el México antiguo. Edited by Luz María Mohar Betancourt. México: Comisión Nacional de los Derechos Humanos, 2004.

Secondary Studies

Anawalt, Patricia. "Costume and Control: Aztec Sumptuary Laws." *Archaeology* 33 (1980): 33–43.

Boone, Elizabeth Hill. "The Aztec Pictorial History of the Codex Mendoza." In *The Codex Mendoza*, edited by Frances F. Berdan and Patricia R. Anawalt, 1:35–54, 152–53. Berkeley: University of California Press, 1992.

——. *Stories in Red and Black: Pictorial Histories of the Aztecs and Mixtecs*. Austin: University of Texas Press, 2000.

Burkhart, Louise M. *The Slippery Earth: Nahua-Christian Moral Dialogue in Sixteenth-Century Mexico*. Tucson: University of Arizona Press, 1989.

Calnek, Edward E. "The Sahagún Texts as a Source of Sociological Information." In *Sixteenth Century Mexico: The Work of Sahagún*, edited by Munro Edmonson, 189–204. Albuquerque: University of New Mexico Press, 1974.

Carrasco, Pedro. *The Tenochca Empire of Ancient Mexico: The Triple Alliance of Tenochtitlan, Tetzcoco, and Tlacopan*. Norman: University of Oklahoma Press, 1999.

Cline, Howard F. "The Relaciones Geográficas of the Spanish Indies, 1577–1648." In *Handbook of Middle American Indians*, edited by Howard F. Cline, 12:183–242. Austin: University of Texas Press, 1972.

Cline, S. L. *Colonial Culhuacan, 1580–1600: A Social History of an Aztec Town*. Albuquerque: University of New Mexico Press, 1986.

Coe, Michael D., and Rex Koontz. *Mexico: From the Olmecs to the Aztecs.* London: Thames & Hudson, 2013.

Dakin, Karen, and Søren Wichmann. "Cacao and Chocolate: A Uto-Aztecan Perspective." *Ancient Mesoamerica* 11 (2000): 55–75.

Durán, Diego. *Historia de las Indias de Nueve España e islas de la Tierra Firme.* Edited by Angel Ma. Garibay K. México: Editorial Porrúa, 1967.

García Martínez, Bernardo. *Los pueblos de la Sierra: el poder y el espacio entre los indios del norte de Puebla hasta 1700.* México: El Colegio de México, Centro de Estudios Históricos, 1987.

Gibson, Charles. *The Aztecs under Spanish Rule.* Stanford: Stanford University Press, 1964.

Gibson, Charles, and John B. Glass. "A Census of Middle American Prose Manuscripts in the Native Historical Tradition." In *Handbook of Middle American Indians,* edited by Howard F. Cline, 15:322–400. Austin: University of Texas Press, 1975.

The Handbook of Middle American Indians. Robert Wauchope, general editor. 16 vols. Austin: University of Texas Press, 1964–.

Haro, Carlos Brokmann. *La estera y la silla: Individuo, comunidad, estado e instituciones jurídicas nahuas.* Mexico: Comisión Nacional de Derechos Humanos, 2006.

Harvey, Herbert R. "The Relaciones Geográficas, 1579–1586: Native Languages." In *Handbook of Middle American Indians,* edited by Howard F. Cline, 12:279–323. Austin: University of Texas Press, 1972.

Harvey, Herbert R., and Hanns J. Prem, eds. *Explorations in Ethnohistory.* Albuquerque: University of New Mexico Press, 1984.

Hicks, Frederic. "Land and Succession in the Indigenous Noble Houses of Sixteenth-Century Tlaxcala." *Ethnohistory* 56, no. 4 (2009): 569–88.

Ixtlilxochitl, Fernando de Alva. *Obras historicas.* [Facsimile]. 2 vols. Mexico City: Universidad Nacional Autónoma de México, Instituto de Investigaciones Históricas, 1975.

Johnson, Benjamin D. "Nezahualcoyotl and a *tlaxilacalli,* 170 Years Later: Tetzcoco, 1581." Paper delivered at the Northeastern Group of Nahuatl Studies Conference at Yale University, May 8, 2015.

Karttunen, Frances. *An Analytical Dictionary of Nahuatl.* 2nd ed. Norman: University of Oklahoma Press, 1992.

Kellogg, Susan. *Law and the Transformation of Aztec Culture, 1500–1700.* Norman: University of Oklahoma Press, 1995.

Klor de Alva, J. Jorge, H. B. Nicholson, and Eloise Quiñones Keber, eds. *The Work of Bernardino de Sahagun: Pioneer Ethnographer of Sixteenth-Century Aztec Mexico.* Albany: Institute for Mesoamerican Studies, University at Albany, State University of New York, 1988.

Lee, Jongsoo. *The Allure of Nezahualcoyotl: Pre-Hispanic History, Religion, and Nahua Poetics.* Albuquerque: University of New Mexico Press, 2008.

——. "Reexamining Nezahualcóyotl's Texcoco: Politics, Conquests and Law." *Estudios de Cultura Náhuatl* 37 (2006): 231–52.

León Portilla, Miguel. *Bernardino de Sahagún, First Anthropologist.* Norman: University of Oklahoma Press, 2002.

Lesbre, Patrick. "Los fuegos del Palacio Real de Tetzcoco (Mapa Quinatzin): ¿una alusión a la realeza sagrada?" *Estudios de cultura náhuatl* 38 (2007): 101–27.

——. "Manumission d'esclaves dans la Mappe Quinatzin?" *Amerindia* 23 (1998): 99–119.

——. "Mapa Quinatzin: las vigas del Tecpan de Tezcoco. Escritura o figuracion?" XXI Convegno Internazionale di Americanistica (session "Codice, glifo e interpretazione: la scrittura mesoamericana"), Pérouse, mai 1999, in *Thule* 6/7 (April–October 1999): 119–37.

Lockhart, James. *The Nahuas after the Conquest: A Social and Cultural History of the Indians of Central Mexico, Sixteenth through Eighteenth Centuries.* Stanford: Stanford University Press, 1992.

Megged, Amos. "Between History, Memory, and Law: Courtroom Methods in Mexico." *Journal of Interdisciplinary History* 45, no. 2 (2014): 163–86.

Mikulska, Katarzyna. "'Secret Language' in Oral and Graphic Form: Religious-Magic Discourse in Aztec Speeches and Manuscripts." *Oral Tradition* 25, no. 2 (2010): 325–63.

——. *Tejiendo destinos: Un acercamiento al sistema de comunicación gráfica en los códices adivinatorios.* Zinacantepec: Colegio Mexiquense, 2015.

Mohar Betancourt, Luz Maria, *Códice Mapa Quinatzin: justicia y derechos humanos en el México antiguo.* Mexico City: Comisión Nacional de Derechos Humanos México, 2004.

Motolinía, Toribio de Benavente. *Memoriales; o, Libro de las cosas de la Nueva España y de los naturales de ella.* [Etc.]. Edited by Edmundo O'Gorman. México, D.F.: Instituto de Investigaciones Históricas, Universidad Nacional Autónoma de México, 1971.

Nicholson, Henry B. "Religion in Pre-Hispanic Central Mexico." In *Handbook of Middle American Indians,* edited by G. F. Ekholm and Ignacio Bernal, 10:395–446. Austin: University of Texas Press, 1971.

Offner, Jerome A. "Aztec Legal Process: The Case of Texcoco." In *Proceedings of the Conference on Late Post-classic Central Mexican Iconography,* edited by Elizabeth Hill Boone, 141–57. Washington, DC: Center for Mesoamerican Studies, Dumbarton Oaks, 1982.

——. "The Distribution of Jurisdiction and Political Power in Aztec Texcoco: Subgroups in Conflict." In *Five Centuries of Law and Politics in Central Mexico,* edited by Ronald Spores and Ross Hassig, 5–14. Nashville: Vanderbilt University, 1984.

———. "Dueling Rulers and Strange Attractors: Some Patterns of Disorder and Killing in Aztec Society." *Political and Legal Anthropology Review* 16, no. 2 (1993): 65–73.

———. "Exploring Three Sixteenth-Century 'Totonac' Pictorial Manuscripts." In *Mesoamerican Memory: Enduring Systems of Remembrance,* edited by Amos Megged and Stephanie Wood, 147–71. Norman: University of Oklahoma Press, 2012.

———. "Household Organization in the Texcocan Heartland." In *Explorations in Ethnohistory*, edited by H. R. Harvey and Hanns J. Prem, 127–46. Albuquerque: University of New Mexico Press, 1984.

———. "Improving Western Historiography of Texcoco." In *Texcoco: Prehispanic and Colonial Perspectives*, edited by Jongsoo Lee and Galen Brokaw, 25–61. Boulder: University Press of Colorado, 2014.

———. "Ixtlilxochitl's Ethnographic Encounter: Understanding the *Codex Xolotl* and Its Dependent Alphabetic Texts." In *Indigenous Historiography in Colonial Mexico: Fernando de Alva Ixtlilxochitl and His Legacy*, edited by Galen Brokaw and Jongsoo Lee, 77–121. Tucson: University of Arizona Press, 2016.

———. *Law and Politics in Aztec Texcoco*. Cambridge: Cambridge University Press, 1983.

———. "On Carrasco's Use of Theoretical 'First Principles.'" *American Antiquity* 46, no. 1 (1981): 69–74.

———. "On the Inapplicability of 'Oriental Despotism' and the 'Asiatic Mode of Production' to the Aztecs of Texcoco." *American Antiquity* 46, no. 1 (1981): 43–61.

———. "Starting from Zero: Overcoming Text-Centrism and Other Western Prejudices." Paper read at the symposium "Indigenous Graphic Communication Systems: A Theoretical Approach," organized by Katarzyna Mikulska, University of Warsaw, March 2015.

Olko, Justyna. "Body Language in the Preconquest and Colonial Nahua World." *Ethnohistory* 61 (2014): 149–79.

Peperstraete, Sylvie. *La "Chronique X": Reconstitution et analyse d'une source perdue fondamentale sur la civilisation Aztèque, d'après l'Historia de las Indias de Nueva España de D. Durán (1581) et la Crónica Mexicana de F.A. Tezozomoc (ca. 1598)*. Oxford: Archaeopress, 2007.

Sahagún, Bernardino de. *Florentine Codex: General History of the Things of New Spain.* Translated and edited by Arthur J. O. Anderson and Charles E. Dibble. Santa Fe, NM: School of American Research, University of Utah, 1963.

Smith, Michael Ernest. *The Aztecs.* Malden, MA: Wiley-Blackwell, 2011.

Supplement to the Handbook of Middle American Indians. Edited by Victoria Reifler Bricker et al. 6 vols. Austin: University of Texas Press, 1981–.

Townsend, Richard F. *The Aztecs.* 3rd ed. London: Thames & Hudson, 2009

Warren, J. Benedict. "An Introductory Survey of Secular Writings in the European Tradition on Colonial Middle America, 1503–1818." In *Handbook of Middle American Indians*, edited by Charles Gibson and John B. Glass, 13:42–137. Austin: University of Texas Press, 1974.

Whittaker, Gordon. "The Identities of Fernando de Alva Ixtlilxochitl." In *Indigenous Historiography in Colonial Mexico: Fernando de Alva Ixtlilxochitl and His Legacy*, edited by Jongsoo Lee and Galen Brokaw, 29–76. Tucson: University of Arizona Press, 2016.

Wilson, Laurel Ann. "Common Threads: A Reappraisal of Medieval European Sumptuary Law." In *Legal Worlds and Legal Encounters*, edited by Elizabeth Lambourn, special issue, *The Medieval Globe* 2, no. 2 (2016): 141–65.

Zorita, Alonso de. *Breve y sumaria relación de los señores, y maneras y diferencias que había del ellos en la Nueva España*. In *Nueva colección de documentos para la historia de* México, edited by Joaquín García Icazbalceta: 3:71–227. Mexico: Andrade y Morales, sucesores, 1891.

Jerome A. Offner (joffner@hmns.org) is Associate Curator of Northern Mesoamerica at the Houston Museum of Natural Science and an expert on the Aztecs, their history, culture, law, and politics. His groundbreaking study, *Law and Politics in Aztec Texcoco* (1983) was the winner of the 1985 Howard F. Cline Prize in Latin American history. More recently, he has turned his attention to the Aztecs' graphic communication system and the study of native pictorial documents from before and after the conquest of 1519 CE. Along with a team of scholars from five European countries and Mexico, he is currently investigating the greatest of the Aztec pictorial histories, the Codex Xolotl, which reports on the remarkable life of the most famous Aztec jurist, Nezahualcoyotl (r. 1431–72 CE).

Abstract This article models a methodology for recovering the substance and nature of the Aztec legal tradition by interrogating reports of precontact indigenous behavior in the works of early colonial ethnographers, as well as in pictorial manuscripts and their accompanying oral performances. It calls for a new, richly recontextualized approach to the study of a medieval civilization whose sophisticated legal and jurisprudential practices have been fundamentally obscured by a long process of decontextualization and the anachronistic applications of modern Western paradigms.

Keywords Aztec, Nahua, Mesoamerica, Mexico, Texcoco, Tenochtitlan, Tlacopan, law, jurisprudence, legal procedure, Fray Bernardino de Sahagún, Fernando Alva de Ixtlilxochitl.

LAND AND TENURE IN EARLY COLONIAL PERU: INDIVIDUALIZING THE *SAPCI*, "THAT WHICH IS COMMON TO ALL"

SUSAN ELIZABETH RAMÍREZ

> By taking away said [native] lands and giving them to Spaniards and forcing the very same Indians to work the same lands that they lost[,] so that they [the Spaniards or Spanish authorities] say that they confiscate the lands because they [the natives] cannot cultivate them; and then they force the same individuals to till them[;] then what can an Indian feel when they take away his land and they deprive him of his freedom to have it worked for him and they force him to work it for the person who confiscated it[?][1]

THIS ARTICLE OUTLINES the transition from indigenous customs regarding land possession and use to European property law as gradually imposed and implemented by the Spanish colonial state in the Viceroyalty of Peru in the sixteenth century. The iconic confrontation between Francisco Pizarro and the Inca ruler Atahualpa on the plaza of Cajamarca in 1532, and its aftermath, has been examined from many different angles over the years. The military advantages of that face-off quickly took center stage.[2] The quest for gold and silver focused many.[3] The attendant evangelization efforts interested multiple researchers.[4] General studies of the negotiation that marked the permanent establishment of Spanish administration in the Andes have yielded insightful perspectives on the process of settlement and reorganization.[5] But one of the least studied aspects of

1 Carta de Fray Diego de Angulo al Rey Phelipe, AGI/AL 316, 25-IV-1584; reprinted in Barriga, *Los mercedarios en el Perú*, 178: "en quitarles las dichas tierras y darles a españoles [. . .] se las hacen labrar a los propios indios a que se las quitaron de manera que dicen se las quitan por que no las pueden labrar y despues se las hacen labrar a los mismos, pues que puede sentir un pobre indio que le quitaron su tierra y le quitan la libertad para hacerla labrar a el para si y se le hacen labrar para quien se la quitó."

2 Hassig, *Aztec Warfare*; Guilmartin, "Cutting Edge"; Chaliand, *Mirrors of a Disaster*.

3 Lockhart, *Men of Cajamarca*; Loredo, *Los repartos*; De la Puente Brunke, *Encomienda y encomenderos*.

4 Ricard, *Spiritual Conquest*; Griffiths, *Cross and the Serpent*; Duviols, *Cultural Andina y represión* and *Procesos y visitas*; Espinoza Soriano, *Juan Pérez de Guevara*; Early, *Maya and Catholicism*; Lippy, Choquette, and Poole, *Christianity Comes to the Americas*.

5 Lockhart, *Spanish Peru*; Ramírez, *World Upside Down*; Ramírez, "Chérrepe en 1572";

this story is the history of land and tenure in this mostly agrarian, peasant society. The anthropologist John V. Murra pioneered studies of native tenure by combing the Spanish chronicles for and listing different categories of native holdings.[6] The ethnohistorian María Rostworowski found, commented on, and published several sixteenth-century manuscripts dealing with land holdings, without questioning the European filters inherent in these recorded proceedings.[7] Silences in the sources led me to wonder about the native perspective on land holding, which I eventually began to investigate in the mid-1990s.

This essay builds and elaborates on this research, incorporating data from further investigations in the archives of Spain (Madrid and Seville), Bolivia (Sucre and La Paz), and Peru (Cuzco, Puno, and Lima), giving it a wider Andean perspective. It argues that the many different ethnic groups under Inca sway regarded the earth as sacred, so sacred that it could not be possessed in perpetuity by anyone. It was considered *sapci* or "that which is common to all."[8] It then focuses on the encounter of radically different conceptions of land and rights of possession and use precipitated by the Spanish conquest of the Andeans in 1532. In so doing, I outline the conflict over rights to use and to appropriate agricultural resources as defined by the unwritten native customs and the imported Iberian laws in the sixteenth century. The sources, summarized here, show that native customary rights remained important in the quotidian lives of peasants despite an overlay of colonial legalities that often, overtime, displaced native peoples and fixed them in place on lands different than those occupied before 1532.[9]

Some of the reasons why this story is so complicated and remains to be delineated are that Spanish descriptions of the colonial process and impositions obscured native practices. Garcilaso de la Vega, a bi-lingual (Quechua-Spanish) and well-educated mestizo[10] born in southern Peru to a rich, upper-class father and a

---

Mumford, *Vertical Empire*; Wernke, *Negotiated Settlements*; Murra, "Derechos a las tierras."

6 Murra, "Vida, tierra y agua."

7 Rostworowski de Diez Canseco, "Nuevos datos;" "Dos manuscritos inéditos;" and "Las tierras reales."

8 Also spelled: sacassi, sapsi, and sapcis. See De la Puente Luna, "That Which Belongs to All"; Ramírez, "Social Frontiers"; Ramírez, *World Upside Down*, ch. 3; Ramírez, "Rich Man, Poor Man."

9 I use the terms "custom(s)" or "customary" to refer to the unwritten, orally-transmitted tenure norms and practices of the natives, as opposed to the "laws," here defined as the written decrees and judicial sentences of the Spaniards. The Crown published a compilation of these in the four-volume *Recopilación de las leyes de los Reynos de las Indias* (hereinafter RLI) in 1681.

10 That is, the offspring of a native and a Spaniard.

native woman, notes in very unambiguous language that contemporary sixteenth-century Spanish chroniclers did not understand what they observed and could not communicate easily with natives because most Andeans did not understand or speak Spanish and the great majority of the Spanish[11] did not speak or understand even one of the Andean languages and dialects.[12] Thus, many of the eyewitness chronicles and later accounts and the information they contain are filtered through prisms of European understandings. Native societies were pre-literate at the time of contact, so they left no written records behind.[13]Most commoners continued to speak their native languages even into modern times. Often, therefore, even after native leaders learned Castilian under colonial rule, the testimonies of most commoners passed through Spanish and mestizo translators, scribes, notaries, lawyers, administrators, and adjudicators onto the page.

Another barrier to understanding is the difference between the late medieval Spanish language and our modern translations of it. The word *tierra*, today, usually equated with land, soil, or ground, was, in the sixteenth century, synonymous with people. The word *pueblo* nowadays means a town; whereas, in indigenous minds it represented a "people," "lineage," or ethnic group.[14]The word "province"(*provincia*) that is ubiquitous in early Spanish sources is never specifically defined there. In sixteenth-century Spain, users of the word understood it to mean "villages ... organized into federations."[15] If the phrase "ethnic groups" is substituted for villages, this meaning accords well with its use in the Andean manuscript sources. Instead of a bounded territory, a "province" in the sixteenth and seventeenth centuries referred to jurisdictions delimited in population and ethnic terms. Viceroy Francisco de Toledo (1569–81), for example, defined a parish as 400 families, enough to support a priest, without regard as to where the families resided. A provincial governor, *corregidor*,[16] had responsibility over an

---

11 I use the term Spaniard or Spanish to refer to peninsular-born individuals and those born in America of Spanish parents; the latter are also known as creoles.

12 Vega, *Royal Commentaries*, 50–51.

13 To record information, the natives used *quipus (khipus)*, knotted and colored strings, as well as drawings, pottery, and textiles. Unfortunately, scholars have not been able to decipher more than the numbers recorded in the knots of the quipus. See Urton, *Signs of the Inka Khipu*, 20; Urton and Quilter, *Narrative Threads*; Salomon, *Cord Keepers*.

14 Ramírez, "From People to Place."

15 Weeks, "European Antecedents," 63–64.

16 There were two types of *corregidores:* municipal and *de indios* (of natives). Both are discussed below.

urban population and/or specific native ethnic groups regardless of where they built their homes.[17]

My discussion begins with a brief overview of the Inca empire, a loose mosaic of ethnic groups, united (at least in theory) by the worship of the sun and its human descendants (the Incas), kinship ties, and mutual obligations. In this empire, rights to agrarian resources were flexible, changing, and all-encompassing. But these customs were gradually replaced by Spanish property rights that proved more inflexible, permanent, and limiting. Attention to colonial institutions and major legal initiatives and their effects on tenure rights and peoples' lives organize the remarks. Examples come from two of the three main Andean geographical regions: the irrigated coastal plains and the mountain sierras. (I have not included the largely hunting, gathering, and gardening populations of the eastern lowland jungles that remained largely unaffected by Spanish colonialism before the nineteenth century.)

Kin-Based Communities, ca. 1532

Spanish chroniclers agree, and later native testimonies support, that Andean populations under the uncertain, unstable hegemony of the Incas on the eve of the Spanish invasions in 1532 lived scattered over the landscape in family compounds and small hamlets, from sea-level on the beaches of the Pacific Ocean to the eastern slopes of the snow-capped Andean mountains. The Incas, the hegemonic ethnic group in the Andes at the time, had been actively incorporating other distinct ethnic groups into their fold during at least the previous century, either by taking captives in "good wars" (by conquest) or inviting these groups to ally with them. Ritual gifts of fine tunics, distinguishing helmets and headdresses, and litters demonstrated the expected generosity of the Inca ruler to compliant ethnic lords. The exchange of women between leaders guaranteed the establishment of blood ties in the next generation and the promise of union and cooperation into the future. Regardless of how they were subjugated, populations had to accept the Inca gods, primarily the Sun (the Inca emperor's father) and the Moon (the emperor's mother); to learn to speak the Inca language of Quechua (if they did not already speak it); and to provide tribute labor when requested, be it for building a ceremonial center, terracing a mountainside, maintaining the roads, constructing storage or burial towers, carrying messages, fighting a war, or running fresh fish from the beaches to wherever the Inca happened to be resting. The Inca ruler and

17 Sahlins, *Boundaries*; Ramírez, "From People to Place"; Vega, *Royal Commentaries*, 50–51; Elden, *Birth of Territory*; Osborne and Van Valkenburgh, "Home Turf"; Mantha, "Shifting Territorialities."

his court often traveled across the landscape maintaining contact and reinforcing the alliance with these distinct groups. Ceremonial centers (at Huánuco Pampa, Quito, Tumipampa, Hatunqolla, Charcas, Vilcasguaman, Incawasi and Cajamarca, for example) with the hallmark features of Inca architecture (trapezoidally-shaped windows and doors, finely-shaped stone construction, storage silos, raised daises (*ushnus*),[18] and monumental structures show the importance and range of this movement to reinforce the personal ties that motivated sometimes distant populations to undertake long pilgrimages to attend ceremonies to venerate the ancestors, enjoy the hospitality of the emperor, and cooperate in imperial goals.[19]

The status of similarly itinerant ethnic leaders, likewise, reflected the number of subjects that would respond to a call for action. A noteworthy chieftain (*curaca*) whose followers numbered 5,000 families, outranked a native lord who held sway over a thousand (*guaranga*) or a hundred (*pachaca*). Kinship ties united hundreds of these family groupings into lineages and these into ethnic groups who each believed that they all descended from one apical-ancestor or couple. Early colonial testimonies from native witnesses on the north coast attest to the fact that leaders at different levels of the administrative hierarchy were joined by exchanging brides.[20] Authority and society itself were relational, based on kinship, not territory.[21] Kin of one ethnic group often lived and cultivated next to members of other ethnic groups, a pattern dubbed *ocupación salpicada* (scattered occupation). Members of each lineage occasionally traveled to their respective ceremonial centers to worship their ancestors and their generosity on significant dates, much as Muslim, Christian, and Jewish neighbors might each attend religious ceremonies in different locations on different days.[22] A hierarchy of hereditary authorities led these events, orchestrating the planning, agenda, and supply of each event. Activities included singing and dancing, sacrifices, storytelling, and feasting—all of which helped to reinforce lineage and ethnic group unity. Individual and group gifts thanked the ancestors for the blessings of health and fertility for themselves, their animals, and their seeds. The population was careful to make appropriate offerings, for to ignore or madden the ancestors by neglect would negatively affect their lives. Drought, disease, earthquakes and other problems could be sent by the ancestors should they become disaffected.

---

18 Ramírez, "The Link."

19 Niles, *Shape of Inca History.* This section is based, in part, on Ramírez, *World Upside Down*; and Ramírez, *To Feed and Be Fed.*

20 Ramírez, "De pescadores y agricultores."

21 Ramírez, "Social Frontiers."

22 With the significant difference that different groups might worship the same gods

Although the term *sapci* is applied to resources (in general) used to benefit a population, early sources clearly show that Andeans regarded land as well as mineral outcrops and *guano* deposits (fertilizer) from offshore islands as open and common for use by all.[23] It was, as the leader of the Guamanes (who lived in the Chimú Valley) stated, in 1566, "a common thing and open to all and which no one could have nor acquire [permanent] possession of,"[24] Individuals freely used as much as they could use for as long as it remained fruitful.[25] Thus, farmers could take possession of any vacant, unused land by working it—clearing it, plowing it, sowing it, watering it (if needed), weeding it, and harvesting it. Rights to a piece of land continued until it was abandoned, due to infertility, prolonged drought, the death of the possessor and his/her descendants, or another cause. In this situation, the land reverted to its natural, wild state, at which point another family could start the process again. Native testimonies recorded by ecclesiastical inspectors to the north-central highlands[26] and the remnants of a native register from the coastal community of Lambayeque dating from the 1580s show that, if anyone remembered a previous possessor, a new user made appropriate sacrifices to his/her memory before beginning to plow the untilled fields anew. One entry from the Lambayeque register records the memories of Pedro Ulcum, Graviel Xecllon, Andres [here the page is torn], Pedro Cupllon, and Miguel Chanan, all born in that town. The lands called Zallan had been planted by their forefathers. Minepoata possessed [*los tuvo*] them first. Then Tequen planted them. They continued to name in chronological order at least eight more tillers of that one piece of land to December of 1611, in order to register their possession.[27] Some fields on the coast and in the highlands had stones (*guancas, huancas, or wank'as*) in their centers that represented preceding cultivators, at which current farmers placed offerings periodically.[28]

---

23 Salomon, *The Cord Keepers*; 2004b, 140–47, 270; Gonzalez Holguín, *Vocabvlario*; Sherbondy, "Organización hidráulica," 142; Pease and Robinson, *Collaguas*; De la Puente Luna, "That Which Belongs to All"; Ramírez, *To Feed and Be Fed*, ch. 3; Guaman Poma de Ayala, *Nueva corónica*, 162 [186], 308 [336], 325 [353], 474 [515], 589 [621], 780 [816], 810 [864].

24 AGI/J458, 1871: "cosa general y como para todos y de que nayde [nadie] podra tener ny adquirir posesion."

25 For an intriguing parallel from Africa, see Elias, *Nigerian Land Law and Custom*, especially ch. 5; and Dike, "Land Tenure System in Igboland."

26 Duviols, *Cultural Andina y represión* and *Procesos y visitas de idolatrías*, 237, 507, 715.

27 ANCR/1586–1611, 14–14v.

28 Dean, *Culture of Stone*, 44–46.

Ideally, peasants cultivated many separate pieces of land in widely dispersed ecological niches. These societies measured plots in *topos*, representing the area needed to provide support for a couple. But the size of each topo was relative. It varied in size, depending on fertility and expected yields.[29] Thus, a smaller piece of maize land under irrigation was needed to support a peasant couple than one, perhaps at a higher elevation, needed to feed the same people. Farmers with large families cultivated many more pieces of land than those with small families. Ideally, these would have been located at various altitudes up and down the Andean slopes in separate fields. Such geographical diversity allowed farmers to match potato varieties[30] with the best field locations to improve productivity and guarantee subsistence. If the crops of one plot became blighted, froze or dried out for lack of rain or irrigation, others would survive to be harvested. Members of the same lineage or ethnic group farmed plots at days' walks away for this reason. At each site, a hut or house provided temporary shelter. Thus, agricultural populations, like their leaders, were mobile, often traveling hours or days from one field to another.[31]

Populations that relied on irrigation may have been somewhat less mobile as the available lands were concentrated along the banks of the river and water canals. Ongoing research suggests that lineages built irrigation ditches and retained rights to the water and the land it irrigated.[32] All members of a group had rights to land and had to participate in communal, periodic canal cleanings to maintain their access. Yet, the same rules prevailed as to the rights to use the ground. Failure to use land to the point that it appeared abandoned signaled that it was open to others. Even outsiders (*forasteros*) could use such land as long as they participated actively in lineage or ethnic activities (*ayni*), be they ceremonies, sacrifices, or irrigation canal cleanings.[33] Indeed, it was advantageous for lords to accept outsiders into their groups and there was keen competition among authorities for the loyalty and labor of peasants, regardless of lineage identity, because as mentioned earlier their status depended on the number of people who they could mobilize for different reasons.[34] The commoners also traveled personally to take advantage of various resources. Thus, farmers might travel to the seashore to burn

29 Rostworowski de Diez Canseco, *Pesos y medidas*.

30 Families had over 600 varieties of potatoes to choose from, for example.

31 Murra, "'El control vertical.'"

32 AGNP/Donaciones D4-8-12, 1722. See also Salomon and Urioste, *Huarochirí Manuscript*.

33 This is evident in the thinking of Felipe Guaman Poma de Ayala. See Adorno, "Court and Chronicle," especially 75.

34 Ramírez, *World Upside Down*, especially 35–36; AGI/J458, 2039–40, 2044–44v.

seashells for lime (needed for releasing the active ingredient in coca leaves), collect salt and seaweed, or hunt sea mammals (sea lions). Others no doubt left their fields to take birds that inhabited back-beach lagoons and lakes. A few walked to mineral outcrops to extract copper, silver, and gold.[35]

Custom obliged each family to also work fertile land for the support of the religio-political authorities and the veneration of ancestral gods. Lords directed native labor. Planting was a celebrated occasion marked with feasting and rituals acknowledging communal efforts and ancestral blessings, which reinforced lineage identity and solidarity. Communal tribute labor (*ayni*: mutual help, reciprocity) embodied a duty and responsibility for the welfare of them all. Evidence from Chincha on the south-central coast shows that these lands, dubbed by the Spaniards the "lands of the Inca" or the "lands of the Sun," were plots designated to be worked by ethnic populations with the produce being designated to be delivered to the Inca storehouses or used to stage ceremonials in honor of one of their many gods. The primary documents on lineage religious practices that span the entirety of the colonial era (published by Pierre Duviols for the north-central highlands, Ana Sánchez on the Lima hinterland, Mario Polia Meconi for the Andes as a whole) show that each bloodline also worked lands to support the veneration of their ancestors. Harvests produced maize that was ground, cooked, and made into cakes and beer to serve as offerings on ritual occasions. These "lands" did not remain in the same place year after year, but were rotated based on fertility and other considerations. This was a point that the Spanish failed to grasp; they assumed that the lands of the Inca and the Sun were fixed in place and immutable over time.[36] Yet, it is apparent that these lands could be any that would serve the purpose and needs of the lineage or ethnic groups at a given season for a particular crop.[37]

Tenuous Tenure

Landholding was not an immediate primary concern for the men who accompanied Francisco Pizarro on their trek south from their landfall in what is now Ecuador in 1531–32. Leaders and men were more focused on the imagined quick wealth that seemed feasible given the gold and silver acquired on a previous expedition. The actions of Pizarro, himself, suggest that, in addition to seeking treasure, he planned on establishing a base from which to initiate contact with the Andean ruler. Thus, in the valley subsequently called after an ethnic chief, Lachira, Pizarro

35 Ramírez, "Ethnohistorical Dimensions."

36 *ACT*, 1:88; ART/CoO l. 148, exp. 46, 13-VII-1565.

37 Castro and Ortega Morejón, "Relación de Chincha."

founded the first Spanish city in the Andes, known as San Miguel de Tangarará (today known as San Miguel de Piura). He chose householders and citizens (*vecinos*) and from their ranks appointed members of a town council (*cabildo*). The city, as was the tradition in Spain, held *propios* (common ground), which could be rented or sold to provide the council with revenue. Each householder received grants (*mercedes*) of a house lot (*solar*) and a suburban garden plot (*huerta*).[38] Pizarro also, most importantly, entrusted to his meritorious followers groups of the indigenous population. He made Hernando de Soto[39] guardian of the population loyal to the native lord of the Tumbes, for example.[40] Juan Roldán became the trustee of the peoples of Túcume on 3 of February 1536 by these words:[41]

> Because you Juan Roldan, citizen of this town of Trujillo, have served his majesty in these kingdoms, [and] are one of the first settlers of them, [and] have married with the intention of remaining in them and have your wife and house like an honorable person; I, Don Francisco Pizarro, precursor, captain general and governor for his majesty ... by this present act in the name of his majesty ... deposit in you the people of Tucome with the person of the cacique principal Conocique [lord of a thousand adult men], ... and with the [subservient] lord named Ponopo with all their Indians and principal persons [....] .

These grants, called *encomiendas*, made the Spaniards masters of the population, able to approximate the Spanish ideal of a gentleman who could not be ordered about (able to say: *a mi no me manda nadie*).[42] In return for protecting their native

38 Ots Capdequi, *España en América*, chs. 1–2.

39 Carlín Arce, *Historia general*, 38, and *Reseña histórica*, 78.

40 For lists of encomendero grants by Pizarro, La Gasca, and others, see De la Puente Brunke, *Encomienda y encomenderos*, 395–497; León Gómez, *Paños e hidalguía*, 73–74; Varallanos, *Historia de Huánuco*, 227–28; Loredo, *Los repartos*, 141–361; Espinoza Soriano, *Juan Pérez de Guevara*, 24, 54–60.

41 AGI/Escribanía 502A, 7: "Don Fran[cis]co piçarro adelantado capp[it]an general e g[overnad]or Por su mag[esta]d en estos rreinos De la nueba castilla. Eta. Considerando que bos Juo[n] rroldan v[e]z[in]o desta billa de truxillo a veis seruido a su mag[es]t[ad] en estos dichos rreinos e que sois de los primeros pobladores della e que os abeis casado con yntençion de permanesçer en ella e tener v[uest]ra mujer e casa como pers[on]a de honrra por e[l] presente en nombre de su mag[esta]d [. . .] os deposito el pueblo tucome con la pers[on]a del cacique prençipal conoçique [. . .] e otro."

42 Pizarro's actions mirrored the Spanish monarchy's practices during the Reconquista of founding municipalities and often granting them privileges, including lands on which families could settle and farm, see Weeks, "European Antecedents." Earlier tenure arrangements and farming practices in Islamic Spain are summarized by Imāmuddin, "Al-Filāhah (Farming)."

charges and teaching them the rudiments of the Christian faith and promising to maintain a horse and arms ready to serve the king, these men and trustees (or *encomenderos*) were to receive the products of native labor as tribute. The *encomiendas* became a basis for the wealth and position of this initial group of Spaniards on the scene and those who were with Pizarro as he made contact with Atahualpa and pushed further afield into and across the Andes. It was an effective institution in a situation where the invaders did not know the geographical extent of Inca hegemony or the population of the realm. The *encomienda* specifically entrusted the subjects under various indigenous lords to Spaniards who then asked or demanded that they produce goods for his own use and that of his family. Land was not mentioned and was not part of the grant. Natives, declared by the Crown to be free, remained in their homesteads to use common resources to produce the food, fiber, and the other products demanded by their *encomendero* and *amo* (lord, master). However, because *encomendero* demands were unregulated until the late 1540s, the institution quickly became a tool of exploitation of the native population and enrichment for the approximately 500 persons who were eventually entrusted with the Andean peoples.[43]

Once Pizarro and his men had captured Atahualpa in mid-November 1532 and had received his gold and silver ransom over the next months, many *conquistadores* requested permission to return to Spain. Still facing thousands of hostile native troops, Pizarro astutely acquiesced to only a handful of these requests. These men departed, loaded down with their shares of treasure. As they traveled overland to Piura and Paita (the fishing village that became Piura's major port) and by sea to Panama and then to Santo Domingo and Seville, news of their fabulous wealth spread, initiating a "gold rush" as merchants and adventurers retraced their paths into the Andes.

Many of these who arrived too late to receive an *encomienda* faced limited options. They could return from whence they came; they could join an out-going expedition to explore new areas for treasure and subject populations; they could seek employment in the house of an *encomendero*; or they could start a business. The last two options proved the most viable for many. Native peoples provided

---

The parallels between tenure arrangements in Spain and the Americas will be discussed below.

43 Lockhart, *Men of Cajamarca*, 12. Data from 1548 shows that *encomienda* incomes (based on the value of the products sold on the open market) varied from 991 to 7206 pesos with the average being slightly over 2000 pesos in one district in the north. Subsequently, *encomienda* labor would enable encomenderos to launch complementary business enterprises that vastly multiplied their wealth. See Ramírez, *Provincial Patriarchs*, 20–24, 37; and Angulo, "Cartulario," 191–206.

their *encomenderos* with fish, maize, potatoes, and animal flesh from ducks, turkeys, camelids, and guinea pigs as tribute; but they had no experience raising European livestock or cereals. So, *encomenderos* hired or established partnerships with these latecomers to raise livestock on the pastures (defined as any vegetation that was not deliberately cultivated [such as crops], including weeds between cultivated plants and stubble left after the harvest in native fields and grasses growing between the rows), which the Crown declared common in the 1530s.[44] A notarial register from 1539 contains an agreement for the establishment of a partnership to raise livestock on the coast near the city of Trujillo (founded in late 1534).[45] No document suggests that the natives were consulted on the locations for these activities. Such latecomers who became some of the first Spanish settlers of rural areas chose sites at which they constructed a shelter for themselves and corrals for the livestock. Horses were the most valuable animal; but, though less valuable per head, the numbers of imported swine, beef cattle, goats, and sheep grew more quickly.[46] As herds and flocks multiplied, shepherds built additional corrals at varying distances from this hub, which later was called an *estancia*, from the verb *estar*, to be or to be located or centered at a place. Some of these Spaniards who served as *mayordomos* (overseers) and custodians of *encomendero* herds, subsequently went into business for themselves. In less than three decades, some had herds numbering in the thousands of head.[47]

Given that royal officials rarely ventured into the countryside, the historical record is mostly silent about early native views on Spanish occupation. Imperial appointees remained concentrated in such cities as Lima and Cuzco. Thus, the most usual interactions between the native population and Spaniards were with their *encomendero* or his agent, a priest, and a growing number of Spanish travelers and vagabonds. What documents exist attest to native discontents, usually in indirect references written by sympathetic Spaniards, especially priests who had frequent contact with native parishioners. Thus, the Bishop of Cuzco, Fray Vicente Valverde, wrote an important letter to His Majesty Carlos I (Emperor Charles V) in 1539, stating that natives came to him asking that he support and defend them because "some Christians take their lands [...] [and] I am no judge with compe-

---

44 Ramírez, *Provincial Patriarchs*, 45; *RLI*, v. 2, leyes 5–7, tit. 17, lib. 4, 112v–113r.

45 Ramírez, *Patriarcs Provinciales*, 64.

46 In 1539, the will of Juan de Barbarán, a member of Pizarro's original company and an *encomendero*, already listed 393 pigs and 586 sheep as patrimony (not counting personal mounts: horses and a mule). Ramírez, *Provincial Patriarchs*, 24; Angulo, "Cartulario," 197–98.

47 Ramírez, *Provincial Patriarchs*, 78–80.

tence to deal with the matter [...] [but this is] an abuse of the Indians."[48] Similar accusations arrived in Spain from another religious who noted, in 1541, that the *encomenderos* kept their charges so busy that they had no time to plant and (in the long run) lost their fields;[49] and that Spaniards took the lands of dead natives (to the chagrin and suffering of their families).[50] The same account related that the Spanish robbed and abused natives to the extent that to defend their families, persons, and possessions the natives killed some of their abusers.[51] Despite the fact that the Crown was concerned and had sent royal orders to appoint "protectors" of the natives,[52] local municipal councils (dominated as they were by *encomenderos*) resisted such nominations. Because these actions would infringe on their prerogatives, the councils invoked bureaucratic delaying tactics to postpone the protectors' involvement with "their" natives. Tragically, also, most natives did not know how to find justice

> [b]ecause the Indians of the land of Peru and their Lords receive many abuses and fatigues and other oppression from their masters [the encomenderos] and other Spaniards, which are not known nor can be known, because the Indians have no understanding [*abilidad,* capacity or knowledge], nor know to whom to complain nor who can remedy and favor them [....][53]

The writer recommended that a "protector" visit the countryside annually to bring justice to these peoples,[54] although this was a practical improbability. Likewise, a

48 Lissón y Chávez, *La iglesia de España*, vol. 1, no. 2, especially 115 : "Le[s] toman sus tierras algunos christianos [. . .] [y] no soi juez para entender en ello [. . .] [era] agrauio de indios [. . .]." Another accusation about Christians taking their lands is on page 69 of the same source.

49 Lissón y Chávez, *La iglesia de España*, vol. 1, no. 3, 62.

50 Ibid., vol. 1, no. 3, 84.

51 Ibid., vol. 1, no. 3, 57.

52 See, for example, the Royal Decree of 1542, published in Lissón y Chávez, *La iglesia de España*, vol. 1, no. 3, 120–22; and the instructions for the protection of the natives sent in another Royal Decree of 1546 to Fray Juan Solano, published in Lissón y Chávez, *La iglesia de España*, vol. 1, no. 4, 148–50.

53 Lissón y Chávez, *La iglesia de España*, vol. 1, no. 3, 72 : "Por quanto los dichos yndios naturales de la tierra del peru e los Señores della reciben muchos agravios e fatigas e otras opresiones de sus amos y de otros españoles, las cuales no se saben ni se pueden saber, por no tener abilidad los yndios ni saber a quien se quexar ni, quien les ha de remediar e favorecer [. . .]."

54 Ibid., vol. 1, no. 3, 74.

Spaniard (Licenciado Martel de Santoyo) wrote a long treatise in 1542, on how to remedy some of Peru's problems in which he suggested that lands that had been appropriated by Spaniards be returned.[55]

Natives were not the only ones vying for land. Herding activities also provoked conflict among the Spanish population. Disputes date to 1541, when some persons occupied an area and tried to keep others from building corrals or grazing their animals nearby. Carlos V and his advisors became worried that if this practice spread all the good pastures would be partitioned within a few years and settlement of Peru retarded. Therefore, the king reiterated that, as was the custom in Spain, pastures were to be held in common.[56]

Simultaneously, disease, overwork, and flight decimated the Andean peoples.[57] The populations of both coast and highlands had already plummeted by 1532, due to disease that spread faster than Spanish exploration. Chroniclers relate that Guayna Capac, the last Inca ruler before the civil war between Atahualpa and his brother Huascar, died from an unknown illness near Quito a few years before Pizarro's invasion. Some scholars estimate that up to 50 percent of the native population had already died by 1532. Historical data from the sixteenth century show that many native lineages suffered declines of up to 90 percent before the end of the sixteenth century.[58] This depopulation left abundant vacant lands that could be and were occupied without title by Spanish immigrants, the *encomenderos*, and their herds.

The Introduction of European Ideas of Property-Holding

Interaction between the Iberian-born population (and the second and subsequent generations) and the natives intensified markedly at mid-century and friction escalated. In response to the combination of the native demographic crisis, high demand for European foodstuffs and wine (which was being supplied by sea from Central America, the Caribbean, and Spain at suitably high prices), and past challenges to royal authority,[59] the central government authorized reform measures

55 Ibid., vol. 1, no. 3, 110.

56 BAH/ML, t. 21, 191–92; see also AGNP/RA, l. 27, c. 95, 1610.

57 Cook, "Indian Population of Peru"; Powers, *Andean Journeys.*

58 Ramírez, *World Upside Down*, especially 26–29; Cook, "Indian Population of Peru."

59 The first Viceroy, Blasco Núñez Vela, intent on introducing legislation that would undercut encomendero power, was defeated in battle by *encomendero* forces and beheaded. This was followed by civil war, which only ended in the late 1540s with the pacification efforts of the King's representative, Licenciado Pedro de la Gasca.

that impacted, directly or indirectly, tenure arrangements. These included founding Spanish towns, beginning officially to grant individuals property with clear title (*mercedes*) for agricultural purposes, appointing new officials (the *corregidor de indios*, an administrator with jurisdiction over natives) who distanced the natives from their *encomenderos* and brought a measure of opportunity for the redress of grievances, concentrating the native population in Spanish-style towns, called *reducciones* (reductions), and commissioning inspectors to take justice into the hinterlands.

The Spanish monarch's authority to make *mercedes* emanated from the "discovery" and "conquest" of the population and his succession to the presumed titles and rights of the Incas. In theory, the Spanish king's claim to eminent domain was based on Pope Alexander VI's bull *Inter caetera divinae magestatis*, issued 4 May 1493, which thus exported an ancient "Old World" doctrine that all land won by conquest could be distributed by the conqueror. It granted the "Most Catholic" monarchs Ferdinand and Isabella and their heirs and successors the lands, cities, forts, places, rights, and jurisdictions to all the islands and continents discovered up to 100 leagues west of the Cape Verde islands. The bull's only restriction was the prohibition against the usurpation of lands belonging to a Christian prince. The Treaty of Tordesillas (4 June 1494) subsequently moved Spanish jurisdiction 270 leagues further to the west.[60]

Using this authority, the Spanish monarchs and their representatives confirmed the natives' communal use and possession of land (*dominio útil*), thus legitimizing their previous tenuous rights, based as they were solely on oral testimonies[61] and occupation and use.[62] According to the climate of opinion, the Crown considered indigenous peoples as minors and dependents to be provided for and

---

60 AGI/AL 101, 1642; Valdez de la Torre, *Evolución*, 50–51.

61 Recorded oral testimonies of provincial peoples, specifically regarding their land use and tenure, start as early as 1565 with references sometimes extending back to pre-Hispanic times. See, for example, Ramírez, "De pescadores y agricultores"; Rostworowski de Diez Canseco, "Etnohistoria," 35–41; AGI/J458, 2125–25v, 2131; ANCR/1586–1611. On native agency in general, see Ramírez, "Chérrepe en 1572"; Ramírez, *Provincial Patriarchs*; Ramírez *World Upside Down*, especially ch. 5; De la Puente Luna, "Into the Heart of Empire"; Noack, "Caciques" (on natives manipulating the written word to secure a desired outcome regarding chiefly succession); and the essays in Drinot and Garofalo, *Más Allá de la dominación*. On Spanish laws (as early as the Laws of Burgos of 1512) confirming native usufruct rights, see Guevara Gil, *Propiedad agraria*, xvii, 129.

62 Oral testimonies are recorded in the 1565 inquiry published in Ramírez, "De pescadores y agricultores"; the testimonies published by Rostworowski de Diez Canseco ("'Mercaderes del Valle de Chincha"); and the unpublished records of the review of an Audiencia judge's activities in 1566–67 (AGI/J458).

protected.[63] Therefore, the monarchs never gave them absolute, fee-simple property rights to the land.

Land grants to Spaniards, in contrast, implied both direct dominion (*dominio directo*) and usufruct rights (*dominio útil*), provided certain provisions were met. Land grants became valid titles, for example, only after the grantee had cultivated the land for a specified number of years. The grantee was also enjoined from selling the land to another individual for a definite period and prohibited indefinitely from selling or donating the land to the Roman Catholic Church.[64] Moreover, land grants were subject to royal confirmation, although few grantees bothered to seek confirmation at this time. Finally, *mercedes* were issued with the condition that they cause no harm to third parties (for example, the natives).[65] The king repeatedly cautioned his representatives not to disturb the possession of lands held communally by the lineages.[66]

The Spanish monarchs delegated their authority to make land grants to governors, viceroys, and certain town councils. Pizarro distributed both urban and suburban real estate around the cities he founded.[67] Town councils later assumed this power, making liberal grants of house sites to encomenderos and non-encomenderos alike. Viceroy Don Antonio de Mendoza (1551–52) made the first known grant of about fifty *fanegas de sembradura* to a non-encomendero of Trujillo for agricultural purposes in 1550,[68] while traveling overland to Lima. In the following years, more *cabildos* partitioned abandoned tracts of land among recent arrivals, sometimes identified as "poor farmers" (*labradores pobres*), on which to grow wheat and other foodstuffs.[69]

---

63 Ots Capdequi, *España en América*, 19, 28, 157.

64 The prohibition against donating lands to the church was unevenly observed in later years. See Guevara Gil, *Propiedad agraria*, 90.

65 For that reason, many early land acquisition records contained an almost requisite clause stating that the lands had belonged to the Inca, sun or moon: Honores, "La asistencia jurídica privada," 6 and 8; Guevara Gil, *Propiedad agraria*, 13, 23 (recording that lands had been of Viracocha Inca and were dedicated to the sun), 172 (recording that these were empty lands of the Inca).

66 *RLI*, v. 2, ley 5, tit. 12, lib. 6, fol. 242; Ugarte, "Los antecedentes históricos," 368–74; BAH/ML, t. 97, 1535, 133–35; Lissón y Chávez, *La iglesia de España*, vol. 1, no. 2, 76; Ots Capdequi, *El estado español*, 39, 135; Guevara Gil, *Propiedad agraria*, 13, 28, 90, 192.

67 Guevara Gil, *Propiedad agraria*, 7; Honores, "La asistencia jurídica privada," 7.

68 A *fanegada* (*de sembradura*) was the land that could be planted with a *fanega* (approximately 1.5 bushels) of seed. This was not an absolute measure, because the amount of land that could be sown with a fanega of seed was a function of the type of seed (e.g., corn, cotton, chilis) and the soil fertility, climate, water availability, and other factors.

69 ART/LC, 1564; *ACT*, 1:11, 177, and 202–3; Ramírez, *Provincial Patriarchs*, 25, 51, 66;

The municipal council of Trujillo, for example, had been making grants since Pizarro's departure without the official sanction of the king or any other authority. In 1558, the Viceroy Marqués de Cañete (1556–61), in an effort to formulate the first coherent land distribution policy, questioned the legality of the council's actions and apparently moved to annul the grants. Pedro Gonzales, with power of attorney from the council, hastily departed for Lima to persuade the viceroy to confirm its previous actions. Under pressure, the Marqués allowed these unauthorized grants to stand in a royal decree issued in Lima on 21 February 1558. The minutes show that the council continued to make grants near the city until at least the end of the 1560s, but rarely outside the immediate vicinity of the city.[70]

One reason for these unauthorized actions was the lack of royal officials in the area. This was effectively remedied in the 1540s, when a *corregidor municipal* (municipal governor with executive, judicial, and administrative jurisdiction over specific populations) was named. His control was weak at best in the early years, given *encomendero* opposition. Most *corregidores* made no pretense of being able to impose their will on all. The multiplicity of his duties forced him to routinely delegate authority to lieutenants when he left town to visit distant settlements to implement royal decrees.[71] Over time, however, his administrative and judicial impartiality was thwarted as, by the mid-1550s, a feeling of common interests between the *corregidor* and Spaniards replaced the initial resistance and distrust of this authority. This was especially true of the *encomenderos* who began to serve as the *corregidor's* guarantors, that is, an *encomendero* guaranteed that the *corregidor* would appear at his *residencia*, a judicial review at the end of his term of office at which he answered any charges of incompetence or misuse of power. Such arrangements made him a less zealous representative and advocate of the crown's interests.[72]

Another reform measure resulting from the mounting intercultural friction between the Spanish and the natives and the fact that there were few authorities outside the cities to whom the natives could appeal to for help, moved Governor García de Castro (1564–69) to appoint a second type of *corregidor*, the *corregidor de indios,* with specific jurisdiction over the natives in 1566. Whereas a *corregidor municipal* exercised jurisdiction over the Spanish and mixed population of the Span-

---

Keith, "Origins of the Hacienda System," 153; Guevara Gil, *Propiedad agraria*, 7–8, 13, 15, 23 (for Cuzco).

70 *ACT*, 1:11, 37, 67, 77, 82, 95, 98, 186–87, 202–3, 264, and 298–99; ART/CoO l. 147, exp. 21, 11-IX-1562. See also Ots Capdequi, *España en América*, 41 (on the *cabildo*'s loss of the right to grant land).

71 Cabero, "El Capitán Juan Delgadillo"; *ACT*, 1:48–50, 59, 371.

72 *ACT*, 1:353, 358, 359; ART/Vega, 1567.

ish cities and towns, the *corregidor de indios* supervised the natives and dealt with the problems of intercultural contact, but at a salary equal to less than half that of the *corregidor municipal* of Trujillo.[73] As a cultural broker and ombudsman in rural areas, the *corregidor de indios* had an ambiguous role. Theoretically, the natives' welfare was one of his primary responsibilities. He was to be an impartial authority who would listen to appeals for justice. His duties included enforcing labor laws, which prohibited natives from working as porters or mill hands; making sure that native laborers were promptly paid; and monitoring the collection of tribute.[74]

But the *corregidor de indios* did not solve all the natives' problems with the Spaniards. Spokesmen for the populations of Chérrepe and Pacasmayo appealed to him for payment of damages to their corn and cotton fields and irrigation network caused by the livestock of Pedro de Morales and Gaspar de Soria. Cabildo officials had ignored their complaints. When they approached the *corregidor*, Don Diego de Valverde, he stalled. To make matters worse, at the insistence of Morales, Valverde ordered the native spokesmen whipped and shaved. To native men, cutting of the hair was second only in severity of punishment to exile. Then, to reassert his authority, Valverde sent them to work as laborers for Morales.[75]

In each of these cases the attitude of both officials and *corregidor* is explained by conflicts of interest. Council magistrates were farmers and livestock raisers, whose own animals damaged the natives' fields and irrigation networks just as the animals of other settlers did. The *corregidor*'s inaction can be explained by his clear identification with such agrarian interests. The *corregidor*, theoretically an outside, impartial representative of the crown and protector of the natives, was by the 1570s and 1580s participating in the agricultural bonanza. Father Toribio de Mogrovejo, the Archbishop of Lima, wrote to King Philip II from the northern valleys in February of 1590 to report that the *corregidores* commonly forced lineages to plant fields for them and grind wheat into flour. Moreover, the *corregidores*, emulating the *encomenderos*, used the natives to generate revenue to supplement their salaries by requiring them to produce commodities on previously unfarmed land or spinning and weaving textiles for sale in the southern markets. Moreover, the lineages constituted a captive market for horses, mules, wine, and other goods, which the *corregidor* could force the natives to buy, sometimes at exorbitant prices.[76]

---

73 *ACT*, 1:249 and 2:147; Eisen, "Indians in Colonial Spanish America," 108; AAT/Causas, 1570; AGNP/R l. 3, c. 7, 1582, 133; ART/Vega, 1587; AGI/AL 464, 1583.

74 Valdez de la Torre, *Evolución*, 63; *ACT*, 1:353; *ACT*, 3:11; ART/O 1591, 144v–45, and 1609; Keith, "Encomienda."

75 ART/Mata 1580; CoO 27-VII-1580; AGNP/R l. 3, c. 7, 1582, 101–3.

76 ASFL/Reg. 9, No. 2, Ms. 11, 1590; and Ms. 2; Lissón y Chávez, *La iglesia de España*, vol.

Furthermore, like the case of the *corregidor municipal*, some of the leading citizens of the towns and largest agrarian interests posted bond so that the *corregidor de indios* could assume office.[77] Being the sponsor of a *corregidor* sometimes gave a guarantor the opportunity to resolve conflicts directly. The *corregidor* often named a guarantor as a lieutenant, thus giving him official jurisdiction over his own interests.[78] Bribes and threats also influenced the *corregidores*' action.[79] It is not surprising, then, that the natives rarely got results when they appealed to the *corregidor* or local officials for help. Long distances and the infrequency of visits by outside authorities regularly allowed *corregidores* and city officials to act, in many cases, with impunity.

Worse, and defying pre-Hispanic traditions, even top native officials were frequently closely allied with local Spanish interests. *Encomenderos*, for example, served as godfathers to native lords' children. Consequently, these children sometimes took the *encomendero*'s name. Thus, Captain Diego de Mora, the first *encomendero* of the Chicamas and Chimús, became the godfather to Don Juan de Mora, the son of Don Alonso Caxahuaman, cacique at the time that Pizarro invaded. According to Jorge Zevallos Quiñones, a prominent local archaeologist and historian, he became the chief and ruled until late in the sixteenth century.[80] In other cases, lords, like Don Antonio of the Chimús, entered into a partnership with Spaniards of the city of Trujillo.[81] Likewise, *encomenderos* and even the viceroy sometimes intervened in the native succession process to impose their choices, which left the newly installed lord subject to his patron's whims.[82] Documentary and secondary sources show that as a result of their inability to find remedies for abuses locally, the natives supported individual leaders' and delegations' trips to the capital (and later to Spain) to present their petitions for justice at court.[83]

At about the same time as the appointment of *corregidores de indios*, a second type of official, a *visitador* or inspector, made tours of rural areas. Visiting

---

3 no. 15 (16-II-1590), 538; ART/CoAG 24-XII-1582; CoR 30-VI-1576; AGNP/R l. 3, c. 7, 1582, 99v–107; AGI/J457 1151–51v; J460, 365v; and J461, 1430v.

77 *ACT,* 2:146; *ACT,* 3:15; AGNP/R l. 2, c. 5, 1582, 27v–28; ART/Vega, 1587.

78 *ACT,* 2:266.

79 ART/MT 1578; *ACT,* 3:11–13; AGNP/R l. 3, c. 7, 1582, 135.

80 Zevallos Quiñones, *Los cacicazgos*, 13–15.

81 Ramírez, "De pescadores y agricultores;" Ramírez, *Provincial Patriarchs*, ch. 5, esp. 132.

82 Ramírez, *Provincial Patriarchs*, 28; Zevallos Quiñones, *Los cacicazgos*, 135.

83 De la Puente Luna, "Into the Heart of Empire"; AGI/J458, 1546–47, 1888v. On the litigiousness of natives in the sixteenth and seventeenth centuries, see Honores, "La asistencia jurídica privada" and "Colonial Legal Polyphony"; Herzog, "Colonial Law."

officials and authorities of the capital were much more sympathetic to natives' complaints than were local authorities who became beholden to local interests. Hundreds of native petitions presented to an Audiencia judge, Dr. Gregorio Gonzales de Cuenca, who spent two years traveling the back trails of the north between Trujillo, Chachapoyas, Piura, and Guánuco, exhibit the level of frustration and conflict experienced by the natives he encountered. These unpublished documents indicate that the natives contested European occupation as early as the 1550s.[84] They complained about harsh treatment, overwork, and occasional water shortages, but rarely because the Spanish usurped unexploited crop land (which was still unusual as long as tribute fed the Spanish and casta population).[85] Instead, they protested most bitterly about the damage caused by imported livestock that destroyed vegetation and infrastructure. Their petitions explained how European animals hurt their fields (*chacras*), pastures, and irrigation canals. Native plots were usually unfenced, because women and children shepherds supervised the camelids, which were their only grazing animals. Furthermore, the animals ate a straw-like *ichu* grass that grew at altitudes that were above most maize and some potato lands. So, they did not threaten most harvests.

European animals, in contrast, roamed in large groups, often with less supervision. They did not distinguish between a weed, a maize stalk, or a potato plant as they wandered, often entering and consuming the crops in native fields. Pigs grazed more rapidly and consumed more than goats, causing the peasants to complain.[86] They also uprooted forage. Sheep nibbled, gnawed, and cropped vegetation close to the ground, causing friction. On the open range, such overgrazing and the loss of plant cover, contributed to erosion and, subsequently, floods. The animals also stumbled and fell as they crossed irrigation canals, breaking down their edges and sending dirt, sand, and vegetation into the bottoms to obstruct the water flow.[87] To prevent damage to the city water supply, the town council of one

84 I found one court case with references back to the late 1550s, recording a dispute over land between Alonso Carrasco and the natives Don Francisco Chuminamo and Xobal Supian (ART/CoPedimento, 22-III-1564).

85 There were, however, conflicts over land between native lineages. See Adorno, "Court and Chronicle," especially 68–69; Rostworowski de Diez Canseco, "Etnohistoria"; ART/CoPedimento 31-VIII-1563 and CoR 3-VI-1564.

86 AGNP/RA, l. 27, c. 95, 1610.

87 The history of the impact of the importation of European livestock has received much recent attention. Most scholars, to date, have focused on Mexico. See, for example, Melville, *A Plague of Sheep* (still the best for central Mexico in early colonial times); and Sluyter, "Landscape Change"; Sluyter, "From Archive to Map." For Spanish Peru, see Wernke, *Negotiated Settlements*.

coastal city ruled that no one could corral animals near irrigation canals above the urban zone; but, in more remote areas, the damage to the irrigation infrastructure continued as the animals multiplied exponentially. The chieftain of the Ferreñafes voiced his despair in September of 1566:

> [I,] Don Fran[cis]co palarreffe lord of this encomienda of ferriñafe declare that the pigs cows and other cattle belonging to Juan Roldan and Lorenço de Camudio encomenderos of Tucume and Illimo and their brothers and servants greatly damage my fields and those of my Indians and the rest of the Indians of this encomienda because the lands of this encomienda are adjacent to the lands of Tucume and Illimo and besides this they [the cattle] break [down the walls of] our irrigation ditches and they damage us in other ways in great detriment to us and of the said fields.[88]

He asked that a local authority place markers on the fields so that boundaries could be recognized and that they order that the said cattle not enter their fields nor damage their irrigation canals nor harm them in any way.[89] To put a stop to such practices, Dr. Cuenca ordered several estancias moved, noting that because of the vast areas of vacant land with abundant grasses this should cause no major hardships to the breeders.[90] He also imposed distance limits between estancias and areas of native cultivation. Subsequent similar complaints show that the 1566 orders to move estancias away from native fields were either not enforced or distance proved a poor deterrent.[91]

These petitions, although written by paid Spanish and mestizo scribes with the help of translators who put words in natives' mouths, show, too, that some of the petitioners had grasped the rudiments of Spanish concepts of proprietorship.[92]

---

88 AGI/J458, 2068: "don fran[cis]co palarrefe prinçipal deste repartimi[en]to de ferriñafe digo que los puercos bacas y demas ganados que Juan Roldan y lorenço de çamudio encomenderos de tucome e Yllimo y sus hermanos y criados tienen hazen muchos daños en mys sementeras e de mys in[di]os y de los demas yn[di]os deste repartimiento por estar juntas las tierras deste repartimi[ent]o con las delos d[ic]hos tucome e yllimo y demas desto nos qyebran y rompen las açequias y nos hazen otros muchos danos y en gran perjuyzio y de las d[ic]has sementeras."

89 AGI/J461, 1554.

90 *ACT,* 1:21–22 and 2: 3–4; AGI/J458, 1840v.

91 Guaman Poma de Ayala, *Nueva corónica*, 944. For other personal complaints, see: ASFL/Reg. 9, no. 2, Ms. 26, 1647; AGI/AL 270, 481 and 589; J461 1443v and 1580v; *ACT*, 2:3; ART/Rios 1582 and Mata 1580; CoO 30-IX-1582; l. 154, exp. 222, 22-II-1585; and 1597.

92 Note that the most widely spoken native language, Quechua, has no words for owner, ownership, or property. Possession and "ownership" of land became issues in the seventeenth

The practice of working for the lineage lord and bringing him gifts of produce began to be called *terrazgo*, which the Spanish translated as rent. One lord asked for title of communal lands that until the visit of Dr. Cuenca had been used "for the corn fields that are worked communally".[93] Furthermore, a few of the native lords' petitions requested titles (*mandamiento de amparo*, *real amparo* or *amparar en posesion*, orders supporting their possession) to the lands that they, and their fathers and grandfathers used, lest someone in the future try to take their fields from them.[94]

The final reform measure was the decision to concentrate the remaining, very dispersed native population in villages called *reducciones*, modeled on Spanish towns with central plazas and perpendicularly intersecting streets in the 1560s-70s.[95] The imperial legislation on which this effort was based made kin-related lineages, living dispersed over large areas and occasionally gathered at ceremonial centers to venerate their ancestors, into concentrated populations living in towns, communities in a physical sense, with Spanish-allotted territories made up of one or more pieces of lands that in later years they had to defend. Kinship and lands thus were melded (at least theoretically) into one institution. Yet, for the natives, the traditional conceptualization of the ground and related customs still governed its use.[96]

The first Crown-mandated, organized efforts in this regard occurred in the 1560s under the direction of Dr. Cuenca, mentioned above. In July of 1566, he ordered that the scattered settlements of Chérrepe be reduced to two.[97] In the next decade, Viceroy Francisco de Toledo extended the program to his entire jurisdiction. Uprooting and re-grouping the natives in a few large settlements, the officials reasoned, would facilitate religious indoctrination and acculturation and help maintain the segregation of natives from Spanish mistreatment and corrupting influences. A less publicized but nonetheless significant reason was

century, especially as native populations began to recover. Wightman, *Indigenous Migration and Social Change*, 54; Adorno, "Court and Chronicle", 68.

93 AGI/J458, 2063v-65: "para las sementeras de maiz que se an de hazer de comunidad."

94 AGI/J458, 2038–29; 2125–25v, 2131; Guevara Gil, *Propiedad agraria*, xxiii, 186–87; Honores, "La asistencia jurídica privada," 8.

95 For the royal decrees governing this institution, see *RLI*, v. 2, tit. 3, lib. 6, f. 198–201.

96 Martínez, "Evolución de la propiedad territorial," 443. Although I disagree with Martínez's characterization of Peruvian land as "territory" and "property" before the *reducciones*, I do agree that the officials in charge of *reducciones* assigned property to native lineages which they subsequently held and defended as corporate holdings.

97 Remy Simatovic, "Los curacas," Appendix 1 (AGI/J459, fols. 3061v–3063r).

administrative expediency—facilitating tribute collection and control.[98] Official statements regarding the *reducción* program stressed its positive features—saving the infidels and protecting them from direct Spanish exploitation through segregation. Laws governing the program promised added safeguards. Lineages were not to lose their lands; and an *ejido*, or reserve, with a diameter of one league for common grazing and future urban expansion, was to be designated around all villages. Other lands were designated for shared cultivation. If the new settlements were far from their traditional fields, making daily access difficult, natives were to receive new ones near the reducción. The lineages on whose land the new town was built were to be recompensed with other land. The few Indian lords with hereditary rights to cultivated land were to be allowed to sell them if they wished. Abandoned land was to be held in common,[99] although Philip II changed his mind on this issue, releasing a royal order in 1568, declaring that vacant lands automatically became the crown's property. He reserved the right to distribute them for himself and his successors.

But there was a great gap between legal theory and actual practice. It did not always produce the expected outcomes. In one case in 1572, Toledo sent Juan de Hoses to resettle the dispersed members of the lineage of Ñoquique (one of three that made up the ethnicity of Chérrepe). He justified his actions stating that the people of Ñoquique lived in unhealthy sites, so isolated that the priest rarely visited, a condition which allowed the natives to meet to practice their pagan rights unmolested. He stressed that the move was for the natives' own physical and spiritual welfare. He ordered the farmers of Ñoquique to rebuild their dwellings around the monastery of Nuestra Señora de Guadalupe and the fishermen in their ranks to reestablish themselves in the town of Chérrepe on the coast.

In this instance, the natives protested. The inhabitants petitioned the viceroy and royal Audiencia almost ten months before the actual order for them to leave their homes was given. They asked that they not be resettled, fearing that a transfer to a different climate would cause them to sicken and die. In fact, the native chronicler Felipe Guaman Poma de Ayala condemns Toledo for the *reducción* policy, writing:[100]

---

98 AGI/P185, r. 24, 1541; J456, 419; J459, 2842 and 3062; J461, 928v; Arroyo, *Los franciscanos*, 34; Ramírez, "Chérrepe en 1572"; Cabero, "El Capitán Juan Delgadillo," 94; Mumford, *Vertical Empire*; Jackson, "Elites indígenas"; Martínez, "Evolución de la propiedad."

99 Valdez de la Torre, *Evolución*, 67, 76 (citing a decree of Philip II, dated 1573); *RLI*, v. 2, tit. 3, lib. 6, leyes 8–9 and 14; fols. 199r–199v; BAH/ML, t. 97, n.d. [1568], 52 and 334).

100 Guaman Poma de Ayala, 1613/1936, 951[965]: "Don Francisco de Toledo, bizorrey, mandó despoblar y rreducir de los pueblos desde rreyno. Desde entonses se a muerto y se ua acauando los yndios deste rreyno por las causas ciguientes: El primero, porque se apartaron

> Viceroy Don Francisco de Toledo ordered the abandonment and resettlement of the people. Since then the Indians of this kingdom have died and are disappearing for the following reasons: the first, because they removed the Indians from some towns, places, and corners that their most important native wise men, doctors and philosophers had selected and were approved by the Incas for their climate, lands and water to [best ensure the] growth of the population. Since then, the Indians in their new towns have died and are disappearing. Where there were ten thousand persons—soldiers of war, without [counting] the women, old men and children—now there are not ten tribute-paying Indians [....] said places are humid and disease prone. And there enter illnesses that the wind brings; in parts stinking, pestilential winds blow in from the sea,[....]in other parts, it is caused by the sun or the moon or the planets [....]

As a result, natives, in some cases, did lose their best lands. Those on the coast, for example, were re-situated closer to the beach, where the low-lying fields were subject to a heavy mist in the winter and fog cover that hindered germination of seeds and fostered such problems as the growth of harmful fungi and insects. Furthermore, these and others lost access to irrigation water, having been moved to the end of the channels, where flows decreased to a trickle in dry years. While natives in many cases did move and rebuild their homes in these new towns, many abandoned them and returned to their traditional homesteads as soon as the Spanish left and they deemed it to be safe to travel.[101]

Where successful, this planned concentration opened up large swaths of fertile lands and shared pastures to Spanish colonization. Estancias, like those informally founded in the immediate aftermath of the invasion, were easy to establish with little capital investment after the initial purchase of a breeding pair and little labor. One shepherd could oversee up to one thousand sheep at a time and earned less than the value of ten head a year. Partnerships, as mentioned above, could ini-

---

los yndios de unos pueblos que tenían escogidos citios, rincones por sus principales sauios y dotores, lesenciados, filósofos y aprouado de los primeros Yngas los tenples y tierras y agua para multiplicar la gente. Adonde auía dies mil personas, soldados de guerra cin las mugeres y biejos y niños, agora no ay dies yndios de tributo ... los quaales [sic] citios causa en partes tierra úmida y pistilenciales y pasa por ella. Y ací entran enfermedades que trae aquella ayre; en partes biene aquella ayre de la mar que es pistilencial y hedor. ... en otras partes, lo causa del sol o de la luna o de las planetas que apunta y da la fuerza en los citios y lugares. Todos los quales es causa, como tengo dicho." Guaman Poma de Ayala, *Nueva corónica y buen gobierno*, 951 [965].

101 Abercrombie, *Pathways of Memory*, 283; Espinoza Soriano, *Juan Pérez de Guevara*, 122–25; Glave, *El virreinato peruano*, 4–5; Duviols, *Cultural Andina y represión*, 403–6; AGI/J458, 942v-43.

tiate breeding on the vast areas of open range which had been abandoned, the so-called *tierras baldías* or *vacas* (wasteland; untilled, uncultivated or empty lands).[102] More open ranges were a great windfall to Spanish cattlemen, but natives benefited less. With the exception of the southern highlands where natives pastured abundant camelids, most natives had fewer livestock.[103] Any advantage to these few did not compensate for the damage done to the majority. Herds of imported animals continued to be a major source of conflict between the natives and the Spanish when the latter allowed their animals to roam freely into the unfenced native fields. Spaniards paid little heed to royal decrees mandating native protection that were against their interests, especially where there was little effective law enforcement by officials representing the king. In fact, Spaniards sometimes purposely allowed their animals to graze in native fields, defending this practice to the bewildered natives by citing the definition of pasture.[104] Breeders knew that if natives could not subsist and produce tribute goods on their traditional lands, they would be forced into the growing labor market.

Crops generally required greater investment than estancias. Spaniards reacted to local grain shortages and growing markets in Tierra Firme and Lima by planting wheat on some of their plots on the edge of town. Continued expansion near the city proved impossible when the decrees that limited the distance which native labor could travel to work began to be implemented. Mixed farms called *labores de pan sembrar* (or *de pan llevar*: the forerunners of the *hacienda*) included land planted in grain and land left as natural pasture for grazing work animals. It required a significant sum to purchase hand tools, plows, oxen, and carts. Wage costs were also greater, because as a labor-intensive activity farming required constant and specific administration to synchronize and coordinate plowing, planting, weeding, and irrigating various fields at once by large numbers of workers. On the coast, as the native labor supply dwindled, those few who could began to spend large sums to purchase slaves to maintain and expand production.

But most farmers still had no title to the lands they used. Similarly, stock-raising did not imply exclusive rights to any, unless the breeder had a *merced*. Most others only acknowledged *de facto* rights to those occupied by the corrals that were built to enclose the animals at night. The question of the ownership of land and pastures was not a predominant preoccupation much of the time.

---

102 Guevara Gil, *Propiedad agraria*, 13, 23.

103 See the analysis of three wills of native lords in Ramírez, "Rich Man, Poor Man," and Diez de San Miguel, *Visita hecha*.

104 AGI/AL 121, 1566, 5; P 185, r. 24, 1541, 75; *RLI*, v. 2, lib. 6, tit. 9, ley 19, f. 231v; and BAH/ML, t. 97, 1541, 181; and t. 21, 191–92.

The First *Visita de la Tierra*, or the Opportunity to Purchase Title

By the last decade of the sixteenth century, a select few Spaniards had acquired titles by gaining *mercedes* from a traveling viceroy or inspector, or their local municipal council. But many more Spanish settlers occupied lands without specific titles. This situation discouraged producers from investing and enlarging their farms. To secure their investments, they began seeking ways to establish their rights to the lands they occupied. At first, Spaniards planted on recently abandoned land that was easy to clear and required relatively little work to restore the irrigation networks, where they existed. Given the native demographic collapse, vacant land was relatively abundant and easy to occupy; there was little need for them to encroach on land still being actively used by natives. They also took advantage of the creation of a forced, rotating labor system (the *mita*) to acquire land. They simply remained in possession of land worked by the natives when temporary workers rotated every few weeks. The land eventually became identified with the Spaniard who occupied it continuously and quietly assumed its control and disposition. The result was a *de facto* transmittal of possession over the years.[105] Some also used an ostensible rental arrangement as another ploy to acquire land. Spaniards leased native lands and later asserted that the rental was a sale, claiming that possession throughout the intervening years constituted proof of ownership.[106]

Gradually, however, the legal uncertainties associated with these stratagems led the Spaniards to prefer formal sales. Some purchased land from native lords for token payments, often paid in kind, despite royal disapproval and at least one decree prohibiting such transactions.[107] In 1566, Dr. Cuenca specifically prohibited the sale of land by native lords and other commoners, unless absolutely necessary.

> Item, because the *curacas*, without having power to do so, sell on their own authority the lands of their communities as their own, thus causing their subjects great harm [...] and because, if the Indian population ever increases in numbers there will be a scarcity of land, it is ordered and mandated that no *curaca* or native official can sell community lands to Spaniards or any other individual, unless the sale is of urgent necessity or of evident utility to the community [...].[108]

---

105 ART/Rios 1979; Mata 1565; Vega, 1567; MT 1578; LC 1559, 10-X-1561 and 16-V-1564; BNP/B871, 1627; and AAT/Causas 1570.

106 ANCR/1586–1611; AGI/J461, 1443–43v.

107 Guevara Gil, *Propiedad agraria*, 19, 21, 23, 103, 126–27, 130, 135–36.

108 *ACT*, 2:16–17: "Yten, porque los caçiques, sin tener poder para ello, venden por su auturidad las tierras de los rrepartimy[ent]os por suyas, siendo de la comunydad, de lo qual

Cuenca realized that if such sales were not banned the native population would lack sufficient land to provide for its own needs if the peoples ever increased to previous levels. But, in later years, natives and Spaniards alike took advantage of the provision's loophole to continue these transactions.[109]

But tenure insecurity and mounting evidence of usurpation of native lands turned viceregal benign neglect and intermittent interventions in the machinations of distant Spanish officials and citizens into affairs of concern.[110] Actions followed. The most noteworthy occasions of direct intervention were the *visitas de la tierra* by viceregal officials sent to the rural areas to review and legalize land titles. These *visitas* were not designed to check on the conditions or the efficiency of rural administration, to alter the local balance of power, or to report on the situation of the native population as much as to simply generate additional revenues for the king, while responding to Spanish demands for secure tenure and native cries for protection against usurpation. These *visitas*, however, often led to abuses as landowners and officials colluded to benefit themselves.

A general review and legalization of landholdings occurred in the 1590s, the first of several more in the decades of the 1640s, 1710s, and 1780s.[111] Only the first is of interest here. The excessive cost of Spain's continental warfare with England, France, and Holland; the destruction in 1588 of the great Armada; the resulting depletion of the royal treasury; and the reports of widespread illegal possession of crown lands in America prompted King Philip II to order the first thorough review of land titles, the *visita de la tierra*, in 1589.[112] Imperial decrees and the accompanying instructions for the *visitas* were designed to generate income for

los yndios a ellos sujetos son danyficados [...] y viniendo los y[ndi]os en avmento avra falta dellas [tierras], se hordena y manda que ningun caçique ny prinçipal pueda bender tierras del rrepartimy[ent]o a españoles ny a otra persona, sino fuere con Urgente nesçesidad de la comunydad o en Evidente utilidad della [....].

109 ART/Mata 1586; 24-X-1563; 1565; 30-IX-1562; CoAG 30-IX-1567; *ACT*, 2:16–17; AGI/P108 r. 7, 1562, 48v; AL 28B; J460, 429v; Guevara Gil, *Propiedad agraria*, 130; and Angulo, "Cartulario," 296.

110 On usurpation, see, for example, Guevara Gil, *Propiedad agraria*, 13, 19, 23, 126; Honores, "La asistencia jurídica privada," 6; Honores, "Colonial Legal Polyphony," 11, especially on the *visita* and *composición*.

111 I am not counting the occasional inspections by special agents sent to remedy the abuses of one of these reviews, like the one conducted in the mid-1650s by a priest Maestro Fray Francisco de Huerta, who came to restore inappropriately expropriated native lands and soothe feelings, and so to restore the legitimacy of the king as father and protector to the native population.

112 Ots Capdequi, *España en América*, 40; Guevara Gil, *Propiedad agraria*, 28, 169, 174; Abercrombie, *Pathways of Memory*, 284–85.

the king's treasury and bring order to the land tenure panorama. Philip II gave the viceroy, in consultation with the Audiencia, the responsibility for appointing visitors to tour the kingdom to conduct the review.[113] The law required all persons, except natives, to exhibit to the visitor for confirmation the titles to the land they occupied. If the titles proved defective[114] or illegal,[115] or if a landholder had no titles, the law provided that proprietary rights to the land in question either revert to the crown or be legalized (or *compuestos*, literally "repaired") by a payment of a "just" and "moderate" sum to the royal treasury. Thus, some had to pay if the visitor found more land than that in the original *merced*. Persons without titles had to pay a fee to legalize possession to all the lands they occupied.

The instructions further stipulated that vacant land—including land which had been assigned to the *reducciones* that was now in excess of that actually needed and used—belonged to the Crown, that is, it was *baldía* (waste, untilled, uncultivated) and *realenga* (royal patrimony: though in practice it appeared ownerless, idle, or unattached). To raise additional funds, Philip II empowered and encouraged the visitor to sell as much of the vacant land as possible, taking care only to reserve the necessary area for the future urban expansion of Spanish towns and cities and for the agricultural needs of the native peoples. The only condition for purchase was that buyers have the means and intent to cultivate it. The law clearly outlined the procedure for such sales. Prospective buyers submitted bids to the visitor for possession of the vacant land of their choosing. After verifying that the land was indeed idle and waste the visitor notified the owners of adjacent property to discover any objections to the sale. The town crier then announced the sale publicly on thirty separate occasions. On the day of the last such advertisement, a candle was lighted and additional bids were accepted as long as it burned. The highest bidder received the right to acquire title to the land. This elaborate procedure was not always followed in practice. There are a few cases when the town crier made fewer announcements than the mandated thirty. But regularly, these were made in Spanish, thus denying news of the sale to non-Spanish-speakers (i.e., the vast majority of the natives).[116]

---

113 A royal decree of 1593 empowered Garcia Hurtado de Mendoza (the first Marqués de Cañete) to review land titles. His commissioners took over and finished the reviews that in some districts had been started on an informal basis by the corregidores. See Bronner, "Tramitación legislativa bajo Olivares," 418–22.

114 For example, they were granted by a town council that did not have the authority to do so or were for less land than the amount presently held.

115 For example, they were bills of sale from natives.

116 BAH/ML t. 97, 1589, 660; BAH/ML 1591, 66; BAH/ML 1592, 49–52; BAH/ML 1598, 768; and BAH/ML 1679–86; AGI/AL 132, [1593–95]; Valdez de la Torre, *Evolución*, 88;

News of these decrees and the impending *visita* unnerved landholders. Many realized that according to the law, the only sufficient titles to land were *títulos originarios*, or titles for concessions, which emanated directly from the king or some person or institution with his explicit authority; for example, the governor, a viceroy, and certain town councils at particular times. Landlords with grants from the town councils worried that their titles might be considered illegal, because the grants had been made without official sanction. Spaniards whose only titles were bills of sale or donations from the natives realized that these titles could be declared defective, since Spanish law regarded the natives as minors. The king had never granted them direct dominion or absolute ownership of the land; natives had purely usufructuary rights (*dominio útil*). *Curacas* had been allowed to sell property, but this practice had been prohibited after the widespread and unauthorized sale of communal lands earlier in the sixteenth century. Consequently, only *mercedes* and bills of sale or donations, dated during the 1560s and accompanied by the sworn statements of the *corregidor* and various informants that the lands were not needed by the natives, would not be challenged as illegal. Finally, cattle raisers worried about their status and continued access to pastures and forests, because by royal decree grazing lands were communal and open to all. Many stockmen had no titles whatsoever, and hence only squatters' rights to the land on which they had built stock pens and huts.[117]

The settlers' fears were intensified by the circulation of exaggerated, near hysterical rumors that the visita was a scheme to return all the land to the lineages and that the land of many Spaniards would be confiscated; in fact, however, the king was willing to sell off large areas of the royal domain to raise cash. Viceroy Cañete's reaction to the order for the visita reflects the landholders' anxieties. He wrote Philip II a strongly worded letter, dated 27 May 1592, outlining the possible disruptive effects of his decrees and suggesting their slow and cautious implementation:

> The landowners are the richest and earliest discoverers and conquerors of the Kingdom, their children and descendants, and other persons to whom they have sold property. All these persons have plowed, cultivated, planted and improved the lands with buildings [...] at first everyone received land without contradiction; the viceroys and governors encouraged and aided those who dedicated themselves to exploiting and plant-

Guevara Gil, *Propiedad agraria*, 90–93, 132.

117 AGI/AL 32, 25-IV-1588. In 1592, a royal decree provided that titles issued by *cabildos* were valid, until the council was specifically prohibited from making land grants. See BAH/ML t. 97, 49.

> ing them [....] Now nothing could cause more scandal and uneasiness in all the Kingdom among the most prestigious, valuable and able citizens [...] than to try to take the land away from them which they possess in perpetuity.[118]

The only lands that should be affected, he argued, were those no longer needed and used by Indian peoples.[119]

The landholders' anxiety was unfounded: none of the *visita*'s predicted dire consequences came to pass. In one case, the visitor, Don Rodrigo de Ampuero, while outwardly maintaining a solemn and disinterested air, probably over-stated the consequences of not regularizing land titles to encourage anxious landholders to come forward and thus accomplish his true and overriding purpose of raising as much money as possible for the royal treasury. Ampuero confirmed as legitimate and sufficient titles the original grants made at the time Spanish cities were founded and their subsequent sale and donations. For a fee, Ampuero issued titles to excess lands and corrected and legalized defective titles. A modest sum also made landholders without titles legal landowners. A few Spaniards took advantage of the opportunity to purchase vacant land at auction. Juan Fragoso, for example, paid 45 pesos for three *fanegadas* of lands and the legalization of the bill of sale for nine others he had previously purchased from the *curaca* of Chuspo-Callanca.[120]

Judging from the *visita*'s extant records, livestock raisers were the group of Spaniards most affected. Ampuero issued clear title to estancias and corrals in one area for sums ranging from 42 to190 pesos per *fanegada*. These titles gave the ranchers ownership of enough land for their center of operations and stock pens, but they excluded exclusive rights to pastures and woodlands. Titles contained the clause that pastures and forests were to remain common. The titles of one estancia, for instance, included land for an administrative center and sites for corrals one-and-one-half to two leagues away. The need to move animals periodically

---

118 AGI/AL 32, 27-V-1592: " Los que poseen estas tierras son los mas ricos y antiguos descubridores y conquistadores del Reyno y sus hijos y descendientes y otras personas aque en estos las han vendido y todas las tienen rompidas, labradas plantadas y mejoradas con edificios ... a principio entraron todos en ellas sin ninguna contradicion dando los virreyes y gouernadores muchas gracias y ayuda a los que se aplicauan a benefiçiarlas y sembrarlas y tratar ora de quitarse las siendo todo su caudal ninguna cosa se podrá ofreçer de tanto escandalo y desasosiego en todo el Reino entre los mas principales y que algo valen y pueden [...] como lo harian quitando les todas las tierras que gozan y tienen por cosa fija y perpetua."

119 AGI/AL 32, 27-V-1592; Mellafe, "Frontera agraria," 39; BAH/ML t. 97, 1589, 654; and 1591, 66.

120 AGNP/TP l. 23, c. 613, 1787, 94.

to fresh pastures made corrals at these sites necessary to minimize the distance the herds had to travel each evening for protection from the prowling mountain lions that populated the rural areas. Subsequent legislation prohibited the establishment of the center of a new sheep and goat operation within one league or that of a new swine enterprise half that distance from an existing center of operations. Because of the recognized distinction between pastures (vegetation) and the lands (soil) on which the plants grew, this regulation did not affect the tenure of the farmers with fields between corrals. But, grazing stock did not differentiate between weeds and stubble and crops, resulting in continuing disputes on this account. Eventually laws were issued specifying that no new estancias could be established within a league of cultivated land and that fields be fenced.[121]

The records show that for, the Spanish, the *visita* merely legalized a *de facto* situation and did not change the pattern of landholding significantly. It made landowners of landholders. For the natives, the *visita* meant yet another lesson in the idea of exclusive property and a loss of "unused" land. The visitor, following his instructions, left the native lineages with enough ground for their current needs, but without sufficient reserves for future population growth. All excess land was publicly declared the domain of the king.[122] The only evidence of change in customs within the communal areas of the *reducciones* comes from the remains of a notarial register, where short entries record oral testimonies of who had occupied a given parcel of land back as far as ten cultivators.[123] In other words, oral testimonies of usage rights were now being supplemented by writing them down. Or, as Guevara Gil has written, "The papers started to talk and, in general, the written word proved superior in truth and authenticity to the spoken word," at least in the minds of the Spanish.[124]

Thus, despite initial misgivings and apprehension, such mandated reviews encouraged investment by regularizing titles and holdings. Landowners borrowed church funds accumulated from charitable works by religious brotherhoods (*cofradias*), monasteries, and convents to intensify production on the cattle-rais-

---

121 ART/Mata 1596; ANCR/[1645]; ASFL/Reg. 9, No. 2, Ms. 26, 1647; AGNP/TH l. 21, c. 131, 1805, 501; Valdez de la Torre, *Evolución*, 86–87; Chevalier, *Land and Society*, 88–90. See Guevara Gil (*Propiedad agraria*, 28, 169) for a discussion of the visita to the Cuzco area.

122 AGI/AL 132, [1593–95].

123 ANCR[1586–1611].

124 "Los papeles comenzaron a hablar y, en general, la palabra escrita sobrepasó en veracidad y autenticidad a la palabra oral." Guevara Gil also noted that, in Spanish law, a written instrument held more proof value than two oral testimonies: *Propiedad agraria*, xxiv.

ing estancias and the crop-producing haciendas. Of special interest was the investment by some in sugar cane and the wheat mills needed to make sugar and flour.

Land, Custom, and Law in the Andes

The history of Spanish colonialism as it affected land and tenure in the "New World" displays strong parallels with the institutions of the *Reconquista* and earlier eras of medieval Iberian history. The carving out of royal domain as patrimony of the Crown, with rights to alienate parts of it; the granting of communal properties to some municipalities; the drive toward private ownership of land; and the guarantee (at least in theory) of freedom to peasants were all elements brought to the Americas.[125] Over time, migrant settlers gradually gained possession and, later, ownership of parts of the royal patrimony. Meanwhile, grasslands remained common and open to all until the eighteenth century. These institutions accompanied the arrival and gradual settlement of the Spanish in such far-flung locations as Piura, Trujillo, Lima, Cuzco, and Sucre. With them came exotic animals that sometimes feasted in native fields and damaged the agricultural infrastructure. Protests against usurpation mounted as natives complained to Spanish priests and local officials, or traveled to the capital to present petitions before royal authorities. But the Spanish predilection for wine, wheat bread, sugar, and olives made agricultural land very valuable, and the crown delegated powers to town councils and royal officials to award land to private individuals. Such grants began as few, relatively small, and sporadic; but the pace of alienation accelerated in the 1560s and at the end of the sixteenth century. Continued loss of traditional lands and conflicts over their use with Spaniards and their descendants further entrenched medieval European notions of property. Indeed, Andean demands for redress of grievances provide evidence that these peoples had grasped the European concepts of usurpation, property, and rent. Though their agency served to negotiate the terms of their colonial existence in the short run, a constant demand for cheap labor further increased the numbers of usurpations and sales, abetted by legal chicanery. Once unable to farm, indigenous peoples survived by joining the labor force, sometimes working lands for a new owner: lands that had formerly been "common to all."

125 Weeks, "European Antecedents," 62.

Archival Sources and Abbreviations

ACT *Actas del cabildo de Trujillo.* Transcribed by Jorge Zevallos Quiñones. 3 vols. Lima: Concejo Provincial, 1969–70.

AAT Archivo Arzobispal de Trujillo

Causas

AGI Archivo General de las Indias (Sevilla, Spain)

Audiencia de Lima (AL)

Escribanía (E)

Indiferente General (IG)

Justicia (J)

Patronato (P)

AGNP Archivo General de la Nación (Lima, Perú)

Donaciones

Residencia (R)

ANCR Archivo Notarial de Carlos Rivadeneira, Lambayeque

ART Archivo Regional de Trujillo (now Archivo Regional de La Libertad, Trujillo, Perú)

Corregimiento, Asuntos de Gobierno (CoAG)

Corregimiento, Ordinario (CoO)

Corregimiento, Pedimento (CoPedimento)

Corregimiento, Residencia (CoR)

López de Córdova (LC)

Mata

Muñoz Ternero (MT)

Obregón (O)

Ríos

Vega

ASFL Archivo de San Francisco (Lima, Perú)

BAH Biblioteca de la Academia de Historia, Madrid

Mata Linares (ML)

BNP Biblioteca Nacional del Perú (Lima)

RLI Spain, Consejo de indias. *Recopilación de las leyes de los Reynos de las Indias.* 4 vols. Madrid, 1681

Legajo (l.), expediente (exp.), manuscrito (ms.), número (no.), folio(s) (f(f).)

Bibliography

Abercrombie, Thomas A. *Pathways of Memory and Power: Ethnography and History among an Andean People.* Madison: University of Wisconsin Press, 1998.

Adorno, Rolena. "Court and Chronicle: A Native Andean's Engagement with Spanish Colonial Law." In *Native Claims: Indigenous Law against Empire, 1500–1920,* edited by Sahiha Belmessous, 63–84. New York: Oxford University Press, 2012.

Angulo, Domingo "Cartulario de los conquistadores del Perú: El Capitán Juan de Barbarán." *Revista del Archivo Nacional del Perú* 4, no. 2 (1926): 187–206.

Arroyo, Luis. *Los franciscanos y la fundación de Chiclayo.* Lima: Private Printing,1956.

Barriga, Víctor M. *Los mercedarios en el Perú.* Vol. 3. Arequipa: Establecimientos Gráficos La Colmena, 1942.

Bronner, Fred. "Tramitación legislativa bajo Olivares: La redacción de los arbitrios de 1631." *Revista de indias* 165–66 (1981): 411–43.

Cabero, Marco A. "El Capitán Juan Delgadillo, encomendero de Saña." *Revista Histórica* 2 (1907): 92–117.

——. "El corregimiento de Saña y el problema histórico de la fundación de Trujillo." *Revista histórica* 1 (1906): 151–91, 337–73, and 486–514.

Carlín Arce, Jorge. *Historia general del departamento de Tumbes: un compendio.* Lima: Private Printing, 1984.

——. *Reseña histórica del departamento de Tumbes.* Lima: Imprenta del Ministerio de Guerra, 1976.

Castro, Fray Cristóbal de, and Diego de Ortega Morejón. "Relación de Chincha [1558]." In *Biblioteca peruana: El Perú a través de los siglos,* 1st ser., 3:465–89. Lima: Editores Técnicos Asociados, 1968.

Chaliand, Gerard. *Mirrors of a Disaster: A Chronicle of the Spanish Military Conquest of America.* Watertown, MA: Blue Crane Books, 1994.

Chevalier, François. *Land and Society in Colonial Mexico.* Berkeley: University of California Press, 1963.

Cook, Noble David. "The Indian Population of Peru, 1570–1620." PhD diss., University of Texas, 1973.

Dean, Carolyn. *A Culture of Stone: Inka Perspectives on Rock.* Durham: Duke University Press, 2010.

De la Puente Brunke, José. *Encomienda y encomenderos en el Perú.* Sevilla: Excma. Diputación Provincial de Sevilla, 1992.

De la Puente Luna, José Carlos. "Into the Heart of Empire: Indian Journeys to the Hapsburg Royal Court." PhD diss., Texas Christian University, 2010.

——. "That Which Belongs to All: *Khipus,* Community, and Indigenous Legal Activism in the Early Colonial Andes." *The Americas* 12 (2014): 1–36.

Diez de San Miguel, Garci. *Visita hecha a la Provincia de Chucuito (1567)*. Lima: Casa de la Cultura del Perú, 1964.

Dike, Azura A. "Land Tenure System in Igboland." *Anthropos* 78 (1983): 853–71.

Drinot, Paulo, and Leo Garofalo, eds. *Más Allá de la dominación y la resistencia*. Lima: Instituto de Estudios Peruanos, 2005.

Duviols, Pierre. *Cultural Andina y represión. Procesos y visitas de idolatría y hechicería. Siglo XVII*. Cuzco: Centro de Estudios Rurales Andinos 'Bartolomé de las Casas', 1986.

——. *Procesos y visitas de idolatrías: Cajatambo, siglo XVII*. Lima: Instituto Francés de Estudios Andinos, 2003.

Early, John D. *The Maya and Catholicism: An Encounter of Worldviews*. Gainesville: University Press of Florida, 2006.

Eisen, Arlete. "The Indians in Colonial Spanish America." In *Spanish Bureaucratic-Patrimonialism in America*, edited by Magali Sarfatti [Larson], 101–23. Berkeley: University of California Press, 1966.

Elden, Stuart. *The Birth of Territory*. Chicago: University of Chicago Press, 2013.

Elias, Taslim Olawale. *Nigerian Land Law and Custom*. London: Routledge and Kegan Paul, 1962.

Espinoza Soriano, Waldemar. *Juan Pérez de Guevara y la historia de Moyobamba, siglo XVI*. Lima: Editora Magisterial Servicios Gráficos, 2003.

Glave, Luis Miguel. *El virreinato peruano y la llamada "crisis general" del siglo XVII*. Lima: Universidad de Lima, 1986.

Gonzalez Holguin, Diego. *Vocabvlario e la lengva general de todo el Perv llamada Qquichua [. . .]*. Ciudad de los Reyes: Francisco del Canto, 1608.

Griffiths, Nicholas. *The Cross and the Serpent: Religious Repression and Resurgence in Colonial Peru*. Norman: University of Oklahoma Press, 1996.

Guaman Poma de Ayala, Felipe. *Nueva corónica y buen gobierno*. Paris: Institut d'ethnolgie, 1936.

Guevara Gil, Jorge Armando. *Propiedad agraria y derecho colonial: los documentos de la Hacienda Santotis, Cuzco (1543–1822)*. Lima: Pontificia Universidad Católica del Perú, 1993.

Guilmartin, Jr., John F. "The Cutting Edge: An Analysis of the Spanish Invasion and Overthrow of the Inca Empire, 1532–1534." In *Transatlantic Encounters: Europeans and Andeans in the Sixteenth Century*, edited by Kenneth J. Andrien and Rolena Adorno, 40–69. Berkeley: University of California Press, 1991,

Hassig, Ross. *Aztec Warfare: Imperial Expansion and Political Control*. Norman: University of Oklahoma Press, 1988.

Herzog, Tamar. "Colonial Law and 'Native Customs': Indigenous Land Rights in Colonial Spanish America." *The Americas* 69 (2013): 303–21.

Honores, Renzo. "La asistencia jurídica privada a las señores indígenas ante la Real Audiencia de Lima, 1552–70." Paper presented at the meeting of the Latin American Studies Association, Dallas, March 27–29, 2003.

——. "Colonial Legal Polyphony: Caciques and the Construction of Legal Arguments in the Andes, 1550–1640." Paper presented at "Seminar on the History of the Atlantic World," Cambridge, MA, August 2–10, 2010.

Imāmuddin, S. M. "Al-Filāhah (Farming) in Muslim Spain." *Islamic Studies* 1 (1962): 51–89.

Jackson, Robert. "Elites indígenas y política española en Cochabamba durante la colonia: La redefinición de la tierra y el poder." In *Elites indígenas en los Andes: Nobles, caciques y cabildantes bajo el yugo colonial*, edited by David Cahill and Blanca Tovías, 243–47. Quito: Abya Yala, 2003.

Keith, Robert G. "Encomienda, Hacienda and Corregimiento in Spanish America: A Structural Analysis." *Hispanic American Historical Review* 51 (1971): 431–46.

——. "Origins of the Hacienda System on the Central Peruvian Coast." Ph.D. diss., Harvard University, 1969.

León Gómez, Miguel. *Paños e hidalguía: encomenderos y sociedad colonial en Huánuco*. Lima: IEP, 2002.

Lippy, Charles H., Robert Choquette, and Stafford Poole. *Christianity Comes to the Americas*. New York: Paragon House, 1992.

Lissón y Chávez, Emilio. *La iglesia de España en el Perú*. 5 vols. Sevilla: Escuela de Estudios Hispano-Americanos, 1943–46.

Lockhart, James M. *Men of Cajamarca*. Austin: University of Texas Press, 1972.

——. *Spanish Peru, 1532–50: A Colonial Society*. Madison: University of Wisconsin Press, 1968.

Loredo, Rafael. *Los repartos*. Lima: n.p., 1958.

Mantha, Alexis. "Shifting Territorialities under the Inka Empire: The Case of the Rapayán Valley in the Central Andean Highlands." *Archeological Papers of the American Anthropological Association* 22 (2013): 164–88.

Martínez, Héctor. "Evolución de la propiedad territorial en el Perú," *Journal of Inter-American Studies* 5, no. 4 (October 1963): 437–50.

Mellafe, Rolando. "Frontera agraria: El caso del virreinato peruano en el siglo XVI." In *Tierras nuevas*, edited by Álvaro Jara, 11–42. México: El Colegio de México,1969.

Melville, Elinor G. K. *A Plague of Sheep: Environmental Consequences of the Conquet of Mexico*. Cambridge: Cambridge University Press, 1994.

Mumford, Jeremy R. *Vertical Empire: The General Resettlement of Indians in the Colonial Andes*. Durham, NC: Duke University Press, 2012.

Murra, John V. "'El control vertical' de un máximo de pisos ecológicos en la economía de las sociedades andinas." In *Visita de la Provincia de León de Huánuco en*

1562, Iñigo Ortiz de Zúñiga, Visitador, edited by John V. Murra, 2:427–76. Huánuco: Universidad Nacional Hermilio Valdizán, 1972.

——. "Derechos a las tierras en el Tawantinsuyu." *Revista de la Universidad Complutense* 28 (1980): 273–87.

——. "Vida, tierra y agua en el Perú antiguo." *Revista Peruana de Cultura* 7–8 (1966), 270–73.

Niles, Susan. *The Shape of Inca History*. Iowa City: University of Iowa Press, 1999.

Noack, Karoline. "Caciques, escribanos y las construcciones de historias: Cajamarca, Perú, siglo XVI." In *Elites indígenas en los Andes: Nobles, caciques y cabildantes bajo el yugo colonial*, edited by David Cahill and Blanca Tovías, 213–27. Quito: Ediciones, Abya-Yala, 2003.

Osborne, James F., and Parker Van Valkenburgh, eds. "Home Turf: Archaeology, Territoriality, and Politics." In "Territoriality in Archaeology," edited by James F. Osborne and Parker Van Valkenburgh, 1–27. Special issue, *Papers of the American Anthropological Association*, 22, no. 1 (2013).

Ots Capdequi, J. M. *España en América: El régimen de tierras en la época colonial*. México: Fondo de Cultura Económica, 1959.

——. *El estado español en las Indias*. Buenos Aires: Fondo de Cultura Económica, 1957.

Pease, G. Y. Franklin, and David J. Robinson. *Collaguas*. 4 vols. Lima: Pontificia Universidad Católica del Perú, 1977–2009.

Polia Meconi, Mario. "Siete cartas inéditas del Archivo Romano de la Compañía de Jesús, 1611–13: Huacas, mitos y ritos Andinos." *Antropológica (Lima)* 14 (1996): 209–59.

——. *Cosmovisión religiosa andina en los documentos inéditos del Archivo Romano de la Compañía de Jesús, 1581–1752*. Lima: Pontificia Universidad Católica del Perú, 1999.

Powers, Karen Viera. *Andean Journeys: Migration, Ethnogenesis, and the State in Colonial Quito*. Albuquerque: University of New Mexico Press, 1995.

Ramírez, Susan Elizabeth. "Chérrepe en 1572: Un análisis de la visita general del Virrey Francisco de Toledo." *Historia y cultura* 9 (1978): 79–121.

——. "De pescadores y agricultores: Una historia local de la gente del valle de Chicama antes de 1565." *Bulletin de l'Institut François de Etudes Andines* 24 (1995): 245–79.

——. "Ethnohistorical Dimensions of Mining and Metallurgy in Sixteenth Century Northern Peru." In *In Quest of Mineral Wealth: Aboriginal and Colonial Mining and Metallurgy in Spanish America*, edited by Alan K. Craig and Robert C. West, 93–108. Baton Rouge: Louisiana State University, 1994.

——. "From People to Place and Back Again: 'Back Translation' as Decentering; An Andean Case Study." *Ethnohistory* 53, no. 2 (2006): 355–82.

——. "The Link: Of Sacred Persons and Places." In *Inca Sacred Space: Landscape, Site and Symbol in the Andes*, edited by Frank Meddens, Katie Willis, Colin McEwan, and Nicholas Branch, 49–56, 279–304. London: Archetype, 2014.

——. *Patriarcas Provinciales: La tenencia de la tierra y la economia del poder en el Perú colonial.* Madrid: Alianza Editorial, 1991.

——. *Provincial Patriarchs: Land Tenure and the Economics of Power in Colonial Peru.* Albuquerque: University of New Mexico Press, 1986.

——. "Rich Man, Poor Man, Beggar Man or Chief: Two Views of the Concept of Wealth in Sixteenth Century Peru." In *Dead Giveaways: Indigenous Testaments of Colonial Spanish Americas*, edited by Susan Kellogg and Matthew Restall, 215–48. Salt Lake City: University of Utah Press, 1998.

——. "Social Frontiers and the Territorial Base of Curacazgos." In *Andean Ecology and Civilization*, edited by Shozo Masuda, Izumi Shimada, and Craig Morris, 423–42. Tokyo: University of Tokyo Press, 1985.

——. *To Feed and Be Fed: The Cosmological Bases of Authority and Identity in the Andes.* Stanford: Stanford University Press, 2005.

——. *The World Upside Down: Cross-Cultural Contact and Conflict in Sixteenth-Century Peru.* Stanford: Stanford University Press, 1996.

Remy Simatovic, María del Pilar. "Los curacas de Cajamarca y el sistema colonial (Siglo XVI, inicios de XVII)." Master's thesis, Pontificia Universidad Católica del Perú, 2011.

Ricard, Robert. *The Spiritual Conquest of Mexico.* Translated by Lesley Byrd Simpson. Berkeley: University of California Press, 1966.

Rostworowski de Diez Canseco, María. "Dos manuscritos inéditos con datos sobre Manco II, tierras personales de los Incas y mitimaes." *Nueva Corónica* 1 (1963): 223–39.

——. "Etnohistoria de un valle costeño durante el Tahuantinsuyu." *Revista del Museo Nacional* 35 (1967–68): 7–61.

——. "'Mercaderes del Valle de Chincha en la época prehispánica: Un documento y unos comentarios." *Revista Española de Antropología Americana [Madrid]* 5 (1970): 135–77.

——. "Nuevos datos sobre tenencia de tierras reales en el incario." *Revista del Museo Nación* 31 (1962): 130–59.

——. *Pesos y medidas en el Perú pre-hispánico.* Lima: Imprenta Minerva, 1960.

——. "Las tierras reales y su mano de obra en el Tahuantinsuyu." In *XXXVI Congreso Internacional de Americanistas, Spain, 1964*, edited by Alfredo Jiménez Núñez, 2:31–34. Seville: ECESA, 1966.

Sahlins, Peter. *Boundaries: The Making of France and Spain in the Pyrenees.* Berkeley: University of California Press, 1989.

Salomon, Frank. "Collca y Sapçi: una perspectiva sobre el almacenamiento inka desde la analogía etnográfica." *Boletín de Arqueología PUCP* 8 (2005): 43–57.

——. *The Cord Keepers: Khipus and Cultural Life in a Peruvian Village*. Durham: Duke University Press, 2004.

———, and George Urioste, eds. *The Huarochirí Manuscript: A Testament of Ancient and Colonial Andean Religion*. Austin: University of Texas Press, 1991.

Sherbondy, Jeannette. "Organización hidráulica y poder en el Cuzco de los Incas." *Revista española de antropología americana [Madrid]* 17 (1987): 117–53.

Sluyter, Andrew. "From Archive to Map to Pastoral Landscape: A Spatial Perspective on the Livestock Ecology of Sixteenth-Century New Spain." *Environmental History* 3 (1998): 508–28.

——. "Landscape Change and Livestock in Sixteenth-Century New Spain." *Yearbook. Conference of Latin Americanist Geographers* 23 (1997): 27–39.

Ugarte, César A. "Los antecedentes históricos del régimen agrario peruano." *Revista universitaria* 1 (1923): 318–98.

Urton, Gary. *Signs of the Inka Khipu: Binary Coding in the Andean Knotted-string Records*. Austin: University of Texas Press, 2003.

———, and Jeffery Quilter. *Narrative Threads: Accounting and Recounting in Andean Khipu*. Austin: University of Texas Press, 2002.

Valdez de la Torre, Carlos. *Evolución de las comunidades indígenas*. Lima: Ed. Euforion, 1921.

Varallanos, José. *Historia de Huánuco*. Huánuco: Empresa Periodística Perú, 1959.

Vega, Garcilaso de la, el Inca. *Royal Commentaries of the Incas and General History of Peru*. Austin: University of Texas Press, 1987.

Weeks, David. "European Antecedents of Land Tenure and Agrarian Organization of Hispanic America." *Journal of Land and Public Utility Economies* 231 (1947): 60–75.

Wernke, Steven. *Negotiated Settlements: Andean Communities and Landscapes under Inka and Spanish Colonialism*. Gainesville: University Press of Florida, 2013.

Whightman, Ann. *Indigenous Migration and Social Change: The Forasteros of Cuzco, 1570–1720*. Durham: Duke University Press, 1990.

Zevallos Quiñones, Jorge. *Los cacicazgos de Lambayeque*. Trujillo: Consejo Nacional de Ciencia y Tecnología, 1989.

——. *Los cacicazgos de Trujillo*. Trujillo: Gráfica Cuatro, S. A., 1992.

Susan Elizabeth Ramírez (s.ramirez@tcu.edu) holds the Neville G. Penrose Endowed Chair in History and Latin American Studies at Texas Christian University in Fort Worth, Texas. Besides dozens of articles and chapters published in the United States, Spain, Peru, England, Italy, Japan, and Australia, she has written several books. Among the most important are *Provincial Patriarchs: Land Tenure and the Economy of Power in Colonial Peru* (1986 and 1991); *The World Upside Down: Cross Cultural Contact and Conflict in Sixteenth-Century Peru* (1996 and 2002); *To Feed and Be Fed: The Cosmological Bases of Authority and Identity in the Andes* (2005); and *Al servicio de Dios y de Su Majestad: Los orígnes de las escuelas públicas para niños indígenas en el norte del Perú en el siglo XVIII* (2014).

Abstract This article compares and contrasts pre-Columbian indigenous customary law regarding land possession and use with the legal norms and concepts gradually imposed and implemented by the Spanish colonial state in the Viceroyalty of Peru in the sixteenth and early seventeenth centuries. Natives accepted oral histories of possession going back as many as ten generations as proof of a claim to land. Indigenous custom also provided that a family could claim as much land as it could use for as long as it could use it: labor established rights of possession and use. The Spanish introduced the concept of private property with the founding of the first colonial city in 1532, but agricultural land did not become immediately important because Europeans were supplied with foodstuffs from the tribute of native communities, produced on native communally worked land. After mid-century, however, royal officials began to grant land to Spanish settlers, and there was also an increase in the usurpation of native lands. Once unable to farm, indigenous peoples were forced into the labor market, sometimes working lands that had formerly been theirs.

Keywords land, tenure, usufruct, usurpation, custom, law, Peru, Andean, native, Spanish, titles, colonialism.

THE EDICT OF KING GÄLAWDÉWOS AGAINST THE ILLEGAL SLAVE TRADE IN CHRISTIANS: ETHIOPIA, 1548

HABTAMU MENGISTIE TEGEGNE

ON 12 FEBRUARY 1548, King Gälawdéwos of Ethiopia (r. 1540–59) issued a royal edict banning the trafficking of Christians and their sale to Arab owners under the penalty of death. The edict sought simultaneously to regulate and centralize the slave trade, protect freeborn Christians from enslavement, and ban the sale of already enslaved Christians to non-Christians. The edict did not, it is important to underline, challenge slavery itself. While the edict banned any trade in Ethiopian Christian slaves outside Ethiopian territory and their transfer to non-Christian masters within the country, it continued to permit the enslavement of adult converts to Christianity and those baptized as infants in slavery. In a pivotal passage, the king declared that the edict was to be the "established law of Ethiopia" and required universal obedience to it.

Currently held in the church of Tädbabä Maryam in northern Ethiopia, this edict has hitherto been unknown to scholars and has never before been published.[1] Furthermore, it is a remarkable text, of a type uncommon in the Ethiopian documentary tradition. Analysis of the edict's content and context sheds light on a broad set of issues concerning slavery, the encounter between medieval legal worlds, and the discrepancy or congruence between actual behavior and documentary norms in late medieval Ethiopia. It also reflects the religious, legal, and ethical precepts already laid down in the law book *Fetha Nägäst* (Law of Kings),

---

Some of the material used to write this essay was gathered on a research grant from the French Center for Ethiopian Studies, which I gratefully acknowledge here. An earlier version of this paper was read before the Seminar on Slavery in Ethiopia at Addis Ababa University on June 5, 2014, and I particularly thank Anaïs Wion and Giulia Bonacci for inviting me to present it and for facilitating my travel to Ethiopia. I would also like to thank the paper's anonymous reviewers, whose constructive comments and suggestions have been very helpful, as well as my former colleagues Nicola Foote, Frances Davey, and Scott Rohr for their comments on earlier drafts. I also owe a debt of gratitude to Mitiku Demele, who helped me with the translation of the Ge'ez text of the edict. Special thanks go to Carol Symes and Elizabeth Lambourn for their insightful comments on several drafts of this essay. The views expressed here, and any remaining errors, are my sole responsibility.

1 Tädbabä Maryam, MS Wängél, image no. 6650. Here, I reference my own digital photograph of the edict, preserved in this Wängél, or Gospel manuscript: see Plate 1.

Plate 1. The Edict of Gälawdéwos in its Manuscript Context: Tädbabä Maryam, MS Wängél. This manuscript page displays seven different texts. The edict begins at the top of the left-hand column and ends on line 13 of the right-hand column. Its scribe has distinguished it from the following charter (also issued by Gälawdéwos, appointing a Muslim governor for the province of Ifat) with a decorative row of alternating black and red dots. Another charter of Gälawdéwos, just below, is a donation to the church of Tädbabä Maryam, where the edict was recorded. However, this document has been partially erased and a later scribe has added a brief charter issued by King Iyasu I (1682–1706), recording his donation of land to one *Fitawrari* Mahdärä Mäläkot. Below it, following the final lines of the deleted charter, is an anathema clause warning the reader not to delete a charter made out in favor of one *Ras* Yämanä Krestos; the clause may refer to the last text in this column, a donation of land to that same man by the clergy of the church. The final text, inscribed in the lower margin of the page, records a donation by King Särṣä Dengel (1563–1596) to soldiers assigned to guard the church of Tädbabä Maryam.

which was transplanted to Ethiopia from Egypt sometime in the late fifteenth or early sixteenth century: a complex blending of elements derived from thirteenth-century Coptic Christian and Islamic laws, as well as from postclassical Roman-Byzantine legal systems.[2] The intricate and hybrid Ethiopian legal system exemplifies the interconnections and translation processes involved in the production of normative texts in many areas of the medieval globe, the result of cross-border communication processes and a special fruit of enduring Coptic-Ethiopian religious ties and interactions. My discovery of the edict now prompts a reconsideration of Ethiopia's slave law as embodied in the *Fetha Nägäst* and also a reevaluation of that text's manuscript history and practical applications.

In this study, I therefore reconsider the whole process of legal encounter in medieval Ethiopia in light of the edict of 1548, focusing the discussion on four areas. First, I explore the legal theory of slavery expressed in the edict and its link to the *Fetha Nägäst*, reexamining the entanglement of Roman-Byzantine, Coptic-Islamic, and Ethiopian legal systems. Second, I consider the circumstances surrounding the edict's making and Gälawdéwos's intentions in publishing it in this textual format. I then provide a Ge'ez edition and English translation, in order to facilitate further research on this important document and its wider implications. Third, I offer a brief analysis of the immediate political context that prompted the promulgation of the edict, arguing that it was the outcome of sustained and violent regional conflicts between the kingdom of Ethiopia and the sultanate of Adal during the fifteenth and sixteenth-centuries, which produced a constant supply of Christian Ethiopian slaves for sale to Egypt, South Arabia, and South Asia. Since Arabs were its particular target, the edict reveals the disjuncture between the Islamic legal theory that exempted Ethiopia from *jihad* and enslavement, and the actual relations between Ethiopians and Arabs within the Muslim world more generally. Finally, I turn to issues of enforcement and to identifying the role that the *Fetha Nägäst* and the edict played in impacting legal decisions, as well as legal and social relations. Ethiopian law is generally assumed by scholars to have been widely violated and ignored. The inaccessibility of the language in which the *Fetha Nägäst* is written and the tenuous records of its practical use are often read as an indication of its limited social relevance. Instead, I suggest that the legal doctrine and principles of the *Fetha Nägäst* concerning slavery, later strengthened by Gälawdéwos's edict, can be shown to have been widely known and to have exercised a measurable influence among a broad spectrum of people in sixteenth-century Ethiopia.

2 It has been translated into English by Abba Paulos Tzadua from the edition of Peter Strauss; cited hereafter as *Fetha Nägäst.*

Medieval Ethiopia as defined here covers the period roughly from 1000 to 1550 CE. Many elements of the civilization of this era were rooted in the Aksumite kingdom (1–800 CE). Named after its capital at Aksum, it developed in the northern highlands of Ethiopia and in the south-central region of what is now Eritrea, where it left a deep social and cultural imprint and a number of well-known institutional practices. Aksum bequeathed to its medieval heirs a script and a language of liturgy and learning, Ge'ez, a Semitic language which worked (and continues to work) in Ethiopia as Latin did in Europe for many centuries, after people stopped speaking it around 1000 CE. It also gave birth to a national church, the Ethiopian Orthodox Church, which is still deeply embedded in the popular culture of the northern and central highlands. Since its emergence in the mid-fourth century CE until 1959, when it became fully autocephalous, the Ethiopian Orthodox Church was headed by an Egyptian Coptic bishop, consecrated by the patriarch of Alexandria. More essentially, Aksum left an enduring church-state institutional relationship. With the rise of Islamic powers in eighth-century Arabia, Aksum abandoned the Red Sea coasts and, over the next seven centuries (a shadowy period of Ethiopian history), the political and cultural center of Ethiopia steadily shifted southwards from Aksum, first to Lalibela and then to the regions of Amhara and Shawa (see **Map 2**). The southward expansion of the state accelerated with the dramatic advent of the new "Solomonic" dynasty in 1270 CE, when Yekuno Amlak (r. 1270–85), who claimed direct descent from Aksumite kings, became emperor of Ethiopia.[3]

Historians such as Marie-Laure Derat, Stephen Kaplan, and Taddesse Tamrat have provided absorbing accounts of the unprecedented political, religious, and literary renaissance experienced during the early Solomonic era (1270–1527). The kings of the new dynasty, which lasted until 1974, revived the Aksumite tradition of charismatic and centralized monarchical rule and made remarkable territorial conquests. In religion, the period witnessed the rapid growth and expansion of the Ethiopian Orthodox Church and the establishment of a new model of church-state relations in which the state dominated. This process eventually made Christianity integral to Ethiopian national identity.[4] Moreover, although medieval Ethiopia remained essentially an oral society, the growth of the Ethiopian Church and royal patronage of art and literature stimulated a rare outburst of literary activity during this period. In particular, King Zärä Yaqob (r. 1434–68) personally

3 Phillipson, *Foundations of an African Civilization*, 51–54, 79–106, 227–43; and Isaac, *The Ethiopian Orthodox Täwahido Church*, 17–26, 109–14, 131–88.

4 Derat, *Le Domaine des rois éthiopiens*; Kaplan, *The Monastic Holy Man*; and Tamrat, *Church and State in Ethiopia*.

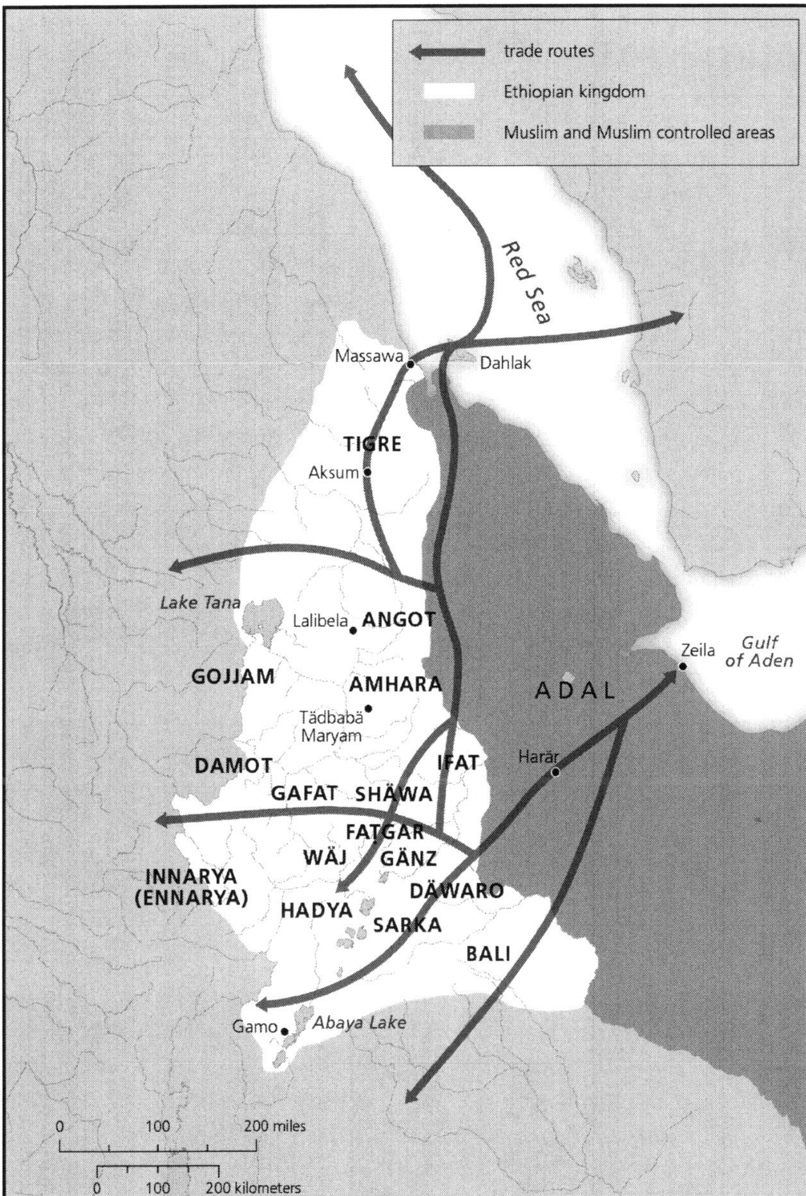

Map 2. Provinces of Ethiopia, Muslim Territories, and Major Trade Routes in the Horn of Africa.
© Habtamu Mengistie Tegegne 2015.

took part in this literary regeneration through writing, promoting, and disseminating juridical and religious books concerned with the regulation of religious life and political rituals.[5]

Despite the expansion of the Ethiopian state and church in the Horn of Africa, it has recently become increasingly clear that medieval Ethiopia remained culturally and religiously diverse. Based on information gleaned from newly discovered Arabic funerary inscriptions and more familiar documentary evidence, François-Xavier Fauvelle-Aymar and Bertrand Hirsch have shown that Islam was an integral part of the cultural landscape, not only of the broad coastal lowlands of the western Red Sea and Gulf of Aden but also in the eastern escapements of the northern and central highlands. Islamic cultural influence on Ethiopia came originally from the Dahlak islands in the Red Sea, where a thriving mercantile Muslim community had developed by the tenth century. The Dahlak and Massawa served as key transit points in a north-south axis of trade route linking Ethiopia to South Arabia and Egypt during the tenth through to thirteenth centuries. Islamic development accelerated in the Horn of Africa with the rapid development of the port of Zeila in the Gulf of Aden and the vibrant east-west axis trade route connecting the highlands of Ethiopia with the lowlands of the western Red Sea area in thirteenth century. Around the same time, the sultanate of Ifat was founded and grew rich from trade and control over Zeila.[6]

In 1332, Ifat and other Muslim polities were absorbed into the expanding Ethiopian state. With the advent of the Solomonids, then, Ethiopia appears to have lost its traditional rapport with Muslims in the Horn of Africa.[7] By the fifteenth century, open rivalry and hostility had largely replaced the peaceful coexistence and economic cooperation between Ethiopia and Muslim powers in the Horn of Africa. In the period 1529–43, Ethiopia was occupied by a *jihadist* army raised from the sultanate of Adal, which grew from the remnants of Ifat in the late fourteenth century. The *jihad* resulted in the looting and destruction of churches and the enslavement of many Christian captives. In 1543, the *jihad* collapsed, its leader was killed, and Ethiopian hegemony in the Horn of Africa was reestablished.[8] As a whole, the rise of the Solomonids animated Ethiopian Christian identity through its conflict against Islam and pagan peoples. This is the backdrop against which the 1548 edict of Gälawdéwos and the issue of legal encounter must be understood.

---

5 *Il libro della luce del negus Zar'a Yaqob*; *The Epistle of Humanity of Emperor Zär'a Ya'eqob*.

6 Fauvelle-Aymar and Hirsch, "Muslim Historical Spaces in Ethiopia"; idem, "Établissements et formations politiques musulmans"; and idem, "En guise d'introduction."

7 Tamrat, *Church and State in Ethiopia*, 231.

8 Uṯmān, *Futūḥ al-Ḥabaša*.

Juridic Precedent and Legal Theory: The Law of Slavery in the *Fetha Nägäst*

The Ethiopian legal system was constituted through complex processes of appropriation, reformulation, and cross-border diffusion of legal institutions and norms: a process which scholars of comparative law call "legal transplant," "legal transfer," or the "translation" of normativity.[9] Initially, postclassical Roman-Byzantine laws were borrowed and subjected to qualifications, then mixed with Coptic-Islamic laws and Ethiopian customs. Ethiopian translators and interpreters used local usage for reformulating the imported laws and norms, resulting in the production of a novel legal system, a mixture of the foreign template and many local elaborations and reconceptualizations. Though a hybrid, the Ethiopian legal system thus remained Ethiopian in its understanding and application. With respect to the legal theory of slavery and the juridical context of the 1548 edict, it is useful, therefore, to ask: How did the precepts of Ethiopian customary law penetrate into Ethiopia's foreign-derived legal system? How was slavery conceptualized in indigenous Ethiopian law? What influences, if any, did the pre-existing laws have on the edict of Gälawdéwos?

Gälawdéwos's edict did not develop in a legal vacuum. Its content was shaped by the juristic precedent of the *Fetha Nägäst* and the political milieu of fifteenth and sixteenth-century Ethiopia. And while the *Fetha Nägäst* bears the strong mark of Ethiopian legal culture and way of life, much of it is derived from Roman laws that found their way into Ethiopia indirectly, by means of truncated Byzantine handbooks written in Greek, which in turn had been translated into Arabic and redacted by Melchite Christians in Egypt in the twelfth and thirteenth centuries. These handbooks were later revised and rewritten, elaborated, and merged in Coptic Church legislation commonly known as the *Nomocanon* (Collections of Canons). Unsurprisingly, perhaps, underlying the *Nomocanon* are also many elements of Islamic law.[10] It was compiled by Abu-l-Fada'il Ibn al-Assal, a Coptic Christian jurist who lived in thirteenth-century Egypt. Prepared to serve as a practical guide for Coptic Christians who lived amidst Muslims, the *Nomocanon* was officially promulgated in 1238 by Patriarch Cyril III ibn Laqlaq of Alexandria (r. 1235–43). It was then transplanted to Ethiopia and translated into Ge'ez from Arabic and renamed the *Fetha Nägäst*.[11] The accepted reasoning behind this change

9 The phrase was originally invented by Watson, *Legal Transplants*. In Watson's words, "legal transplants" mean "the moving of a rule or a system of law from one country to another, or from one people to another" (21).

10 Sand, "Roman Origins of the Ethiopian Law," xlii–xlix.

11 Tzadua, foreword to *Fetha Nagast*, xvi-xvii.

of name, as given by its nineteenth-century translator Ignazio Guidi, is that the ecclesiastical portions (chapters 1–22) already existed in Ethiopia in the book titled *Sinodos*, long before the coming of the *Nomocanon*. The *Sinodos* is a canonical work of Egyptian Melchite Christian origin with great prestige and authority in the Ethiopian Orthodox Church to this day. What was new to Ethiopians was the secular law sections or the "Canons (or Laws) of the Kings," chapters 23–51, from which the code derived its Ethiopian name.[12]

Much remains uncertain about the date, the motives, and the circumstances in which the *Fetha Nägäst* came to Ethiopia. There is no evidence of its formal promulgation. Some scholars have speculated that the Egyptian archbishop of the Ethiopian church, Abunä Sälama (1350–90), was responsible for its translation,[13] but this interpretation has lately fallen from favor. Ignazio Guidi has dated the translation to the sixteenth century, based on information gleaned from philological evidence,[14] and records of *Fetha Nägäst's* practical use in courts during the reign of King Särṣä Dengel (r. 1563–94) conforms to this later dating. But it is unlikely that the principles, institutions, and norms of a complex legal system have been translated, received, studied, and applied in court all at once during such a short period of time, a period marked by profound political upheavals and disruption of social and religious life. The training of jurists in its legal principles and their effective application in courts must have required a long gestation period. This can be illustrated with reference to the better known history of the *Sinodos*, whose Ethiopian reception was not immediately followed by its effective application. It was King Zärä Yaqob (r. 1434–68) in the fifteenth century who resolutely started the practical use of the *Sinodos*. Guidi, again, has used the evidence of its practical application to date the *Sinodos*'s introduction to the early fifteenth century. But there is conclusive evidence of its existence in the fourteenth century, offered by the royal chronicle of King Amdä Ṣeyon (1314–44).[15] In both cases, we can conclude that the long process of translation and reception began much earlier.

According to Ethiopian tradition, the *Fetha Nägäst* was introduced into the juridical system of the country in the fifteenth century at the initiative of King Zärä Yaqob, the very promulgator of the *Sinodos*.[16] The larger historical developments of this period would seem to fit this scenario: Ethiopia appears to have stood at

---

12 *Il Fetha Nagast o "Legislazione dei Re,"* 37–38.

13 Brietzke, *Law, Development, and the Ethiopian Revolution*, 32.

14 Guidi, "Der æthiopische Senodos."

15 Bausi, "Heritage and Originality in the Ethiopic *Sinodos*," 16 and 21–23.

16 Tzadua, foreword to *Fetha Nagast*, xvii; and Sand, "Roman Origins of the Ethiopian Law," xlii.

the threshold of a legislative development under Zärä Yaqob. It is known that the king was the author a number of Ethiopian religious-juridical traditions, and his reign placed unprecedented emphasis on reform in religious practice, centralized authority, and legislative uniformity. His aspirations, and the widely felt inadequacy of the reliance on customary law to administer a diverse empire, influenced the king to seek the codification of a new law for the use of his subjects. Church scholars were called upon, and yet the ecclesiastical code they produced, *Fäwsä Mänfäsawi* (Spiritual Remedy), was not comprehensive and fell into disuse. According to tradition, it was the absence of a satisfactory indigenous law code that motivated Zära Yaqob to borrow a more sophisticated foreign legal system, the Coptic-Islamic Arabic language *Nomocanon*, to best serve the demands of his centralizing state.[17] In Ethiopian tradition, the translator of the *Fetha Nägäst*, who gives his name in the colophon as "Peṭros son of Abdä Säyd," was the same person who brought the text from Egypt at the expense and order of Zära Yaqob.[18] Although this cannot be confirmed by any independent source, this tradition cannot be dismissed lightly.

Ibn al-Assal divided the *Fetha Nägäst* into two broad parts arranged by subject and divided into chapters treating, on the one hand, ecclesiastical law and ritual; on the other, secular law. I am concerned here with the secular law sections, which cover a broad range of human affairs, including slavery, property law, succession, criminal law, commercial law, family law, sumptuary and dietary law, and so on. Beside chapter 30, which deals exclusively with matters of slavery and freedom, references to slaves are found scattered across several other chapters.[19] Thanks to the exacting investigations of legal historians, the main sources of the *Fetha Nägäst* have now been identified. For the provisions regarding slavery and manumission, Ibn al-Assal drew directly upon the two handbooks of Roman-Byzantine law known as the *Syro-Roman Law Book* and the *Procheiros Nomos*. The former was originally written in Greek in 480 CE and later translated into Syriac in about 750. Although assumed to have a Syriac contribution, it was essentially a work of Roman jurisprudence. The *Procheiros Nomos* was enacted in 878 by the Byzantine emperor Basilios I the Macedonian (r. 867–86). Ibn al-Assal was able to access both handbooks via the Arabic translations of various Egyptian Melchite Christians made around 1100. The *Syro-Roman Law Book*, which is cited eighty-nine times in the *Fetha Nägäst*, formed the basis for many of the enactments relating

17 Jembere, *Introduction to the Legal History of Ethiopia*, 187–89.

18 *Fetha Nagast*, 319; Jembere, *Introduction to the Legal History of Ethiopia*, 188.

19 *Fetha Nagast*, 175–78. References to slaves are too many to list here, but the most important ones are on 54, 186–90, 196–98, 204, 216, 224, 225, 227, 231, 232, 245, 258, and 317.

to slavery, such as the provisions against the traffic in Christians. By contrast, Ibn al-Assal's debt to the *Procheiros Nomos* was negligible, and it is cited infrequently. However, it is the source for his statements regarding natural law and justice, the origins of slavery, and the provisions about the methods and justification for manumission.[20]

The third and the oldest source of Romano-Byzantine law available to Ibn al-Assal was the *Ecloga* (Selection). This handbook was written in Constantinople in 726 and is specifically ascribed to Emperor Leo III Isauricos (r. 717–41) and his son and successor Constantine V Copronimos (r. 741–75). The citations of the *Ecloga* in the *Fetha Nägäst* are, according to P. H. Sand, "based on an excerpt made by Melchites in the thirteenth century from a previous Arabic translation of the *Ecloga*, into which the Nicaean canons were incorporated."[21] The *Ecloga* provided the direct basis for the *Fetha Nägäst*'s statement about the methods of manumission and return to slavery, offences by and punishments against slaves.[22]

These three handbooks, which contain bits and pieces of the sixth-century Justinianic Code, were ultimately redacted into the *Nomocanon*, which in its transfer from Egypt to Ethiopia and translation into Ge'ez became the *Fetha Nägäst*. This was the primary means through which Roman legal thought entered Ethiopia. But the *Fetha Nägäst* was not entirely Roman in its essence. Although Ibn al-Assal does not directly credit other sources, he clearly had a knowledge of, and borrowed freely from, Islamic law. Thus, there are many examples in the *Fetha Nägäst*, of terminologies, punishments, jurisprudential concepts, legal formulae, and commentary that present striking similarities with the Islamic law of slavery and manumission. This becomes apparent by comparing, for example, *Fetha Nägäst*'s provisions relating to the method of manumission of a jointly owned slave with a comment attributed to the Prophet Muhammad. The hadith records that "[w]hoever frees [his share of] a slave owned by two persons shall be charged [for the other half] if he is well off; then [the slave] shall be [completely] freed."[23] The *Fetha Nägäst* states that "[i]f a man is part owner of a slave, so that there is another who shares ownership, if one of them is a rich man, he must buy him entirely and

20 Sand, "Roman Origins of the Ethiopian Law," xlv–xlvi; *Fetha Nägäst*, 175–77, 224, 231–32, and 245; and *Manual of Eastern Roman Law*, ed. Freshfield, 90–91, 137–41. Ibn al-Assal cited the *Procheiros Nomos* and *Syro-Roman Law Book* (in that order) using the abbreviations TS and MAK, citations repeated in the Ge'ez version.

21 Sand, "Roman Origins of the Ethiopian Law," xlvii.

22 *Fetha Nagast*, 176–77, 302, and 303; and *Manual of Roman Law*, ed. Freshfield, 88–90. *The Ecloga* appears in the *Fetha Nägäst* as MAG, citation repeated in the Ge'ez version.

23 Quoted in Hunwick and Powell, *The African Diaspora*, 6 (citing the recension by Muhammad al-Bukhari, *al-Jami al-sahih*).

set him entirely free."[24] I would contend that a considerable part of the provisions about manumission and slavery in the *Fetha Nägäst* reflect Islamic law even more than Roman-Byzantine practices. The source of the theory of natural liberty in the *Fetha Nägäst*, together with the presumption that slavery derives from warfare, were not of Ethiopian and Roman-Byzantine origin alone. In Muslim legal theory, too, it is also believed "that the innate condition of people is freedom" and slavery originated in war.[25] Evidence suggests that the *Fetha Nägäst* also exhibits elements of Malikite Islamic jurisprudence (which was very popular in Egypt during the author's time) in its form, literary and legislative style, and arrangement of materials.[26] Such Islamic touches are to be expected in a text compiled for Coptic Christians who had been living within Islamic lands since 642 AD.

It has been argued that the *Fetha Nägäst* contains many judicial precepts and terminologies which were largely unfamiliar and irrelevant to the Ethiopian experience. A more accurate assessment is that of Abba Paulos Tzadua, the most highly regarded authority on the subject, who sees a great "influence of the Ethiopian way of life on the *Fetha Nägäst*."[27] As noted above, the Ethiopian reception of Roman-Byzantine and Coptic-Islamic legal systems was neither unqualified nor wholesale. Even if the *Fetha Nägäst* reflects what might be seen as alien, its interpretation and application were thoroughly Ethiopian. For example, as noted by Tzadua, the understanding of the notions of mandate in the Ge'ez version is divergent from the Arabic version. He finds that the chapter on mandate was "relegislated" and reconceptualized to refer to "stewardship in the house of the Emperor or some member of the nobility."[28] In this and countless other instances, Ethiopian customs and legal principles were blended and reconciled with the foreign body of law, thereby facilitating its reception.

To take one salient example, "the [state of] liberty" is understood in the text of the *Fetha Nägäst* to be "in accord with the law of reason, for all men share liberty on the basis of natural law."[29] It follows that liberty is a universal and natural right. This conception of natural law is founded partly on the local customary law and usages of Ethiopia, existing since at least the introduction of Christianity in the fourth century CE, and partly on Roman law and Greek philosophical precepts. The customary law commonly held in learned ecclesiastical circles, in

24 *Fetha Nagast*, 177.

25 Hunwick, "Islamic Law and Polemic," 44.

26 Sand, "Roman Origins of the Ethiopian Law," xlvii–xlix.

27 Tzadua, foreword to *Fetha Nagast*, xxi.

28 Ibid.

29 *Fetha Nagast*, 175.

particular, was natural law, with "natural justice" recognized by the technical term *fethe feṭerätawi*. Aberra Jembere, the author of an important book on the legal history of Ethiopia, maintains that "a conception of natural law—as the law of reason 'inborn by nature' and as such perceived in Ethiopia—was considered to be the source of many of the old laws of the country that was elaborated and solidified later on the basis of Christian beliefs and values."[30] Jembere adds that "Ethiopian legal culture is consistent with" the view that "human rights [...] are an endowment from a 'natural fact' to any person, as the result of he/her being created as a human being."[31]

While the Ethiopian notion of natural law and human rights therefore has a long history, its elaboration and articulation in writing came only later in the seventeenth century as a critique of slavery and the slave trade. The notion of equality, justice, and belief in the shared humanity of all God's children, profoundly rooted in the teaching of the Ethiopian Orthodox Church, was then expounded by Wäldä Heywät in a treatise entitled *Hatäta Zärä Yaqob* (The Treatise of Zera Yacob):[32]

> Moreover, God created all men equal just like brothers, sons of one father; our creator himself is the father of all. Therefore, we should love one another and observe this eternal precept which God engraved upon the Tables of our heart and which says: "Love your fellow men as yourself, and do to them what you wish others to do to you; do not do to them that which you do not want to be done to you"; observation of this primary precept is the perfection of all other deeds and of all justice. Do not think that the doctrine of fools who say the following is good: "the word 'fellow men' is confined only to relatives, or our neighbors, or our friends, or members of the same faith." Do not say the same as they do; for all men are our fellow men whether they are good, or evil, Christians, Mohammedans, Jews, pagans: all are equal to us and our brothers, because we are all the sons of one father and the creatures of one creator. Therefore we ought to love one another, and to behave well with all as much as we can and not to inflict evil on anyone.[33]

---

30 Jembere, *Introduction to the Legal History of Ethiopia,* 31.

31 Ibid.

32 Quoted in Sumner, *Ethiopian Philosophy*, 225.

33 Lacking any literary precedent or classic model, the *Hätata's* originality has resisted any classification, and for this reason its authorship was questioned by Conti Rossini, "Lo Hatata Zaraa Ya'qob." He attributes the work to a nineteenth-century Catholic missionary to Ethiopia, Giusto da Urbino. This view has never been adequately elucidated, much less universally accepted.

Since they sprung from a common origin, Wäldä Heywät teaches that all men are natural kinsmen and members of a great family. Therefore, there is no inherent distinction between human beings and every man by nature is a born free and equal to other men. From this argument of universal fraternity, it follows that "there can be no chosen people, no more than there is the right of the stronger over the weaker, and the priority of man over woman!" [34] Since no one is created slave or master by nature, the slave trade was accordingly an affront to the fundamental rights and liberties of individuals. Although this treatise was written centuries after the *Fetha Nägäst*, it echoes ideas that had already penetrated into the *Fetha Nägäst*, which considers slavery to be unnatural and without any ethical foundation. Not only is slavery unnatural but also it is unwarranted, for the inequality inherent in the system extinguishes justice.

If slavery was dishonorable and incompatible with human nature, the inevitable question is: Why was it accepted as a legitimate institution in Ethiopia in the first place? The *Fetha Nägäst* gives an explanation for this: slavery was the function of war and violence, because the strongest and the victorious used violence and coercion to make the weakest and vanquished accept it: "[b]ut war and the strength of horses bring some to the service of others, because the law of war and victory makes the vanquished slaves of the victors."[35] This closely corresponds to the explanation of the origin of slavery given in the *Procheiros Nomo*, where it is stated that "[s]lavery is consequent upon the *jus gentium* [law of nations] whereby one man is made subject to another man. By nature all men were made free; by war men were made slaves. For the law of war prescribes that the conquered shall be the property of the conquerors."[36] By the manmade law of war, those defeated in war are held to belong to the victor; slavery was therefore justified on moral grounds: that is, it accorded with human *mores*. The *Fetha Nägäst* therefore joined other legal traditions in conceding the morality of the institution of slavery. Indeed, in one of several similar provisions it treats slaves with cool indifference, as objects: "The price of a slave is like that of an object at any given time. It may increase or decrease."[37] The Bible is also cited as an authority on the religious and political conditions that justified slavery. The proof text quoted in the *Fetha Nägäst* is Leviticus 25:44 and following: "[t]hose whom you take from the

34 Sumner, *Ethiopian Philosophy,* 232. The legal and ethical precepts on liberty and universal right were based on the Judeo-Christian belief in that man was made in the image and likeness of God.

35 *Fetha Nagast*, 175.

36 *Manual of Eastern Roman Law*, ed. Freshfield, 138.

37 *Fetha Nagast*, 177.

people who dwell around you and the aliens who dwell among you, let them, men and women, be your slaves. You shall buy [slaves] from among them, and from their offspring born in your land, and they shall be for you and your children after you, as an inheritance."[38] Religion determined who fell within the boundaries of those protected from enslavement and those who could legitimately be enslaved. Based on this, freeborn Christians were a priori of free status and off-limits, while non-Christians captured in war could be enslaved. Slavery was therefore caused by unbelief, and yet the conversion of pagan slaves to Christianity subsequent to the establishment of the right of ownership by masters did not extinguish slavery. In this way, the code provided the ground for a religiously justified exclusion and enslavement of non-Christians and Christians whose slavery was caused by previous unbelief.[39]

While granting legitimacy to the institution, the *Fetha Nägäst* insists that slavery should be confined within the boundaries of Christian conduct and civilized values. First, it imposes a ban on the sale of "a [Christian] slave accustomed to the usages of a country to a foreigner; unless the slave gives his consent."[40] The Amharic gloss is more specific and goes further, stating that Christian slaves were not to be sold to aliens, "especially if the buyer belongs to another faith and speaks another language."[41] Second, it discusses the many circumstances under which slaves might be given freedom. It encourages individuals to buy Christian slaves from the *ahzab* or infidels and praises manumitting slaves as an act of charity and compassion "that must be done for it is an excellent form of alms."[42] Entailing as it does "the granting to a man of the right to become master of himself, according to the original law of his natural liberty," releasing a slave from bondage is deemed "a deed of perfection."[43] Freedom from transfer to non-Christians was acquired from the moment of baptism, so while it was acceptable to make a pagan slave a Christian, it was flatly forbidden to sell a Christian slave to infidels.[44] The *Fetha Nägäst* also imposed capital punishment against those who stole children, be they free or slave. The trade in Christian slaves (whose servitude was caused by a previous

38 Ibid., 175.

39 Ibid.

40 Ibid., 190.

41 Ibid., 190, n. 61.

42 Ibid, 175. The *Fetha Nägäst* also states that "A buyer may not return to the seller, invoking their defects, a slave who was bought from an infidel and then baptized or a Christian female slave whom he married or give away in marriage" (187).

43 *Fetha Nagast,* 175.

44 Ibid., 188.

unbelief) to infidels such as Muslims was offensive because these Christian slaves could thereby be converted to a despised religion, and their souls could not be saved. In the end, it was only the slavery of freeborn Christians that was considered inconsistent with humanity and natural law.

The newly discovered edict of Gälawdéwos was structured around the same legal and religious principles found in the *Fetha Nägäst*. As will be discussed below, the king considered slavery exclusive to non-Christians and thereby recognized a link between religion, slavery, and freedom. But before discussing Gälawdéwos's intention in publishing the edict, the impetus for its promulgation, and the manner of its preservation and transmission, the text deserves to be published in its entirety.

The Edict: Text and Analysis

So far as I am aware, this is the only written edict by an Ethiopian king prior to the twentieth century. Indeed, African scholarship has not brought to light anything like the edict of Gälawdéwos, which also constitutes the first documented articulation of something analogous to anti-slavery sentiment generated in reaction to the slave trade. It also has implications for the study of Arab-Ethiopian/African relations and the history of law.

King Gälawdéwos's edict is preserved in a sixteenth-century parchment Wängél, or Gospel manuscript, held by the Tädbabä Maryam church in Amhara, a major foundation of Gälawdéwos.[45] The manuscript is undated, but the main text is datable to the sixteenth century date and thus roughly contemporary with the edict. Remarkably, it also contains a rich variety of texts written on its front and back flyleaves, dating from the sixteenth through to the late eighteenth centuries and covering a broad range of issues, though mainly concerned with land and its control.[46] I recently had direct access to this manuscript and was able to photograph the edict and other historical sources at the church. The edict is written in Ge'ez, on parchment. It is only 340 words long in the original and is written as one continuous text consisting of four basic parts: the proem; general provisions regulating the slave trade and prohibiting the traffic in Christians; the anathemas and

45 A contemporary chronicle details the circumstances leading to the founding of the church. See *Chronique de Galâwadêwos*, 49–54, 58–59, and 123.

46 Tädbabä Maryam, MS Wängél, image nos 6597–6654 (the author's own digital photographs of documents in this Wängél).

the date on which the edict was issued; and finally the provisions concerning the regulation of the slave trade in Damot and Gamo provinces, specifically.[47]

> በስመ ሥሉስ ቅዱስ ዘይሴባሕ ስሙ ወይትሌዐል ዝክሩ ወውእቱ ረዳእየ ወቦቱ እትዌከል ወበረድኤቱ እስምከ ወበኃይሉ እትፌሣሕ ሎቱ ኃይል ወስብሐት ወሎቱ ክብር ወዕዘዝ በኵሉ ዓለማት ለዓለመ ዓለም አሜን።
>
> አነ ንጉሥ ገላውዴዎስ ወልደ ንጉሥ ወናግ ሰገድ አዘዝኩ እምይእዜ ከመ ኢይረድ ነጋዴ ኢእስላም ወኢክርስቲያን ኀበ ባሕረ ወኀበ አዳል አው ኀበ ኵሉ መካን ዘየሐውሩ ውስቴታ ነጋድያን ዘእንበለ ይብፀሕ ኀበ ዴዴየ። ወያምጽእ ኵሎ አግብርት ዘውስቴቱ ተባዕተ ወአንስተ ኀቤየ። ወዘእንበለ ይጽሐፍ ሎቱ ክታበ ኊልቆሙ ለአግብርቲሁ ከመ ያርኢ ለመኳንንት ወለመሳፍንት ወለስዩማን ሀገር ዘውስተ ፍኖት። ወኵሉ ዘተረክበ ምስሌሁ ምንትኒ ዘይተርፍ እምኊልቍ ዘተጽሕፈ ይንሥኡ እምኔሁ፣ ፣ ወኵሉ ዘተረክበ ምስሌሁ ገብር ክርስቲያናዊ ወእመ ኮነ ውእቱ እምደቂቀ ዓረብ ይንሥኡ ኵሎ ንዋዮ ወይፈንው ኀቤየ። ወዘሤጠ ለገብር ክርስቲያናዊ በውስተ ምስያጥ ይቅትልዎ። ወእመሰ ኮነ ነጋዴ ዘሤጠ ለክርስቲያናዊ እመሂ እስላም ወእመሂ ክርስቲያን እምሰብአ ሀገረ ኢትዮጵያ ይቀትል ዘሤጦ። ወለተሳየጦሂ እምደቂቀ ዐረብ እንዘ የአምር ከመ ውእቱ ክርስቲያናዊ ይንሥእዎ ኵሎ ንዋዮ።
>
> ወኵሉ አዛዥ አው ፈታሕት አው መኮንን አው ሰዩመ ሀገረ ዘኢይፈትሕ በዘ አዘዝነ ቦቱ ይትቀተል ዘእንበለ ምሕረት ወይትበርበር ኵሉ ንዋዩ ወይኩን ውጉዘ በአፈ አብ ወወልድ ወመንፈስ ቅዱስ ወበአፈ ኵሎሙ አበው ዘተወከፈቶሙ ቤተ ክርስቲያን።ወአነ ንጉሥ ገላውዴዎስ ፈታህኩ ፍትሐ ወአጽናዕኩ ዘንተ ክታበ። ወትኩን ዛቲ ሕገ ወሥርዓት ጽንዕተ በምድረ ኢትዮጵያ እስከ ለዓለመ ዓለም። ወኵሉ ዘተዐደዋ እምነገሥታት እምድኅሬየ አው እምፈታሕት ይኩን ታሕተ ግዘት ወኢይኩን ሎቱ ኅድገት ኢበሞቱ ወኢበሕይወቱ። ወኵሉ ዘይደመስስ ዘንተ መጽሐፈ አው ዘያደርያ እምድረ ኢትዮጵያ እግዚአብሔር ይደምስስ ስሞ እመጽሐፈ ሕይወት ወይኩን መክፈልቱ ምስለ ሐና ወቀያፋ ወይሁዳ አስቆሮታዊ ወሴሞን መሠሪ ወትፍታሕ ምድር አፈሃ ወትሐጦ በአምሳለ ዳታን ወአቤሮን። ወዝንቱ ብርዐ እዴየ ትኩን ስምዐ ላዕሌየ። ወተጽሕፈት ዛቲ ክታብ በዓመተ ሰማዕታት ፲፻ወ፭፻፷ወ፱ወአመ ፲ወ፰ ለወርኃ የካቲት ቡሩክ በ፳ዓመት ወበ፳ ወርኀ እምአመ እንገሠኒ እግዚአብሔር። ስብሐት ለእግዚአብሔር በሰማያት ወሰላም በምድር ሥምረቱ ለሰብእ ለዓለመ ዓለም አሜን።
>
> ወእመቦ ዘተሣየጠ ገብረ እምዳሞት አው እምገሞ ይጽሐፍ ስመ ብእሲ ዘሤጠ ሎቱ ። ወይጽሐፍ ካዕበ ኊልቆሙ ለአግብርቲሁ ውኆልቈ ንዋይ ዘወሀበ ወያርኢ ለመኳንንት ወለመሳፍንት ወለሥዩማነ ሀገር ዘውስተ ፍኖት። ወለእመ ኮነ ነገሩ እሙነ ሐቲቶሙ ይፈንውዎ። ወእመሰ ሞተ ገብር ዘተሣየጦ ውእቱ ብእሲ እምዳሞት ወገሞ ወአምጽአ ከልአ ገብረ ክርስትያናዌ ከመ ይምላእ ሎቱ በኊልቍ። ወእመ ተአውቀ ወተጠየቀ ቦቱ ዝንቱ ነገር ይንሥእዎ ኵሎ ንዋዮ። ወኪያሁሰ አሢሮሙ ያምጽእዎ ኀቤየ። ወሶበሰ ይጽሐፍ ይበል ከመዝ ኆላቋ አግብርት ዘተሣየጥኩ እምዳሞት የአከል ዘንተ ወዘተሣየጥኩ እምገም የአከል ዘንተ።ወይፍልጥ ኵሎ በበስመ ብሔሩ።[48]

47 For the sake of convenience, I have divided the edict into paragraphs and have disregarded the punctuation marks in the original text in favor of the current conventional system used by the *Journal of Ethiopian Studies*.

48 Tädbabä Maryam, MS Wängél, image no. 6650.

Praise be, Blessed Trinity, to Your name and exalted be Your memory. He is my Helper and I trust in Him. I delight in His power and shelter in His grace. Praise and power be to Him. Glory and rule over all worlds be to Him. Forever and ever. Amen.

I, King Gälawdéwos, son of Wänag Sägäd,[49] have ordered that from now onwards any merchant [traveling with slaves], whether he be Muslim or Christian, shall not proceed to the sea, to Adal, and to other market places visited by merchants, without coming to my gate [for inspection]. Let him bring both female and male slaves before me. Let him write down the number of slaves [he is traveling with] and report them to the *mäkwanent,*[50] *mäsafent,*[51] and *seyuman*[52] of the district along the route they pass through. When any captive who is not in the list reported to the [*mäkwannent, mäsafent,* and *seyuman*] is discovered, let them take him into custody. If the captive turns out to be Christian and the one [who knowingly bought him] is an Arab, let them deprive him of all his merchandise and send him to me. Let them kill the seller who [knowingly] puts up for market and sale [to the Arab merchant] the Christian slave. If the seller who [knowingly] sold a Christian is a merchant, whether he be Muslim or a Christian Ethiopian compatriot, let them kill him. If an Arab [merchant] knowingly purchases a Christian, let them confiscate all his property. Any *azaj,*[53] whether he be *fätahit* (judge), or *mäkonnen*, or *seyum* of the district, who [slacks on his obligation] and does not follow our commands, deserves to be killed without mercy and his house ransacked; and let him be damned by the mouth of the Father, the Son, and the Holy Ghost, and by the mouth of all Church Fathers.

---

49 Wänag Sägäd is the regnal name of King Lebnä Dengel (r. 1508–40), Gälawdéwos's father.

50 *Mäkwannent* is generic term, which historical sources from the thirteenth to the twentieth centuries use to refer to the higher nobility collectively. Modern Amharic dictionaries conform to usage of the historical sources. See, for instance, Kane, *Amharic-English Dictionary*, 1443; Wolf Leslau, *Comparative Dictionary of Ge'ez*, 287; and Baetman, *Dictionnaire Amarigna-Français*, 734.

51 *Seyuman* (sing. *seyum*) is a general term for officials appointed by the monarch. It is derived from the root word *säyyämä* "to designate (appoint), give the title of" (Kane, *Amharic-English Dictionary*, 571).

52 This word is generally used to refer to the hereditary nobility or princes. Kane renders its singular form *mäsfen* as "prince" (Ibid., 599).

53 Kane (Ibid., 1281) defines *azaj* as "commander, chief, intendant, major-domo." Baeteman's dictionary shows that the word has a connotation of legal authority (*Dictionnaire Amarigna-Français*, 614). He renders the word as "juge de tribunal supreme" or "supreme court judge."

> I, King Gälawdéwos, legislated this law and sanctioned this writing. Let it be the established law and regulation of the land of Ethiopia forever and ever. Anyone who violates my decree, whether they be future kings, or judges, is under perpetual anathema both in his life and after his death. Whosoever destroys this book, or takes it away from Ethiopia, may God delete his name from the Book of Life; may his lot be with Caiaphas and Annas, Judah of Iscariot and Simon the Magician; may the earth open her mouth, and swallows him up like Dathan and Abiram. My handwriting shall be my testimony. This was written down in the year of the martyrs 1264; on the 18th day of the blessed month of Yäkatit, 7 years and 7 months after God made me king [February 12, 1548].[54] "Glory to God in the highest heavens, and peace on the earth, [and] His good will to men" [Luke 2: 14]. Forever and ever. Amen.
>
> If one buys a slave, whether be it from Damot, or Gamo, [first], let him write down the name of the seller; second, let him write down the number of slaves and the price of purchase and report it to the *mäkwannent*, *mäsafent*, and *seyumanä hagär* along the routes the [caravan] is passing through. If, upon examination, the matter is found to be true, they shall let him [the merchant] go. When a slave bought from Damot and Gamo dies, and the owner subsequently buys a Christian slave as replacement, let them deprive such a person so offending and duly convict all his property; let them handcuff and bring him to me. When he [the slave merchant] writes down his merchandise, let him [use this formula "I hereby specify that] the slaves I purchased from Damot numbered this many; the slaves I purchased from Gamo numbered this many." Let him classify them by regional origin in this way.

It is difficult to determine precisely where and how this edict was promulgated. My conviction is that it was passed in the presence of many higher officers at the royal court whose principal residence in 1548 was at a place named Agraroha. By far the strongest evidence comes from the Tädbabä Maryam Gospel itself. Our

---

54 Two methods of dating are used here. First, the document is dated by the era of martyrs, named for Christians killed by the order of the Roman emperor Diocletian, the beginning of whose reign is the first day of the year of martyrs: a convention used by the Coptic and Ethiopian Churches. The second is the regnal year of Gälawdéwos, who came to the throne after the death of his father on September 3, 1540 (the source for this is Perruchon, "Notes pour l'histoire d'Éthiopie," 278 and 280). There seems to be an error in calculating the number of years and months since the first day of the king's reign and the date of the decree. The edict could not have been issued seven years and seven months after he came to power unless Gälawdéwos had started to exercise power at least one month before the demise of his father.

edict is inscribed just before another copy of a royal document, in this case a charter recording Gälawdéwos's appointment of a local Muslim governor over the province of Ifat. Recorded in the Gospel is also Gälawdéwos's land charter issued sometime after the foundation of Tädbabä Maryam in 1552, for the support of the memorial services of a deceased royal servant named Besratä Mikael.[55] Although the handwriting is identical to the other two documents, the land charter is not helpful in determining the manner in which the edict was promulgated. However, the edict and the charter of appointment were not only written by the same scribe but at the same time, because both the handwriting and the ink are identical; the charter of appointment appears in the middle left column next to the edict and is stated to have been issued while the king was staying in Agraroha.

Since the charter of appointment appears at the end of the edict, the edict was the first to be written. What is more, both documents were issued on the same day and in the same month and, although the year is not given in the charter of appointment, it is highly probable that the two royal decrees were issued together at Agraroha.[56] A contemporary chronicle confirms that at this period the king's court was based here, in the province of Däwaro, although the exact location of this capital has yet to be identified.[57] The Tädbabä Maryam church was not established until 1552, and it seems clear that the manuscript through which the edict comes down to us must antedate the foundation of the Tädbabä Maryam church by at least five years. The manuscript thus had a special association with Gälawdéwos's court and originally belonged, it appears, to the king before its subsequent transfer to Tädbabä Maryam's collection at a later date.

This conclusion would fit what we know from the fourteenth-century *Seratä Mängest* (Law of the State) about the appointments and coronations of officials and governors. This source attests that the appointment of dignitaries was made in the royal court and with a lot of pageantry.[58] The king therefore deliberately chose the auspicious occasion of the appointment of a governor of a key province to advertise and strengthen the authority of this new law. Ifat was the Ethiopian province with the longest history of Islamic presence, and it was the birthplace of militant leaders of Islam in the Horn of Africa. Gälawdéwos's issuance of this edict at this particular time and place was therefore a politically astute move.

The structure of the edict reflects many elements of analogous legal documents found in Ethiopian manuscripts of the thirteenth through sixteenth cen-

55 Ibid., image no. 6626.

56 Ibid., image no. 6650.

57 *Chronique de Galâwadêwos,* 33.

58 *Serata Mangest: An Early Ethiopian Constitution,* 35–36, 38, and 40.

turies.[59] The document is formulaic in its assumption of the first person. The king assumed the first person in the land charters he issued for three monasteries and two individual beneficiaries.[60] In the case of the anti-slavery edict, Gälawdéwos went further and underlined his intimate involvement in the production of the text by noting that it was in "my handwriting." Conventionally, though, kings dictated to professional scribes, and so Gälawdéwos's statement that he is the author of his edict is metaphorical and intended only to strengthen its authority. The language of the proem and the anathema clauses are unusually flowery and lengthy, but by no means unique.[61] The method of dating is also conventional, but its precision and the two styles of dating is uncommon

In terms of its substance, legal diction, the procedures set in place for the enforcement of the law, and the death penalty imposed against violators regardless of social rank, the edict fundamentally departs from many legal documents issued in late medieval Ethiopia. It is, moreover, singular in taking up issues related to *gäber*, a generic word for "slave," to illegal traffic in Christians, and to the regulation of the slave trade more generally. This is not to say that a demographically significant number of slaves did not exist in medieval Ethiopia: although slaves were not ubiquitous, trade in slaves and slavery was an old Ethiopian institution.[62] Nor was the idea of a Christian slave a paradox. Yet slaves rarely make it into written sources of any genre. In a key passage where the king sums up his new regulation of the slave trade, the crucial words *fetha* and *hegg* appear: "I, king Gälawdéwos, legislated this law (*fetha*) and sanctioned this writing. Let it be the established law (*hegg*) and regulation of the land of Ethiopia forever and ever."[63] The literal meaning of both words is "law." The word *fetha* also perfectly matches with the notion of justice.[64] Use of such words in the document is revelatory of the legislative character of Gälawdéwos's deed. There is no doubt that the document was intended to have the force of law. We are dealing with what was meant to be a new slave code, but my rendering of "edict" best characterizes the substance of the document and

59 For analysis of the structure of legal documents from the thirteenth to the seventeenth century, see Huntingford, *Land Charters of Northern Ethiopia*.

60 Ibid., 54–55; and Tädbabä Maryam, MS Wängél, image no. 6626.

61 Ibid., 6–7 and 20–21.

62 For the traffic in Ethiopian slaves, see Medard et al., *Traites et esclavages en Afrique orientale*; Jayasuriya, *African Identity in Asia*, 3–7 and 19–32; Erlich, *Ethiopia and the Middle East*, 11–14; Pankhurst, *Ethiopian Borderlands*, 18, 28, 122–23, 167–69; idem, *Introduction to the Economic History of Ethiopia*, 3–44, 54–57.

63 Tädbabä Maryam, MS Wängél, image no. 6650.

64 Kane, *Amharic-English Dictionary*, 33 and 2308.

avoids the anachronism implied in the notion of a fully fledged slave code. Before discussing its political contexts and social effect, it is worth examining the thrust of its terms and provisions.

Objectives of the Edict

The primary intentions of Gälawdéwos's edict were twofold. First, the edict aimed at *protecting freeborn Christians from enslavement and preventing the export of Christian slaves from the country*. Gälawdéwos's edict does not make a distinction between freeborn Christians and Christian slaves who were born into slavery or who became Christian while subject to the ownership of their master. It appears that he was strongly opposed to the commercial traffic in freeborn Christians and the transfer of any Christian slaves to non-Christians. The king found both crimes so offensive that he condemned any transgressor to death. Buying a captive while being aware of his true Christian religious identity fell under the penalty of the law. A merchant was under the obligation to avoid buying a Christian. A captive could not be deported unless he or she was proven to be non-Christian. Although the word is not used in the edict, *ahzab* was the generic term for pagans found in contemporary documents, including Gälawdéwos's regnal chronicle;[65] in our edict instead it is simply *gäber* or "slave" that is used without additional religious marker.

The decree also imposed heavy burdens of proof on merchants. How could merchants and captors establish the religious identity of a person and prove that their captives were non-Christians? The sumptuary regulations and religious rules to which Christian Ethiopians were subjected produced recognizable physical markers of religious identity which merchants could use to distinguish Christians from non-Christians. Circumcision was a requirement of religious law in the Ethiopian Orthodox Church. As part of his religious reform, King Zärä Yaqob had also required every Christian to "bear the names of 'the Father, the Son, and the Holy Ghost' branded on his forehead" as well to fasten the emblem of the cross "on all the belongings of the Christians—on their dress, their instruments of war, and even on their ploughs."[66] As a norm, Christian Ethiopians wore a cross necklace, or *matäb* (neck chord) given at the rite of baptism to distinguish themselves from non-Christians. Furthermore, Christians in the highland areas of rural northern and northwestern Ethiopia used to get a cross-shaped tattoo permanently etched on their faces as a marker of their religious identity. These and similar religious attributes could help merchants to identify a Christian from a non-Christian. The

65 *Chronique de Galâwadêwos*, 51 and 54–56.

66 Tamrat, *Church and State in Ethiopia*, 239.

penalties on Ethiopian merchants, Muslim and Christian alike, convicted of illegally trading in Christians was confiscation of property and death. Moreover, if a non-Ethiopian Arab merchant knowingly purchased a Christian captive, and that fact was concealed, the king instructed government officials to "deprive him of all his merchandise and send him to me."

The edict neither advocates nor condemns slavery itself, but takes it for granted. It should be firmly born in mind that Gälawdéwos was not opposed to the traditional idea that one Christian could hold another Christian in a state of bondage. He certainly owned slaves without qualms, and his chronicler tells us that the king occasionally raided *ahzab,* or pagans, for captives, some of whom he distributed among his kinsmen.[67] Since the *Fetha Nägäst* required masters to convert their nonbelieving slaves to Christianity, the majority of slaves in the country were thus very likely Christians.[68] The conversion to Christianity therefore did not eliminate slave status. Nor did conversion exempt slaves from being purchased and sold, as long as the transacting parties were Christians. The intention of Gälawdéwos was not to end trade in Christian slaves completely, *it was their trade to local non-Christian owners and their export abroad which the king regarded as outrageous.*

The second objective of Gälawdéwos's edict was to regulate and control the slave trade. Any merchant traveling with slaves must register and make a report of their names and numbers to government officials before proceeding to the coast, to Adal and other markets. Merchants operating in the only partially Christian provinces of Damot and Gamo (the former long the most important source of slaves)[69] were specifically required to record the name of the seller, the price of purchase, and the origins of the slaves. The slaves that had gone through customs and official inspection in this way could be exported to South Arabia and Egypt. Here, as well as in other sections of the edict, Arab and local Muslim merchants appear to have been its particular targets. This is not surprising because Arabs and Muslim merchants had almost single-handedly run the trade in slaves for a considerable period. Arabs and Africans, in this case Muslims and Christians in Ethiopia and the Horn, alike participated in the enslavement of enemies and the commercial trade of slaves for centuries.[70] Ethiopian slaves show up in South Arabian records as early as the mid-seventh century. As will be discussed later, the number of slaves being exported from Ethiopia increased particularly in the late fifteenth

67 *Chronique de Galâwadêwos*, 33 and 40–41

68 Gardiner, "Law of Slavery in Abyssinia," 183.

69 Bouanga, "Le Damot dans l'histoire de l'Ethiopie," 78, 82–86.

70 Pankhurst, "The Ethiopian Diaspora to India."

and first half of the sixteenth centuries, when local Muslim merchants and slave raiders captured and sold them or send them as gift to Arabs in South Arabia. Trading in Ethiopian slaves also increased after the Dahlak islands, Massawa, and the ports of the southern Red Sea and Somali coast became accessible to Arab merchants beginning in the tenth century. In the fifteenth and sixteenth centuries, the port of Zeila on the Somali coast (modern Somaliland) was the largest market for slaves in the Horn of Africa, where merchants from Arabia acquired slaves.[71]

Even though Christian Ethiopians perhaps did not engage in slave trading as actively as Muslims and Arab merchants did, Marie-Laure Derat has shown that Christian Ethiopians were involved in capturing, transporting, and selling human cargo from the Ethiopian region, for which they are duly targeted by the edict. In fact, without the active participation of Christians in the kidnapping and selling of slaves, there could not have been Arab and Muslim slave trade in the first place. According to Derat, the Christian kingdom did in fact try to "take a more direct role in long-distance trade and therefore in the slave trade in the fifteenth and sixteenth centuries."[72] The edict provides concrete evidence of this.

The edict further explicates the obligations of government officials and states that it was incumbent upon them to prevent the enslavement of freeborn Christians. Authorities seen as negligent and complacent towards merchants who enslaved and sold freeborn Christians and trafficked Christian slaves to non-Christian masters were considered as culpable as the merchants who operated illegally. The edict thus provided for measures by which state officials would monitor the activities of merchants and protect the rights of Christians, be they freeborn or servile. Noblemen, princes, judges, and local officials are instructed to inspect merchants traveling with slaves, and if anything was found amiss, they were to take necessary measures. If merchants were found transporting enslaved freeborn Christians, Gälawdéwos instructed officials to confiscate their caravan's merchandise and to send them in chains to the king himself for investigation. State officials were to enforce the free release of Christians wrongly taken captive. The king asked his officials to obey the new law, mixing threats with pleas. If officials neglected their duties and failed to take action against illegal enslavement, they would be regarded as committing a culpable offence. The edict required them to be put to "death without mercy and [their] house ransacked."[73]

---

71 Francois-Xavier and Hirsch, "Muslim Historical Spaces in Ethiopia," 39–42; Tamrat, "Ethiopia, the Red Sea and the Horn"; Fauvelle-Aymar et al., "Le Porte de Zeyla et son arrière-pays au Moyen Âge."

72 Derat, "Chrétiens et musulmans d'Éthiopie," 124.

73 Tädbabä Maryam, MS Wängél, image no. 6650.

Gälawdéwos stops far short of calling for the abolition of the slave trade altogether. As long as merchants did not illegally capture Christians and followed the rules, they could trade in non-Christian slaves. So the edict does not signify a change in political and public feeling towards slavery. However, the very fact that such an edict was drafted at all commands our attention. Clearly, the *Fetha Nägäst* provided the basis for Gälawdéwos's idea of the freedom of freeborn Christians from slavery and the ban on the sale of Christian slaves to non-Christians. But despite the conceptual link between them, the tone of Gälawdéwos's edict is very different from that of the *Fetha Nägäst.* Gälawdéwos toughened the restrictions on slave dealers and went much further than the *Fetha Nägäst* by criminalizing not only the enslavement of freeborn Christians and the trade in Christian slaves to non-Christians but also acts of negligence by government officials. The following pages attempt to understand the contextual pressures that inspired Gälawdéwos's edict.

Political Context: *Jihad* and Enslavement

Gälawdéwos's edict of 1548 suggests the new legal strategies adopted by Ethiopian rulers to address the perennial problem of an illegal slave trade. This was not a sign of any humanitarian sensibility, which arguably did not emerge among Ethiopian elites until the twentieth century.[74] But if slavery and the slave trade had been established systems for so long a period, and there was public indifference to them, then Gälawdéwos's edict begs several urgent questions. What was it that inspired legislative action? Why did the protection of freeborn Christians and the sale of Christian slaves to non-Christians become a major policy concern? If there was a preexisting law regulating slavery, the *Fetha Nägäst,* why then did the king issue the edict? This section attempts to answer these questions. In doing so it will investigate the political, economic, religious factors that propelled the illegal slave trade in Ethiopia and how the slave trade, in turn, affected those factors. Furthermore, since Arabs are specifically targeted in the edict, the dynamics of the Arab-Ethiopian encounter in this era require assessment. Any understanding of the making of the 1548 edict needs to take into account the Adal's *jihad* war of the sixteenth century.

The simplest reason behind the edict's promulgation might be the king's sense of justice and a personal abhorrence of the enslavement of freeborn Christians and the sale of Christian slaves to nonbelievers. Gälawdéwos is depicted by con-

---

74 Gardiner, "Law of Slavery in Abyssinia"; Whyte, "'Everyone Knows'"; and Coleman, "Gradual Abolition or Immediate Abolition?"

temporary sources as a just, clement, and intelligent young monarch. The king is deemed by Merid Wolde-Aregay, a specialist on the period, as the most "remarkable" and one of the few "humane persons to ascend the throne."[75] Yet personal outrage alone cannot in itself explain why he acted decisively against the illegal slave trade. Recent scholarship has shown that it was often the flagrant breach of old laws that justified the enactment of new laws. The historian Jill Harries, for instance, found that in the Roman Empire of late antiquity a flood of new laws were issued by emperors primarily because of the need "either to clarify and/or supplement existing legislation, or because an existing law was being broken or got round, or in order to reclassify anti-social or inconvenient behavior as a legal offence." She added that "[i]n a sense, therefore, laws existed because they were broken. What is not established by their existence is the scale on which they were broken, not enforced, got round or ignored."[76] This explanation applies to the Ethiopian experience as well. The edict of Gälawdéwos was issued because the law protecting freeborn Christians from enslavement and Christians slave from being trafficked was being widely breached. So it is of the utmost importance to understand the reasons for the violation of the law and the expansion of the traffic in Christians.

Normally, as noted above, slaves were captured in war and slaving raids and taken from the pagan inhabitants of Ethiopia's weak neighboring states and borderland societies.[77] The traffic in Christians prior to the reign of Gälawdéwos was therefore probably so negligible that Ethiopian kings felt no urgent need to legislate specifically against it. Hence, something else happened during the reign of Gälawdéwos, or shortly before, that led to a substantial expansion of the illegal slave trade and spurred the promulgation of our edict. Between 1527 and 1543, Ethiopia faced repeated attacks and then military occupation by the sultanate of Adal to its east and northeast. These attacks, termed *jihad* by the sultanate, controverted traditional Islamic legal doctrine which had long exempted Ethiopia from *jihad*. This war resulted in heavy material, human, and territorial losses and the enslavement of large numbers of Christian Ethiopians.[78] While the Sultanate of Adal and its occupying army was defeated in 1543, I propose that this edict was intended to reaffirm the law against illegal trade in Christians and reestablish order following this long period of disturbance.

---

75 Wolde Aregay, "Southern Ethiopia and the Christian Kingdom," 164–65.

76 Harries, *Law and Empire in Late Antiquity*, 80.

77 Bouanga, "Le Damot dans l'histoire de l'Ethiopie," 78, 82–86; and Pankhurst, *Ethiopian Borderlands,* 18, 28, 122–23, 167–69.

78 Uṯmān, *Futūḥ al-Ḥabaša*.

The fifteenth and first half of the sixteenth centuries were marked by incessant conflict and competition between Ethiopia and the Islamic state of Adal over the control of the trade routes of the lowlands and the resources of the highland regions of Ethiopia. The Christian kingdom was in control of "the *resources* of the highlands" while "Muslims were in charge of the *routes.*"[79] These conflicts produced a continuous stream of new slaves as both sides supported the raiding, seizing, and sale of captives. The army of Adal had the upper hand in these conflicts and most of those captured and sold into slavery were Christian and pagan Ethiopians.[80] But we must go back a few centuries in order to understand the broad shifts in the balance of power between the Ethiopian state and the sultanate of Adal, as well as Islamic doctrines concerning *jihad* and Ethiopia's historical role in them.

The term *jihad* has multiple and complex meanings, but one prominent significance of the term (from the point view of some Islamic jurists) was that *jihad* signified a just war against non-Muslims who had refused the call to join Islam. Islamic legal theory also recognized the legitimacy of enslaving captives in a legally perpetrated *jihad*. In theory, therefore, *jihad* was waged against non-Muslims, and slavery was the price for refusing to accept Islam. By definition, slaves were to be exclusively non-Muslims or their descendants, since Muslims could not enslave fellow Muslims. But according to Muslim tradition, the Prophet Muhammad had exempted Ethiopians and Turks from *jihad*. One of the medieval legal opinions concerning this immunity was given by Ibn Rushd (d. 1198), better known as Averroes, a famous physician, judge, and philosopher from Córdoba in Al-Andalus (modern Spain). In 1167, he wrote an influential legal handbook which discusses *jihad* and Ethiopia as follows. [81]

> Scholars agree that all polytheists should be fought. This is found on [Qur'an 8:39]: "*Fight them until there is no persecution and the religion is God's entirely.*" However, it has been related by Malik that it would not be allowed to attack the Ethiopians and the Turks on the strength of the tradition of the Prophet: "*Leave the Ethiopians in peace as long as they leave you in peace*" [*Utruku al-habasha ma tarakukum*]. Questioned as to the authenticity of this tradition, Malik did not acknowledge it, but said: "People still avoid attacking them."

79 Fauvelle-Aymar and Hirsch, "Muslim Historical Spaces in Ethiopia," 42.

80 Pankhurst, "Ethiopian Diaspora to India."

81 Quoted in Peters, *Jihad in Classical and Modern Islam*, 30.

According to tradition, the Prophet granted Ethiopia immunity from *jihad* and legal tolerance out of gratitude for its ruler having given asylum to some of his early followers. The crucial role played by Bilal ibn Rabbah during Islam's formative history further contributed to the positive image of Ethiopia among Muslims. In Muslim tradition, Bilal was a slave of Ethiopian origin and belonged to the father-in-law of the Prophet. Bilal was the first male convert to Islam and had the dignity to become the first muezzin.[82] Furthermore, the most famous leaders of early Islam such as Caliph Umar and Amir Ibn al-As, conqueror of Egypt, and the greatest Arab poet-warrior in pre-Islamic time, Antara, all had Ethiopian ancestry and contributed to Ethiopia's positive image among Muslims.[83] In the words of Haggai Erlich, who has studied this subject extensively, "Ethiopia was to become the only 'land of neutrality,' a proclaimed state of political immunity positioned midway between the concept of the 'land of Islam' and that of the infidels' 'land of war.'"[84]

Malik ibn Anas (d. 795), founder of the Malikite school of Islamic law whose opinions were referenced by Averroes, was responsible for collecting and spreading the Prophet's instruction to leave Ethiopia in peace. Hence, Averroes believed that Muslims "avoid[ed] attacking Ethiopians" because of Muhammad's requirement that they be left alone. It is true that this legal theory was not often translated into practice, but the strength of this tradition is not to be taken lightly. It no doubt influenced the action and policy of some stratum of Muslim legists and leaders in dealing with Ethiopians, particularly during the era of Islam's phenomenal expansion in the two centuries after its rise. However, in later centuries, the message of tolerance was either forgotten, ignored, or circumvented. Arab owners purchased Ethiopian slaves and received them as gifts from their Muslim counterparts in the Horn of Africa without qualm. Šihāb ad-Dīn Aḥmad bin Abd al-Qāder bin Sālem bin Uṯmān, a Yemeni lawmaker who accompanied and chronicled a *jihad* war against Ethiopia in the sixteenth century, never questioned its legitimacy and the enslavement of thousands of Ethiopians. In fact, in the late fifteenth and sixteenth centuries, *jihad* was a primary method of obtaining Ethiopian slaves.[85]

Muslim leaders and scholars in the Horn of Africa could justify the war and enslavement of Ethiopians on the grounds of Ethiopian aggression against Muslims in the Horn of Africa. As we have seen earlier, in 1332, a resurgent Ethiopian kingdom had subdued most of the Muslim principalities in the Horn of Africa.

82 Cerulli, "Ethiopia's Relations with the Muslim World," 575–76.

83 Lewis, *Race and Slavery in the Middle East*, 24–25.

84 Erlich, *The Cross and the* River, 25.

85 Uṯmān, *Futūḥ al-Ḥabaša*.

Later in the fourteenth century, the most militant leaders of Islam in the Horn of Africa moved further east and established the kingdom of Adal in the Harar plateau. For over two centuries after 1332, raiding and counter-raiding marked the relations between the rulers of Adal and the Ethiopian kingdom.[86] As the fifteenth century progressed, the Christian state declined. The death of King Bädä Maryam (r. 1468–78), which left his six-year-old son Eskender (r. 1478–94) as heir, opened up a troubled period in which the Ethiopian kingdom was plunged into internal power struggles while constant Muslim raids of the frontier provinces continued down to the 1520s. Morale in the Ethiopian army dropped sharply as the result of the political disorganization and confusion in the kingdom.[87]

While Ethiopia was fragmenting and without its traditional military strength, the kingdom of Adal was growing stronger and more united. In the late fifteenth and early sixteenth centuries, in particular, the weakness of the Ethiopian army encouraged Adali raiders to intensify their raiding campaigns. In the fourteenth century, slaves had been primarily the consequences of war; during this new era, booty in the form of captives and cattle was the primary motivation. A fifteenth-century sultan of Adal, Jamal ad-Din II (d. 1433), is said to have boasted that he "flooded Middle Eastern markets, India, Greece, and Persia with Abyssinian slaves."[88] Adali raiders under the leadership of a capable general, Mahfuz, conducted more successful and protracted slave raiding campaigns throughout the late fifteenth and early sixteenth centuries. Most of the captives were probably sold to merchants while some were sent as gifts to the ruler of Yemen. This can be illustrated by the case of an important Ethiopian military commander, who was captured by Adali forces sometime during the reign of King Eskender: this unnamed commander and fifty other captives were sent as presents to Yemen, where the former commander became the servant of Abu'l Fatḥ, who was born to a Jewish mother and Arab father. In 1498, probably accompanied by his Ethiopian slaves, Abu'l Fatḥ immigrated to Ethiopia as a merchant, where he converted to Christianity and was renamed Embaqom (Habakkuk), subsequently becoming abbot of a major monastery and authoring a polemical work against Islam.[89] This instance shows that Christian populations in frontier areas and in Muslim-controlled ports along the Red Sea coast increasingly found themselves vulnerable to enslavement because of frequent raids. During the reign of King Lebnä Dengel (r. 1508–40), the balance of power between the Ethiopian kingdom and the sultanate

86 Tamrat, "Ethiopia, the Red Sea and the Horn."

87 Tamrat, "Problems of Royal Succession in Fifteenth-Century Ethiopia."

88 Derat, "Chrétiens et musulmans d'Éthiopie," 139.

89 Ibid., 135; and *Anqaṣa Amin (La Porte de la Foi)*, 18–19.

of Adal tipped decisively in favor of the latter, and Ethiopia was overwhelmed by the *jihad*.[90]

Ahmad ibn Ibrahim al-Ghazi, the Adali ruler and the son-in-law of Mahfuz, escalated the raids, culminating in the battle of Shembra Kuré in 1529, in which the Ethiopian army was trounced. Ahmad followed up his victory by launching a *jihad* and occupying the highlands of Ethiopia for fifteen years. In the 1530s, his army of Somali and Afar tribesmen, some seventy al-Mahra Arab tribesmen from the Arabian Peninsula and two Indian mercenaries (who served as gunners) swept into the highlands of Ethiopia. By 1540, Ahmad controlled all the regions previously under Ethiopian rule. The Muslim seizure of Ethiopian provinces led to a tremendous expansion in the slave trade within the region, and included the enslavement and forced conversion of Christians. Before the *jihad*, Christians had had special protected status within the Ethiopian kingdom. During the *jihad* and immediately afterward, their legal protection against enslavement was lifted. The *jihad* of Ahmad ultimately had as its object the conversion of Ethiopia to Islam. Šihāb ad-Dīn, Ahmad's Yemeni follower and chronicler, constantly referred to Ethiopians as "infidels", "polytheists," and "idol-worshipers" who deserved to be fought, converted, and enslaved. With the exception of those located in inaccessible areas, all churches and monasteries were looted and razed to the ground and an estimated nine out of every ten Christians converted to Islam.[91]

In his discussion of Adali's *jihad* war, Vô Vân David underscores that medieval Islamic legal theory about *jihad* and slavery, especially the Shafite jurisprudence, goes far to account for, and shed light on, the motivations of the *jihadists* and their treatment of the Christian population. In Shafite law, a leader of *jihad* had the options of enslaving and killing prisoners as well as pardoning and releasing them either on ransom or as non-Muslim subjects of the Islamic state in return for paying tax.[92] Ahmad used all these options. Sometime Ahmad showed finesse in his treatment of Christian captives, releasing them on ransom. Frequently he killed and enslaved captives while sparing and sending some of them as gifts to his friends and allies in southwestern Arabia. Šihāb ad-Dīn records that, in a single minor raiding campaign in 1527, 484 Ethiopians were taken prisoners, some of whom were killed and some others were "enslaved to the emir of Zabid," a commercial town and political center of southwest Arabia.[93] In another of several instances, Šihāb ad-Dīn describes that following a triumphant raiding campaign in

90 Tamrat, "Ethiopia, the Red Sea and the Horn," 163–76.

91 *Chronique de Galâwadêwos*, 5; and Abd al-Qader, *The Conquest of Abyssinia*, 11–385.

92 David, "À propos du Ǧihâd dans le Futuh al-Habasha, " 137–38.

93 Uṯmān, *Futūḥ al-Ḥabaša*, 26.

1528, Ahmad himself took a fifth of the booty which included, among other things, "five-hundred heads of slaves" and distributed it "among the eight categories that the Most High God described in his illustrious book [Qur'an]."[94] It appears that this raid had yielded in a total of 2500 captives.

Besides ordinary captives, several high-ranking noblemen and women were also taken prisoner and sold as slaves or sent as gifts. Among these captives were the future king Minas and his two cousins. In 1542, Ahmad presented them as gifts to the ruler of Zabid. The experience of Minas and his cousins demonstrates that practically everyone faced the possibility of enslavement after the Muslim conquest. In 1543, when Gälawdéwos finally defeated the army of Adal and killed its leader, with the help of a small contingent of Portuguese soldiers, Minas and two other high-ranking captives were eventually ransomed in 1544.[95] Not all of the Christians taken as captive to the Arabian Peninsula and elsewhere could have been ransomed and returned to their families, however. This is, then, the immediate context in which the edict regulating the slave trade and banning the enslavement of freeborn Christians and the export of Christian slaves must be placed.

The victories of the Sultanate of Adal had shaken Ethiopian confidence in their army, religion, and self-esteem. Gälawdéwos's edict emerged as a legal force in this atmosphere of trauma and profound political and spiritual crisis in Ethiopian society. Regulating the slave trade and banning the enslavement of freeborn Christians were therefore among the more prominent of royal concerns for Gälawdéwos. The captivity of Minas and his cousins in particular touched a raw nerve and drove the issue of Christian enslavement home. Furthermore, there was probably public pressure on the king, especially from those who had lost family members and relatives to slavery, to take up the cause of illegal enslavement and act decisively. In this way the pre-*jihad* complacency about the unregulated slave trade and illegal enslavement gave way to the stern political and legislative action and edict of 1548. It remains now to explore the question of how well the edict was implemented.

The Enforcement of the Edict and of the *Fetha Nägäst*

How well the *Fetha Nägäst* and the edict were implemented is a good question. This section deals with the complex relationship, or the huge gulf, between the legal principles and norms expressed in the *Fetha Nägäst* and in our edict, and actual practices. How enforceable was Ethiopian law concerning slavery? To what

---

94 Ibid, 41.

95 *Chronique de Galâwadêwos*, 34–35 and 123; and *Historia de Minas*, 22–23.

extent was the law known among the people at large? In anticipation of fuller elaboration below, suffice here to say that there was a general reluctance to enslave freeborn Christians among Ethiopian slave raiders, such as government officials and soldiers who derived their wealth partly from the slave trade in the sixteenth century. It is hardly surprising, therefore, that throughout the second half of the sixteenth century, the various *ahzab* or pagan subjects of Ethiopia fervently implored authorities to convert them to Christianity. Equally unsurprising is the fact that slave raiders were entirely averse to evangelization during the same period. However, in the long run, the law could not be rigorously enforced—in southern Ethiopia in particular. With the withdrawal of the Ethiopian state from southern Ethiopia by the end of the century, the general insecurity of life and the difficulty of reporting a captive's religion and origins all played a part in the eventual failure of the law to protect Christians from enslavement.

As I mentioned at the outset, scholars have generally assumed that Ethiopia's various laws have been widely violated and ignored throughout the country's history. Royal edicts are thought to be valid so long as "an emperor had the means to enforce them physically" and many proclamations "have been lost or disregarded."[96] According to the historian Aṣmä Giyorgis: "In Ethiopia a law is legislated, but not put into practice."[97] The practical use of the *Fetha Nägäst* in courts is believed to have been limited in scope, an argument enhanced by the acute poverty of evidence on its application in the century after its introduction around 1450 and the tenuous records of its actual use in the sixteenth century and thereafter. But this verdict is too sweeping. Drastic differences between written law and real behavior doubtless existed, but how far laws were enforced cannot be ascertained simply by using the records of their practical use alone. A people's knowledge of a particular law is a better guide to its applicability and social effect. I propose here that the law in question (that freeborn Christians could not be enslaved, and once baptized slaves could not be resold to non-Christians) was widely known and largely observed in the sixteenth century.[98] Even on the basis of the fragmentary evidence

---

96 Brietzke, *Law, Development and the Ethiopian Revolution,* 32–33.

97 *Asma Giyorgis and His Work,* 119.

98 The history of the actual role of the *Fetha Nägäst* in the legal life of Ethiopia is yet to be written. Largely unknown to scholars are the records of private individuals, held in church archives, which show the *Fetha Nägäst's* relevance in the daily realities of people's lives. This evidence comes largely from recent centuries and consists chiefly of brief references to the use of the *Fetha Nägäst* in administrative manuals, charters, land registers, and wills. See Mengistie, *Lord, Zega and Peasant,* 113, 115–16. See also Märtulä Maryam, MS Däqiqä Näbeyat (the Minor Prophets), fol. 219r; and Illinois/IES 89. II. 16, Däbrä Wärq Maryam, *Tarikäa Nägäst.* This last reference is to a microfilm catalogued and on deposit at the Univer-

we possess, it is certain that the edict of Gälawdéwos and the *Fetha Nägäst* were of great social and legal relevance in sixteenth century Ethiopia.

Knowledge of the *Fetha Nägäst* was kept alive through its study in church schools up to the twentieth century. The administration of justice was placed in the hands of higher government official as well as jurists, who were often ecclesiastics trained in the study of the *Fetha Nägäst* via schools attached to churches and monasteries. These legists of the Ethiopian church were distinguished from other clergy by the bestowal of an honorific title: *liqé* or *liqä ma'emran*, "one who excelled others, one who is versed in the studies of law."[99] The *Fetha Nägäst* was studied as part of the "study of the [works of Saintly] Doctors [and the Fathers of the Church]," a curriculum which included theology, the highest rank of learning in Ethiopian church schools.[100] It was also studied as a field of specialization in its own right. Church scholars wrote commentaries on the *Fetha Nägäst* and its practice and developed a complex system of teaching and exposition called *andemta*—the first of its kind in Ethiopian history. Individuals trained in the *Fetha Nägäst* were professional jurists in the accepted sense of the term. In the lands beyond the reach of Church administration, most appear to have served only occasionally as itinerant judges when they were summoned to the courts of the emperors and higher officials to administer justice in important decisions.[101]

Gradually, then, knowledge of the *Fetha Nägäst* spread among the nobility and ordinary people. Chronicle sources demonstrate that some strata of the nobility were acquainted with the *Fetha Nägäst* as early as the sixteenth century. The earliest certain point for the practical application of the *Fetha Nägäst* recorded in chronicle sources comes during the reign of Särsä Dengel (r. 1563–97), when criminals were condemned to death by "the great men of the kingdom and the chief of the people" by referring to the *Fetha Nägäst*.[102] In the second oldest written instance, recorded in the chronicle of Susenyos (1607–32), higher govern-

---

sity of Illinois, Urbana-Champaign, and at the Institute of Ethiopian Studies in Addis Ababa University. It was made by the late Donald Crummey; however, it should be noted that the Däbrä Wärq material catalogued by Crummey is actually an administrative manual rather than a copy of the *Tarika Nägäst*.

99 Tzadua, foreword to *The Fetha Nagast*, xx; and Jembere, *Introduction to the Legal History of Ethiopia*, 37–38. In the manual of the Däbrä Wärq monastery, they bore the title of *liqä ma'emran*: Illinois/IES, 89. II. 16, Däbrä Wärq Maryam, *Tarikäa Nägäst*.

100 Tzadua, foreword to *The Fetha Nagast*, xx.

101 Jembere, *Introduction to the Legal History of Ethiopia*, 37–38.

102 Quoted in Tzadua, foreword to *The Fetha Nagast*, xxi. The reference is to *Historia regis Sarsa Denegel*, 87.

ment officials along with "the learned men of the Church who were versed in the *Fetha Nägäst*" were summoned to a royal assembly and there condemned a rebel to death.[103] Some of the royal justices referred to as "the great men of the kingdom" could presumably be laymen unfamiliar with the legal principles of the *Fetha Nägäst,* but others may have been familiar with it. And more would become so, as custom that had the force of law and was applied side by side with the *Fetha Nägäst.* Gradually, the legal principles and the doctrines of the *Fetha Nägäst* became fossilized into custom in their own right.[104]

There is evidence, direct and indirect, that shows the observance of the ban on the traffic in freeborn Christians. Two of the clearest indications of the law's influence come from the reign of Särṣä Dengel in the second half of the sixteenth century. The first indication may be found in the oppositions put up by soldiers and noblemen of Särṣa Dengel against evangelization, since pagan slaves constituted one element of the wealth of the military class at that time; the regnal chronicler records how these court officials and soldiers rejected conversion of the pagan subjects of Ethiopia by explaining that they feared that Christianity would allow the pagans to become too similar to them. Once they became Christians, soldiers and noblemen argued, by law the pagans could not be made to serve them.[105] Clearly, these arguments remind us of the provisions in the *Fetha Nägäst* and of Gälawdéwos's edict. This opposition to conversion by soldiers can therefore be attributed to knowledge of the law.

The second piece of evidence that points to the observance of the edict is the frequent requests for conversion to Christianity from the pagan subjects of Ethiopia attested throughout the second half of the sixteenth century. This indicates a popular knowledge of the edict especially in the region where captives were most often taken, including Damot, which the chronicler of King Särṣä Dengel described as "the land of slaves."[106] Among those who requested conversion were the Gafat people in the former district of Shat in Damot; Särṣä Dengel granted their request in 1581. Similarly, the people of Ennarya in southwest Ethiopia turned to Christianity to avoid enslavement. But tellingly, the conversion of Ennarya was preceded by strong argument and resistance from soldiers and noblemen at the king's court, as discussed above. After several years of procrastination, Särṣä Dengel

---

103 Quoted and translated in Tzadua, foreword to *The Fetha Nagast,* xxi. The reference to this court ruling is found in Pereira, *Chronica de Susenyos,* 298.

104 Gardiner, "Law of Slavery in Abyssinia," 181–82.

105 *Historia Regis Sarsa Dengel,* 136–44.

106 Ibid., 35; and Wolde Aregay, "Southern Ethiopia," 278–79.

finally allowed the people of Ennarya to convert to Christianity which they did en masse in 1587.[107]

The chronicler of Särṣä Dengel was neither the first nor the last to report the fervent requests for conversion by pagans. For instance, a letter which the Jesuit missionary Gonçalo Rodrigues wrote from Ethiopia to Rome in 1556 corroborates the details provided by the chronicler.[108] Similarly, in 1564, the head of the Jesuit missionaries in Ethiopia, Bishop Andre de Oviedo, wrote that the Shinasha people in Bizamo, in western Ethiopia, implored members of the royal family to convert them to Christianity in order to avoid enslavement.[109] What is important for us here is that the soldiers and court officials, as well as the pagans of Ethiopia, knew that the law of the land protected freeborn Christians from enslavement and equated Christianity with the condition of liberty. The opposition of slave raiders to evangelization and the request for conversion can therefore be regarded as an indication of the enforcement of the edict.

All this is not to say that Ethiopian laws were always effective. The observance of the law banning the traffic in freeborn Christians was not entirely successful. The slave trade left virtually no further documentation in Ethiopia, but there can be no doubt that Christians continued to be swept into slavery through the breach of the law. The Jesuit missionary Lusi de Azevedo, for instance, reports the following incident which illustrates the breach of the law during the reign of Susenyos (r. 1607–32):

> A rich Muslim trader was subsequently accused of exporting slaves from Ennarya, and on being found guilty was executed, his head being stuck on a pole in the market-place as a warning against future law-breakers. The emperor reiterated his opposition to the trade, declaring that anyone caught trading in slaves with either Moor or Turk would be sentenced to death and have all his property confiscated. At the same time, he summoned all his governors, the ministers of the court, and instructed them, on pain of severe penalty, to enforce the law, as God wished to protect the unfortunate Ethiopians, who, we are told, were then being transported in large numbers to Arabia, India, Cairo and Constantinople.[110]

107 *Historia Regis Sarsa Dengel*, 136–44; and Wolde Aregay, "Southern Ethiopia," 299–302.

108 Wolde Aregay, "Southern Ethiopia," 104.

109 Ibid., 298–99.

110 *Rerum Aethiopicarum Scriptores Occidentales*, 421. The text is quoted and translated by Pankhurst, *Introduction to the Economic History of Ethiopia*, 378.

The punishment, as recorded by Azevedo, against an illegal trader was meant to deter potential violators and demonstrate the consequences of disregarding the law. Yet the deterrent effect of such public punishment is uncertain. Slaves from the Ethiopian region continued to be distributed in Middle Eastern markets down to the twentieth century. The legal system regulating slavery in sixteenth-century Ethiopia was deeply destabilizing and hypocritical, intending to prevent illegal enslavement of Christians while encouraging the expansion of slave raiding activities by wholly legitimizing and supporting the trade in non-Christians. Some of the elaborate provisions of the edict were almost certainly wildly ambitious and unenforceable. It should be recalled that the edict required slave traders to avoid buying a Christian slave and called for reporting the names of slaves, their purchase price, origins, and vendor to government officials—in writing. This provision presupposes the use of documents and the existence of literate merchants and government officials; but in actual fact, such widespread literacy cannot be assumed to have existed in sixteenth-century Ethiopia.

Reporting the origins and religious affiliation of slaves was also a difficult matter. We have already seen how the sumptuary regulations and laws instituted by King Zärä Yaqob, which required Christians to put religious symbols on their dress and body, could have been used by merchants to differentiate Christians from non-Christians. But it is not clear at all if these religious requirements were effectively met by Christians. Some experienced local traders might have easily distinguished between slaves of differing origins by language and other identifying features. But although we may expect some merchants to have been well informed about the identity of their human merchandise, this was an impossible demand for many of them, especially those of foreign origin, because of the stunning linguistic and ethnic diversity of the country. In most cases, they had to rely on what their local suppliers told them about the identity of their captives. Slave raiders could thus deliberately falsify the true identity and origins of their captives and the merchants would have had no way of knowing it.

For much of this period, in sum, the compliant governors and noblemen, the political stability, and well-regulated administration taken for granted in the edict never existed. Gälawdéwos began the long process of picking up the pieces of Ethiopia's shattered defense system and royal administration after the end of the wars with the sultanate of Adal. He died prematurely in 1559, while repulsing another slaving raid from the sultanate. The Christian court was then in the midst of upheaval throughout the reigns of Gälawdéwos's brother Minas (1559–63) and his nephew Särsä Dengel (1563–97).[111] It was thus relatively easy to evade the

111 Wolde Aregay, "Southern Ethiopia," 174–94, 204–30.

regulations of the slave trade set down in the edict of 1548 because of the chronic insecurity and political instability of the period. In this situation, only their sense of morality—rather than the fear of punishment—could prevent individuals from buying and selling Christians.

By the turn of the seventeenth century, southern Ethiopia was largely out of the political control of Ethiopian rulers. With the withdrawal of the Ethiopian state from these areas, whatever protection this edict could have provided to the Christians of the region was lifted. Most Christians, left to fend themselves, did not survive the new Oromo invasions and the attendant slave traders.[112] The enslavement of the region's inhabitants persisted into the nineteenth century, by which time the Gamo, Damot, and Ennarya Christians had disappeared entirely.

Conclusion

Gälawdéwos's edict of 1548 shows that the sixteenth century witnessed a serious, if ultimately unproductive, effort to protect Christian Ethiopians from illegal enslavement. And it is arguably the first Ethiopian document to take up the issue of illegal enslavement prior to the twentieth century. The edict gives us an idea of the scale and strength of the illegal slave traffic and the legislative act it elicited. The king sought to prevent the enslavement of freeborn Christians while simultaneously allowing for the long-distance slave trade in non-Christians to go on. Economic necessities prevented the king from a wholesale ban on all forms of slave trade, including the trade in non-Christian slaves. In the areas under the firm control of the state, the ban on the traffic in freeborn Christians was generally respected. Nevertheless, in the long run, the political and legal environment which recognized the raiding and enslaving of pagans rendered Gälawdéwos's legal pronouncements ineffectual. Some aspects of the edict were also unenforceable or out of touch with the political and administrative realities of sixteenth-century Ethiopia. In the southern part of the kingdom, especially, the state was not in a position to enforce the law after the end of the sixteenth century. Despite their theoretically protected status, Christians in this region appear to have been taken captive along with non-Christians through politically sanctioned raids, warfare, and illegal slave raiding.

Nevertheless, the edict of 1548 was effective and also a reaffirmation of the older *Fetha Nägäst*. It therefore holds significant value for the study of comparative slavery while providing a new perspective on the struggle for domination between the sultanate of Adal and the kingdom of Ethiopia, and the larger encoun-

---

112 *Some Records of Ethiopia*, 111–33.

ter between Arabs and Africans in the region. My recent discovery of Gälawdéwos's edict also has important methodological implications for the study of Ethiopian history. The edict and the establishment of the church of Tädbabä Maryam were key events in Gälawdéwos's reign. The contemporary royal chronicle discusses the circumstances of Tädbabä Maryam's establishment at unusually great length, but the edict is not mentioned in the chronicle itself.[113] And accordingly, Ethiopian historians have often looked at narrative sources such as this chronicle for evidence of the origins and impact of legislation; and they have drawn conclusions based on that. Gälawdéwos's edict indicates that anything can be left out from such chronicles, and that nothing conclusive can be said about legal developments in medieval Ethiopia without further archival research.

113 *Chronique de Galâwadêwos*, 49–54, 58–59, and 123.

Bibliography

Manuscripts

Amhara, Tädbabä Maryam, MS Wängél

Gojjam, Märtulä Maryam, MS Däqiqä Näbeyat

Urbana-Champaign, University of Illinois [Institute of Ethiopian Studies, Addis Ababa University], Illinois/IES, 89. II. 16, Däbrä Wärq Maryam, *Tarikäa Nägäst*

Primary Sources

Anqaṣa Amin (La Porte de la Foi): apologie Éthiopienne du Christianisme contre l'Islam a partir du Coran: introduction, texte, critique, and traductic. Edited and translated by E. J. Van Donzel. Leiden: Brill, 1969.

Chronique de Galâwadêwos (Claudius) Roi d'Éthiopie. Edited by William Conzelman. Paris, 1895.

The Epistle of Humanity of Emperor Zär'a Ya'eqob (Ṭomarä Tesbet). Edited by Getachew Haile. Corpus Scriptorum Christianorum Orientalium 523, Scriptores Aethiopici, 95. Louvain: Peteers, 1991.

The Fetha Nagast: The Law of Kings. Translated by Abba Paulos Tzadua from the edition of Peter Strauss. Addis Ababa: Haile Selassie I University Faculty of Law, 2009.

Il Fetha Nagast o "Legislazione dei Re," Codice Ecclesiastico e Civile di Abissinia. Edited and translated by Ignazio Guidi. Roma: Casa Editrice Italiana, 1899.

Historia de Minas (Ademas Sagad) Rei de Ethiopia. Edited by Esteves Pereira. Texto Ethiopico, Publicado, Traduzido a Annotado. Lisbon, 1888.

Historia regis Sarsa Denegel (Malak Sagad) accredit Historia Gentis Galla, curante I. Guidi. Edited by Carlo Conti Rossini. Coprus Scriptorum Christianorum Orientalium, Scriptores Aethiopici, Series Altera, 3. Paris, 1907.

Huntingford, G. W. B. *The Land Charters of Northern Ethiopia.* Addis Ababa: Institute of Ethiopian Studies and Faculty of Law, Haile-Selassie I University, 1965.

Il libro della luce del negus Zar'a Yaqob (Maṣhafa Berhan). Edited and translated by Carlo Conti Rossini and L. Ricci. Corpus Scriptorum Christianorum Orientalium 250–51 and 261–62; Scriptores Aethiopici, 47–48 and 51–52. Louvain: Peteers, 1964–65.

A Manual of Eastern Roman Law: The "Procheiros Nomos," Published by the Emperor Basil I at Constantinople between 867 and 879. Edited by Edwin Hanson Freshfield. Cambridge: Cambridge University Press, 1928.

A Manual of Roman Law: The "Ecloga," Published by the Emperors Leo III and Constantine V of Isauria at Constantonple in 726 AD. Edited by Edwin Hanson Freshfield. Cambridge: Cambridge University Press, 1926.

Pereira, Esteves. *Chronica de Susenyos, rey de Ethiopia.* Lisboa: Imprenza Nacionale, 1892.

Rerum Aethiopicarum Scriptores Occidentales Inediti a Saeculo XVI ad XIX. Edited by Camillo Beccari. Vol. 11. Rome, 1911.

Serata Mangest: An Early Ethiopian Constitution. Edited and translated by Bairu Tafla and Heinrich Scholler. Addis Ababa: Faculty of Law and IES at Haile-Selassie I University, 1973–74.

Some Records of Ethiopia, 1593–1646. Edited by C. F. Bechingam and G. W. B. Huntingford. London: Hakluyt Society, 1954.

Uṯmān, Šihāb ad-Dīn Aḥmad bin Abd al-Qāder bin Sālem bin. *Futūḥ al-Ḥabaša: The Conquest of Abyssinia, [16th century].* Edited and translated by Paul Stenhouse. Hollywood: Tsehai Publishers, 2003.

Secondary Studies

Abir, Mordechai. *Ethiopia and the Red Sea: The Rise and Decline of the Solomonic Dynasty and Muslim-European Rivalry in the Region.* New York: Cass, 1980.

Alpers, Edward, Gwyn Campbell, and Michael Salman. *Slavery and Resistance in Africa and Asia.* London: Routledge, 2005.

Asma Giyorgis and His Work: The History of the Galla and the Kingdom of Shawa. Edited by Bairu Tafla. Stuttgart: Steiner, 1987.

Baeteman, Joseph-Émile. *Dictionnaire Amarigna-Français.* Dire-Daoua: Imprimérie Saint Lazare, 1929.

Bausi, Alessandro. "Heritage and Originality in the Ethiopic *Sinodos.*" *Journal of Ethiopian Studies* 25 (1992): 15–33.

Bouanga, Ayda. "Le Damot dans l'histoire de l'Ethiopie (XIIIe–XXe siècles): recompositions religieuses, politiques et historiographiques." Unpublished doctoral thesis, Université Panthéon-Sorbonne, 2013.

Brietzke, Paul H. *Law, Development, and the Ethiopian Revolution.* Lewisburg: Bucknell University Press, 1982.

Cerulli, Enrico. "Ethiopia's Relations with the Muslim World." In *General History of Africa: Africa from the Seventh to the Eleventh Century,* edited by M. El Fasi, 3:575–85. London: Heinemann, 1988.

Conti Rossini, Carlo. "Lo Hatata Zara Ya'qob e il Padre Giusto da Urbino." *Rendiconti della Reale Accademia dei Lincei, Classe di scienze fisiche, matematiche e naturali* 29, no. 5 (1920): 213–23.

Coleman, Sterling Joseph, Jr. "Gradual Abolition or Immediate Abolition of Slavery? The Political, Social and Economic Quandary of Emperor Haile Selassie I." *Slavery and Abolition* 29, no. 1 (2008): 65–82.

David, Vô Vân. "À propos du Ğihâd dans le Futuh al-Habasha: de la lecture d'Alfred Morabia à la relecture d'Arab-Faqih." *Annales d'Ethiopie* 17 (2001): 127–39.

Derat, Marie-Laure. "Chrétiens et musulmans d'Éthiopie face à la traite et à l'esclavage aux XVe et XVIe siècles." In *Traites et esclavages en Afrique orientale et dans l'océan Indien,* edited by Henri Medard et al., 121–48. Paris: Karthala et CIRESC, 2013.

——. *Le Domaine des rois éthiopiens (1270–1527): espace, pouvoir et monachisme.* Paris: Publications de la Sorbonne, 2003.

Erlich, Haggai. *The Cross and the River: Ethiopia, Egypt and the Nile.* Boulder: Lynne Rienner, 2002.

——. *Ethiopia and the Middle East.* Boulder: Lynne Rienner, 1994.

Fauvelle-Aymar, François-Xavier, et al. "Le Porte de Zeyla et son Arrière-pays au Moyen Âge: investigations archéologiques et retour aux sources écrites." In *Espaces Musulmans de la Corne de l'Afrique au Moyen Âge: études d'archéologie et d'hstoire,* edited by François-Xavier Fauvelle-Aymar and Bertrand Hirsch, 53–70. Addis Ababa: Centre Français des Études Éthiopiennes, 2011.

Fauvelle-Aymar, François-Xavier, and Bertrand Hirsch. "En guise d'introduction sur les traces de l'Islam ancien en Éthiopia e Corne L'Afrique." In *Espaces Musulmans de la Corne de l'Afrique au Moyen Âge: Études d'archéologie et d'hstoire,* edited by François-Xavier Fauvelle-Aymar and Bertrand Hirsch, 11–26. Addis Ababa: Centre Français des Études Éthiopiennes, 2011.

——. "Établissements et formations politiques musulmans d'Éthiopie et de la corne de l'Afrique au Moyen Âge." *Annales Islamologiques* 42 (2008): 339–75.

——. "Muslim Historical Spaces in Ethiopia and the Horn of Africa: A Reassessment." *Northeast African Studies* 11, no. 1 (2004–2010): 25–54.

Gardiner, A. L. "The Law of Slavery in Abyssinia." *Journal of Comparative Legislation and International Law* 15, no. 4 (1933): 180–202.

Guidi, Ignazio. "Der aethiopische Senodos." *Zeischrift dec Deutschen morgenländischen gesellschaft* 55 (1901): 495–502.

Harries, Jill. *Law and Empire in Late Antiquity.* Cambridge: Cambridge University Press, 1999.

Hunwick, John. "Islamic Law and Polemic over Race and Slavery in North and West Africa (16th-19th Century)." In *Slavery in the Islamic Middle East,* edited by Shaun E. Marmon, 43–68. Princeton: Wiener, 1999.

Hunwick, John, and Eve Trout Powell. *The African Diaspora in the Mediterranean Lands of Islam.* Princeton: Wiener, 2002.

Isaac, Ephraim. *The Ethiopian Orthodox Täwahido Church.* Trenton: Red Sea Press, 2012.

Jayasuriya, Shihan De Silva. *African Identity in Asia: Cultural Effects of Forced Migration.* Princeton: Weiner, 2009.

Jembere, Aberra. *An Introduction to the Legal History of Ethiopia, 1434–1974.* Hamburg: Lit, 2000.

Kane, Thomas L. *Amharic-English Dictionary.* Wiesbaden: Otto Harrassowitz, 1990.

Kaplan, Steven. *The Monastic Holy Man and the Christianization of Early Solomonic Ethiopia.* Wiesbaden: Coronet, 1984.

Leslau, Wolf. *Comparative Dictionary of Ge'ez (Classical Ethiopic): Ge'ez-English, English-Ge'ez, with an Index of the Semitic Roots.* Wiesbaden: Otto Harrassowitz, 1987.

Lewis, Bernard. *Race and Slavery in the Middle East: An Historical Inquiry.* Oxford: Oxford University Press, 1990.

Medard, Henri, et al., eds. *Traites et esclavages en Afrique orientale et dans l'océan Indien.* Paris: Karthala et CIRESC, 2013.

Pankhurst, Richard. *The Ethiopian Borderlands: Essays in Regional History from Ancient Times to the End of the Eighteenth Century.* Lawrenceville: The Red Sea Press, 1997.

——. "The Ethiopian Diaspora to India: The Role of Habshis and Sidis from Medieval Times to the End of the Eighteenth Century." In *The African Diaspora in the Indian Ocean*, edited by Shihan De Silva Jayasuriya and Richard Pankhurst, 189–222. Trenton: Africa World Press, 2003.

——. *An Introduction to the Economic History of Ethiopia from Early Times to 1800.* London: Lalibela House, 1961.

Perruchon, Jules. "Notes pour l'histoire d'Éthiopie: le règne de Lebna-Dengel." *Revue Sémitique* 1 (1892): 274–86.

Peters, Rudolph. *Jihad in Classical and Modern Islam: Updated edition with a Section on Jihad in the 21st Century.* 2nd ed. Princeton: Wiener, 2009.

Phillipson, David. *Foundations of an African Civilization: Aksum and the Northern Horn 1000 BC–AD 1300.* New York: Boydell and Brewer, 2012.

Sand, P. H. "Roman Origins of the Ethiopian Law of the Kings (Fetha Nagast)." In *The Fetha Nagast: The Law of Kings,* translated by Abba Paulos Tzadua from the edition by Peter Strauss, xxxix–li. Addis Ababa: Haile Selassie I University, Faculty of Law, 2009.

Sumner, Claude. *Ethiopian Philosophy: The Treatise of Zära Ya'eqob and of Wäldä Heywat: An Analysis.* Vol. 3. Addis Ababa: Commercial Printing Press, 1978.

Tamrat, Taddesse. *Church and State in Ethiopia, 1270–1527.* Hollywood: Tsehai, 2009.

——. "Ethiopia, the Red Sea and the Horn." In *The Cambridge History of Africa: From c. 1050 to c. 1600,* edited by Ronald Oliver, 3:98–182. Cambridge: Cambridge University Press, 1977.

——. "Problems of Royal Succession in Fifteenth-Century Ethiopia, Presentation of the Documents." In *Quatro Congresso Internazionale di Studi Etiopici*, 1:501–35. Rome: Problemi Atuali di Scienza e di Cultura 191, 1974.

[Tegegne,] Habtamu Mengistie. *Lord, Zèga and Peasant: A Study of Agrarian and Social Relations in Rural Eastern Gojjam.* Addis Ababa: United Printers, 2004.

Vernet, Thomas. "Slave Trade and Slavery on the Swahili Coast, 1500–1750." In *Slavery, Islam and Diaspora,* edited by Behnaz A. Mirzai, Ismael Musah Montana, and Paul E. Lovejoy, 37–76. Trenton: Africa World Press 2009.

Watson, Alan. *Legal Transplants: An Approach to Comparative Law.* 2nd ed. Athens, GA: University of Georgia Press, 1993.

Wolde Aregay, Merid. "Southern Ethiopia and the Christian Kingdom 1508–1708, with Special References to the Galla Migrations and Their Consequences." Unpublished doctoral thesis, University of London, 1971.

Whyte, Christine. "'Everyone Knows that Laws Bring the Greatest Benefits to Mankind': The Global and Local Origins of Anti-Slavery in Abyssinia, 1880–1942." *Slavery and Abolition* 35, no. 4 (2014): 1–18.

Habtamu Mengistie Tegegne (ht254@rutgers.edu) holds a doctoral degree in history from the University of Illinois at Urbana-Champaign (2011). He is currently Assistant Professor of History at Rutgers University at Newark and is the author of *Lord, Zèga and Peasant: A Study of Social and Agrarian Relations in Rural East Gojjam* (Addis Ababa, 2004). He is also the author of "Rethinking Property and Society in Gondärine Ethiopia," *African Studies Review* 52–53 (2009), 89–106; this article was based on an essay that won the 2007 Graduate Student Paper Prize of the African Studies Association.

Abstract This study explores the relationship between documentary-legal prescriptions of slavery and actual practice in late medieval Ethiopia. It does so in light of a newly discovered edict against the enslavement of freeborn Christians and the commercial sale of Christians to non-Christian owners, issued in 1548 by King Gälawdéwos. It demonstrates that this edict emerged from a dramatic and violent encounter between the neighboring Sultanate of Adal, which was supported by Muslim powers, and the Christian kingdom of Ethiopia, which had the support of expanding European powers in the region. The edict was therefore issued to reaffirm and clarify the principles and doctrines of preexisting legislation codified in the *Fetha Nägäst* (Law of Kings). The study includes a full transcript and translation of the edict and also analyzes its place within the broader framework of Ethiopia's encounter with other legal traditions, including older Romano-Byzantine and Coptic-Islamic systems. This study further argues that the legal principles enshrined in the *Fetha Nägäst* were strengthened by the edict and were more widely known than previous scholarship has been able to establish, and that the edict did inspire actual legal practices that affected daily life in sixteenth-century Ethiopia.

Keywords Ethiopia, slavery, *Fetha Nägäst*, Gälawdéwos, Christianity, Islam, law, jihad

MUTILATION AND THE LAW IN EARLY MEDIEVAL EUROPE AND INDIA: A COMPARATIVE STUDY

PATRICIA SKINNER

IN HER SURVEY *Crime and Punishment in Ancient India*, Sukla Das highlights the occurrence—in religious texts, literary material, and legal digests—of the use of branding and mutilation of the face and body to punish specific misdemeanors, including theft, the sexual violation of women, female adultery, defamation, and assault. Moreover, mutilation (including blinding of the eyes) might also be prescribed instead of the death penalty for acts of treason, and was considered a lenient alternative to death.[1] Such penalties, the rhetoric surrounding their use, and the circumstances in which they were prescribed sound very familiar to a historian of early medieval Europe, where the language and targets of such precepts were similar to those set out in the Indian material.[2] Yet drawing a comparison between the two regions, or even suggesting that their similarities constitute a "legal encounter," is fraught with methodological problems. First, there is a clear chronological mismatch between the development of the prevailing legal norms of India and Europe; second, neither region can be treated as an undifferentiated whole; third, there is an important qualitative difference between "legal" texts in Europe and India; and finally, even if points of similarity and difference are identified in the texts, these represent not so much a dialogue as a shared recognition that the human body has always been an effective target for coercive and corrective practices.[3] All of this leads to an inevitable conclusion that the corresponding passages in Hindu and Western European texts should not surprise us at all.

Yet the apparent incommensurability of the two regions in the period before 1200 CE has not deterred historians from demanding and attempting comparative work. Susan Reynolds, for example, recently has called specifically for more comparative research on the laws of medieval Europe and India, and set out some

I should like to thank the editors for their invitation to write for *TMG*, the anonymous readers for their constructive criticism, and the Wellcome Trust for the grant (no. 097469) that supported research for this paper and my wider project on medieval disfigurement.

1 On blinding, see Bührer-Thierry, "'Just Anger'"; and Wheatley, *Stumbling Blocks*.

2 Skinner, *Living with Disfigurement*, explores the evidence for Western Europe in detail.

3 Miller (*Eye for an Eye*) and Geltner (*Flogging Others*) articulate this point from legal and historical perspectives.

questions surrounding the relationships between the royal authority and the law, the role of legal professionals, and the process of justice.[4] This essay, whilst not addressing all of those broader issues directly, will first highlight the problems of comparison across time and place, before examining in detail a specific element of the legal culture of both regions, the use of corporal punishment. It will ask whether the representations of facial and bodily mutilation, in particular, suggest similar ideas in each region about royal authority, honor (and, if so, whose), and gender relations, and how these might have developed and changed between the third and twelfth centuries CE.

Problems of Comparison, Slippages in Time, Fragmentation of Space

The "comparative turn" in medieval history is no longer affecting only European regions, and its expansion has been marked—and fueled—in the past two decades by the appearance of serials such as *The Medieval History Journal,* edited and published out of India, and thus complicating the category "medieval," and now by *The Medieval Globe*.[5] To take just one example, the model of medieval "feudalism," which Marc Bloch envisioned might be tested on Japanese as well as European society,[6] is still being used to think through extra- as well as intra-European political frameworks in a way that stretches its validity (itself contentious) as a tool of analysis.[7] As Reynolds and other historians of medieval Europe have commented, however, comparison is hard work, and particularly so when one is exploring a new area (for the present author, India) in which one has relatively little previous research experience.[8] Lack of linguistic training, in particular, limits the survey of Indian texts used in this survey to those accessible in English translation, which significantly compromises the study of technical or descriptive words and phrases. (The English word "disfigurement," for example, is regularly used as a catch-all term to translate a range of injuries to the face reported in Latin and Greek source texts in the medieval West, highlighting the potential pitfalls of relying on translated texts alone.) Bloch himself, however, was

---

4 Reynolds, "Early Medieval Law."

5 Reuter, "Medieval: Another Tyrannous Construct?"; Mukhia, "'Medieval India.'"

6 Bloch, *La société féodale*, 610–12.

7 Bagge, *Feudalism: New Landscapes of Debate*; Hendricz, "Is There Evidence?"; Heirbaut, "Not European Feudalism"; Sharma, *Early Medieval Indian Society*; Chattopadhyaya, *Making of Early Medieval India*, 212–14.

8 Reynolds, "Early Medieval Law." See also Wickham, "Problems in Doing Comparative History" and "Historical Transitions."

an advocate of comparison as a means of better understanding one's *own* area of expertise, and exposing assumptions that a model developed in one part of the world was applicable, uncritically, elsewhere.[9] (The subtlety of *La société féodale* in this respect has often been overlooked by subsequent commentators and generations of undergraduate students.) This caution is particularly applicable to the present study: as J. Duncan Derrett pointed out long ago, one of the difficulties for British colonial rulers in India was their assumption that Hindu *dharmaśāstra* (the teaching or science of righteousness) could be equated with Western canon law and separated from the secular concerns of the state.[10] This assumption, in turn, affected the early Anglophone historiography of India. We shall return to the nature of "law" below.

The first problem of comparison for the present study is the time frame expressed by the term "early medieval." In Europe, it has traditionally been seen as the period from ca. 500 to ca. 1100, although the starting date is contested by those who champion "late antiquity" as a specific period of transition, and the eleventh century often appears in surveys of the "central" Middle Ages. Such mutability is also visible in the historiography of early India. Brajadulal Chattopadhyaya situates the "early medieval" from the seventh to thirteenth centuries CE,[11] and this estimation is echoed by Upinder Singh, who relates the start and end dates to the fall of the Gupta Empire (ca. 550 CE) and the establishment of the Muslim Delhi sultanate (1206), respectively.[12] This periodization incorporates the Ghaznavid conquest of parts of northwestern India under Mahmud (998–1030). But, as Singh points out, alternative "early Middle Ages" have existed in Indian scholarship: eschewing political frameworks, R. S. Sharma's model of Indian feudalism places the period as 400–1200 CE.[13] The period of the Delhi Sultanate (1206–1526 CE) has also been termed "early medieval" or "medieval" to distinguish it from the "later medieval" Mughal state that lasted into the nineteenth century. (It is possible to posit a "medieval" period extending this late in Jewish history as well, as I have argued.[14]) But as Kesavan Veluthat points out, these are all chronologies largely driven by northern Indian political developments, and largely ignore the existence of the polities of the Rashtrakutas (ca. 750–1000 CE) and the Cholas (ca. 850–1280 CE, at its height till 1044 CE), whose hostilities in the early tenth cen-

9 Bloch, *Apologie pour l'histoire*, 107.

10 Derrett, *Dharmaśāstra and Juridical Literature*, 2–4.

11 Chattopadhyaya, *Making of Early Medieval India*, 1–37.

12 Singh, *Rethinking Early Medieval India*, 1.

13 Sharma, *Early Medieval Indian Society*.

14 Skinner, "Viewpoint. Confronting the 'Medieval.'"

tury impacted kingdoms such as the Cheras in Kerala, which is documented as a kingdom by the early ninth century.[15] With these *caveats* in mind, the discussion that follows will focus on the period from the fifth to the eleventh centuries, and compare Christian and Hindu precepts. It will exclude discussion of imported Muslim norms but may utilize examples falling outside those beginning and ending dates.

Veluthat's work exposes the second problem of comparing Europe and India in this period: the shifting and heterogeneous political map of the latter. This, however, should not cause undue concern. Just as temporal boundaries were being challenged in the late 1990s as a hegemonic and Eurocentric historiographical construct, so Martin Lewis and Kären Wigen challenge the spatial organization of historical enquiry, the value-loaded terms "West" and "East," and the assumption of coherence in organizing the world into seven "continents."[16] Drawing on this work for their own study of medieval India, Catherine Asher and Cynthia Talbot comment that "we can view the presence of numerous kingdoms [in India] in 1000 CE as a normal course of affairs," and suggest that, "like Europe, South Asia had a common elite 'civilization' that served to unify it culturally in a general sense prior to 1200, although there were many different local practices and beliefs."[17]

One element of such elite "civilization" was religious culture as expressed in the Hindu *dharmaśāstra*, the teaching of righteousness, which Derrett terms an overarching, systematic presentation of precepts suited to the diversity of Indian society. This framework, underpinning Indian jurisprudence in the medieval period, was already centuries old, dating back to well before the Common Era, and some have cautioned against treating it as "law" in the English sense of the word.[18] Moreover, it was not unified or consistent.[19] Surviving texts and commentaries (*smṛti*) range in date from ca. 600 BCE onwards, though precise dating, attribution, and place of composition remain vexed problems. Early Hindu law (even the term "Hindu" is problematic) encompassed not only the impetus to punish a criminal act, often with corporal punishment, and so to restore social order, but also a desire to encourage the individual to perform penitential acts that would rectify her/his offence against the moral order.[20] As Patrick Olivelle comments, the correlation between the two is often indistinct, but both were tied up in a reli-

---

15 Veluthat, *Early Medieval in South India*, 1–3, 185, 196.

16 Lewis and Wigen, *Myth of Continents.*

17 Asher and Talbot, *India before Europe*, 9.

18 Lubin, Davis, and Krishnan, *Hinduism and Law: An Introduction.*

19 *Dharmasūtras*, xxv–xxxiv; Olivelle, "*Dharmaśāstra*: A Textual History."

20 Lubin, Davis, and Krishnan, *Hinduism and Law: An Introduction*, 1–4.

gious ideology that envisioned creating a virtuous human being and ensuring a positive rebirth, since the fate of the transgressor who failed to perform penance for her or his deeds would be to lose status between this life and the next.[21] This religious dimension, it seems to me, opens up a point of comparison straightaway. Early law from the Visigothic, Lombard, and Anglo-Saxon kingdoms, and from the Byzantine Empire (included as a further comparator) certainly prescribe corporal punishments alongside monetary compensation, but they do not explicitly look to encourage the transgressor to repent. This, in large part, was the responsibility (at least after the conversion period in the fifth and sixth centuries) of the Church, not the king or state, and Western Europe provides numerous examples of early penitentials underpinning that duty.[22] Yet, as numerous scholars have pointed out, this apparent separation between punishment/law and penance/religion in Western society is anything but: as Christianity became more institutionally embedded within Western European kingdoms, laws were drafted by, and/or with the assistance of, members of the clergy, and they incorporate, in a more or less explicit fashion, biblical concepts of right and wrong.[23] Whilst the replacement of tit-for-tat violence with monetary payments might speak to Christian ideals, the ruler's right to inflict a corporal punishment—whether beating, branding, or mutilation—draws upon not only Old Testament ideas of reciprocal injury but also expresses an explicit reservation to the ruler of the right to punish physically in order to enforce authority and make an example of the offender. The replacement of capital penalties with corporal ones, however, also signals that concern for an offender's soul demanded that he or she be given the opportunity to repent.[24] Looking forward to the next life, therefore, was a core consideration in the judicial cultures of both regions.

Ashutosh Dayal Mathur has argued for what he terms the secularization of Hindu law between the eighth and seventeenth centuries, as commentators sought to move away from law as *dharma* (righteousness)—the model described by Olivelle for earlier centuries—and towards an understanding of law as a state matter (*vyavahāra*), rather than a question of personal religious or moral conduct.[25] The pace of such change varied according to region, however, and *vyavahāra* is in fact visible in much earlier material.[26] But whereas earlier *dharmaśāstras* had

21 Olivelle, "Penance and Punishment"; see also Davis, "Before Virtue."

22 Meens, *Penitentials*; McNeill and Gamer, *Medieval Handbooks of Penance*.

23 Wormald, *Legal Culture*; Evans, *Law and Theology*.

24 Gates and Marafioti, *Capital and Corporal Punishment*.

25 Mathur, *Medieval Hindu Law*.

26 Derrett, *Dharmaśāastra and Juridical Literature*, 31 and 36.

made little distinction between civil or criminal disputes, later digests and commentaries paid more attention to offences that disturbed the order of the state and/or might be brought to the king's attention. The process that Mathur outlines, therefore, is roughly contemporary with the period in European history when the Germanic successor-states to the Roman Empire were beginning to produce codified books of law. Written law *mattered* in both geographical spheres, it seems, and functioned as a symbol of rulers' authority. The plurality of early medieval kingdoms and their law codes in Europe did not prevent similarities in their written forms, and this is also a useful way to think about the multiple commentaries existing across different Indian polities. The key difference lies in the fact that whilst the texts of most early medieval law codes in Europe are datable to within about a century (and some in fact carry dating clauses emphasizing when, in the ruler's reign, the codes were compiled), the complete and fragmented works of law surviving from early India are hard to date because their purpose was entirely different. Early Hindu texts, such as Kautilya's *Arthaśāstra* (recently redated to the fourth century CE, rather later than previously thought) had of course explicitly set up some of the qualities and duties expected of the king, still framed in religious terms; but medieval European laws varied in how much attention they paid specifically to him, since the very existence of the codes themselves marked out the king's concern with the limitation of violence.

It is unlikely that the two historical developments—a more "state-like" king in India, a focus on the king's responsibility to keep peace in Europe—were linked.[27] It is also debatable whether the transition outlined by Mathur for India led to anything like a fully secularized law code replacing older customs and practices. Chattopadhyaya comments that part of the process of change was the need for "constant validation of power," against the background of political fragmentation among multiple kingdoms.[28] The temporal and the sacred domain were too interdependent to permit a clear split, however. Thus the priestly validation of temporal power continued beyond the period of the so-called Hindu dynasties. The full secularization of Indian law is, some commentators argue, not something that even the modern Indian state has achieved.[29] But it is clear that the Hindu laws retained far more than they discarded, whilst the various law codes in Western Europe are often distinguished by how much, or little, of preceding Roman (or Germanic) law is visible in their provisions.

---

27 Kershaw, *Peaceful Kings.*

28 Chattopadhyaya, *Making of Early Medieval India*, 196–97.

29 Menski, *Hindu Law*, 24–25.

For our purposes, the main issue to keep in mind is the rather obvious point that no law is static: the written codifications and commentaries that historians now use were more a starting point in a negotiation, rather than the end game, and it is clear that legal precepts in India—and corresponding prescriptive texts in Western European kingdoms and the Byzantine Empire—set up ideals of behavior that were, often, unenforceable. In both regions, however, the process of revising and updating opinions allowed for flexibility as new situations arose. Reynolds highlights the wealth of legal commentaries in India that medieval Europe does not have (at least, until the twelfth century onwards), each shaping and offering possibilities for new interpretations of older texts.[30] In this sense, India seems more akin to the medieval Islamic world.[31] But in Europe, codes of law were supplemented and updated when regimes changed, and some of this material shows signs of having responded to real situations. Overall, however, the picture presented by these texts is explored here without any assumption (or "naïve acceptance," as Don Davis puts it)[32] that it represents the social reality on the ground. (As Davis notes, different texts served different purposes.) Some older, nationalist historians of India have emphasized the durable nature of the Hindu achievement, focusing particularly on the areas of India that were not subject to Muslim conquest. For example, Ishwari Prasad stresses that the medieval period saw "some of our best [legal] commentaries" emerge in south India.[33] Yet even in areas that did come to be under Muslim rule, Hindu culture seems to have been valued rather than suppressed, and links were forged between the Mediterranean Sea and Indian Ocean that permitted the transmission not only of goods but of ideas.[34]

Approaching Disfigurement as Injury: Honor and Shame

One way, perhaps, of drawing meaningful comparisons is to focus in on a very specific manifestation of the law and/or social custom and/or moral compass in each region, and to explore whether it occurs in similar circumstances as reported by the texts, as was done for instance by Richard Larivière for ordeals.[35] This essay is interested in the phenomenon of facial appearance and disfigurement, which appears most often in the context of legal codes and narrative sources. Both

30 Reynolds, "Early Medieval Law."

31 See Reid, *Law and Piety*.

32 See Davis, "Toward a History of Documents," in this issue.

33 Prasad, *History of Medieval India*, 549.

34 Wink, *Al-Hind*, 10.

35 Larivière, "Ordeals in Europe and India."

European and Indian cultures appear to have placed great importance on facial appearance, including the presence, absence, or removal of facial hair. Barry Flood comments that "the differentiation of ethnic and religious groups through the prescription of appropriate hairstyles or modes of facial hair was common to both Indic and Islamic cultures," and European historians, too, have noted its charged qualities as a signifier of status.[36] They might have added that facial perfection or impairment was similarly loaded with meaning. As a comparative topic, therefore, it seems a worthwhile seam to mine, and what follows is largely drawn from the ostensibly "legal" texts, although set alongside narrative sources.

The historic mutilation of the face and body in Indian and European cultures has already attracted the attention of some scholars. F. Barry Flood, for instance, explores the meeting of Indian and Islamic cultures in records of the Indian practice of cutting off little fingers or fingertips as a sign of submission to one's lord.[37] The removal of digits also features in some European texts, but there it is either as a highly visible personal injury[38] or as an extreme sign of tyrannical or even diabolical behavior, as when the monastic chronicler Amatus of Montecassino says that Gisulf II (1052–76/77), prince of Salerno, cut off the fingers and toes of his wealthy hostage, Maurus of Amalfi, and made him eat them.[39] (This was *after* Gisulf had had Maurus's eye gouged out.) Writing to please Gisulf's eventual conquerors and the patrons of his own abbey, the Norman lord Robert Guiscard and his wife Sichelgaita, Amatus was implacably opposed to Prince Gisulf, which clearly colors his narrative. And yet a report of finger-cutting in India is no less problematic. Although its former attribution to the Persian sea-captain Buzurg ibn Shahriyar (in a work commonly known as *The Wonders of India*) has now been discarded, the account's real author, a Cairene scholar named Abū 'Imrān Mūsā ibn Rabāh al-Awsī al-Sīrāfī, was still writing with the perspective of an outsider.[40] Is either report therefore to be trusted? This is a problem that dogs the evidence surrounding mutilation, since its very prospect tended to induce fascination or horror in those recording it. The same fascination, arguably, has shaped later historians looking for evidence of the "barbarity" of the medieval period, drawing

---

36 Flood, *Objects of Translation*, 63. See also Leyser, "Long-Haired Kings"; Bartlett, "The Symbolic Meanings of Hair"; Dutton, *Charlemagne's Mustache*.

37 Flood, *Objects of Translation*, 85.

38 As in the laws of King Æthelberht of Kent (Æthelberht's code (Abt), § 53–58). See also Oliver, *Beginnings of English Law*, 72–73.

39 Amatus of Montecassino, *History of the Normans*, 189–90.

40 Ducène, "Review."

upon not only reports such as these, but also folkloric and religious tales that are hardly reliable indicators of social "norms" (see below).

Injuries in Indian law were classified as verbal (*vākpāruṣya*) or physical (*daṇḍapāruṣya*). A similar categorization is found in European codes: the Salic law from Francia lists penalties for both physical injuries (*De debilitatibus*) and insults (*De convitiis*).[41] The latter, mainly consisting of calling a person by the name of an animal, was undoubtedly insulting to honor. Calling a man a coward, informer, or liar threatened rather more damage to the reputation, requiring substantial monetary compensation (as in the law of the Kentish kings Hlothere and Eadric on calling someone a perjuror or "shamefully accosting him using mocking words").[42] Such transgressions, however, were largely limited to the social class in which the offender and victim belonged: the balance of honor needed to be restored, but vertical social ties do not appear to have figured in such offences. Other Western European cultures, however, posited insults as a serious challenge to vertical authority: in Ireland, in particular, close attention was paid to the respective rank of perpetrator and victim, and the high visibility of the poet in Irish society led to multiple tales of physical facial blemishes spontaneously appearing on kings and other social superiors by the effects of satirical verse.[43] Even publicizing a physical blemish by talking about it was regarded as an injurious act.[44]

In the Indian context, however, the effects of all verbal and physical injuries were complicated by *varna* or caste. Transgression often meant loss of caste or even rebirth as a non-human, and this may explain why punishments handed out to the lowest group, the Śūdra, were, and remain over time, so severe. Already at the bottom of the pile, they were threatened with the most gruesome of punishments, often leading to death. For example, Gautama's code orders that if a Śūdra uses violent language or violence against any member of the three upper classes, the body part that committed the crime should be cut off. If a Śūdra listens to a Vedic recitation, his ears should be filled with molten metal; and if he repeats the recitation, his tongue should be cut off.[45] This treatment was in contrast to that of other castes, who were more frequently fined for their transgressions. Yet the difficulty rests in knowing whether this very ancient law retained its purchase in later recapitulations. It would be tempting to see a parallel here with the frequent distinctions in European law codes between those of different status—the free

---

41 *Pactus legis Salicae*, 112–20 (§ 29–30).

42 Translated in Oliver, *Beginnings of English Law*, 131.

43 Kelly, *Guide to Early Irish Law*, 43–44.

44 Ibid., 137.

45 *Dharmaśūstras,* 98 (Gautama 12).

and the unfree, those with official titles and those without.[46] Certainly slaves who committed offences were punished more severely than the semi-free or free. Thus in an addition to the Salic law of the Franks, a slave who struck a free woman or untied her hair would lose his hand; but—and this is the crucial difference—slaves were *owned* by someone else, and that person could, if they wished, mitigate the threatened damage to their property by paying a fine.[47] The Salic law also permitted the master of a slave who was about to be castrated or tortured to withhold the slave's punishment by paying the penalty plus the slave's value, though it is debatable how often such a substitution might happen in practice.[48]

Turning to physical injuries, the classifications found in the later medieval Indian commentary *Vivāda Ratnākara* (ca. 1300) have strong resonance with similar lists of injuries found in earlier European texts. In ascending order of seriousness, physical offences in *Vivāda Ratnākara* included: defiling with touch; raising a hand or weapon with intent; hurting without drawing blood; blood-shedding injuries that were skin-deep, muscle-deep, or bone-deep; breaking of bones; and severing or mutilation of organs.[49] Defilement with touch was an injury particular to Brahmin status, where impurity lurked in inanimate objects and everyday gestures and actions as well as in physical contact between persons. Such religious defilement is not visible in the legal texts of medieval Europe, but it is notable that some early codes did classify touching women in certain ways as injuries to be compensated. A rather closer comparison can be drawn in the distinction between bloodless and bloody injury, and the grading of the latter. This has strong parallels in early medieval European laws such as the Visigothic code of the seventh century, which categorized wounds as slight, drawing blood, or down to the bone;[50] or the probably contemporary Ripuarian and the slightly later Alamannic codes, which retained the distinction between bloodless and bloody wounds (both adding the detail "if the blood touches the ground") and, in the case of the Alemannic code, added further distinctions of seriousness for head injury.[51] Later still, in medieval Welsh law, the three "dangerous wounds"—a blow to the head exposing the brain, a blow to the body exposing the bowels, or the breaking of a limb—are again distinguished from other types of injury.[52] In both Indian and European cul-

46 Geltner highlights this issue for ancient societies: *Flogging Others*, 37 and 44.

47 *Pactus Legis Salicae*, 260 (Capit. Addita 104.3).

48 *Pactus Legis Salicae* 58 (§ 12).

49 Mathur, *Medieval Hindu Law*, 177.

50 *Leges Visigothorum*, 262–63 (VI.4.1).

51 *Lex Ribvaria*, 73 (II); *Pactus Legis Alamannorum*, 116–17 (LVII [LIX]).

52 *Laws of Hywel Dda*, 24–26 (book I.3).

tures, the visible wound or scar clearly threatened status:[53] Baudhāyana asks, "If a Brahmin has an open wound filled with pus and bloody discharge and a worm appears in it, what penance should he observe?"[54] Here, though, the problem might well be the "worm"—a sign of decay and thus of degradation?—rather than the original wound. Infection of wounds was, of course, also a sign of guilt associated with medieval ordeals involving hot metal or water, so there may be a common understanding of bodily corruption indicating corruption of the soul in these parallel examples.

Disfigurement as Punishment

Facial mutilation as a *punishment*, however, was not as ubiquitous in Indian law as Das seems to suggest (and in fact is something of a rarity as a punishment in European texts as well). Certainly some very serious capital offences, such as someone from the lowest caste speaking rudely to a Brahmin, could be commuted to mutilation (in this case, the removal of the offending tongue).[55] But early laws forbid the capital or severe corporal punishment of Brahmins, limiting penalties to the placing of permanent marks on their foreheads indicating their crimes[56] in a process explicitly described as branding.[57] Similar markings in Western Europe were prescribed, for example, in the case of a recidivist thief: the Lombard laws say that one "should put a mark" (*ponat ei signum*) on his forehead and face, probably by branding.[58] In Byzantium (according to hagiographic sources, and thus not specifically "legal" ones) tattooing was used in specific cases, such as that of the martyred saints Theodore and Theophanes, known as the *Graptoi* ("those written upon").[59] The Brahmins' privilege, however, was withdrawn in later medieval commentaries, and it is by no means clear that all corporal punishment of this class was banned earlier on. The ancient code of Āpastamba, for example, states that a Brahmin guilty of theft should not be executed but "he should be blindfolded"[60] Olivelle does not believe this should be translated as "blinded"

53 Skinner, "Visible Prowess?"

54 *Dharmasūtras*, 152 (Baudhāyana 1.11.37).

55 *Dharmasūtras*, 71 (Āpastamba 2.27.14); Mathur, *Medieval Hindu Law*, 178.

56 *Dharmasūtras*, 53 (Āpastamba 2.10.16); Das, *Crime and Punishment*, 75.

57 *Dharmasūtras*, 160 (Baudhāyana 1.88.17).

58 *Leges Langobardorum*, 140 (Liutprand, LXXX [11]).

59 *Byzantine Defenders of Images*, 204.

60 *Dharmasūtras*, 71 (Āpastamba 2.27.17).

because this would be inconsistent with the ban on corporal punishment.[61] Yet surely being convicted of theft when one occupied the highest caste was a matter of extreme disgrace, and the alternative punishment that the translator suggests is not really credible—unless the blindfold was to symbolize the thief's moral blindness? Such an idea would not be implausible: with the Āpastamba, we are still in an age when the religious and the secular were intertwined, and a similar rhetoric of metaphorical blindness suffuses the writings of Christian commentators, too.[62] In any case, law codes and religious precepts work on the basis of the *threat* of mutilation, and its attendant social exclusion, and this was far more common than its actual *execution*.

Medical care was sometimes prescribed in the codes for the victim of an illegal, disfiguring assault. Such care, however, only amounted to staunching a bleeding or continuously running wound (in Salic law)[63] and/or removing bone splinters from injuries to the head and body in a number of other codes.[64] Although the legal precepts of early medieval Europe seem to have been very focused on the appearance of the victim of an attack, the medical assistance that is described does not seem to have extended to any form of cosmetic intervention. In contrast, it has been claimed that the sheer prevalence of actual cases of judicial and vendetta-fuelled mutilation in India gave rise to precocious and sophisticated practices of surgical reconstruction of the face, centuries before such procedures were "discovered" in Europe in the early modern era.[65] This is a highly problematic contention, however. Although early Sanskrit texts, such as that of Suśruta (ca. 600 BCE), do suggest that ancient Indian surgical techniques were highly sophisticated—at least in theory—and Indian barbers of the early Middle Ages have been characterized as "celebrity surgeons,"[66] linking the development of surgical competence to a perceived need arising from judicial mutilation ignores the social disgrace inherent in being convicted, and the challenge to authority that such restorative surgery might represent. Even if the written record of Indian surgical practice does indeed point to a precocious art (or knowledge) of techniques of facial reconstruction, this does not, I would argue, derive from the prevalence of queues of mutilated patients. Ancient expertise in surgical techniques was already well-established

---

61 *Dharmasūtras*, 373.

62 Wheatley, *Stumbling Blocks*, 18–19, 65–72.

63 *Pactus Legis Salicae* 78 (XVII.7).

64 *Pactus Legis Salicae.* 77 (XVII.5); *Pactus Legis Alamannorum*, 21 (I.4); *Lex Baiwariorum*, (IV.5, V.4, VI); *Leges Frisionum*, 71–74 (XXII).

65 Gilman, *Making the Body Beautiful*, 76.

66 Narayana and Subhose "Evolution of Surgery."

in Egypt long before the Sanskrit texts of Suśruta and others, as the Edwin Smith papyrus (ca. 3000 BCE) illustrates.[67] That said, recourse to a surgeon might in fact represent resistance to authority on the part of elite victims. The challenge to legal authority inherent in undertaking to fix a criminal's face, moreover, is plausible when we look at the occurrence of doctors in ancient Indian legal codes. Offering medical assistance, indeed being a doctor at all, does not appear to have been a particularly honorable role, in notable contrast to the apparent high status of the early medieval doctor or *medicus* in Western European texts.[68] Practicing medicine was "a secondary sin causing loss of caste,"[69] and selling medicines was forbidden to the householder.[70] If the medic was indeed something of a marginal figure, perhaps the idea of reconstructing the mutilated faces of criminals is not so far-fetched.

As in Western Europe, the contexts within which we find evidence of corporeal and/or facial mutilation in India indicate it to have been a punishment interchangeable with the death penalty. Das, drawing upon the seventh-century *Tale of Ten Princes/Young Men* (*Daśakumāracarita*), highlights the gouging out of eyes as a substitute for the death penalty in a case of treason.[71] Mathur cites a surviving twelfth-century inscription from the village of Lāhadpura, in the Gahadwal kingdom, threatening robbers with blinding or death.[72] These crimes by definition disturbed the peace of the kingdom. There is one area, however, that does not seem quite to fit this pattern, and that is the inflicting of facial mutilation on women.

Gender and Disfigurement

Early medieval European laws concerning women have been extensively studied and are best characterized as heterogeneous when it comes to women's agency and freedom of action. At one end of the spectrum were those women "living according to Roman law," enjoying legal identity and a certain degree of autonomy in the ownership and disposal of property. At the other end were women in Lombard society (in northern Italy) who seem to have enjoyed no separate legal personality at all, at least according to the law of King Rothari:[73]

---

67 Demaitre, *Medieval Medicine*, 2.

68 Pilsworth, "Could You Just Sign This?"

69 *Dharmasūtras*, 169 (Baudhāyana 2.13).

70 Ibid., 89 (Gautama 7.12).

71 Das, *Crime and Punishment*, 71.

72 Mathur, *Medieval Hindu Law*, 33.

73 *Leges Langobardorum*, 50 (Edictus CCIV).

> No woman living in our kingdom according to Lombard law may live under her own control, that is *selpmundia*, but should always be under the power of some man or the king; nor does she have the right to give away or alienate any movable or immovable property, except with the permission of him in whose guardianship (*mundium*) she is.[74]

This is extraordinarily similar in language to chapter 9 verse 3 of Manu's *Authoritative Teaching of the Laws*, which says:

> When she is a girl, her father guards her; when she is a young woman, her husband guards her; when she is an old woman her sons guard her. A woman should never be on her own.[75]

Manu's text, although very early (dating to ca. 200 CE), certainly has resonances with Western European laws that establish guardianship over women (effectively, power over their property and bodies) as a central aspect of male legal competence. Stephanie Jamison has commented that Manu's position—or at least the language in which he articulated the law (he describes women as "whores")—was by far the most extreme statement of women's legal incapacity in Indian jurisprudence.[76] It is tempting to deduce that the close guardianship is in fact an admission of women's relative *agency*. Jamison links Manu's position, for instance, to the rise of ascetic women in India who answered to no guardians.

At the heart of this apparently stringent supervision of women was anxiety about female sexuality, and in particular of inappropriate liaisons outside of marriage. These are expressed in the laws in two forms—punishments for sexual liaisons across caste boundaries, and for adulterous relationships. The former are articulated in many early recensions of Indian law, including the *Arthaśāstra*, where a low-status man (*śvapāka*) having relations with an *Ārya* woman was killed, while she had her nose and ears cut off.[77] Yet other early codes omit explicit mention of the mutilation of the woman: Āpastamba simply states that such a union makes her "sordid" and returns to the subject to prescribe death for the man and "emaciation" for her.[78] Whether this meant starving her to death or inflicting a fasting penance (of which there were many versions in Indian law) is unclear. In either case, however—mutilation or emaciation—the idea appears

74 Translation adapted from *Lombard Laws*, 92.

75 Quoted in *Mahābhārata*, 11.

76 Jamison, "Women 'between the Empires.'" Others are included the law code of Baudhāyana, 2.3.45: see *Dharmasūtras*, 175.

77 Cited by Parasher-Sen, "Naming and Social Exclusion," 421.

78 *Dharmasūtras*, 32 and 70 (Āpastamba 1.21.1 and 2.27.8–9).

to be to deprive the woman of her beauty, as punishment for her inappropriate liaison.

We can compare this to the censure of free women who had sex with male slaves in European laws. The earlier laws of the Lombard king Rothari condemned both partners to death, although the woman could also be sold outside the kingdom by her family, or become the property of the palace.[79] King Liutprand later modified this by removing the death penalty, and allowed for the woman's relatives to deal with her before the penalty of enslavement was imposed.[80] Such unequal unions, however, could and did occur in medieval Western Europe: Suzanne Wemple has pointed out that free Frankish women who married below their station, whilst similarly condemned by the laws of that region, may have stood to gain economically from such choices (living as a bound peasant might have been more secure than living as a poor freewoman, for instance), particularly since their lords usually guaranteed the free status of any children born of the union.[81] It is notable, of course, that unequal relationships the other way (lower status woman, higher-status man) attracted far less attention in European than in Indian legislation, the latter being concerned with questions of the caste of the potential offspring.[82]

Turning to adultery, the mutilation of women's faces certainly seems to feature as one extreme measure in a spectrum of punishments. Das gathers some tenth-century evidence for punishment of this type having been carried out.[83] But the inscription she cites from Kogali, in the western Chalukya kingdom (dated 992), only *prescribes* that "the nose of the woman guilty of adultery is to be cut off and the adulterer put to death."[84] There is no evidence that this was actually done. And Das's other piece of evidence, like that used by Flood for the finger-cutting cited above, comes from an external observer. Moreover, the practice does not appear in all of the ancient law codes, suggesting that—like the punishment for sexual relations across caste—this type of punishment divided opinion. If anything, the developing legal framework discouraged such acts: the late twelfth-century jurist Devaṇṇabhaṭṭa (fl. ca. 1150–1225) opposed the practice of husbands cut-

79 *Leges Langobardorum*, 53–54 (Edictus CCXXI).

80 *Leges Langobardorum*, 118 (Liutprand XXIV [6]).

81 Wemple, *Women in Frankish Society*, 71–72.

82 For example, Gautama 4.16–28, which sets out the various combinations of parentage and condemns children of "reverse" unions to illegitimacy: *Dharmasūtras*, 85.

83 Das, *Crime and Punishment*, 65–67.

84 *Kannada Inscriptions from the Madras Presidency*, no. 77.

ting off their adulterous wives' noses and ears.[85] This suggests that such punishments were, if not "private," then certainly not a measure condoned in the legal world. Indeed, thinking back to women's legal incapacity, it seems that adulterous women were considered to have been more acted *upon* than the male actors in Indian law (the Kogali inscription's more severe punishment for the male partner seems to underline this); and so we find penance, rather than punishment, prescribed in early codes such as Baudhāyana.[86] The punishment of adulterous wives in Western Europe was certainly, in some early laws, seen as the husband's prerogative, extending to permission to kill both the woman and her lover without penalty.[87] A number of later codes, however, did threaten facial mutilation as the appropriate punishment for sexual transgression: Byzantine laws of the eighth century, Cnut's English law of the eleventh, and southern Italian laws of the twelfth century (as codified by Frederick II in the mid-thirteenth) all include such punishments.[88] But I have suggested that these references ultimately derive from Old Testament precedents, specifically the story of the prostitute sisters Oholah and Oholibah in Ezekiel 23, and do not reflect contemporary practices, particularly since these penalties are not actually recorded as having been carried out in those regions.[89] We could equally well posit three very specific contemporary contexts for these metaphorical laws. Byzantium was suffering the pain of the iconoclast controversy, and the faces of icons were being erased just as the threat to erase facial features was issued; meanwhile, many saints of this era are said to have been mutilated and marked for defending icons, as in the cases of Theodore and Theophanes mentioned above. The law of King Cnut (990–1035) might have been inspired by the biblical knowledge of his bishop, Wulfstan, but it could also have derived from Viking traditions in his Danish homeland, where mutilation was often preferred to the killing of kin.[90] And the mutilation of women in twelfth-century southern Italian law could have taken its cue either from the pre-existing Byzantine model (though the applicability of Byzantine law in this region was by then rather diluted) or from the same biblical model. Southern Italy and Sicily, of course, also had histories of Muslim rule and influence, though again the "evi-

85 Cited by Mathur, *Medieval Hindu Law*, 187.

86 *Dharmasūtras*, 175 (2.3.48–50).

87 For example, *Leges Visigothorum*, 149 (III.4); *Leges Langobardorum*, 51–52 (Edictus CCXII).

88 *Manual of Roman Law*, ed. Freshfield; *English Historical Documents*, 458–59; *Die Konstitutionen Friedrichs II.*

89 Skinner, "Gendered Nose."

90 Van Eickels, "Gendered Violence," 593.

dence" for the treatment of adulteresses in Islamic culture may have derived from literary, rather than legal, sources.

Imagining Disfigurement?

These evidentiary uncertainties suggest that laws themselves can only take us so far. However, it is significant that the facial mutilation of women seems to have been a popular theme in medieval story-telling traditions throughout Eurasia.[91] Famously, it features as an episode in the ancient story of Rama in the epic *Mahabharata*, surviving in numerous versions and strands of early Indian literature, and owing its continued popularity to the transformation of Rama from human to supernatural figure early in the story's development.[92] Whilst in exile, Rama persuades his half-brother Laksmana to disfigure the malignant demon *rākṣasī* (fem.) Ravana's sister Surpanakha. In revenge, Ravaṇa captures and takes away Rama's wife Sita, who is only rescued with the aid of an army composed of monkeys and bears. But what had Surpanakha done to merit such a violent act as the removal of her nose and lips? Scharf explains that she is blamed for hostility between Rama and Ravaṇa's brother Khara, whom Rama in fact kills. One version of Rama's story goes further, suggesting that Rama and Laksmana engage in a game of teasing Surpaṇakha when she proposes marriage to one or the other; and then, when she rushes towards Sita, threatening to eat her, Laksmaṇa mutilates her with Rama's encouragement.[93] As Peter Scharf comments, "the ethical propriety of some of Rama's actions is less than ideal."[94] Kathleen Erndl, too, has reflected upon the incident involving Surpanakha, commenting that she had "gotten a raw deal in a world where the rules were made by men."[95]

The *Mahabharata* even contains a specific word for "one whose nose and lips have been cut," *nikṛttanāsauṣṭhī*.[96] Given the popularity of the tale from its ancient origins throughout the medieval period in India, would such a figure have been familiar in real life, or was it just the most fantastical horror that could be imagined? I would suggest the latter, given the limited evidence in the legal codes as attesting to this as a practice. Story-telling was a much better way to communicate the boundaries of the acceptable to an audience, and it was perhaps useful to imag-

91 Girón-Negrón, "How the Go-Between Cut Her Nose"; Skinner, "Gendered Nose."

92 *Rāmopākhyāna*, 2.

93 Ibid., 9.

94 Ibid., 8.

95 Erndl, "Mutilation of Śūrpaṇakhā," 68.

96 *Rāmopākhyāna*, 227.

ine Surpanakha as a woman behaving badly. Did her inappropriate approaches to men, and threat to Sita, justify her cruel punishment? Or does the disfiguring of Surpanakha function as a means of deflecting attention away from Sita's own reputation, compromised as it now was by Ravana's capture of her, and requiring a drastic ordeal (walking on fire) to rehabilitate her in her husband's eyes?

Storytelling may in fact represent the one concrete link between South Asia and medieval Europe, via the Middle East. Singh has highlighted that the expansion of the Arab world gave rise to a sharp increase in the collection and translation of Sanskrit (and other) texts, an initiative focused on the court of the Abbasid caliph Al-Ma'mum (r. 813–33) at Baghdad. As a result, many stories which circulated in the medieval Arab and European worlds ultimately derived much of their material from Indian fables, in particular the Khalila-wa-Dimna collection, which includes similar episodes of disfigurement.[97] Violent or assertive women were often characterized as stepping outside an acceptable norm of behavior and punished violently in turn. We might think here of legal examples of females (though not demons) whose engagement in violent or transgressive acts open them up not only to corporal punishment but also to being disbarred from seeking compensation for injuries suffered. In Europe, Lombard law treated women involved in sinful or unseemly violence (*scandalum*) harshly,[98] whilst Irish law dismissed injuries inflicted in a fight between women as inactionable.[99]

Conclusion

Was facial mutilation an "oriental" punishment that travelled West, or is it yet another example of that nebulous category of "Indo-European" cultural practices whose origins are lost to us but go back well before the Common Era? To take another example, there are the parallels between stoning and burning as punishments for adultery in Aztec law[100] and in the Bible (Leviticus 21:9; John 8:7). But Reynolds cautions against accepting apparent similarities at face value and suggests that differences are the more thought-provoking elements in the substance and processes of law, since "human beings find different solutions to similar problems."[101] Perhaps it is best to think about the question another way: if the death of a perpetrator was, for whatever reason, not an option, damage to the face

97 Girón-Negrón, "How the Go-Between Cut Her Nose."

98 Balzaretti, "'These Are Things That Men Do, Not Women.'"

99 Kelly, *Guide to Early Irish Law*, 79.

100 Offner, "Future of Aztec Law," in this issue.

101 Reynolds, "Early Medieval Law," 11.

was the most visible way of indicating religious defilement, inflicting shame, or signaling loss of status. The inspiration for European law codes that include this practice might ultimately derive from a common, Old Testament model, or might in fact be the coincidental product of different contexts. As Reynolds has pointed out, it was probably *local* pressure that decided whether and how a miscreant should be punished, and this may explain the apparent slippage between law and practice regarding adulterous women.[102] (Eventually, the paths followed by Indian and European laws diverged in the former culture's continued inclusion of penance within punishment.) The linking of the two regions by trade connections opens up the possibility that ideas about *how* to disfigure traveled with material goods. Certainly, there is no doubt that Muslim geographers, whose "journeys" were sometimes entirely virtual and whose texts often adhered to quite rigid generic frameworks, may have inadvertently spread knowledge of exotic "wonders" that were already centuries out of date.

The assumption that mutilation was ubiquitous in Indian culture, then, is at best an over-reading of the often unreliable evidence, perhaps shaped by the fact that the best-known product of Indian culture, the epic of the *Mahabharata*, prominently features an episode of facial cutting. In both India and Europe, the threat or the idea of facial disfigurement occurs far more frequently in the surviving evidence than actual examples of the practice being carried out. In both regions, mutilation attracted the attention of lawmakers who wanted to express the extremity and "otherness" of the practice, but few actually wanted to see it in the flesh.

102 Ibid.

Bibliography

Primary Sources

Æthelberht's code (Abt). Edited by Lisi Oliver. <http://www.earlyenglishlaws.ac.uk/laws/texts/abt/> [accessed September 16, 2015]

Amatus of Montecassino, *History of the Normans*. Translated by Prescott N. Dunbar. Woodbridge: Boydell, 2004.

The Book of the Wonders of India: Mainland, Sea, and Islands. Translated by G. S. P. Freeman-Grenville. London: East-West Publications, 1981.

Byzantine Defenders of Images: Eight Saints' Lives in English Translation. Edited by Alice-Mary Talbot. Washington: Dumbarton Oaks, 1998.

The Dharmasūtras: The Law Codes of Ancient India (Āpastamba, Gautama, Baudhāyana and Vasiṣṭha). Edited and translated by Patrick Olivelle. Oxford: Oxford University Press, 1999.

English Historical Documents. Volume 1. Translated by Dorothy Whitelock. 2nd. ed. London: Routledge, 1979.

Kannada Inscriptions from the Madras Presidency. Edited by R. Shama Sastry. South Indian Inscriptions 9. New Dehli: Archaeological Survey of India, 1941 (repr. 1986). <http://www.whatisindia.com/inscriptions/south_indian_inscriptions/volume_9/index.html> [accessed November 26, 2014].

Die Konstitutionen Friedrichs II für das Königsreich Sizilien. Edited by Wolfgang Stürner. Monumenta Germaniæ Historica: Constitutiones et Acta Publica Imperatorum et Regum 2 (supplement). Hanover: Hahn, 1996.

The Laws of Hywel Dda: Law Texts from Medieval Wales. Edited and translated by Dafydd Jenkins. Llandysul: Gomer, 1986.

Laws of the Salian and Ripuarian Franks. Translated by T. J. Rivers. New York: AMS, 1986.

Leges Langobardorum. Edited by Friedrich Bluhme. Monumenta Germaniae Historica: Leges (in Folio) 4. Hanover: Hahn, 1868.

Leges Visigothorum. Edited by Karl Zeumer. Monumenta Germaniae Historica: Leges Nationum Germanicarum 1. Hanover: Hahn, 1902.

Lex Baiwariorum. Edited by Ernst von Schwind. Monumenta Germaniae Historica: Leges Nationum Germanicarum 5.2. Hanover: Hahn, 1926.

Lex Frisionum. Edited by Karl von Richthofen in *Leges Alamannorum. Leges Baiuwariorum. Leges Burgundionum. Lex Frisionum*, edited by Georg Heinrich Pertz, 631–711. Monumenta Germaniae Historica: Leges (in Folio) 3. Hanover: Hahn. 1863.

Lex Ribvaria. Edited by Franz Bayerle and Rudolf Buchner. Monumenta Germaniae Historica: Leges Nationum Germanicarum 3.2. Hanover: Hahn, 1954.

The Lombard Laws. Translated by Katherine Fischer Drew. Philadelphia: University of Pennsylvania Press, 1973.

The Mahābhārata 11: The Book of the Women; 12: The Book of Peace, part I. Edited and translated by James L. Fitzgerald. Chicago: Chicago University Press, 2004.

Manu's Code of Law: A Critical Edition and Translation of the Mānava-Dharmaśāstra. Edited and translated by Patrick Olivelle. Oxford: Oxford University Press, 2005.

Pactus legis Alamannorum. Edited by Karl Lehman. Monumenta Germaniae Historica: Leges Nationum Germanicarum 5.1. Hanover: Hahn, 1966

Pactus legis Salicae. Edited by Karl August Eckhardt. Monumenta Germaniae Historica: Leges Nationum Germanicarum 4.1. Hanover: Hahn, 1962.

Rāmopākhyāna: The Story of Rāma in the Mahābhārata. Edited by Peter Scharf. London: Routledge, 2003.

Secondary Studies

Asher, Catherine B., and Cynthia Talbot. *India before Europe*. Cambridge: Cambridge University Press, 2006.

Bagge, Sverre, ed. *Feudalism: New Landscapes of Debate*. Turnhout: Brepols, 2011.

Balzaretti, Ross. "'These Are Things That Men Do, Not Women': The Social Regulation of Female Violence in Langobard Italy." In *Violence and Society in the Early Medieval West*, edited by Guy Halsall, 175–92. Woodbridge: Boydell, 1998.

Bartlett, Robert. "The Symbolic Meanings of Hair in the Middle Ages." *Transactions of the Royal Historical Society*, 6th ser., 4 (1995): 43–60.

Bloch, Marc. *Apologie pour l'histoire, ou, métier d'historien*. Paris: Colin, 1949 [1944].

——. *La société féodale*. Paris: Michel, 1939.

Bührer-Thierry, G. "'Just Anger' or 'Vengeful Anger'? The Punishment of Blinding in the Early Medieval West." In *Anger's Past: The Social Uses of an Emotion in the Middle Ages*, edited by Barbara Rosenwein, 75–91. Ithaca: Cornell University Press, 1998.

Chattopadhyaya, Brajadulal. *The Making of Early Medieval India*. Oxford: Oxford University Press, 1994.

Das, Sulka. *Crime and Punishment in Ancient India, ca. A.D. 300 to A.D. 1100*. New Delhi: Abhinav, 1977.

Davis, Donald R. "Before Virtue: Halakhah, Dharmaśāstra and What Law Can Create," *Law and Contemporary Problems* 71 (2008): 99–108.

——. "Toward a History of Documents in Medieval India: The Encounter of Scholasticism and Regional Law in the *Smṛticandrikā*." In *Legal Worlds and Legal Encounters*, edited by Elizabeth Lambourn, special issue, *The Medieval Globe* 2, no. 2 (2016): 167–98.

Demaitre, Luke. *Medieval Medicine: The Art of Healing from Head to Toe*. Santa Barbara: Praeger, 2013.

Derrett, J. Duncan M. *Dharmaśāstra and Juridical Literature*. Wiesbaden: Otto Harrassowitz, 1973.

Ducène, Jean-Charles. "Review of Abū 'Imrān Mūsā ibn Rabāh al-Awsī al-Sīrāfī, Al-sahīh min ahbār al-bīhār wa-'ağā'ibihā, edited by Y. Al-Hādī (Damascus, 2006)." *Journal Asiatique*, 298 (2010): 579–84.

Dutton, Paul Edward. *Charlemagne's Mustache and Other Cultural Clusters of a Dark Age*. New York: Palgrave Macmillan, 2004.

Erndl, Kathleen M. "The Mutilation of Śūrpaṇakhā." In *Many Rāmāyanas: The Diversity of a Narrative Tradition in South Asia*, edited by Paula Richman, 67–84. Berkeley: University of California Press, 1991.

Evans, G. R. *Law and Theology in the Middle Ages*. New York: Routledge, 2002.

Flood, F. Barry. *Objects of Translation: Material Culture and Medieval "Hindu-Muslim" Encounters*. Princeton: Princeton University Press, 2009.

Freshfield, Edwin Hanson, ed. *A Manual of Roman Law: The "Ecloga," Published by the Emperors Leo III and Constantine V of Isauria at Constantonple in 726 AD*. Cambridge: Cambridge University Press, 1926.

Gates, Jay Paul, and Nicole Marafioti, eds. *Capital and Corporal Punishment in Anglo-Saxon England*. Woodbridge: Boydell, 2014.

Geltner, Guy. *Flogging Others: Corporal Punishment and Cultural Identity from Antiquity to the Present*. Amsterdam: Amsterdam University Press, 2014.

Gilman, Sander. *Making the Body Beautiful: A Cultural History of Aesthetic Surgery*. Princeton: Princeton University Press, 1999.

Girón-Negrón, Luis M. "How the Go-Between Cut Her Nose: Two Ibero-Medieval Translations of a *Kalilah wa Dimnah* Story." In *Under the Influence: Questioning the Comparative in Medieval Castile*, edited by Leyla Rouhi and Cynthia Robinson, 231–59. Leiden: Brill, 2005.

Heirbaut, Dirk. "Not European Feudalism, but Flemish Feudalism." In *Galbert of Bruges and the Historiography of Medieval Flanders*, edited by Jeff Rider and Alexander Murray, 56–88. Washington, DC: Catholic University of America Press, 2009.

Hendrickz, Benjamin. "Is There Evidence for a Medieval Nubian Feudalism?" *Acta Patristica et Byzantina* 21 (2010): 256–69.

Jamison, Stephanie. "Women 'between the Empires' and 'between the Lines.'" In *Between the Empires: Society in India 300 BCE to 400 CE*, edited by Patrick Olivelle, 191–214. Oxford: Oxford University Press, 2011.

Kelly, Fergus. *A Guide to Early Irish Law*. Dublin: Dublin Institute for Advanced Studies, 1988.

Kershaw, Paul. *Peaceful Kings: Peace, Power and the Early Medieval Political Imagination*. Oxford: Oxford University Press, 2011.

Larivière, Richard W. "Ordeals in Europe and India." *Journal of the American Oriental Society* 101 (1981): 347–49.

Lewis, Martin T., and Kären Wigen. *The Myth of Continents: A Critique of Metageography.* Berkeley: University of California Press, 1997.

Leyser, Conrad. "Long-Haired Kings and Short-Haired Nuns: Writing on the Body in Caesarius of Arles." *Studia Patristica* 24 (1993): 143–50.

Lubin, Timothy, Donald R. Davis, Jr., and Jayanth K. Krishnan, eds. *Hinduism and Law: An Introduction*. Cambridge: Cambridge University Press, 2010.

Mathur, Ashutosh Dayal. *Medieval Hindu Law: A Study of Post-Smṛti Changes in Hindu Law*. Oxford: Oxford University Press, 2007.

McNeill, John T., and Helena M. Gamer. *Medieval Handbooks of Penance*. New York: Columbia University Press, 1990.

Meens, Rob, ed. *Penitentials*, special issue, *Early Medieval Europe* 14, no. 1 (2006).

Menski, Werner. *Hindu Law: Beyond Tradition and Modernity*. Oxford: Oxford University Press, 2009.

Miller, William Ian. *Eye for an Eye*. Cambridge: Cambridge University Press, 2006.

Mukhia, Harbans. "'Medieval India': An Alien Conceptual Hegemony?" *The Medieval History Journal* 1 (1998): 91–105.

Narayana, A., and V. Subhose. "Evolution of Surgery: Śuśrta's Innovative Skills." *Bulletin of the Indian Institute for the History of Medicine Hyderabad* 34 (2004): 17–39.

Offner, Jerome A. "The Future of Aztec Law." In *Legal Worlds and Legal Encounters*, edited by Elizabeth Lambourn, special issue, *The Medieval Globe* 2, no. 2 (2016): 1–32.

Olivelle, Patrick. "*Dharmaśāstra*: A Textual History." In *Hinduism and Law: An Introduction*, edited by Timothy Lubin, Donald R. Davis, Jr., and Jayanth K. Krishnan, 28–57. Cambridge: Cambridge University Press, 2010

——. "Penance and Punishment: Marking the Body in Criminal Law and Social Ideology of Ancient India." *Journal of Hindu Studies* 4 (2011): 23–41.

Oliver, Lisi. *The Beginnings of English Law*. Toronto: University of Toronto Press, 2002.

Parasher-Sen, Aloka. "Naming and Social Exclusion: The Outcast and the Outsider." In *Between the Empires: Society in India 300 BCE to 400 CE*, edited by Patrick Olivelle, 415–56. Oxford: Oxford University Press, 2011.

Pilsworth, Claire. "Could You Just Sign This for Me, John? Doctors, Charters, and Occupational Identity in Early Medieval Northern and Central Italy." *Early Medieval Europe* 17 (2009): 363–88.

Prasad, Ishwari. *History of Medieval India from 647 AD to the Mughal Conquest.* Allahabad: Indian Press, 1925.

Reid, Megan H. *Law and Piety in Medieval Islam.* Cambridge: Cambridge University Press, 2013.

Reuter, Timothy. "Medieval: Another Tyrannous Construct?" *Medieval History Journal* 1 (1998): 25–45.

Reynolds, Susan. "Early Medieval Law in India and Europe: A Plea for Comparisons." *Medieval History Journal* 16 (2013): 1–20.

Sharma, R. S. *Early Medieval Indian Society: A Study in Feudalisation.* Delhi: Orient Longman, 2001.

Singh, Upinder, ed. *Rethinking Early Medieval India: A Reader.* Oxford: Oxford University Press, 2011.

Skinner, Patricia. "The Gendered Nose and Its Lack: 'Medieval' Nose-Cutting and Its Modern Manifestations." *Journal of Women's History* 24 (2014): 45–67.

——. *Living with Disfigurement in Early Medieval Europe.* New York: Palgrave Macmillan, forthcoming.

——. "Viewpoint. Confronting the 'Medieval' in Medieval History: The Jewish Example." *Past and Present* 181 (2003): 219–47.

——. "'Visible Prowess? Reading Men's Head and Face Wounds in Early Medieval European Sources to 1000 CE." In *"His Brest Torbrosten": Wound and Wound Repair in Medieval Culture,* edited by K. deVries and L. Tracy. Leiden: Brill, forthcoming.

Van Eickels, Klaus. "Gendered Violence: Castration and Blinding as Punishment for Treason in Normandy and Anglo-Norman England." *Gender and History* 16 (2004): 588–602.

Veluthat, Kesavan. *The Early Medieval in South India.* New Delhi: Oxford University Press, 2009.

Wemple, Suzanne Fonay. *Women in Frankish Society: Marriage and the Cloister, 500–900.* Philadelphia: University of Pennsylvania Press, 1981.

Wheatley, Edward. *Stumbling Blocks before the Blind: Medieval Constructions of a Disability.* Ann Arbor: University of Michigan Press, 2010.

Wickham, Chris. "Historical Transitions: A Comparative Approach." *Medieval History Journal* 13 (2010): 1–21.

——. "Problems in Doing Comparative History." In *Challenging the Boundaries of Medieval History: The Legacy of Timothy Reuter,* edited by Patricia Skinner, 5–28. Turnhout: Brepols, 2009.

Wink, André. *Al-Hind: The Making of the Indo-Islamic World 1: Early Medieval India and the Expansion of Islam.* Leiden: Brill, 1990.

Wormald, Patrick. *Legal Culture in the Early Medieval West.* London: Bloomsbury, 1999.

Patricia Skinner (p.e.skinner@swansea.ac.uk) is Research Professor in Arts and Humanities at Swansea University. She is currently engaged on a long-term project tracing the history of medical and social responses to facial difference. Her book *Living with Disfigurement in Early Medieval Europe* will be published by Palgrave Macmillan in 2016.

Keywords medieval Europe, India, mutilation, adultery, jurisprudence, Christianity, Hinduism, Islam, face, law and religion, gender.

Abstract This essay examines the similarities and differences between legal and other precepts outlining corporal punishment in ancient and medieval Indian and early medieval European laws. Responding to Susan Reynolds's call for such comparisons, it begins by outlining the challenges in doing so. Primarily, the fragmented political landscape of both regions, where multiple rulers and spheres of authority existed side-by-side, make a direct comparison complex. Moreover, the time slippage between what scholarship understands to be the "early medieval" period in each region needs to be taken into account, particularly given the persistence of some provisions and the adapatation or abandonment of others. The paper goes on to consider how the body and face are presented as sites of injury and punishment, and asks whether the prescriptive measures actually played out in practice. Despite tangible links between the Indian subcontinent and Europe during the period under review, it is concluded that direct influence of one set of laws upon the other is unlikely.

COMMON THREADS: A REAPPRAISAL OF MEDIEVAL EUROPEAN SUMPTUARY LAW

LAUREL ANN WILSON

IN THIRTEENTH-CENTURY SPAIN, no one other than the king was legally permitted to wear a scarlet rain cape; in 1356, the city of Florence proclaimed it illegal for women to have buttons on their clothing without corresponding buttonholes; while in England in 1363, Parliament decreed that only knights and clerics with incomes above a certain amount were permitted to wear linen in the summer.[1] As puzzling as these restrictions may seem to the modern mind, they were profoundly meaningful to contemporaries, since sumptuary laws such as these were enacted in great numbers throughout Western Europe from the mid-thirteenth century on; there are more than three hundred examples from the Italian city-states alone.[2]

Although scholarly interest in sumptuary law has increased in recent decades, the laws hold far more potential as a historical resource than has yet been realized. To date, moreover, the various bodies of sumptuary law have been studied in geographic and temporal isolation from one another, rather than as a whole, as a large corpus with local variations. It is time to approach sumptuary law on a comparative basis, to allow internal similarities and differences to suggest new meanings and new avenues of research.[3]

---

1 Spain: Cortes de Valladolid, 1258: "que ninguno non traya capa aguadera descarlata sinon el Rey" in *Cortes de los antiguos reinos*, XIV (14), 57. Florence: "Pragmatica of 1356," 2 ("De abottonaturis,"), cited in Rainey, "Sumptuary Legislation in Renaissance Florence," 669. England: Parliament of 1363 (30); cited by Ormrod, "Edward III: October, 1363." It should be noted that, with the possible exception of "England," geographical terms such as "Spain" are anachronistic; here, they allowed to stand as shorthand because they have been the categories that have framed most research on sumptuary law—which is, of course, part of the problem.

2 Killerby, *Sumptuary Law in Italy*, 28–29 (Table 1). Neithard Bulst and his researchers ("Les ordonnances somptuaires," 771) have amassed more than 3,500 sumptuary laws from German-speaking areas.

3 Maria-Giuseppina Muzzarelli has published a plea for less circumscribed study of sumptuary law: "Reconciling the Privilege of a Few"; and Bulst has repeatedly urged the importance of comparative study, for example, in "La legislazione suntuaria." Catherine Kovesi Killerby's *Sumptuary Law in Italy* compares laws among the various city-states. The only attempt to examine sumptuary law comparatively in all eras and cultures is Hunt, *Governance of the Consuming Passions.* Hunt is a legal sociologist rather than a historian, but

What Is Sumptuary Law?

Sumptuary law is often defined rather vaguely, as laws intended to regulate any kind of consumption of any kind of commodity. Some recent legal scholarship even classifies intellectual property law as sumptuary law, for instance, or describes the 1979 Archaeological Resources Protection Act in the United States as a form of sumptuary law.[4] Even the word "sumptuary," which strictly speaking should be applied only to sumptuary laws, is now often used to describe goods of widely differing types.[5] In actuality, sumptuary law was always narrowly focused on personal consumption and almost always aimed at its public display. It might be directed at the construction of lavish houses, as in medieval Japan or precolonial Burma, or, as in many cultures, it might regulate public or semi-public events such as banquets, weddings, and funerals.[6] Laws governing dress appear to be universal to all sumptuary laws.

Not all sartorial law is sumptuary law, however. One must be careful to distinguish between sumptuary laws and dress codes, as there are substantive differences between the two. Sumptuary law is *prohibitive*: that is, it claims to prohibit certain groups of people from acquiring and/or displaying certain commodities. Dress codes, however, are *prescriptive*, that is, they require a certain group, usually a group defined as outsiders, to wear specific clothing (thus, by implication, proscribing other garments): all Jews must wear a particular kind of hat, for example, or all prostitutes must wear yellow; a member of the clergy must wear the dress prescribed for his rank; and so on.[7] Most important, prohibitive sumptuary law differs sharply from prescriptive dress codes in terms of its enforcement: sumptuary law, which is a society's attempt to discipline itself, is enforced only ambivalently, if at all; while prescriptive dress codes, which generally apply to outsiders and the non-elite, or operate within strictly hierarchical institutions such as the clergy or the military, are relatively easily to enforce and generally are enforced. Thus, although both sartorial codes combine symbolic and instrumental func-

---

his comparative approach is productive; he is particularly insightful in defining sumptuary law as symbolic rather than instrumental.

4 Beebe, "Intellectual Property Law"; Goddard, "Anticipated Impact."

5 The meaning of "sumptuary goods" ranges from a synonym for luxury goods to "sinful" goods (Moeti and Khalo, *Public Finance Fundamentals*, 36) to "items of wide distribution not used in daily sustenance" (Miller, *Chieftains of the Highland Clans*, 10).

6 Shively, "Sumptuary Regulation and Status"; Ware, "Origins of Buddhist Nationalism."

7 In speaking of Islamic laws which make Muslims distinguishable from non-Muslims by their dress, one scholar calls these "laws of differentiation": Schick, "Some Islamic Determinants of Dress," 25.

tions, sumptuary law is primarily symbolic, while dress codes have a stronger instrumental component.[8]

Sumptuary Law as a Historical Resource

Sumptuary law provides us with remarkable primary source material. In addition to furnishing details of material goods, it illustrates lawmakers' conceptions of an ideal society. The material details provide insight into patterns of production, consumption, and trade, while the tensions between the actual and the ideal enable us to trace the dynamics of changing class distinctions. The laws make visible changes in the meaning of clothing and other material signifiers, while also providing profound insights into gender and social relations. Relationships between the governing and the governed, strategies of contestation, the connection between law as normative statement and law as practice, along with glimpses of the workings of law courts: all can be investigated via sumptuary law.

Appreciation of sumptuary law as a valid historical source is a relatively recent phenomenon, however. Until the final decades of the twentieth century, many references to sumptuary law treated it as little more than an illustration of the quaint habits of earlier times.[9] More recently, as interest in the meanings of material culture has grown, sumptuary law has received an increasing amount of attention from medievalists, including literary scholars and art historians as well as economic and social historians.[10] In addition, feminist historians have been particu-

8 On the distinction between sumptuary laws and dress codes, see Wilson, "Status." Like sumptuary laws, dress codes would repay comparative study, particularly given that certain of them, such as dress codes imposed on religious outsiders, have a wide geographical and chronological range.

9 Susan Vincent, in *Dressing the Elite* (117), describes the historiography of sumptuary law as "slight, and on occasion slighting." The primary exceptions, other than among historians of dress, are Italian historians who published many medieval sumptuary laws during the nineteenth century, those French historians who included sumptuary laws in their studies of luxury (such as Henri Baudrillart's *Histoire du luxe*), and a small school of American historians at Johns Hopkins who saw sumptuary laws as akin to Prohibition: Baldwin, *Sumptuary Legislation and Personal Regulation*; Greenfield, *Sumptuary Law in Nürnberg*; Vincent, *Costume and Conduct.*

10 Although this essay is limited to thirteenth- and fourteenth-century sumptuary laws, historians studying later centuries have made considerable use of sumptuary law as a resource. To cite just a few examples: Hayward (*Rich Apparel*) has used Tudor sumptuary laws to examine changing social structures and the uses of display in reinforcing royal power; Bulst, as mentioned earlier, has examined sumptuary laws as part of the process of state formation (e.g., "Zum Problem städtischer und territorialer"), while Anderssen's recent study of sumptuary laws in seventeenth-century Sweden ("Foreign Seductions") positions

larly prominent in the more recent studies of sumptuary law, inspired, at least in part, by the almost exclusive focus on women in the laws of the Italian city-states. The earliest work of this kind was done by Diane Owen Hughes, and it continues to be influential.[11]

In addition to exploring gender through the medium of sumptuary laws, Hughes was the first to ask some of the obvious questions: Why were these laws, which their legislators described as ineffective, still passed over and over again? And why in some places and not others? Hughes suggested that urban governments in medieval Italy, and perhaps in southern France as well, enacted sumptuary laws as a way of containing aristocratic display, but that royal governments had different motives.[12] This suggestion has been followed up to some degree by other scholars, including Neithard Bulst and Sarah-Grace Heller. But there is much more work to be done, since local sumptuary laws from regions that had both municipal and royal or imperial governments (such as southern France, southern Italy, and imperial Germany) are not yet widely available.[13] Hughes was also the first to voice the crucial idea that it might be the *process* of legislating rather than the function of the legislation which is significant, that is, that sumptuary law should be considered as symbolic rather than instrumental, an insight which calls for far more attention than it has received to date.[14]

Subsequent to Hughes's work, many Anglophone historians have concentrated on the sumptuary laws of the Italian city-states, notably Catherine Kovesi Killerby.[15] Carole Collier Frick's work on fifteenth-century Florence has used fashion and dress as historical categories of analysis and thus has touched on sumptuary law as well.[16] Applying Hughes's feminist approach, Susan Mosher Stuard has

---

them as a tool for strengthening national identity. Riello has also written extensively on European sumptuary law, primarily from the fifteenth century on (e.g. Riello and Parthasarathi, *Spinning World*, and Lemire and Riello, "East and West"). See also the essays in Muzzarelli and Campanini, *Disciplinare il lusso*, which cover European sumptuary laws from the thirteenth century on.

11 Hughes, "Sumptuary Law and Social Relations," "Distinguishing Signs," and "Regulating Women's Fashion."

12 Hughes, "Sumptuary Law and Social Relations," 99.

13 Bulst, "La legislazione suntuaria"; Heller, "Limiting Yardage"; Killerby, *Sumptuary Law in Italy*, 25.

14 Hughes, "Sumptuary Law and Social Relations," 99. The distinction between symbolic and instrumental legislation is summarized in Gusfield, "On Legislating Morals," 56–59.

15 Killerby, *Sumptuary Law in Italy*, "Practical Problems in the Enforcement of Italian Sumptuary Law," and "Heralds of a Well-Instructed Mind."

16 Frick, *Dressing Renaissance Florence*.

looked at fashion and the marketplace in fourteenth-century Italy, in addition to studying consumption through the lens of sumptuary law.[17] Carol Lansing's work uses the funeral laws of medieval Orvieto as a means of exploring both gender and political relationships, suggesting that the men who governed the city were attempting to establish new, regulated patterns of behavior for themselves, but were, in Claude Lévi-Strauss's phrase, "using women to think with."[18] Another gender-based approach comes from Kim Phillips, who has used English sumptuary laws, directed primarily at men, as a means of studying gender relations and the construction of masculinity.[19] A sign of the new interest being aroused by this topic was the republication of Stella Mary Newton's *Fashion in the Age of the Black Prince*, in which Newton (an English costume historian) gathered together European sumptuary laws from the 1340s to the 1360s and used them in conjunction with literary, pictorial, and documentary sources to argue for the revolutionary nature of the fashion changes in this era.[20] (At the time of its initial release, in 1980, it failed to attract attention beyond a very specialized circle of experts.)

Given sumptuary law's symbolic importance, it is not surprising that literary scholars such as Clare Sponsler, Susan Crane, and Andrea Denny-Brown have also been attracted to the subject of English sumptuary law, introducing theoretical techniques and concepts that have broadened the ways in which sumptuary law has been approached.[21] Sarah-Grace Heller, a literary scholar specializing in medieval France, has also been extremely influential.[22] French historians interested in social history and material culture have also been drawn to sumptuary law, for example, Françoise Piponnier, Agnès Page, and, for a later period, Daniel Roche.[23] Many recent scholars of sumptuary law elsewhere in Europe elide the

17 Stuard, *Gilding the Market.*

18 Lansing, *Passion and Order.*

19 Phillips, "Masculinities and the Medieval English Sumptuary Laws." Compare Lansing, *Passion and Order.*

20 Newton, *Fashion in the Age of the Black Prince.*

21 Sponsler, "Narrating the Social Order"; Crane, *Performance of Self*; Denny-Brown, *Fashioning Change.*

22 Heller, "Limiting Yardage," "Anxiety, Hierarchy, and Appearance," and *Fashion in Medieval France*. Aside from Heller, there has been little Anglophone study of French sumptuary law, with the exception of an American doctoral dissertation on the subject in 1996, of which Bulst justly says that it produced "rather modest results"; Bulst, "La legislazione suntuaria," 121. See also n. 24 below.

23 Piponnier, *Costume et vie sociale;* Page, *Vêtir le prince*; Roche, *La culture des apparences.* Curiously, Michel Pastoureau, although he devotes considerable attention to the ordering of

medieval and the early modern in their investigations,[24] including Neithard Bulst and Gerhard Jaritz, who have examined sumptuary laws of both French- and German-speaking areas as a means of investigating state formation.[25]

There is, in other words, a valuable body of research on medieval European sumptuary laws. But the work done to date has concentrated on discrete geographical areas and chronological periods, almost without exception.[26] The virtue of this approach is to enable study of local laws in depth, and much of the published source material which is now available has also resulted from state- or city-state-based studies of sumptuary laws.

Nonetheless, the circumscribed focus of these studies is problematic. Like the parable of the blind men and the elephant (where one man feels the trunk and says the creature is a tree, while another feels the tail and says it is a rope), the limited scope of these individual studies has led to contradictory conclusions. Sumptuary laws are directed primarily at men; sumptuary laws are directed primarily at women. They represent the efforts of the nobility to control the bourgeoisie; they represent the efforts of the bourgeoisie to restrain the nobility; they emanate from the king in an attempt to control the bourgeoisie, the nobility, or both. Sumptuary laws are rarely/never/always enforced. Their primary motive is anti-luxury, economic, mercantilist, paternalistic, moralistic, religious, and so on. And indeed, all of these conclusions are accurate for one or another time or place—but none of them are universally true. The only way to discover the universals is to examine sumptuary law on a macro level, to treat it as an integrated whole with regional and chronological variations.

Comparative Views

Sumptuary law is an ideal subject for comparative study on a global basis, since it is a widespread phenomenon, both geographically and chronologically: there have been attempts to regulate the display of consumption in many societies, including ancient Greece and Rome, Imperial China, Tokugawa Japan, the Islamic world, Aztec Mexico, and Colonial America. I have limited this article to the earliest post-

---

medieval dress in terms of color, fabric, mottos, heraldry, and so on, has paid surprisingly little attention to sumptuary law.

24 See the articles in Muzzarelli and Campanini, *Disciplinare il lusso*, for summaries of scholarship on sumptuary law as of 2003.

25 Examples include Bulst, "Zum Problem städtischer und territorialer"; Jaritz, "Kleidung und Prestige-Konkurrenz."

26 See notes 1 and 3 above.

classical sumptuary laws of Western Europe, specifically the laws which appeared in the territories of Spain, Italy, France, and England in the thirteenth and fourteenth centuries.[27] This was the formative period for the templates of European sumptuary law on which most later laws were based; by the fifteenth century, the meaning and uses of these legal templates had changed considerably, and would do so even more in later centuries. I have further limited myself to clothing-related laws, in part because they are the most common, but also because they offer a way of investigating the drastic changes in the meanings of dress and its materials in this period.[28] I have also chosen to study the form and content of the laws themselves, and not the preambles attached to them, which require a different sort of analysis because they are filled with rhetorical tropes, many of which are common to sumptuary laws in general, and they often reflect contemporary "moral panics" that have little to do with the subject of the laws. In short, the preambles to sumptuary laws deserve a comparative study of their own, which space does not permit here.

Cross-regional comparisons of medieval sumptuary laws raise many questions that have not yet been explored. Why was there more legislation of sumptuary law in one area than in another: hundreds of laws in the Italian city-states versus single-digit numbers in England and in northern France, for example? Why was there no sumptuary law in Flanders until 1497, despite the fact that Flanders was a center of commerce and industry, boasting many powerful and rich members of the urban elite? Judging from the visual evidence, Flanders was also a center of elaborate fashion and rapid fashion change, making the absence of sumptuary law even more intriguing.[29] Comparative investigation also raises many questions related to gender. The Italian city-states targeted women almost exclusively in their sumptuary laws, and the laws in Germany and southern France were often

27 On the inevitable anachronism of these geo-political categories, see note 1. In this article, "medieval" sumptuary laws refer specifically to the laws which fall within these chronological limitations, for the reasons noted above. There is one known twelfth-century law restricting the wearing of fur, enacted in Genoa in 1157: Killerby, *Sumptuary Law in Italy*, 24; Stuard, *Gilding the Market*, 4. There was also thought to have been a sumptuary law enacted in France by Louis VIII in 1229, but Heller has proven that it did not exist: "Anxiety, Hierarchy, and Appearance," 317, n. 23.

28 See below on the relation of sumptuary laws to the development of the so-called "Western fashion system" during this period.

29 On the chronology of Flemish sumptuary law, see Buylaert, DeClerq, and Dumolyn, "Sumptuary Legislation." For visual evidence of the fashionableness of Flemish dress, see, for example, the Magic Carole in *Lancelot du Lac*, illustrated in Hainaut, 1344 (Paris, Bibliothèque nationale de France, MS fr. 122, fol. 137v), or almost any illustration in the *Roman d'Alexandre* illustrated in Flanders ca. 1340 (Oxford: Bodleian Library, Ms. Bodl. 264).

aimed at women, too—so far as can be known from the sparsely published evidence—while in other places the laws were directed primarily, although not exclusively, at men. Is there a connection between the power of municipal governments and sumptuary laws which focus on women?[30] More generally, is it possible to relate the ways in which gender is targeted to a specific system of government?[31] The first step towards answers to these questions is to compare the structure and content of the laws.

Patterns of Difference

The earliest European sumptuary laws can be roughly divided into two groups according to their structure, content, and chronology (see Table 2). One group, the French and English laws, show striking similarities in chronology, with gaps in both cases of a century or more between the first sumptuary laws and subsequent ones. Two extensive sumptuary laws were enacted in France, in 1279 and 1294 respectively; the next substantive law was passed in 1485. In England there was a limited sumptuary law in 1337 and an extensively detailed one in 1363; the law of 1363 was repealed in the next Parliament, and the next sumptuary law was not enacted until 1463, although unsuccessful attempts were made to pass similar laws in the intervening years. The structural similarities are equally striking. In both the French and English laws, the actual objects being regulated, though they may be specified, are secondary to a detailed focus on permissions and prohibitions expressed in terms of status categories, which are defined in both cases by a combination of social status and income.[32] The English law mentions approximately thirty socio-economic categories, from knights with a certain income on down to oxherds; it ignores the upper nobility entirely. At the top are two categories of knight, divided by wealth, followed by two categories of esquire,

30 See Lansing, *Passion and Order*. Lansing suggests that the communes were in the process of creating their own ideal democratic societies, and were thus very concerned with sources of disorder, including their own violent emotions, which they then projected onto women.

31 This is a suggestion originally made by Hughes ("Sumptuary Law and Social Relations," 73–74), but no conclusive answer has been reached.

32 The similarity between these two groups of laws is perhaps not accidental, as suggested by an undated memorandum addressed to Edward I at the end of the thirteenth century. The anonymous writer suggests that a law similar to the recent French sumptuary laws would be an effective way of raising money for the war, and supplies possible details based on the French laws. There is no evidence that this memorandum ever reached Edward, and it is clearly meant as a project for taxation, but it does suggest that the French laws were known in England. See Langlois, "Project for Taxation."

Table 2. A Comparative Survey of Western European Sumptuary Laws, Thirteenth and Fourteenth Centuries*

	SPAIN	ITALY	FRANCE	ENGLAND
Gender: directed at	primarily men	women	primarily men	primarily men
Material details	ornamentation and color	ornamentation and cut	cloth and cost	cloth and cost, some ornament
Number of status categories	variable	n/a	30+	±25
Income level included for categorization	no	no	yes	yes
Classes affected	variable; primarily nobility and knights, some bourgeoisie	knights, doctors, lawyers	aristocrats, knights, upper bourgeoisie; no lower classes	knights down through peasants; no nobility
Enacted by	king	towns	king	Parliament
Enforced by/via	unknown; fines specified	fines and an enforcement apparatus	unknown; fines specified	no
Knightly classes	mentioned most often	specifically excluded	described in detail	described in detail

* This table is illustrative, not exhaustive, and it excludes many regions of Europe that regularly enacted sumptuary laws, such as German-speaking lands. Information on sumptuary laws repeatedly enacted in the territories of Spain and Italy has been derived and synthesized from Gonzalez Arce, *Apariencia*; Sempere y Guariños, *Historia del Luxo*; Rainey, "Sumptuary Legislation"; Killerby, *Sumptuary Law in Italy*. In France and England, where the laws were not repeatedly enacted during this period, data is limited to the French law of 1294 (Heller, "Anxiety, Hierarchy, and Appearance") and the English law of 1363 (see the introduction to *Edward III, 1351–1377*, ed. Ormrod).

two categories of clergy, and two categories of urban dwellers, all divided similarly.[33] There are also three lower ranks, of which the lowest specifically includes carters, plowmen, wagoners, oxherds, cowherds, shepherds, pigherds, threshers, and so on. Careful and specific equivalencies have been set up between groups. Urban bourgeoisie on the one hand, and the "esquires and *gentils gens*" on the other, are allowed the same clothing and ornaments if the income of the bourgeois is five times that of the esquire; meanwhile, upper clergy are equivalent to the lower rank of knights and lower clergy to the lower ranks of both esquires and bourgeoisie. Even the income qualifications show subtle class distinctions: knights' income is measured in marks, which was a money of account rather than actual specie, and their income was to be from "lands or rents"; the income of the esquires is also specified as "land and rents" but measured in pounds; while the clergy's income is simply stated as marks per year. The incomes of the bourgeoisie are measured in pounds, but not calculated annually. Instead, the law specifies that they must "clearly" (*clerement*) possess goods and chattels of the appropriate value. There is a certain amount of material detail, though far less than that found in the Spanish and especially Italian laws. Particularly in the lower categories of society, the descriptions of forbidden items are rather general, although the maximum price of the cloth which may be worn by each group across the spectrum is finely graded, with permitted prices differing between categories by as little as half a mark per ell.[34]

It is somewhat more difficult to summarize the patterns discernible in the French laws.[35] Like the English regulations, they stipulate the maximum cost of permissible cloth, but the French regulations also prescribe the maximum number of *robes*, or sets of garments, permitted per social category per year, and the groupings are not always parallel. For example, a baron with an annual revenue of 6,000 *livres tournois* may have four sets of robes, spending a maximum of 25 *sols tournois* per year, while a prelate (of unspecified income) may use the same cloth but is only permitted two sets of robes per year. As may be seen from this example, the construction of socio-economic categories is remarkably complex, as is the breakdown of permissible expense. By my count there are eight separate prices per *aune* (a unit of measure) listed, with a wealthy *bourgeois* being permit-

33 This law marks the first official appearance of "esquire" as a recognized status: Coss, "Knights, Esquires, and the Origin of Social Gradation in England," 155–56.

34 An *ell* is a unit of measurement roughly equivalent to a yard, as is the *aune* used in French laws.

35 I have used the law of 1294 for purposes of this discussion: it is quite similar to the law of 1279, but lists a larger number of ranks. See Heller, "Anxiety, Hierarchy, and Appearance," for tabular breakdowns of both laws.

ted material costing 12½ *sols tournois* per *aune*, exactly half of the 25 *sols* per *aune* permitted to the highest ranks. However, these early French laws are unique in that they contain no material details of clothing, cloth or ornamentation at all; it is the number of garments and the cost of materials that is at issue. Indeed, the law is aimed primarily at the nobility, from dukes down to *vavassors*, or sub-feudatories, who are ranked even below the bourgeoisie. Only two ranks are accorded to the latter: those with income of over 2,000 *livres tournois*, and those with income below that figure, with a separate category in each rank for their wives.[36] By contrast, the upper ranks are broken down with particular precision. One-fourth of the categories, eight ranks, are devoted to the clergy alone; an even greater proportion of the categories are devoted to the "knightly" ranks: there are ten different gradations covering knights, bannerets, squires, and their companions (eleven including the *vavassors*).

Although women were clearly not an afterthought in this law, they make up a relatively small proportion of the total categories: six ranks, less than one-fifth of the total, are devoted to women. There are three categories of wives (in the higher ranks and in the two categories of *bourgeois*) and, unusually, three exclusively female categories, confined to the higher ranks alone (*dame*, *damoiselle*, and *chatelaine*), which are not dependent on marital status. And while the wealthy *bourgeois* mentioned above was limited to fabric costing 12½ *sols* per *aune*, his wife was permitted to spend up to 16 *sols* per *aune*; no such gender gap exists for the higher ranks.

The early sumptuary laws enacted in England and France, then, itemize rank and socio-economic categories with great specificity, while treating the material objects in question with far less detail. The structure of the early laws in the other contemporary group, exemplified by the Spanish and Italian laws, is the inverse. Here, the objects rather than the status categories are itemized in detail, concentrating on specific types of clothing, ornamentation, or color.[37] And unlike the sporadically enacted laws of England and France, these laws began in the mid-thirteenth century and thereafter were passed repeatedly. Given the resultant number of laws, their content cannot be compared as systemically as that of the smaller sample of French and English legislation. Still, comparisons are possible if we focus on two locales which typify the whole: the laws of Castile and the laws of Florence as the primary Spanish and Italian examples respectively.

---

36 The *livre tournois* was not actual specie but a money of account, comprising 20 *sous/sols/solidi tournois*.

37 See note 1 above, on the clause entitled *de abottonaturis* in a mid-fourteenth century Florentine law.

Spanish sumptuary law is obsessively focused on banning certain kinds of ornamentation. For example, in the earliest legislation, which emanated from Jaime I of Aragon in 1234, there are prohibitions against clothing which has been cut, or which trembles (*vestas incisas* [. . .] *vel trepatas*)—that is, clothing with slashes or possibly dags—striped clothing, orphreys, fringe, and so on.[38] In addition, the wearing of fur which has been cut or worked over (*aliam pellum fractam, vel recoctam*) was prohibited, and whole ermine or otter furs were permitted only as trimming on hoods and sleeves.[39] Other things which clothing may not display include gold and silver, various kinds of gold and silver thread and embroideries, all very specifically described, and several other kinds of fur. Another area of detail, which is almost unique to the Spanish laws, is a focus on color, as exemplified by this passage from the Cortes de Valladolid of Castile in the mid-thirteenth century: "no squire may wear white furs or scarlet stockings; or wear scarlet, green, dark brown, pale green, brown, orange, pink, blood-red, or any dark-colored clothing."[40] Similarly, in a slightly later compilation from Castile, the *Siete Partidas*, there is a list of colors (red, dark yellow, green, and purple) which knights should wear when young because they confer lightheartedness (*diesen alegría*), and a proscription against darker colors because they bring sadness.[41]

The social categories of Spanish sumptuary law are also described with some specificity. Although there are some references to different ranks of city dwellers, it is on the nobility that the thirteenth-century laws find their focus. The highest nobility—the king's brothers, dukes, marquesses, princes, counts, and viscounts—are the *ricos homes*; the king is actually included in many of these laws, albeit in ways which set him apart from the *ricos homes*, including his brothers,

38 Dags are ornamental shapes cut into the borders of garments, made possible by the heavily fulled broadcloth developed in the later Middle Ages, which did not fray when cut or notched. Dagging was increasingly popular from the thirteenth century on, and considered very fashionable; at the same time, it was often associated with marginal groups and outsiders. See Denny-Brown, "Rips and Slits," and Friedman, "Iconography of Dagged Clothing." Orphreys are bands of rich embroidery, usually done with gold thread, and most often used on ecclesiastical clothing.

39 Transcribed in Juan Sempere y Guariños, *Historia del Luxo*, 72–73. All translations are mine unless otherwise indicated.

40 Real Academia, *Cortes de los antiguos reinos*, XIV, (22), 59: "ningun escudero non traya penna blanca ni calcas descarlata, nin uista escarlata nin uista verde nin bruneta nin pres nin morete nin narange nin rrosada nin sanguina ninningun panno tinto."

41 Castile, *Les siete partidas*, 211–12. There are similar laws in some of the Italian city-states, requiring the wearing of bright colors to dispel sadness or increase prestige. Muzzarelli gives examples from Reggio Emilia and Ferrara ("Una società nello specchio," 26).

to whom certain laws and prohibitions were specifically directed.[42] Below these are the lower nobility, including noble knights, non-noble knights, and even bourgeois knights, with various urban categories below them. As in France, and to a lesser degree in England, the categories of knights increased over the thirteenth and fourteenth centuries.

Aside from their chronology, what the representative Italian laws have in common with the Spanish is a preoccupation with the details of dress and ornamentation, carried to an even greater extreme. For example, the Florentine statutes of 1322–25 prohibited (under penalty of a high fine) "clothes with cut, worked, or superimposed images or likenesses of trees or flowers, animals or birds, or any other figures," while the Florentine Pragmatica of 1356, which contained the regulation on buttons quoted at the beginning of this essay, also contained detailed specifications governing the conditions under which it was permissible to wear one "single-layered fringe [*fregiaturam fregii simplice*] with gold or silver but without enamel or anything else ornamenting it."[43] Moreover, this ornament could not be larger than a certain size and it could only be worn in certain places on certain garments, each one of which is specified. It is also specified that this type of fringe may not be worn on

> robes which are *dimecçate*, that is single or double samite or made of samite and wool cloth or samite and silken cloth or camel's hair [. . .] nor on any tucked [?*rimbocchatura*] cloth of camel's hair or sindon [light silk] or ermine or rabbit [. . .] except that tucked cloth may be worn with impunity over a mantel.[44]

This level of detail is devoted only to clothing and ornamentation, however; when it comes to social classifications, the Italian laws are notably concise. In contrast to all the other laws we have examined, knights, doctors, and lawyers are the only categories mentioned, and then only to exempt them from the laws to which everyone else is subject. More correctly, I should say the *wives* of knights, doctors, and lawyers are exempt, since the Italian sumptuary laws were directed primarily at women, in contrast to most other European sumptuary laws. Men are mentioned occasionally, and there were even a few prosecutions of Florentine men in the

---

42 Note the distinction between *ricos homes*, who are the uppermost level of the nobility, up to and including the king's brothers, and *hombres ricos*, who are simply rich men. Gonzalez Arce, *Apariencia y poder*, 133.

43 Statutes of 1322–25, from Rainey, "Sumptuary Legislation," 97. The Pragmatica of 1356 is reproduced in full on pages 667–93.

44 Rainey, "Sumptuary Legislation," 668–69.

1340s for wearing pleated garments, which seem to have been a cause of particular anxiety for both women and men. But essentially, the laws concerned the clothing and ornaments of women.[45]

Commonalities: Enforcement and Effectiveness, Status and Social Change

Having examined some of the differences in content and structure among the earliest medieval sumptuary laws, it is time to explore some of the common features which emerge when they are considered as a group. Two areas are of particular interest: questions of effectiveness and enforcement, approached comparatively, offer insight into the nature and function of the laws themselves; while a comprehensive view of the treatment of social rank opens up a number of perspectives into changes in social dynamics.

Almost without exception, European sumptuary laws were accompanied by weak, inconsistent, or nonexistent enforcement, followed by complaints that the laws had been impossible to enforce, coupled with repeated and often increasing attempts to pass new laws, which would prove unenforceable in their turn. Although such complaints are clearly rhetorical tropes, and appear even in the preamble to the English law of 1463 (when there had been no prior laws in effect for a century), they must still be subject to careful scrutiny.[46] They cannot simply be regarded as evidence that sumptuary laws were intended to be instrumental, did not affect behavior, and therefore were failures. When sumptuary laws are approached on their own terms, it becomes clear that their paradoxes and ambivalences are a function of their symbolic importance and idealism. Rather than being indications of failure, these inconsistencies are valuable clues to the meanings ascribed to these laws and evidence of the resistance and contestation which invariably arose in response to their enactment and publication.

One indication of the laws' symbolic nature is precisely the fact that enforcement efforts ranged from nonexistent to ambivalent; nowhere do we see a pattern

45 Gender is an obvious target for the kind of comparative approach which I am suggesting, but at this point it seems to me that there is not yet enough information available to undertake such a study. Until we have gathered a substantial number of the municipal laws from southern Italy and southern France, which may well have been focused on women, it is difficult to make any systematic comparisons. And, as with the other areas of comparison which I have suggested, a representative sample of the sumptuary laws from German lands, both municipal and imperial, is sorely needed.

46 Doda, "'Saide Monstrous Hose,'" 178.

of consistently enforced obedience.[47] Among the laws we have just examined, the English law contains no specified punishment or enforcement mechanism; while the French and Spanish laws contain schedules of fines, in some cases quite hefty, but, again, no enforcement mechanism. During this early period there is little in the known records of England, France, or the Christian areas of Spain to suggest that people were changing their behavior in order to avoid contravening the sumptuary laws—indeed, it is possible that we are more aware of the existence of these laws than many of the groups who would have been affected by them.[48]

This is not the case in the Italian city-states, where there are records of prosecutions, as well as documented forms of resistance and efforts to circumvent the laws.[49] Nonetheless, even here the laws were ambivalently enforced and the prosecutions relatively few. Sometimes, the laws gave rise to a licensing system: in Florence, for example, as early as 1290, we find a reference to registering garments and recording a payment, a kind of commodity tax or *gabella*, for the privilege of wearing forbidden objects. But this system, too, was practiced inconsistently: licensing fees were more prevalent when the commune was in need of money, while at other times the fines were clearly intended as actual punishments. Nonetheless, the practice of paid exemptions continued to the point where, in 1373, what had been *ornamenta vetita*, "forbidden ornaments," were now *gabellata*, taxable.[50] And although stricter laws, permitting no exemptions, did make a brief reappearance later in the century, the licensing system ultimately prevailed.[51]

---

47 This is not a universally held view; the evidence of enforcement is sufficiently patchy that it has been variously interpreted as evidence both for and against regular enforcement. Killerby, for example, who refers to Italian sumptuary law as a "manifest failure," nonetheless believes that the Italian laws were generally enforced, and that they were passed repeatedly precisely because they were being obeyed: as individuals continually found ways to get around the laws, the laws required continual rewriting: *Sumptuary Law in Italy*, chapter 7, "Problems of Enforcement and the Failure of Sumptuary Law."

48 Attempts have been made to compare wills and inventories with the sumptuary laws in force in a given area, e.g., Burkholder, "Threads Bared," but I find that the documents do not consistently give enough information to firmly fix the person's status according to the laws.

49 See Sacchetti, *Novelle*, 137, in which he describes some of the ways that women evaded officials attempting to enforce the laws. According to Rainey, Sacchetti based his *novella* on the actual experiences of one of the *uffiziali delle donne*, the "women's officials" charged with enforcing the law. See Rainey, "Sumptuary Legislation," 234.

50 Rainey, "Sumptuary Legislation," 206.

51 The licensing/money-raising aspect of the laws appears elsewhere as well: compare, for example, the statute in Munich which required a man who wished to wear colored shoes to supply an archer to the city. Bulst, "Les ordonnances somptuaires," 779.

If sumptuary laws were indeed largely ineffective in the instrumental sense, as measured by enforcement and compliance, the effectiveness of symbolic legislation is not related to enforcement or to the impact of the legislation on behavior. Rather, its purpose was to demonstrate or affirm certain values, to elevate the values of a particular group, to create or underscore group or national identities.[52] For example, in ancient Rome, rulers enacted sumptuary laws to demonstrate that they were still in touch with the traditional virtues, the *mos maiorum* of their ancestors.[53] Given that another common trope in the preambles to medieval sumptuary laws is a lament that the traditional virtues of an earlier golden age have vanished, it is likely that this was one of the major motivating forces behind the repeated enactments of sumptuary law in the thirteenth and fourteenth centuries, for kings and municipal governments alike.

But if the primary meaning of sumptuary law—to lawmakers and citizens alike—was as a symbolic statement about virtue and social order, it is clear that the common conception of sumptuary law as a means of social control, or restriction of goods to one or another class, must be completely re-examined.

The other common characteristic which is immediately noticeable in looking at Western European sumptuary laws as a group is that all are focused in one way or another on knights and the bourgeoisie. The nobility may or may not be involved; the lower classes may or may not be involved; but the laws always include knights and urban merchants and professionals. The focus may have been on strengthening the knightly ranks, as in the Spanish laws; knights may have been exempted from the laws, as in Italy; knights may have been made subject to the laws through a carefully graded and increasing series of ranks, as in England and France. Urban populations, too, are targeted. They may be divided into groups by income, as in England and France; referenced as comprising the *bourgeoisie* (France); specified as merchants and/or the wealthy (England and Spain); or inclusive of doctors and lawyers (Italy). And one or both groups may also be driving the actual legislative process (England and Italy). But, regardless of the shape which their involvement takes, the knightly ranks and the bourgeoisie were always at the center of thirteenth- and fourteenth-century sumptuary law.

Indeed, because the focus on these two groups remains constant, changes over time are more easily visible. One of the most obvious is the change in the number of ranks, on all levels. For example, in the French sumptuary law of 1279, there

52 Gusfield, "Moral Passage," 228.

53 Zanda, *Fighting Hydra-Like Luxury*, 159. Compare Diane Owen Hughes's suggestion that urban sumptuary laws might be seen as "a symbol of republican virtue": "Sumptuary Law and Social Relations," 74.

are fourteen categories listed. The only knightly rank listed is *escuier* (squire or esquire), and it is divided into two groups by income level. Fifteen years later, when the second law was enacted, the total number of categories had increased from fourteen to thirty-two, of which eleven were gradations of knightly status. In England, the sumptuary law of 1363 contains the first mention of the category of "esquire."[54] In, Spain from the thirteenth century on, there were a variety of levels within the noble knightly groups, with the knights who carry banners (*rico home que haya pendón*) being the highest status, and further distinctions among knights who may wear sashes (*caballeros de la banda*) and non- or less noble knights.[55] In the fourteenth century, urban knights (*caballeria villana*: knightly members of the bourgeoisie) became more powerful, though they had existed for some time; and here, too, additional gradients were added as time went on.[56] Once again, Italy appears to be the exception, since the only social categories mentioned—with the exception of servants and slaves—are those listed as exempt. Despite the lack of the subtle gradations found elsewhere, however, the Italian laws share with all the others a focus on the knightly and professional classes, since these were precisely the groups exempted from the laws.[57]

All of the bodies of sumptuary laws we have considered, whether royally promulgated or stemming from a municipal government, display an intense focus on the interzone shared by the knightly class and the upper bourgeoisie, including professionals such as doctors and lawyers, as well as the lower nobility in many cases. The formation of this status bracket into a relatively self-aware group is often described as the rise of the "urban elite" (though I prefer the wider English term "gentry") and it has been a subject of much scholarly interest in recent decades.[58] And while sumptuary laws have not been overlooked entirely in the resultant studies, they have not been considered on a comparative basis. Once again, a number of avenues remain to be explored. For example, outside of Eng-

54 Similarly, the 1463 sumptuary law contained the first use of "gentleman" as a specific rank.

55 Gonzalez Arce, *Apariencia y poder.*

56 Although the articles in Asenjo-Gonzalez, *Urban Elites*, are primarily devoted to urban elites in the Christian Spanish kingdoms of the fifteenth century, they show, if only by implication, the increase and permeability of social categories in the previous centuries.

57 Catherine Kovesi Killerby has summarized the exempt statuses listed in the group of laws which she studied; out of a total of nearly two hundred mentions, well over half are of knights, doctors, and judges; counting mentions of related statuses such as "magistrate," the proportion is even higher: *Sumptuary Law in Italy*, 85 (Table 4.2).

58 See Coss, *Origins of the English Gentry*; and Lachaud, "La 'formation de la gentry,'" for the history of the construct of the gentry in the English context. Dumolyn, "Later Medieval and

land, the rise of the gentry is often thought to have occurred in the fifteenth and sixteenth centuries. While the dynamics may have become more obvious or taken on a different character in later centuries, the attention paid to this very group in the thirteenth- and fourteenth-century sumptuary laws suggests that the chronology deserves another look.

The focus on the gentry also helps to elucidate the frictions and contestations which were taking place *within* this grouping, as exemplified by the history of the English sumptuary law of 1363. Like all Parliamentary legislation at the time, this law originated with a petition to the king from the Commons, a body which was composed of two knights from each shire, and two citizens or burgesses from each city or borough—in other words, a representative group of gentry.[59] And yet it was presumably an equally representative group of gentry who were responsible for the immediate repeal of the statute, in the following Parliament, alleging that the statute had caused great financial harm, though there is no evidence that it was either enforced or obeyed. It seems likely that the immediate repeal, as well as the initial passage of the statute, resulted from conflict among the various segments of the gentry which made up the Commons. The friction and contestation among the various components of the gentry are rarely so clearly demonstrated, but a comparative examination of the multiple iterations and occasional repeals of sumptuary laws offers another way of making those dynamics more visible.[60] A comparative study of the preambles to thirteenth- and fourteenth-century sumptuary laws might offer insights as well.

Another area of evident interest is the connection between sumptuary law and fashion. The emergence of the so-called "Western fashion system" in the later Middle Ages is now generally accepted by most medievalists and fashion scholars.[61]

Early Modern Urban Elites," is an extended discussion of the various terminologies applied to the powerful as a group (such as elite, aristocracy, patriciate), including a consideration of the general application of "gentry."

59 There is an enormous literature on English Parliamentary legislation. For the origin of legislation in the Commons, see, most recently, Dodd, *Justice and Grace*. For the composition of the Commons, see Brown, *Governance of Late Medieval England*, 180.

60 There seem to have been repeals of the Spanish regulations from time to time for similar reasons. Gonzalez Arce gives an example from Madrid in 1339: *Apariencia y poder*, 98.

61 Representative fashion scholars include Laver, *Concise History of Costume*; Wilson, *Adorned in Dreams*; Lipovetsky, *L'Empire de l'éphémère*; Breward, *Culture of Fashion*; Hollander, *Sex and Suits*. Representative medievalists include Heller, *Fashion in Medieval France*; Blanc, "From Battlefield to Court"; Newton, *Fashion in the Age of the Black Prince*; Stuard, *Gilding the Market*; Crane, *Performance of Self*. Early modernists have located the advent of a fashion system somewhat later, generally in the eighteenth century.

This system is generally thought to have been fully developed by the mid-fourteenth century, although medievalists have variously located its beginnings in the thirteenth, fourteenth, or fifteenth centuries.[62] But the chronological connection is clear, and continues to be throughout the lifespan of sumptuary law: as fashion spread down the social scale, sumptuary laws dwindled, disappearing altogether in the eighteenth century at a point when fashion had become both universal and feminized, that is, less serious.[63]

Conclusion

Comparative study of the varieties of medieval sumptuary law can suggest many new approaches through which to understand an array of topics relevant to the mission of *The Medieval Globe*, and part of my purpose in writing this article was to join fellow historians in urging scholars in many fields to consider approaching sumptuary law and its underpinnings comparatively.[64] Examined as a complex phenomenon, and treated with what Carol Symes calls "the dignity of being considered relevant and fully real," it becomes very clear that these laws had no instrumental function and were not really intended to.[65] Sumptuary law has long been considered a "paradox," but we perceive it that way in part because we do not yet understand it.[66] Analyzing sumptuary law as symbolic and aspirational, laden with hidden meanings and contests, is one step towards clarifying our understanding; considering sumptuary law as a global phenomenon with multiple variants, and thus approaching it comparatively, is another.

62 In my view, the system was not manifest until the fourteenth century, when the crucial component of continual rapid change was added. See Wilson, "'De Novo Modo.'"

63 See Belfanti and Giusberti, "Clothing and Social Inequality," who describe fashion as "taking the place" of sumptuary law in establishing social categories (362).

64 See note 3 above.

65 Symes, "When We Talk about Modernity," 717.

66 Hunt, *Governance of the Consuming Passions*, 355.

Bibliography

Manuscript Sources

Oxford, Bodleian Library, MS Bodl. 264
Paris, Bibliothèque nationale de France, MS fr. 122

Primary Sources

Cortes de los antiguos reinos de León y de Castilla. Vol. 1. Madrid: Real Academia de la Historia, 1861.

Edward III, 1351–1377. Edited by W. Mark Ormrod. Vol. 5 of *The Parliament Rolls of Medieval England, 1275–1514*. Woodbridge: Boydell, 2005.

Sacchetti, Franco. *Novelle di Franco Sacchetti*. Edited by Giovanni Silvestri. Vol. 3. Milan, 1815.

Las siete partidas del Don rey Alfonso el Sabio, contejadas con varios codices antiguos por la Real academia de la historia. Vol. 2. Madrid: Real Academia de la Historia, 1807.

Secondary Studies

Anderssen, Eva I. "Foreign Seductions: Sumptuary Laws, Consumption, and National Identity in Early Modern Sweden." In *Fashionable Encounters: Perspectives and Trends in Textile and Dress in the Early Modern Nordic World*, edited by Tove Engelhardt Mathiassen, Marie-Louise Nosch, and Maj Ringgard, 15–30. Oxford: Oxford Books, 2014.

Asenjo-Gonzalez, Maria, ed. *Urban Elites and Aristocratic Behaviour in the Spanish Kingdoms at the End of the Middle Ages*. Turnhout: Brepols, 2013.

Baldwin, Frances E. *Sumptuary Legislation and Personal Regulation in England*. Baltimore: Johns Hopkins University Press, 1926.

Baudrillart, Henri. *Histoire du luxe privé et public depuis l'antiquité jusqu'à nos jours*. Vol. 3, *Le Moyen âge et la Renaissance*. 2nd ed. Paris: Hachette et Cie, 1881.

Beebe, Barton. "Intellectual Property Law and the Sumptuary Code." *Harvard Law Review* 123 (2010): 810–89.

Belfanti, Carlo Marco, and Fabio Giusberti. "Clothing and Social Inequality in Early Modern Europe: Introductory Remarks." *Continuity and Change* 15 (2000): 359–65.

Blanc, Odile. "From Battlefield to Court: The Invention of Fashion in the Fourteenth Century." In *Encountering Medieval Textiles and Dress: Objects, Texts, Images*, edited by Désirée Koslin and Janet E. Snyder, 157–72. New York: Palgrave Macmillan, 2002.

Breward, Christopher. *The Culture of Fashion: A New History of Fashionable Dress.* Manchester: Manchester University Press, 1995.

Brown, A. L. *The Governance of Late Medieval England, 1272–1461.* Stanford: Stanford University Press, 1989.

Bulst, Neithard. "La legislazione suntuaria in francia (secoli XIII–XVIII)." In *Disciplinare il lusso: la legislazione suntuaria in Italia e in Europa tra medieoevo ed età moderna*, edited by Maria Giuseppina Muzzarelli and Antonella Campanini, 121–36. Rome: Carocci, 2003.

——. "Les ordonnances somptuaires en Allemagne: expression de l'ordre urbain (XIVe–XVIe siècle)." In *Comptes rendus des séances de l'année,* 771–84. Paris: Académie des Inscriptions et Belles-Lettres, 1993.

——. "Zum Problem städtischer und territorialer Kleider-, Aufwands- und Luxusgesetzgebung in Deutschland (13. - Mitte 16. Jahrhundert)." In *Renaissance du pouvoir législatif et genèse de l'État,* edited by André Gouron and Albert Rigaudière, 29–57. Montpellier: [Société d'histoire du droit et des institutions des anciens pays de droit écrit], 1988.

Burkholder, Kristen M. "Threads Bared: Dress and Textiles in Late Medieval English Wills." *Medieval Clothing and Textiles* 1 (2005): 133–53.

Buylaert, Frederik, Wim DeClerq, and Jan Dumolyn. "Sumptuary Legislation, Material Culture and the Semiotics of 'Vivre Noblement' in the County of Flanders (14th–16th Centuries)." *Social History* 36 (2011): 393–417.

Coss, Peter R. "Knights, Esquires, and the Origin of Social Gradation in England." *Transactions of the Royal Historical Society,* 6th ser., 5 (1995): 155–77.

——. *The Origins of the English Gentry.* Cambridge: Cambridge University Press, 2003.

Crane, Susan. *The Performance of Self: Ritual, Clothing, and Identity During the Hundred Years War.* Philadelphia: University of Pennsylvania Press, 2002.

Denny-Brown, Andrea. *Fashioning Change: The Trope of Clothing in High- and Late-Medieval England.* Columbus: Ohio State University Press, 2012.

——. "Rips and Slits: "The Torn Garment and the Medieval Self." In *Clothing Culture, 1350–1650,* edited by Catherine Richardson, 223–37. Aldershot: Ashgate, 2004.

Doda, Hilary. "'Saide Monstrous Hose': Compliance, Transgression and English Sumptuary Law to 1533." *Textile History* 45 (2014): 171–91.

Dodd, Gwilym. *Justice and Grace: Private Petitioning and the English Parliament in the Late Middle Ages.* Oxford: Oxford University Press, 2007.

Dumolyn, Jan. "Later Medieval and Early Modern Urban Elites: Social Categories and Social Dynamics." In *Urban Elites and Aristocratic Behaviour in the Spanish Kingdoms at the End of the Middle Ages,* edited by Maria Asenjo-Gonzalez, 3–18. Turnhout: Brepols, 2013.

Frick, Carole Collier. *Dressing Renaissance Florence: Families, Fortunes & Fine Clothing.* Baltimore: Johns Hopkins University Press, 2002.

Friedman, John Block. "The Iconography of Dagged Clothing and Its Reception by Moralist Writers." *Medieval Clothing and Textiles* 9 (2013): 121–38.

Goddard, Jennifer. "Anticipated Impact of the 2009 Four Corners Raid and Arrests." *Crime, Law, and Social Change* 56 (2011): 175–88.

González Arce, José Damián. *Apariencia y poder: la legislación suntuaria castellana en los siglos XIII y XV.* Jaén: Universidad de Jaén, 1998.

Greenfield, Kent Roberts. *Sumptuary Law in Nürnberg: A Study in Paternal Government.* Baltimore: Johns Hopkins University Press, 1918.

Gusfield, Joseph R. "Moral Passage: The Symbolic Process in Public Designations of Deviance." *Social Problems* 15, no. 2 (1967): 175–88.

——. "On Legislating Morals: The Symbolic Process of Designating Deviance." *California Law Review* 56 (January 1968): 54–73.

Hayward, Maria. *Rich Apparel: Clothing and the Law in Henry VIII's England.* Aldershot: Ashgate, 2009.

Heller, Sarah-Grace. "Anxiety, Hierarchy, and Appearance in Thirteenth-Century Sumptuary Laws and the *Roman de la rose.*" *French Historical Studies* 27 (Spring 2004): 311–48.

——. *Fashion in Medieval France.* Cambridge: Brewer, 2007.

——. "Limiting Yardage and Changes of Clothing in Thirteenth-Century France, Languedoc, and Italy." In *Medieval Fabrications: Dress, Textiles, Cloth Work, and Other Cultural Imaginings,* edited by E. Jane Burns, 122–36. New York: Palgrave Macmillan, 2004.

Hollander, Anne. *Sex and Suits.* New York: Knopf, 1994.

Hughes, Diane Owen. "Distinguishing Signs: Ear-Rings, Jews and Franciscan Rhetoric in the Italian Renaissance City." *Past & Present* 112 (1986): 3–59.

——. "Regulating Women's Fashion." In *Silences of the Middle Ages,* edited by Christine Klapisch-Zuber, 136–58. (Vol. 2 of *A History of Women in the West,* edited by Georges Duby and Michelle Perrot.) Cambridge: Cambridge University Press, 1992.

——. "Sumptuary Law and Social Relations in Renaissance Italy." In *Disputes and Settlements: Law and Human Relations in the West,* edited by John Bossy, 69–100. Cambridge: Cambridge University Press, 1983.

Hunt, Alan. *Governance of the Consuming Passions: A History of Sumptuary Law.* New York: St. Martin's Press, 1996.

Jaritz, Gerhard. "Kleidung und Prestige-Konkurrenz: unterschiedliche Identitäten in der städtischen Gesellschaft unter Normierungszwängen." *Saeculum: Jahrbuch für Universalgeschichte* 44 (1993): 8–31.

Killerby, Catherine Kovesi. "Heralds of a Well-Instructed Mind: Nicola Sanuti's Defence of Women and Their Clothes." *Renaissance Studies* 13 (1999): 255–82.

——. "Practical Problems in the Enforcement of Italian Sumptuary Law, 1200–1500." In *Crime, Society and the Law in Renaissance Italy*, edited by Trevor Dean and Kate Lowe, 99–120. Cambridge: Cambridge University Press, 1994.

——. *Sumptuary Law in Italy, 1200–1500*. Oxford Historical Monographs. Oxford: Clarendon Press, 2002.

Lachaud, Frédérique, " La 'formation de la gentry,' XIe–XIVe siècle: un nouveau concept historiographique?" In *Histoires d'outre-Manche: tendances récentes de l'historiographie britannique*, edited by Frédérique Lachaud, Isabelle Lescent-Giles, and Francois-Joseph Ruggiu, 13–36. Paris: Presses de l'Université de Paris-Sorbonne, 2001.

Langlois, Charles V. "Project for Taxation Presented to Edward I." *English Historical Review* 4 (1889): 517–21.

Lansing, Carol. *Passion and Order: Restraint of Grief in the Medieval Italian Communes*. Ithaca: Cornell University Press, 2008.

Laver, James. *A Concise History of Costume*. London: Thames and Hudson, 1969.

Lemire, Beverly, and Giorgio Riello. "East and West: Textiles and Fashion in Early Modern Europe." *Journal of Social History* 41 (2008): 887–916.

Lipovetsky, Gilles. *L'Empire de l'éphémère: la mode et son destin dans les sociétés modernes.* Paris: Gallimard, 1987.

Miller, Robert D. *Chieftains of the Highland Clans: A History of Israel in the Twelfth and Eleventh Centuries B.C.* Eugene: Wipf & Stock, 2012.

Moeti, Kabelo, and T. Khalo. *Public Finance Fundamentals*. Cape Town, South Africa: Juta, 2007.

Muzzarelli, Maria Giuseppina. "Una società nello specchio della legislazione suntuaria: il caso dell'Emilia-Romagna." In *Disciplinare il lusso: la legislazione suntuaria in Italia e in Europa tra medieoevo ed età moderna,* edited by Maria Giuseppina Muzzarelli and Antonella Campanini, 17–32. Rome: Carocci, 2003.

——. "Reconciling the Privilege of a Few with the Common Good." *Journal of Medieval and Early Modern Studies* 39 (2009): 597–617.

Muzzarelli, Maria Giuseppina, and Antonella Campanini, eds. *Disciplinare il lusso: La legislazione suntuaria in Italia e in Europa tra medieoevo ed età moderna.* Rome: Carocci, 2003.

Newton, Stella Mary. *Fashion in the Age of the Black Prince: A Study of the Years 1340–1365.* Woodbridge: Boydell, 1980; repr. 1999.

Ormrod, W. Mark. "Introduction, Edward III: October 1363." In *Parliament Rolls of Medieval England*, edited by Chris Given-Wilson et. al. <http://www.british-history.ac.uk/no-series/parliament-rolls-medieval/october-1363> [accessed 15 September 2015].

Page, Agnès. *Vêtir le prince: tissus et couleurs à la Cour de Savoie, 1427–1447*. Lausanne: Section d'histoire, Faculté des lettres, Université de Lausanne, 1993.

Phillips, Kim M. "Masculinities and the Medieval English Sumptuary Laws" *Gender & History* 19 (2007): 22–42.

Piponnier, Françoise. *Costume et vie sociale; la cour d'Anjou XIVe–XVe siècle*. Paris: Mouton, 1970.

Rainey, Ronald. "Sumptuary Legislation in Renaissance Florence." PhD diss., Columbia University, 1985.

Riello, Giorgio, and Prasannan Parthasarathi. *The Spinning World: A Global History of Cotton Textiles, 1200–1850*. Oxford: Oxford University Press, 2009.

Roche, Daniel. *La culture des apparences: une histoire du vêtement (XVIIe–XVIIIe siècle)*. Paris: Fayard, 1989.

Schick, Irvin Cemil. "Some Islamic Determinants of Dress and Personal Appearance in Southwest Asia." *Khil'a* 3 (2007–9): 25–53.

Sempere y Guarinos, Juan. *Historia del Luxo y de las Leyes Suntuarias de España*. Vol. 1. Madrid, 1788.

Shively, Donald. "Sumptuary Regulation and Status in Early Tokugawa Japan." *Harvard Journal of Asiatic Studies* 25 (1964–65): 123–64.

Sponsler, Claire. "Narrating the Social Order: Medieval Clothing Laws," *Clio* 21 (1992): 265–83.

Stuard, Susan Mosher. *Gilding the Market: Luxury and Fashion in Fourteenth-Century Italy*. Philadelphia: University of Pennsylvania Press, 2006.

Symes, Carol. "When We Talk about Modernity." *American Historical Review* 116 (2011): 715–26.

Vincent, John Martin. *Costume and Conduct in the Laws of Basel, Bern, and Zurich, 1370–1800*. Baltimore: Johns Hopkins University Press, 1935.

Vincent, Susan. *Dressing the Elite: Clothes in Early Modern England*. Oxford: Berg, 2003.

Ware, Anthony. "Origins of Buddhist Nationalism in Myanmar/Burma? An Urban History of Religious Space, Social Integration and Marginalisation in Colonial Rangoon after 1852." In *Religion and Urbanism: Reconceptualising Sustainable Cities for South Asia*, edited by Yamini Narayanan. London: Routledge, 2015.

Wilson, Elizabeth. *Adorned in Dreams: Fashion and Modernity*. London: Virago, 1985.

Wilson, Laurel Ann. "'De Novo Modo': The Birth of Fashion in the Middle Ages." PhD. diss., Fordham University, 2011.

———. "Status." In *Fashion in the Medieval Age (500–1450)*, edited by Sarah-Grace Heller. [Vol. 2 of *A Cultural History of Dress and Fashion*, edited by Susan Vincent.] London: Bloomsbury, forthcoming.

Wood-Legh, K. L. "The Knights' Attendance in the Parliaments of Edward III." *English Historical Review* 47 (1932): 398–413.

Zanda, Emanuala. *Fighting Hydra-Like Luxury: Sumptuary Law in the Roman Republic*. London: Bloomsbury 2011.

Laurel Ann Wilson (lwilson@fordham.edu) earned her PhD from Fordham University and is currently a Visiting Fellow at the Center for Medieval Studies at Fordham. Her interests include medieval textile technology and the emergence of fashion as a social phenomenon: the subject of her doctoral dissertation, as well as of many conference papers given under the auspices of the Pasold Research Fund, the North American Conference on British Studies, the Medieval Academy of America, and the International Congress on Medieval Studies. Her current research involves changes in the meaning of clothing in the later Middle Ages as reflected in sumptuary law, liveries, and dress codes. Forthcoming publications include "Status," in *Fashion in the Medieval Age (500–1450)*, edited by Sarah-Grace Heller.

Abstract Medieval sumptuary law has been receiving renewed scholarly attention in recent decades. But sumptuary laws, despite their ubiquity, have rarely been considered comprehensively and comparatively. This essay calls attention to this problem and suggests a number of topics for investigation, with specific reference to the first phase of European sumptuary legislation in the thirteenth and fourteenth centuries. It argues that comparative study demonstrates that this chronology closely parallels the development of the so-called "Western fashion system" and that the ubiquity of sketchy or nonexistent enforcement is evidence for the symbolic importance of sumptuary legislation, rather than its instrumentality. Comparison across (modern) national boundaries further reveals intriguing patterns of similarity and difference that require further exploration and contextualization; for example, such research reveals that only one social category, that of knights, emerges as universally important during this period.

Keywords Sumptuary law, clothing, luxury, gentry, symbolic legislation, social classification, status, knight, Western fashion system

TOWARD A HISTORY OF DOCUMENTS IN MEDIEVAL INDIA: THE ENCOUNTER OF SCHOLASTICISM AND REGIONAL LAW IN THE *SMṚTICANDRIKĀ*

DONALD R. DAVIS, JR.

A PERENNIAL CHALLENGE in the study of law in medieval India concerns the encounter of scholastic legal discourse and local and regional practices of law. Composed over a period of roughly two thousand years, the notoriously ahistorical Sanskrit textual corpus called *dharmaśāstra* contains systematized discussions of all major legal topics, codified and elaborated through centuries of scholastic commentary and compilation.[1] Datable, locatable evidence for the practice of law in similar topical areas and over a similar length of time, however, is either scarce, nonexistent, or unstudied. Indologists have approached this divide in several ways, ranging from naïve acceptance of the scholastic corpus as evidence of historical practice to the total rejection of the texts as a fantasy of luxurious Brahmins.

The present article takes up the use of documents as a revealing focus for approaching the encounter of text and practice in the laws of medieval India (ca. 600–1500 CE, though no one agrees about these limits). The range of written material available from medieval India may be roughly classified into three groups: 1) texts, substantial writings by eponymous authors of uncertain dating that contain treatises or original works of literature, theology, law, science, and so forth, generally preserved on palm-leaf, or later paper, manuscripts that were continually recopied; 2) inscriptions, short and medium-length writings by notable political figures and donors that record a specific event, giving the relevant names, places, and inscribed on durable substances such as stone or copper; and 3) documents, typically short records of particular transactions, agreements, contracts, and so on that specify the parties' names, the materials involved, and other transactional details, written on less durable materials such as palm leaf, birch bark, or prepared fabric and rarely recopied.[2] Within the last group, many types

I acknowledge with gratitude the valuable feedback and suggestions for improvement given to me by Elizabeth Lambourn, Patrick Olivelle, and the two anonymous reviewers of the journal.

1 Lingat, *Classical Law of India*; Olivelle, *Dharmasūtras.*

2 These large categories and the subcategories within them are all conveniences that are belied by regular categorical crossovers. So, the poetic preambles of Sanskrit inscriptions

of "document" are spoken about and sometimes copied into "texts" in the special sense above, though we do not have preserved examples of all types outside of the texts. From the other side, the types of historical documents actually known from medieval India far exceed the categories described in *dharmaśāstra* or in other textual sources.

The focus here will be a fresh translation of the description of documents in the twelfth-century digest of Hindu law called the *Smṛticandrikā*, (Moonlight on the Laws) and its possible historical value.[3] Its author, Devaṇṇabhaṭṭa, came from South India and some of his views (for example, the idea of inheritance by birth) reflect regional views, but beyond this fact we know only his name and that of his father. His digest of laws is one of the most comprehensive and thoroughly explained in the entire corpus of *dharmaśāstra*. Like all digests of law in Sanskrit, the *Smṛticandrikā* collects relevant legal rules from "root-texts"—undated earlier texts by eponymous authors—arranges them topically, and provides explanations and clarifications in the form of scholastic commentary. As such, it provides a reliable and intelligent discussion of every major topic of Hindu law, from daily and occasioned ritual practice to legal procedure and substantive law to penance and punishment.

The thoroughness and comprehensive intent of the *Smṛticandrikā* make it an ideal starting point for a more detailed examination of the use of documents within medieval South Asian legal practice because this scholastic text categorizes myriad types for which historical examples exist. The discussion of documents that will be presented here is found within a larger section on legal procedure and state policy (*vyavahāra*)—more precisely as part of the description of evidence accepted in courts—and it describes thirteen different document types under the twin rubrics of "royal" and "popular" documents.[4] Therefore, historical legal practice is recorded in the special idiom of Sanskrit scholasticism, even though

are often on par with the best poetry found in texts. Inscriptions likewise can function like documents, legal and/or political. Salomon (*Indian Epigraphy*, 110) discusses such overlap in the context of his now standard survey of the Indo-Aryan inscriptional corpus.

3 Srinivasacharya, *Smṛticandrikā by Devaṇabhaṭṭa.*

4 The distinction between "royal" (*rājakīya*) and "popular" (*jānapada, laukika*) is basic to all discussions of documents in Sanskrit. The first is easier to grasp as the set of documents initiated and executed by the state. The second refers to ordinary documents used for the transactions of private people. One reviewer suggested "civil" instead of "popular," but this carries too many connotations of citizenship and connection to a political body. "Popular" documents are those relating to or generated by the general public as opposed to the government. Unfortunately, no single adjective is ideal in translation.

such practice can only be situated in place and time through other evidence.[5] More importantly, however, the way in which different documents are placed into categories reveals cultural understandings of the distinct functions and purposes of those documents. Legal documents themselves do not come with a guide on how to interpret them, but the scholastic texts do, even if one must also read their taxonomies with a critical eye. The *Smṛticandrikā* discloses political, social, religious, and economic functions of legal documents, giving us a window into the cultural significance of documents beyond the legal arrangements described in the documents themselves. The important conclusion to be drawn here is that the scholastic tradition of *dharmaśāstra* helps us to do more than speak of generic "documentary culture" and rather helps to draw meaningful historical and cultural distinctions between the materials and functions of different documentary types in medieval India. Although they may seem to be straightforward carriers of information, documents are no more transparent than other types of writing, and we must, therefore, attend to their contexts and social construction.

The history of law is in part the history of legalism, the processes by which rules and categories are used to order a conceptual world, typically one invested with religious or moral value. Paul Dresch writes, "Legalism means the world is addressed through categories and [explicit] rules that stand apart from practice."[6] What *dharmaśāstra* texts offer historians is an important Indian articulation of the salient categories of legal thought and rule formation. As one of the most cogent and clear categorical presentations of the rules for documents in Sanskrit, the *Smṛticandrikā*, therefore, gives us insight into how practical documents may have been received: that is, how they fit into the conceptual frameworks of the time. The scholastic nature of the *Smṛticandrikā*, however, limits how much history we can read into the text.[7] On the one hand, we feel the author's scholastic compulsion to be true to the commentarial tradition by not elaborating further categories of document beyond those mentioned in the accepted root-texts; on the other, the author is also frustrated by knowing how many more types of document actually existed "in accordance with local standards."

The Social History of Documents in Medieval India

In an important way, this is the story of law: the formation of endless practical legal arrangements, the creation of rules and categories to tame them, and the subse-

5 See Lariviere, "*Dharmaśāstra*, Custom, 'Real Law,' and 'Apocryphal' *Smṛtis*."

6 Dresch, "Legalism, Anthropology, and History," 15.

7 Rocher, *Studies in Hindu Law*.

quent mutual development of (and tension between) both as an ongoing encounter.[8] Within that story, I provide first a very cursory overview of documents from medieval India, relying on existing syntheses of various sources for the history of written materials in India. I then give a full translation of the chapter defining documents in the *Smṛticandrikā*, in order to make one influential systematization of rules and categories available to a wider audience. The idea is to lay out a preliminary scheme for what it would take to write a fuller history of legal documents in medieval India. What we need in South Asian history is a volume like M. T. Clanchy's classic *From Memory to Written Record*. Essentially, I would like to sketch here how it might be done and to relate that sketch to the question of legal encounters.

The most comprehensive work to date on forms of documentation in medieval India is Ingo Strauch's edition and translation of the *Lekhapaddhati*,[9] a formulary of written exemplars of nearly one hundred types of document compiled between the thirteenth and fifteenth centuries. Here, we have letters addressed to figures ranging from an honored teacher to family members to friends; "public documents" such as royal instructions, decrees, tribunal decisions, charters, seizure notices, official communications, and ordeal certificates; "private documents," including commercial contracts, sale deeds, mortgages, receipts, gift records, and bills of safe passage; and "additional documents," covering tax notices, court judgments, bills of credit, and diplomatic communiqués. The huge number of document types modeled in a regional form of Gujarati-Sanskrit immediately tells us that, by the fifteenth century, documents of considerable variety were known to formulary compilers and, we can safely assume, in practice. Because they provide exemplar-like models—with names, amounts, and other details—formularies like the *Lekhapaddhati* get us close to practice without containing the records of actual legal transactions.

In addition to excellent work on the formulary itself, Strauch also provides a thorough study of the development of *dharmaśāstra* rules concerning documents in ancient Indian law.[10] He stops, however, with the last major root-text in approximately the seventh century, ignoring all of the commentarial literature that followed down to the eighteenth century. While understandable, given his purposes, it is precisely in the commentarial syntheses of the root-text material that we find a more coherent and complete view of the rules and categories for documents in

8 For a description of an exemplary regional case of this encounter in late medieval Kerala, see Davis, "Recovering the Indigenous Legal Traditions," 166–67.

9 An English translation, but much less reliable than Strauch's edition and German translation, can be found in Prasad, *Lekhapaddhati*.

10 *Die Lekhapaddhati-Lekhapañcāsikā*, 19–52.

medieval India. However, it is Strauch's impulse to move between documentary instance and categorical reflection that I want to emphasize.

The other essential starting point for a history of documents in medieval India is the work of Richard Salomon, and D. C. Sircar before him, on India's large corpus of inscriptions. Salomon is the latest in an illustrious line of epigraphy scholars whose fundamental work made South Asian historiography possible in the first place. Pertinent to both documents and epigraphy, Salomon notes that "the history of ancient and medieval (i.e., pre-Islamic) India must for the most part be reconstructed from incidental sources; that is, sources whose original intent was something other than the recording of historical events as such."[11] The line between document and epigraph is not always clear. Thus, Salomon's typological, chronological, and geographical surveys of the inscriptions in Indo-Aryan languages include contracts, donations, and charters, among other genres that might be classed as documents. The principal distinction lies rather in the material form, documents usually being written on palm leaf, birch bark, and (later) paper. The almost total lack of self-consciously historical texts in India, which is not the same as a lack of historical sense or orientation, has made epigraphy into "a primary rather than a secondary subfield within Indology" not a "corroborative and supplementary source" as in other areas of the world.[12] The challenges of Indian epigraphy for historians are unique: "Not only is the material vast, voluminous, and inherently difficult; it also requires a command of a range of languages, dialects, and script forms far greater than that needed for epigraphic studies in most other parts of the world."[13]

Together, Salomon, Strauch, and others supply a promising baseline for a richer history of documentary cultures in medieval India. Through their work, one finds important earlier studies of epistolary writing,[14] of regional and dynastic collections of inscriptions,[15] and of temple and royal archives.[16] If combined with analy-

---

11 Salomon, *Indian Epigraphy*, 3.

12 Ibid., 4.

13 Ibid., 5–6.

14 For an overview, see Michaels, "Practice of Classical Hindu Law," 63–67. Among many collections and studies of formularies and epistolary writing, see also Thakur, "Documents in Ancient India"; *Sanskrit Documents*; Banerji, "Study of the Epistolary and Documentary Literature"; Vidyāpati Ṭhākura, *Likhanāvalī*; Salomon, "*Ukti-Vyakti-Prakarana*." In a recent study of the *Likhanāvalī*, Jha ("Beyond the Local and the Universal," 35) makes the very plausible suggestion that collections of models for different types of writing for Indic languages were triggered in part by the influence of Persian *inshā* texts.

15 Salomon's bibliography (*Indian Epigraphy*, 311–27) is indispensable as a reference for general, regional, and specific studies of Indian epigraphy.

16 Archival studies focused on law include Gune, *Judicial System of the Marathas*; *Documents*

ses of *dharmaśāstra* and other textual material, at least two important types of documentary histories could emerge. First, more regionally focused histories that describe the typology and chronology of documents in relation to political, legal, economic, religious, and other social historical themes would bring the documents out of their incidental historical connection and into an interpretive framework. The narrower range of languages and scripts involved make such work possible and would, in turn, create the conditions for a macroscopic overview of document usage. The goal of this second type of history would be a story about the impact of documents throughout the medieval period in India, but with the necessary attention to differences of pace and usage that regional histories reveal.

By attending to the specificities of documentary categories, of regional patterns, of narrative depictions of document use, and of textual prescriptions for documents and their authentication, we could move beyond vague invocations of literacy and documentary culture in the singular.[17] Writing itself, of course, produced momentous changes in India as it did everywhere, but its introduction was neither definitive nor suddenly widespread. In fact, only careful collation of existing enumerations of inscriptions and documents can yield a sense of when the use of writing per se accelerated, and which specific types of writing emerged when. The key for any history of documents, in my view, is the desperate need for better interpretive theoretical frameworks within which one can make sense of writing from medieval India. Exemplary work, usually based on inscriptions, does exist,[18] but so much more is waiting to be studied and, further, to be synthesized beyond the few regional frameworks that have paved the way for future work.

Legal Encounters of Text and Document

One important source of guidance for a social history of documents will be their interface with textual traditions like *dharmaśāstra*. While always suspicious in their highly systematic and list-oriented presentation, *dharmaśāstra* texts, especially medieval commentaries and digests, give us a preliminary schema of categories and rules within which to place the dated documents of practice. A study of the connections and disconnections between texts and documents, therefore, helps us avoid imposing anachronistic or culturally strange assumptions on the

from the Rudravarṇa-Mahāvihāra; *Vanjari Grandhavari*; and Davis, *Boundaries of Hindu Law*.

17 As in Gurukkal, "Shift of Trust from Words to Deeds."

18 So, for example, Stein, *Peasant, State, and Society*; Chattopadhyaya, *Studying Early India*; Orr, *Donors, Devotees, and* Daughters; Talbot, *Precolonial India in Practice*; and Veluthat, *Early Medieval in South India*.

material. This dilemma is nothing new, of course, being a version of a central problem of the modern debate over law in action *versus* law in books and the conflicts among positivists, naturalists, and realists, each of whom adopts a distinctive attitude toward the value of written law and its encounter with practical legal problems.[19] When it comes to the role of documents, the *Smṛticandrikā* suggests that their legal functions are better captured in texts while their historical valences are better seen in practical examples.

Consider, for instance, the opening distinction made between royal and popular documents in the *Smṛticandrikā*. The legal effect of this distinction is still not fully understood. For example, to interpret a copper-plate inscription sealed with wax by a king or a royal inscription on stone as a legal document is to place it in a culturally and historically incongruous category. The *śāsana*, decree or edict (most often a donation), was first of all a political act that had religious and legal side effects. In the name of magnifying the king's glory and political power, decrees generated religious merit for the donor(s), and they conveyed legal privileges, exemptions, and protections on the beneficiaries. However, a royal decree in medieval India was neither a legislative declaration of a general law nor a record of legal arrangements intended for evidentiary use in courts.[20] As the *Smṛticandrikā* suggests, the main threat to a royal decree was a later king (see 1a below), whose violation of the gift would undermine both its religious and legal value. Contravention by a later king, moreover, would allow no legal recourse through the evidence of the decree. That is to say, there was no way to take the new king to court, if he

---

19 Lon Fuller's classic satire, "Case of Speluncean Explorers," is as good a place as any to discern the real difficulties of adopting any rigid, inflexible attitude, no matter how principled, toward the authority of written law.

20 This strong statement relies on a distinction of political and legal actions that I see as important and basic in the legal categories of *Dharmaśāstra*. Consider the recently examined example of the eighth-century Vēḷvikuṭi copper plates: Gillet, "Dark Period," 294–97. The inscription portrays a Pāṇḍya king restoring a grant of land that had been seized by the notorious Kalabhra kings to a group of Brahmins, after they had produced a document showing the antiquity of the grant (*nāṭṭāl niṉ paḻamai (y) ātal kāṭṭi*). In my view, the scene conforms well to the future political threats against land grants by later kings described in the *Smṛticandrikā*. The aggrieved Brahmins make an appeal to the current, benevolent king to restore a lost grant, and the king in turn "magnanimously accepted [their appeal and document] as a royal act of grace" (*cemmānt' avaṉ eṭutt' aruḷi*). There is no legal case against anyone, least of all the offending kings. Rather, the plea is for the new king's grace and beneficence. If the circumstances were legal in nature, we could imagine the Brahmins having some other recourse, in case the king did not accept their plea and proof. The fact that they obviously do not have any such legal option leads me to characterize this and similar situations as primarily political in nature. Any legality in such cases is fragile at best.

chose to violate the terms of the old king's decree. Only political and moral appeals were possible. In this way, the difference between royal and popular documents is nontrivial and shapes how we should understand the reception of different document types in context.

By contrast, the verdict or "victory-document" (*jayapatra*)[21] at the conclusion of a full-blown trial is also classed as a "royal" document (see 1b below), but it is intrinsically legal as well. One might expect that the frequent injunction to provide a written verdict to a successful litigant would have generated many historical examples of litigated case law for medieval India.[22] Unfortunately, I am not aware of a single example of a *jayapatra* from India that delineates a full trial prior to the eighteenth century.[23] To find them, we have to travel to Java and to Mason Hoadley's essay on the transplantation of the *jayapatra* to Java, which remains the best survey and study of *jayapatra*s, even for India.[24] While acknowledging that some link to India and some practical presence of verdicts there must have existed, Hoadley shows that the evidence for written verdicts in Java (and Cambodia) begins in the tenth century, at least three centuries before any Indian attestation. Even allowing for the inevitable loss of the majority of such verdicts due to the fragility of writing material and environmental factors, the paucity of examples for medieval India still suggests that document production by Indian courts was neither vibrant nor prolific. Nevertheless, the transplanted and modified forms found outside India do help soften the argument from silence and seem to allow us to justify the use of extensive *dharmaśāstra* discussions of verdicts in describing the practical legal use of writing in the medieval period.

If the adjudication of civil matters was meant to produce a written verdict, how then were evidentiary documents used in those judicial contexts? Here again, in addition to cataloging their various types (*lekhyanirūpaṇam*), *dharmaśāstra*

---

21 Sanskrit orthography would normally require *patra*, "leaf, document," to be written *pattra*. However, the usage of *patra* with a single "t" is so ubiquitous in both inscriptional and manuscript evidence of medieval India that it seems artificial to "correct" what was obviously an accepted spelling in this period. I have retained the spelling *patra*, exclusively used in the *Smṛticandrikā*, throughout.

22 Similarly, one would expect the *Dharmaśāstra* texts to refer to the ubiquitous Indian practice of inscription on stone, but they do not.

23 In addition to the *jayapatra* of 1794 which he translates, Lariviere ("Witness as the Basis," 53–57) tries valiantly to adduce reasons why we would not find *jayapatra*s (decay of manuscript materials and transfer of cases to Mughal courts), but manages to find only two ordeal-related (and very truncated) examples from seventeenth-century Karnataka and nine additional examples from the eighteenth and nineteenth centuries.

24 Hoadley, "Continuity and Change."

supplies extensive discussions of the verification of documents' legal validity (*lekhyaparīkṣā*),[25] including the required elements, restrictions on who may have documents made, and many faults which nullify their evidentiary value. A desire for authenticity and avoidance of forgery drives the discussion. Indeed, one senses a mistrust of documents as legal evidence throughout. That same mistrust shows up in the premium placed on the testimony of witnesses. In fact, as Richard Lariviere has argued, documents of many kinds fail without the support of witnesses, to the point that the witness becomes the paradigmatic mode of proof in Hindu law.[26] Unlike in Islamic law, however, documents always retained explicit doctrinal sanction as evidentiary proof in *dharmaśāstra*.[27] The effects of this cultural suspicion led to the abundant use of witnesses to documents in both theoretical discussions and practical examples. Royal documents written by the king himself and sealed with the royal seal, however, were accepted even without witnesses' signatures.[28] Without this interpretive frame about the role of witness made possible by *dharmaśāstra*, we run the risk of succumbing to the "prejudice in favor of literacy" which Clanchy warns us against.[29] In order to see the interpretive help offered by *dharmaśāstra* in greater detail, let us now examine the full discussion of documents in the *Smṛticandrikā*.

Translation of the Chapter entitled "Definition of Documents" in the *Smṛticandrikā*

My translation below is based primarily on the text edited by Srinivasacharya,[30] but occasional textual emendations have been made using a compendium known as the *Dharmakośa*. I have benefitted greatly from the earlier, hard-to-find translation of J. R. Gharpure and from suggestions by Patrick Olivelle. In general, Gharpure's translation is good, but it leans heavily toward an off-putting hybrid of Sanskrit and English and consists too often of paraphrase rather than translation. As a result, a new translation was essential.

25 This section of the *Smṛticandrikā* follows immediately after the one translated here.

26 Lariviere, "Witness as the Basis."

27 Compare the well-known proscription of documents as evidence in classical Islamic law and its practical encounter with Muslim communities. See, for example, Messick, "Just Writing." The broad emphasis of the two traditions seems reversed while the practice appears closer.

28 Lariviere, "Witness as the Basis," 67; see also 1a, 1c–e, below.

29 Clanchy, *From Memory to Written Record*, 7.

30 Srinivasacharya, *Smṛticandrikā by Devaṇabhaṭṭa*, 3:125–39.

The chapter opens with a preamble on the two categories of documents and is subdivided thereafter into two sections, royal (section 1 in this translation) and popular documents (section 2). Under royal documents are discussed decrees (1a), verdicts (1b), orders (1c), instruction documents (1d), and "documents of gratitude" (1e). The section on popular documents, by contrast, departs from this typological classification to discuss "types of popular document" (2a), followed by a concluding discussion of "the utility of popular documents" (2b). The names of the eponymous authors of the legal root-texts structure the exposition, with the commentator's elaborations bringing these disparate sources together.

Following Indological conventions, I have placed cited root-texts in bold, along with words and phrases glossed from them. Sanskrit commentaries often simply gloss one word with another, making an elegant English rendering difficult in many places. Page numbers to the Srinivasacharya edition are indicated in brackets for ease of reference.

Preamble: The Two Categories of Documents

[125] Among the three forms of evidence,[31] Vasiṣṭha[32] states:

> **One should know that documents (*lekhya*) fall into two categories: common and royal.**

Common is also called "popular." So says the maker of the Collection:[33]

> **The traditional texts state that what is written is of two types: royal and popular.**

31 Namely, documents, witnesses, and possession, first mentioned in the *Vasiṣṭhadharmasūtra* 16.10: see *Dharmasūtras*, trans. Olivelle, 413. However, Strauch considers this a later interpolation belonging likely to the period of the *Laws of Yājñavalkya* or the *Laws of Nārada*, made perhaps in fourth or fifth century CE, in which documents become more prominent: *Die Lekhapaddhati-Lekhapañcāsikā*, 51.

32 This name of a reputed author of a root-text of *Dharmaśāstra* is the first of many mentioned in the ensuing discussion. Most are names of legendary sages of the Hindu tradition. Apart from relative chronology and mythological associations, we know very little about the dates of the texts or the biographies of their authors.

33 The author of the *Smṛtisaṃgraha* (The Collection of Traditional Texts) is simply known as Saṃgrahakāra, the "maker of the Collection," in the *Smṛticandrikā* and elsewhere. The collection is known to us only through its citation in later digests and commentaries. See Kane, *History of Dharmaśāstra*, 1:537–41.

1. Royal Documents

Of these, Vasiṣṭha states that the royal is of four types by dividing them into the decree, and so on.

> **The royal is of four types: 1) the first is known as the decree (*śāsana*), 2) the next is the verdict (*jayapatra*), 3) the order (*ājñā*), and 4) the instruction-document (*prajñāpanapatra*).**

1a. Decrees

Among these, Yājñavalkya proceeds to define the decree.

> **When a king grants land or creates an endowment, he should have an inscription (*lekhya*) made in order to inform good kings of later times.**

An **endowment** is property that is to be acquired through an arrangement with the king, for example: yearly or monthly, those who are engaged in commerce and the like shall give a certain amount of wealth to this Brahmin or to this deity. Here, even though it is the people engaged in commerce who actually give the property, the merit nevertheless belongs to the one who makes the endowment, because the actions of the former happen only because of the latter. The word **land** serves to indicate sub-varieties such as villages, gardens, and so on. From this, Bṛhaspati:

> **After he donates land and such, the king should have a charitable (*dharmya*) decree executed on copper-plate or on cloth[34] that contains the place, dynastic lineage, and other details.**

Have executed, by the official in charge of peace treaties, war declarations, and the like[35]—this completes the sense, because in this case there is a restriction on who may be an executor of his writings. Vyāsa says the same:

---

34 *Paṭe*, "on cloth," seems to refer to a specially prepared cloth, usually cotton, made somewhat stiff or sized "through the application of pastes and then inscribed with a stylus": Sircar, *Indian Epigraphy*, 66–67. Unfortunately, not a single example of such a cloth bearing a royal decree has survived to the present, though similar types of canvas are widely used for ritual text production and sacred art: see Kapstein, "Weaving the World"; Hatley, "Paṭa." It may also have been the case that such canvases were used for "archival" copies of royal decrees kept by a king's officials or for draft copies of grants eventually inscribed on more permanent surfaces. For further description, see Salomon, *Indian Epigraphy*, 132. My thanks to several members of the Indology listserv for clarifying this term.

35 The term *saṃdhivigrahādikāriṇā* likely indicates the scribe of a minister of peace and war, but it may refer to the minister himself. The two are clearly distinguished in a passage

> **As instructed by the king himself, the scribe in charge of peace treaties and war declarations [126] should write out the king's decree on copper-plate or else on cloth, detailing the connection of the action and the agent, including the action taken and the brief purpose.**

The connection of the action and the agent, meaning a decree which includes the connection between the action and the agent.[36] **Including the action taken and the brief purpose** means that the decree should incorporate the action taken along with a brief statement of its purpose.[37] Yājñavalkya states what details should be written at the beginning of a copper-plate:

> **The lord of the earth should inscribe his own lineage ancestors and himself and then a description of the grant, the extent, and the delineation of the gift.**

At the beginning, he **should inscribe** in the customary manner a benediction communicating the gift of boons by the glorious king, whose realm is the whole raised earth, and who is the very body of Lord Varāha. And then, he **should inscribe** the names of his **three lineage ancestors**—great-grandfather, grandfather, and father, in that order—by means of a description of their virtues such as heroism and so forth, **and himself** as the fourth. Then he should have written the grant, the extent, and so on. **Grant** in this case means what is being granted, that is the land or the endowment.[38] Its **extent** means the quantity. **The delineation of the gift** signifies the boundaries of the land and such that is being given.[39] Vyāsa too states:

---

of Vyāsa below, but not elsewhere. In any case, this ministry is regularly given responsibility for drafting royal decrees. See Scharfe, *State in Indian Tradition*, 151–52; and Sircar, *Indian Epigraphical Glossary*, 295.

36 The gloss in this case simply clarifies that the connection should be written as part of the decree itself and not separately, which is not perfectly clear from the root text. The compound *kriyākārakasaṃbandhaṃ* must be interpreted as a *bahuvrīhi*, which means literally, "in which there is a connection of action and agent," in order to link it to the word *śāsana*, "decree." The action refers to the detailed terms of the grant or decree and the agent specifies that it is the king himself who takes the action.

37 Grants of the sort being described often include a short statement assigning the spiritual merit or beneficiary of the donation or indicate another purpose for making the gift. The verse from Vyāsa below provides an example.

38 The word in question is *pratigraha*, which can signify both the acceptance of a gift and the gift itself. Devaṇṇabhaṭṭa ensures that the latter meaning should be understood here.

39 The gloss in this case is sensible, but the term *dānaccheda*, literally "cutting the gift," is also regularly used to refer to imprecations against those who might violate or renege on the gift in the future. See the texts from Bṛhaspati and Vyāsa below.

> **Indicating the year, the month, the fortnight,[40] the day, and the name of the king, as well as the caste and other details, and the kin-lineage and Vedic school of the recipient.[41]**

The second half of this verse means that one should also write the caste (*jāti*), family, and Vedic school, in order to make clear the unique character of this donation.[42] Similarly, other things should also be written, as Vyāsa himself states:

> **He should write down the locale, lineage ancestry, region, village, and what is received, informing the Brahmins[43] and all other dignitaries, officials, [127] heads of important families, managers, envoys, physicians, and village headmen, all the way down to foreigners and outcastes: "For the merit (*puṇya*) of my mother and father and of myself, I give this gift to so-and-so of this Vedic school, the son of so-and-so."**

So also, Bṛhaspati:

> **A gift should never be divided or taken away; it should be free from all interference;[44] it should endure for as long as the moon and sun shall last; and it should pass down from son to grandson and to all descendants. The donor and the protector of a gift shall enjoy heaven, but the one who rescinds it shall suffer hell for sixty thousand years—these are the rewards of giving and violating that he should write down.**

To complete the sense, he does this in order to admonish future kings and others. Vyāsa has exactly this in mind:

---

40 Indian calendars, especially ritual calendars, recognize both a bright and a dark half of the month, or lunar fortnight, following the phases of the moon.

41 The compound *sagotrabrahmacārikam* refers to the *gotra*, one of several Indic kinship groups, and *śākhā*, the special branches or schools of Vedic recitation. The *Smṛticandrikā* makes this identification clear below, but see also *Mitākṣarā* on *Yājñavalkya* 2.85. See the similar requirement in section 2 below.

42 In other words, as Gharpure's translation suggests (*Smṛticandrikā*, 101), the decree should be written to allow the gift, the donor, and the recipient to be uniquely and completely identified.

43 Read *brāhmaṇāṃs tu* for *brāhmaṇasya*. See *Dharmakośa* 1.375.

44 The compound *sarvabhāvyavivarjitam*, unexplained in the *Smṛticandrikā*, is taken by one commentator to mean *devabrāhmaṇanāpitādilabhyavarjitam*, "exempt from the dues normally given to gods, Brahmins, barbers, and so forth" (*Dharmakośa* 1.365). Another digest offers the easier reading *sarvabhāgavivarjitam*, "exempt from all taxes," especially those levied to support the maintenance of the king's military (*Dharmakośa* 1.365).

> **The king should write the rewards of giving and violating that shall last for sixty thousand years in order to admonish future kings and governors.**

Similarly, another verse, recorded only by him, should also be written.

> **This bridge of the Law is shared by all kings. May you protect it time upon time, as the good Lord Rāma calls anew upon all the illustrious lords of the earth.**

Now, the king himself should write his signature (*svahasta*). And, thus, the same author:

> **He should himself write the location and extent of the grant and his signature.**

This means he should himself write something like, "I, king so-and-so the son of so-and-so, affirm what is written here above." But, the scribe should also write his own name, as the same author states: [128]

> **The minister of peace and war or else his scribe shall at the instruction of the king himself write the king's decree. At the end, he should write his own name and seal it with the royal seal. This is the kind of royal decree relating to villages, fields, homes, and so forth.**

And, this should be entrusted to the recipient because he is the one to whom it is useful.[45] On this point, Viṣṇu:

> **He should give a document on cloth or copper plate and marked with his seal in order to inform future kings.**

The maker of the Collection also:

> **Having the mark of the king's signature and containing his command; bearing the royal name and sealed with the royal seal; in the local script,[46]**

---

45 The phrase *tasyopayogitvāt*, "because he is the one to whom it is useful," indicates that the author anticipated situations in which a decree would need to be produced to verify the arrangements established by the decree itself. The kind of situation the author has in mind is noted in the next passage, namely, the failure of future kings to uphold the grant.

46 The legal validity and necessity of writing in a local script is also confirmed in section 2 below, in cases where "foreign" parties are directed to write in their own script. In fact, royal inscriptions in India almost always employ the script used in that region. The use of multiple scripts in epigraphy is rare (Salomon, *Indian Epigraphy*, 70–71), and the use

> **expressed without grammatical errors, and with complete ligatures and letters—what is granted by the king through the scribes in charge of peace treaties and war declarations is to be known as a decree.**

This means that what is **given** by the king to another in the stated form and written down **by the scribes in charge of peace treaties and war declarations** shall be given the name **decree**. But, this decree is not for the purpose of making the grant legally valid (*dānasiddhyartham*), because its validity occurs only through the act of acceptance. Rather, it is for the purpose of making the grant permanent, as the unending rewards promised depend on its permanence (*sthiratva*).[47] For, similarly,

> **For as long as his radiant fame outshines all heaven and earth shall the doer of good dwell at the foot of the divine.**[48]

With exactly the same intention, Yājñavalkya too states:

> **[129] He shall have a permanent[49] decree bearing his signature and the time executed.**

Bearing the time means describing the gift or other grant specified by a particular year, etc. Similarly, Vyāsa also:

> **The donor should write "I approve" in plain letters. It should also be marked with the year, month, fortnight, day, and with the royal seal. Following this procedure, he should write the document called a royal decree.**

---

of more than one script in documents is unstudied, to my knowledge. Cox ("Scribe and Script," 17–22) discusses the strategic use of the non-local Nāgarī script in several royal charters of the western Cālukyas in the eleventh century, though without the use of two or more scripts in any single inscription.

47 Devaṇṇabhaṭṭa seems to intend here that only an irrevocable grant of unending duration produces the everlasting spiritual merit desired by the donor.

48 Devaṇṇabhaṭṭa emphasizes the effect of the correlative *tāvat*, "to this extent," in this verse to connect it with the issue of a grant's permanence. He implies that a king's merit lasts only as long as he continues to make gifts and protect them.

49 The word *sthira*, "permanent, fixed," and its derivatives are used several times in this section. It seems to refer, in the first place, to a longlasting material form: that a grant should be written on a permanent or durable substance, such as copper or stone. The permanence of a gift's religious reward is thus said to depend on its material permanence.

1b. Verdicts

And, similarly, the same author proceeds to define the verdict (*jayapatra*).

> **After he himself conducts legal procedures or has been briefed by the chief judge, the king should then give a verdict for the information of others.**

If one asks, to whom it should be given, he himself states:

> **A successful litigant is one who uses evidence to prove himself the owner of moveable or immoveable property in the face of a doubt raised by an accusation about a portion of it. The king should confer upon him a definitive verdict.**

Bṛhaspati, also:

> **When a king confers upon a successful litigant a document that ends with the decision and incorporates the plaint, reply, and evidence, that is called a verdict.**

Incorporates the plaint, reply, and evidence is for the purpose of providing a summary of the proceedings, because the same author also states:

> **What occurs in a legal procedure—the plaint and reply, as well as the evidence and decision—all of this should be written in a verdict.**

Vyāsa, also:

> **The plaint, the reply, the proof-stage, the adducing of evidence, the testing of it, [130] the depositions, the traditional texts, and the determination according to the assessors (*sabhya*)—all of this should be summarily written down in a verdict.**

Proof-stage refers to the phase for assigning the burden of proof also known as the determination of the burden of proof. **Depositions** means the testimony of witnesses. **According to the assessors** means without contravening the assessors. **Summarily**, briefly. Kātyāyana, also:

> **The statements of the claimant and respondent, the plaint, the witnesses' statement, and the decision that he has himself determined—this should be successively entered letter by letter on a document.**

The same author elaborates what is meant by **successively**.

> **First, the statements of the plaintiff and defendant should be entered. Then, on the same document, he should have written the determina-**

> **tions of the assessors, the chief judge, or, beyond these, of the families,**[50] **as well as of the traditional legal treatises,**[51] **and the line of thought.**

The line of thought, of the king and the others—that completes the sense. The writing of this line of thought, however, is to be done by one's own hand, because the author had just previously enjoined the writing of a judgment in another's hand in the phrase above **that he has himself determined**. Following this, the same author states:

> **A litigant should be awarded with the amount proven in law and the king should, with the appropriate courtesies, give him a document containing his signature. The assessors knowledgeable in the traditions and treatises who were present for the case should likewise be required to provide their signatures, in accordance with the rules for documents.**

The meaning is: In the case of verdicts, the king should require the judges to provide their signatures, as if it were a popular document.[52] Vṛddhavasiṣṭha, also:

> **[131] When a case has been won, the winning party should be given a verdict marked in the hand of the chief judge and other judges and sealed with the royal seal.**

Kātyāyana calls this kind of verdict by the name conclusive-document (*paścātkāra*):

> **The wise know a document created according to this procedural rule as a conclusive-document.**

But this **conclusive-document** is given only in a special type of judicial decision and not in every case, as the same author states:

> **A conclusive-document is given in a case where one party meets the burden of proof by means of evidence itself, but this is not prescribed for all cases.**

---

50 *Kulānām* seems to refer to cases in which the court of jurisdiction is an extended family or *kula*. See *Yājñavalkya* 2.30.

51 These are the *Dharmaśāstra* texts themselves, the *smṛtis*. Unlike most legal writing, the few extant verdicts or victory-documents we have do in fact cite relevant *Dharmaśāstra* rules.

52 *Jānapadalekhyavat*, "as if it were a popular document," is an important simile that emphasizes the distinction to be made between most types of royal document and ordinary documents in other contexts. *Jayapatras*, however, resemble the day-to-day documents described below in their specifically judicial and evidentiary use in courts and in their use of signatures.

Burden of proof means what is to be proven. By saying **by means of evidence itself**, he intends to say that a conclusive-document is given only in a legal procedure with all four phases, not in a proceeding with just two phases. And Bṛhaspati makes this clear:

> **In a legal victory, one should prove the matter to be proven through all four phases of the trial. And, a verdict including the royal seal is then required.**

In a two-phase proceeding, a verdict consisting of the plaint and reply is still given, and it is only the label "conclusive-document" that is prohibited as it would not reflect an accurate summary in this case. The same author describes yet another verdict.

> **A verdict complete with a full account of the proceedings is to be given to those other than the five types of losing parties, starting with the one who changes his plea.**[53]

Those other means the party that did not lose.[54]

1c. Orders

Both the order and the instruction-document have been explained by Vasiṣṭha.

> **A document that instructs vassal kings, retainers, or regional governors and the like about what to do is called an order.**

1d. Instruction-documents

> **[132] A document that informs a sacrificial priest, a family priest, a teacher, a religious dignitary, or other honorable person about what to do is an instruction-document.**

---

53 The *Laws of Nārada* (Mā 2.33) lists these five types of defeated litigants: "There are five kinds of losers: one who changes his plea, one who shows contempt for the proceedings, one who does not appear, one who does not reply, and one who absconds when he has been summoned" (*Nāradasmrti*, 460). See also *Mitākṣarā* on *Yājñavalkya* 2.6.

54 Read *ahīnavādinām* for *hīnavādinām*. See *Dharmakośa* 1.366.

1e. Documents of Gratitude

Bṛhaspati describes yet another type of royal document called the document of gratitude.

> **When a king, being pleased with someone's service, valor, and so forth, grants in writing a locality or the like, that is a document of gratitude.**

Therefore, royal documents are of five types; one should understand the earlier statement by Vasiṣṭha that they are of four types as stated carelessly.

2. Popular documents

Now, Vyāsa defines the popular.

> **A scribe in a well-known location should write popular documents, incorporating the order of the king's lineage along with the year, month, fortnight, and time.**

Incorporating is to be read also with list beginning with the word **year**. **Time**, day. The same author states what else should be required in a document.

> **He should write the name and caste of the creditor and debtor,**[55] **as well as the names of their fathers and ancestors, along with the extent and the classification of the property and the interest agreed upon by both parties.**

Agreed upon by both is a specification that also modifies both of the words **property** and **interest**. Relatedly, Yājñavalkya:

> **In regard to any matter concluded willingly and mutually, a document should be drawn up containing the witnesses, preceded by the creditor.**

Containing the witnesses means including the names of impartial people knowledgeable about the **matter concluded**. Similarly, insofar as what is to be written with respect to the time, creditor, debtor, witnesses, and so forth possesses legal validity for its specific arrangement through specific details, a document should be drawn up that provides those details. Thus, the same author says:

> **A document should indicate the year, month, fortnight, day, name, caste, common kinship-lineage, common Vedic school, and one's own father's name, etc.**

---

55 From the outset, we see that the prototypical "popular" document is a contract of loan, mortgage, or other interest-bearing financial instrument that creates a legal debt.

[133] **Common Vedic school** refers to the secondary name given to a branch of Vedic recitation such as the Bahvṛca or Kaṭha.[56] **One's own father's name** indicates the father's name of the creditor, debtor, and witnesses. The word **etc.** should be understood to mean that the inclusion of, for example, the day of the week and similar details should follow local standards. In this connection, Vyāsa:

> **In accordance with local law, the document (*kriyā*) should clearly note the actions taken, what is mortgaged, and what is received.**

In accordance with local law means the legal instrument (*karaṇa*) should follow local law.[57] **What is mortgaged** is the mortgaged property. Nārada, also:

> **A document including the witnesses should be made, in which neither the order nor the letters are broken, that follows the standards required by local law, and that is complete with respect to all required elements.**

Vasiṣṭha, also:

> **One should enter the time, the king, the locale, the residence, the names of the donor and recipient, as well as the names of their fathers, the caste, the kinship-lineage, the Vedic branch, the property, the mortgage, including the amount, the interest, the signature of the recipient, and two witnesses who know the transaction.**

Yājñavalkya states the manner in which the recipient should enter a signature.

> **When a transaction has been concluded, the debtor should enter his name in his own hand, "I, the son of so-and-so, affirm all that is written here above."**

By saying **written above**, he shows that the section of letters in one's own hand comes below the section of letters written previously. **Debtor** is intended to also indicate the witnesses. Thus, the same author:

> **And, an even number of witnesses should write their names preceded by the names of their fathers in their own hand, "I, so-and-so, am a witness to this."**

---

56 Branches (*śākhā*) of the Ṛgveda and Yajurveda, respectively. Indian inscriptions regularly record the Vedic affiliations of the Brahmins when they receive grants and gifts.

57 The sense is that the form of the legal instrument should include details as dictated and expected by local custom, even if those deviate from the specific lists given in the texts.

[134] In documents requiring that the witnesses be written down, they too should each write, "I, **so-and-so**, son of so-and-so, **am a witness to this** transaction." And, they should be enumerated in an **even** number, such as two, etc. The meaning is that the enumeration should not be in an odd number such as three, etc. Some read the restriction about the number of witnesses contrarily by assuming that the negative prefix "a-" has been elided.[58] One should understand the rule to conform to the law as observed in a particular locality, and not elsewhere, for this might lead to doing as one pleases. The plural form **witnesses** refers to documents that record a very important matter,[59] because we have the statement of Hārīta that there should be just two witnesses in an ordinary document:

> **A document should be made that includes the combination of each of the following: the creditor and debtor, the two witnesses, and the scribe—and not otherwise.**

Thus, because a document written by another involves five people, namely the creditor, debtor, two witnesses, and scribe, its common designation among people is the "fiver" document. Where the number of witnesses required is more, however, that designation is considered secondary.[60] With reference to the ordinary document, Vyāsa also states:

> **It should be in the debtor's hand, including the names of the two witnesses and of their fathers.**

From this, we can see that the restriction that documents should have an even number of witnesses should be followed in a way that does not conflict with local law. But, Nārada explains what to do when a witness or debtor is illiterate.

---

58 The text reads *te samāḥ*, "they being even (in number)." The contrary view, plausible due to simple scribal elision in manuscripts, would read *te 'samāh* (that is, *te a-samāḥ*), "they being odd (in number)." Two opinions are thus recorded as to whether witnesses should be even or odd in number. Unless an independent criterion is established, there is no way to determine which reading is correct. Therefore, Devaṇṇabhaṭṭa insists that local customary law should control the required number of witnesses. This allows both contradictory readings of the rule to be possible and yet still binding in practice.

59 In Sanskrit, "plural" must mean at least three, according to the simple grammatical existence of the dual number, but it might also mean exactly three according to the Mīmāṃsā maxim of the *kapiñjala-nyāya*: see *Laukikanyāyāñjali*, 29–30.

60 If a locality requires more than two witnesses, then the label "fiver" (*pañcārūḍha*, literally, "ascended by five"), in which only two witnesses appear, becomes "secondary" (*gauṇa*), perhaps a "secondary alternative."

An illiterate debtor should have his attestation written for him, and an illiterate witness should have it written by another witness in the presence of all the witnesses.

A person who knows only a foreign script should also write for himself because he is literate, [135] as the statement of Kātyāyana maintains:

Written scripts from all localities may be entered on a document.

Yājñavalkya explains what happens immediately after the witnesses have written their signatures.

Finally, at the end, the scribe should write, "As requested by both parties, I, so-and-so, the son of so-and-so, have written this.

Vyāsa, also:

At the end, the scribe should write his own name in his own hand attesting, "I, so-and-so, the son of so-and-so, being asked by both parties." Thus, Vyāsa has laid down the rule in regard to popular documents.

At the end of the document, which completes the sense.

2a. Types of Popular Document

The same author then states that the documents thus described are of eight types.

The eight types of common document are as follows: basic (*cīraka*),[61] self-written (*svahasta*), acknowledgement (*upagata*), mortgage (*ādhi*), purchase (*kraya*), local convention (*sthiti*), reconciliation (*saṃdhi*), and purification (*viśuddhi*).

In this context, the precise number is not the point intended, because other documents such as the partition deed also fall in the common category. The maker of the Collection now defines the basic.

Basic is the name for what is written by the elder scribes of a town, selected by the parties involved, and praised as the best around. It

61 The precise meaning of *cīraka*, or *ciraka*, here is uncertain. It is mentioned at *Yājñavalkya* 2.22 as one of two major categories of writing, with *śāsana*, or decree, being the other. It may refer to a particular style of writing that was used for ordinary documents which employed "strokes" (*cīra*) or produced documents that resemble rags or tattered cloth, the usual denotation for *cīra*. I have opted for a neutral translation that tries to indicate the ordinary character discernible from the context.

should bear all the respective personal names of the two parties and of the witnesses, preceded by the names of their fathers, and others, as well as the signatures of the initiating party and the witnesses. It should be clear and understandable with all the characteristics required according to the traditional texts.

Praised, celebrated. Now, Kātyāyana defines the self-written.

[136] A document written by the recipient in his own hand, but lacking any witness, is known as a self-written document. The wise accept it as legal evidence.

Similarly, a document written by the donor but acknowledged by the recipient is known as an acknowledgement. Nārada describes the mortgage deed.

When a creditor receives property as a mortgage and lends his own money in return, the document made in this case is called a mortgage deed.

Prajāpati states a specific rule relating to a sub-mortgage.

If a creditor contracts a higher mortgage with that same money, he should draw up a document for the new mortgage and provide both the new and the original to the first mortgagor.[62]

Pitāmaha defines the purchase deed.

When particular property is purchased, what is executed for the sake of publicizing the purchase as approved by the buyer and known to the seller is known as a purchase deed.

Kātyāyana has defined the deed of local convention (*sthitipatra*).

A convention may belong to a group of knowers of the four Vedas, a town, a guild, a corporate group, or a group of citizens. A document intended to legally effect that convention should be known as a deed of local convention. [When an accusation is leveled before an assembly of dignitaries, the document giving a legal summary of what happened

62 Although not fully clear, the rule seems to apply to two scenarios: a mortgage to the same mortgagor in which the terms have been renegotiated or that has been refinanced; or a mortgage to a new mortgagor in which the terms are more advantageous to the creditor. In either case, both the mortgage deed with the original terms and the new mortgage deed should be given to the first mortgagor, presumably to avoid confusion or conflict around the continuing terms of the new mortgage.

> **is known as a document of reconciliation. When the reconciliation has been reached, the document is called a reconciliation.]**[63] **When an accusation has been settled by persons performing a ritual penance, the document containing the witnesses to it is known to them as the document of purification.**

Bṛhaspati also declares the division of document-types.

> **Common documents are of seven types: partition, gift, sale, mortgage, local convention, slavery, debt, etc. Royal decrees are of three types.**

Here, again, the precise number is not the point, because he also illustrates additional documents beyond these. [137] He uses the word **etc.** for this very reason. Otherwise, because by simple counting the fact that seven are enumerated, the use of the word **etc.** would become pointless. By this fact, we know that the mention of a certain number of documents is for the purpose of limitation. As a result, there is no contradiction between rules that give variant numbers. The same author himself explains documents of partition, and so on.

> **When brothers who have willingly and mutually divided their inheritance make a document of the division, it is called a document of partition. The document made when land is gifted to a worthy recipient for as long as the moon and sun last and which is never to be divided or seized is known as a gift deed. When one buys a house, field, or something similar, the document made furnishing in writing the original payment price is called a purchase deed. When one gives moveable or immoveable property as collateral for a loan, the document one makes indicating whether the mortgage is custodial or usufructuary is called a mortgage deed. When a village or locality makes a mutual agreement for a purpose of the Law and it does not contravene the king, they call that a document of convention. What is written down in a desolate place when someone who lacks clothing or food says, "I shall perform work for you," is called a deed of servitude. When one receives money on loan at interest and either makes or has made a document with the terms for repayment, the wise call this a document of debt.**

Kātyāyana describes yet another common document.

> **When a dispute over a boundary has been legally resolved, a boundary deed is prescribed.**

---

63 The bracketed verses do not appear in the printed edition of Srinivasacharya but are found in the *Dharmakośa* and complete the description of different documents.

[138] Yājñavalkya, also:

> **When one has paid off a debt, one should either tear up the original document or have another made attesting to the acquittance.**

2b. The Utility of Popular Documents

Marīci states the usefulness of documents.

> **When selling or mortgaging immoveable property, partitioning inheritance, and making a gift, one should both secure its legal validity and prevent any dispute about it by means of a document.**

Mortgaging, a mortgage. The first occurrence of the word **and** refers to the whole range of such transactions concluded, such as debts and so on. **Prevent any dispute** means that even at some later time, what happened with regard to the concluded transaction cannot be claimed to be otherwise. Thus, having considered the legal validity secured through preventing disputes about the immoveable property, and so forth, one should determine what to include and what to remove among the various elements to be written—the royal lineage, the year, and so on—because these serve a visible purpose.[64] As a result, it is not necessary to write the name of the creditor or debtor in a gift deed, or the like, nor even what is received, and so forth in a document of debt, or similar contract. Moreover, even in other types of document, what should actually be written down is a matter for modification (*ūhanīya*) because the whole point of documents is to accomplish a practical, worldly goal. Therefore, when a document, the terms of which have not yet been fulfilled, becomes incapable of use or is destroyed, another document must be drawn up. For this very reason, Yājñavalkya states:

> **When a document is located in a faraway place, has been poorly inscribed, destroyed, effaced, stolen, ripped, burnt, or cut, another should be created to replace it.**

---

64 Following Indian hermeneutical principles, the *Dharmaśāstra* tradition draws a distinction between properly dharmic actions that have no visible purpose (*adṛṣṭārtha*) and essentially mundane acts that function to accomplish some visible purpose (*dṛṣṭārtha*) in the world itself. The author here classifies almost everything discussed in this section under the heading of "visible purpose." The point for Devaṇṇabhaṭṭa is clearly the freedom afforded by the possibility to rationally decide which elements should be required in a document, since those are not subject to the unalterable obligation imposed by actions done for unseen, transcendental purposes.

Located in a faraway place indicates a place from which it is utterly impossible to retrieve. **Poorly inscribed**[65] refers to handwriting that is unintelligible. **Ripped**, in two parts. **Cut** means torn apart. Kātyāyana, also:

> **A document that is damaged by filth, burnt, perforated, or misplaced, or erased through perspiration should be replaced by another.**

Misplaced, lost. **Erased**, effaced. As to what Nārada has stated:

> **When a document is located in a faraway place, ripped, poorly written, or stolen, [139] then, if the document still exists, one should allow a delay. If it no longer exists, then one should rely on the testimony of those who have seen it.**

This refers to a situation in which the debtor is prepared to repay the owed amount right away. In this case, there is no point in making another document. **Allow a delay** for the purpose of producing it: that is, fixing an allotment of time sufficient to produce the document. **The testimony of those who have seen it** is what can be made known by the witnesses to the transaction recorded in the document as it would be available in the document itself, meaning specifically what is supposed to be done about the repayment of the money. This, of course, should also be done, even when a document is impossible to tear up, so that witnesses may discharge their obligation to witness. And, a settlement deed should be received in order to publicize the repayment. One should only create a new document when there is money still to be repaid at a later time. For this reason, the same author states:

> **A new document should be made if a document is ripped, cut, stolen, effaced, burnt, or poorly written. This is the traditional rule for documents.**

Concluding Observations

The foregoing translation confirms several points of legal encounter between scholastic writing and unwritten regional laws in medieval India.[66] First, royal or

65 *Durlekhya* can also, and perhaps more commonly, signify a forgery. See the same in the Nārada verses below. On forgery in Indian inscriptions, see, most recently, Salomon, "Fine Art of Forgery."

66 Very recently, Lubin, "Writing and the Recognition of Customary Law," has analyzed the function of writing in several new epigraphical sources in relation to the Sanskrit texts. His nuanced study of varying legal purposes for written materials is a model of the kind of history that is possible for India.

state documents differed functionally and conceptually from ordinary documents. Royal decrees, orders, instructions, and judicial verdicts depend on the imprimatur of the king or an official acting in his name. The only material guarantee that matters is his seal and signature. Such writing is a political act. By contrast, the requirement of signatures by witnesses, assessors, and judges in verdicts signals that signing is a legal act. Ordinary documents, too, require signatures and/or witnesses in a way that confirms their legality. On this point, we have two modes of practical writing distinguished through legal categories. When we find royal inscriptions that contain lists of signatures, therefore, we are obliged to rethink the scholastic categories and to what extent, whether, and how they may help us understand the inscriptions.[67]

A second prominent emphasis in the translation is the recurrence of requirements to consider and follow local or regional law. More than ten invocations of local law in the discussion indicate that the specified legal requirements for documents had to yield to local expectations. Even royal writings were required to use a local script as a way to further their acceptance. In the case of popular documents, local law is constantly called upon to fill in any gaps or clarify ambiguities in the textual laws. Signatures can and should be written in whatever script is known to the transacting parties. Scribes should employ ordinary local language in conveying the details of the contract. And, most importantly, the precise elements required to make a document legal depend more on local standards than on the several lists given in the texts. Here, the texts nevertheless give a reliable impression of the kinds of details we actually find in both royal and popular documents, but Devaṇṇabhaṭṭa gives the strong impression that what counted legally were the expectations of local people, what local law required. The scholastic legal texts acknowledge a lawmaking power outside of themselves, even as they attempt to codify norms that undoubtedly influenced local legal expectations.

Finally, in several places, the discussion highlights aspects of the material form of writing that were considered critical, even essential, to its legality. Simple requirements of legibility and continuity (that is, clear, legible handwriting and unbroken text) obviously serve to thwart forgery and fraudulent manipulation of both royal and ordinary documents. However, the discussion also suggests that more than textual integrity is at stake in the repeated insistence on clean, continuous writing. Writing is the material extension of the persons writing and transacting and witnessing. Its form, therefore, is bound up with their personalities and the transaction itself. A sloppy, broken, torn, or otherwise damaged or shoddy document portends problems, legally and morally. The text thus insists that great

67 Davis, "Law-Stuff: Content and Materiality."

care be taken in the preparation of documents. That care invests the writing with the seriousness and good intention of the parties involved, thus achieving a congruence of form and content.

With these points in mind, our interpretation of the huge corpus of documents from medieval India described above can begin from a contemporaneous set of legal categories and generalizations. The contextual meaning of such documents should start from what others at the time thought of them. Their significance does not end there, but the interplay of scholastic legal discourse and regional documentary practices demands that we consider both together.

In sum, contrary to the usual lamentations about lack of evidence (I myself have often cried loudest), sources for a legal history of medieval India do exist in great abundance, so great that they exceed the capacity of any individual to study them all. What they seem not to provide, however, is the legal history that we want to write, because there is very little familiar intrigue or entertaining conflict of the courtroom variety in a hundred thousand land tenure documents or in a statistical analysis of interest rates on mortgages or in ten thousand more endowments of perpetual lamps for temples. What we need—what I want—is more information about dispute resolution through legal channels. But, this information we will not find in any great measure. We are left, therefore, with the possibilities of writing a different type of legal history. One could approach the economic history of medieval India with law in mind by drawing conclusions from the aggregation of documentary data about taxation, interest rates, endowment sizes, and/or corporate and domestic production for a specific place and time.[68] More in line with my argument here, however, would be histories of law that draw upon both documents and correlative textual and epigraphic sources, especially sources like *dharmaśāstra* that are centrally concerned with law. Names, dates, and details are necessary for any history, and this alone requires us to work from historical legal documents first, but our understanding must be shaped by the legal encounter with the textual tradition of *dharmaśāstra* which, if nothing else, represents an Indian effort to systematize the rules and categories of law. The prestige and longevity of that tradition demands our attention. An abundance of ripe fruit awaits scholars willing explore the encounter of text and practice in the law of medieval India; we just need more laborers in the field to pick it.

68 Excellent studies of some of these issues already exist, but none focuses on the question of law or legal encounter. The call of this essay asks for more work that addresses the history of law in India in a direct way. See, for example, Sinopoli, *Political Economy of Craft Production*; Chattopadhyaya, *Studying Early India*; Heitzman, *Gifts of Power*.

Bibliography

Primary Sources

Dharmakośa: Vyavahārakāṇḍa. Vol. 1, pt. 1, *Vyavahāramātṛkā*. Edited by Laxmanshastri Joshi. Wai: Prajñā Pāṭhaśālā Maṇḍala, 1937.

Dharmasūtras: The Law Codes of Āpastamba, Gautama, Baudhāyana, and Vasiṣṭha. Translated by Patrick Olivelle. Delhi: Motilal Banarsidass, 2000.

Documents from the Rudravarṇa-Mahāvihāra, Pāṭan I: Sales and Mortgages. Edited by Bernhard Kölver and Hemrāja Śākya. Sankt Augustin: VGH Wissenschaftsverlag, 1985.

Laukikanyāyāñjali: A Handbook of Popular Maxims Current in Sanskrit Literature. Edited by G. A. Jacob. 2nd rev. ed. Bombay: Nirnaya Sagar Press, 1911.

Die Lekhapaddhati-Lekhapañcāsikā: Briefe und Urkunden im Mittelalterlichen Gujarat. Edited by Ingo Strauch. Berlin: Reimer, 2002.

The Nāradasmṛti. Edited and translated by Richard W. Lariviere. Delhi: Motilal Banarsidass, 2003.

Sanskrit Documents Being Sanskrit Letters and Other Documents Preserved in the Oriental Collections at the National Archives of India. Edited by Surendranath Sen and Umesha Mishra. Allahabad: Ganganatha Jha Research Institute, 1951.

The Smṛticandrikā: Vyavahārakāṇḍa, Part I. Collection of Hindu Law Texts XXIX. Edited by J. R. Gharpure. Bombay: Aryabhushan Press, 1948.

Srinivasacharya, L. *Smṛticandrikā by Devaṇabhaṭṭa*, 6 vols. Mysore: Government Press, 1914–21.

Vanjari Grandhavari. Edited by M. G. S. Narayanan. Calicut: University of Calicut, 1987.

Vidyāpati Ṭhākura. *Likhanāvalī*. Edited by Indrakānt Jhā. Paṭanā: Indrālaya Prakāśana, 1969.

Secondary Studies

Banerji, S. C. "A Study of the Epistolary and Documentary Literature in Sanskrit." *Indian Historical Quarterly* 34 (1952): 226–50.

Chattopadhyaya, Brajadulal. *The Making of Early Medieval India*. Oxford: Oxford University Press, 1995.

——. *Studying Early India: Archaeology, Texts, and Historical Issues*. Delhi: Permanent Black, 2003.

Clanchy, M. T. *From Memory to Written Record: England, 1066–1307*. 3rd ed. Oxford: Wiley-Blackwell, 2013 [1979].

Cox, Whitney. "Scribe and Script in the Cālukya West Deccan." *Indian Economic and Social History Review* 47 (2010): 1–28.

Davis, Donald R., Jr. *The Boundaries of Hindu Law: Tradition, Custom, and Politics in Medieval Kerala*. Torino: CESMEO, 2004.

——. "Law-Stuff: Content and Materiality of the Kollam Plates." In *The Copper-plates from Kollam: Global and Local in Ninth Century South India,* edited by Elizabeth Lambourn, Kesavan Veluthat, and Roberta Tomber. Delhi: Primus, forthcoming.

——. "Recovering the Indigenous Legal Traditions of India: Classical Hindu Law in Practice in Late Medieval Kerala." *Journal of Indian Philosophy* 27 (1999): 159–213.

Dresch, Paul. "Legalism, Anthropology, and History: A View from Part of Anthropology." In *Legalism: Anthropology and History*, edited by Paul Dresch and Hannah Skoda, 1–37. Oxford: Oxford University Press, 2012.

Fuller, Lon L. "The Case of Speluncean Explorers." *Harvard Law Review* 62 (1949): 616–45.

Gillet, Valérie. "The Dark Period: Myth or Reality." *Indian Economic and Social History Review* 51 (2014): 283–302.

Gune, V. T. *The Judicial System of the Marathas: A Detailed Study of the Judicial Institutions in Maharashtra from 1600–1818 AD, Based on Original Decisions Called Mazhars, Nivadpatras, and Official Orders*. Pune: Deccan College, 1953.

Gurukkal, Rajan. "Shift of Trust from Words to Deeds: Implications of the Proliferation of Epigraphs in the Tamil South." *Indian Historical Review* 34 (2007): 16–35.

Hatley, Shaman. "Paṭa." In *Tāntrikābhidhānakośa*, 371–72. Vienna: Austrian Academy of Sciences, 2013.

Heitzman, James. *Gifts of Power: Lordship in an Early Indian State.* Delhi: Oxford University Press, 1997.

Hoadley, Mason C. "Continuity and Change in Javanese Legal Tradition: The Evidence of the *Jayapattra*." *Indonesia* 11 (1971): 95–109.

Jha, Pankaj. "Beyond the Local and the Universal: Exclusionary Strategies of Expansive Literary Cultures in Fifteenth-Century Mithila." *Indian Economic and Social History Review* 51 (2014): 1–40.

Kane, P. V. *History of Dharmaśāstra*. 5 vols. Poona: Bhandarkar Oriental Research Institute, 1962–75.

Kapstein, Matthew. "Weaving the World: The Ritual Art of the 'Paṭa' in Pala Buddhism and Its Legacy in Tibet." *History of Religions* 34 (1995): 241–62.

Lariviere, Richard W. "*Dharmaśāstra*, Custom, 'Real Law,' and 'Apocryphal' *Smṛtis*," *Journal of Indian Philosophy* 32 (2004): 611–27.

——. "Witness as the Basis for all other Modes of Proof in Hindu Law." *Adyar Library Bulletin* 51 (1987): 60–70.

Lingat, Robert. *The Classical Law of India*. Translated by J. Duncan M. Derrett. Berkeley: University of California Press, 1973.

Lubin, Timothy. "Writing and the Recognition of Customary Law in Premodern India and Java," *Journal of the American Oriental Society* 135 (2015): 225–59.

Messick, Brinkley. "Just Writing: Paradox and Political Economy in Yemeni Legal Documents." *Cultural Anthropology* 4 (1989): 26–50.

Michaels, Axel. "The Practice of Classical Hindu Law," In *Hinduism and Law: An Introduction*, edited by Timothy Lubin, Donald R. Davis, Jr., and Jayanth K. Krishnan, 58–77. Cambridge: Cambridge University Press, 2010.

Olivelle, Patrick. "Dharmaśāstra: A Textual History," In *Hinduism and Law: An Introduction*, edited by Timothy Lubin, Donald R. Davis, Jr., and Jayanth K. Krishnan, 28–57. Cambridge: Cambridge University Press, 2010.

Orr, Leslie. *Donors, Devotees, and Daughters of God: Temple Women in Medieval Tamilnadu.* Oxford: Oxford University Press, 2000.

Prasad, Pushpa. *Lekhapaddhati: Documents of State and Everyday Life from Ancient and Early Medieval Gujarat.* Delhi: Oxford University Press, 2007.

Rocher, Ludo. *Studies in Hindu Law and Dharmaśāstra*. London: Anthem, 2012.

Salomon, Richard. "The Fine Art of Forgery in India." In *Écrire et transmettre en Inde classique*, edited by Gérard Colas and Gerdi Gerschheimer, 107–34. Paris: École française d'Extrême-Orient, 2009.

——. *Indian Epigraphy: A Guide to the Study of Inscriptions in Sanskrit, Prakrit, and the other Indo-Aryan Languages.* Oxford: Oxford University Press, 1998.

——. "The *Ukti-Vyakti-Prakaraṇa* as a Manual of Spoken Sanskrit." *Indo-Iranian Journal* 24 (1982): 13–25.

Scharfe, Hartmut. *The State in Indian Tradition*. Handbuch der Orientalistik. Leiden: Brill, 1989.

Sinopoli, Carla. *The Political Economy of Craft Production: Crafting Empire in South India, c. 1350–1650*. Cambridge: Cambridge University Press, 2003.

Sircar, D. C. *Indian Epigraphical Glossary*. Delhi: Motilal Banarsidass, 1966.

——. *Indian Epigraphy*. Delhi: Motilal Banarsidass, 1965.

Stein, Burton. *Peasant, State, and Society in Medieval South India*. Delhi: Oxford University Press, 1980.

Talbot, Cynthia. *Precolonial India in Practice: Society, Region, and Identity in Medieval Andhra*. Oxford: Oxford University Press, 2001.

Thakur, Anantalal. "Documents in Ancient India." *Annals of the Bhandarkar Oriental Research Institute* 9 (1928): 49–81.

Veluthat, Kesavan. *The Early Medieval in South India*. New Delhi: Oxford University Press, 2007.

Donald R. Davis, Jr. (drdj@austin.utexas.edu) is Associate Professor of Sanskrit and Indian Religions in the Department of Asian Studies at the University of Texas at Austin. His research focuses on the history of law and religion in medieval India, especially the tradition known as Hindu law. His major publications include *The Boundaries of Hindu Law: Tradition, Custom, and Politics in Medieval Kerala* (CESMEO, 2004) and *The Spirit of Hindu Law* (Cambridge University Press, 2010).

Abstract In order to understand the legal use and significance of documents in medieval India, we need to start from the contemporaneous legal categories found in the Sanskrit scholastic corpus called *dharmaśāstra*. By comparing these categories with actual historical documents and inscriptions, we gain better insight into the encounter of pan-Indian legal discourse in Sanskrit and regional laws in vernacular languages. The points of congruence and transgression in this encounter will facilitate a nuanced history of documents and their use beyond unhelpfully broad categories of written and oral. A new translation of one major scholastic discussion of documents is presented as a way to raise issues relevant to any historical description of the legal encounter text and practice.

Keywords documents, India, Hindu law, *dharmaśāstra*, scholasticism.

CHINESE PORCELAIN AND THE MATERIAL TAXONOMIES OF MEDIEVAL RABBINIC LAW: ENCOUNTERS WITH DISRUPTIVE SUBSTANCES IN TWELFTH-CENTURY YEMEN

ELIZABETH LAMBOURN and PHILLIP ACKERMAN-LIEBERMAN

LEGAL TEXTS ARE increasingly proving to be valuable sources for the study of the material culture of the medieval Middle East and the Islamicate world more broadly. Innovative monographs (such as Leor Halevi's *Muhammad's Grave: Death Rites and the Making of Islamic Society*) and articles (such as Tziona Grossmark's study of glass within Jewish law and Ruba Kana'an's use of Islamic legal sources in the interpretation of medieval metalwork production) exemplify the new perspectives that emerge from the dialogue between legal texts and material things.[1] As Don Davis proposes in this issue, we can see the "story of law" as "the formation of endless practical legal arrangements, the creation of rules and categories to tame them, and the subsequent mutual development of (and tension between) both as an ongoing encounter."[2] Hence, the objects of material culture offer us a new opportunity to explore the encounter between the theory and the praxis of law. Nevertheless, the slow pace at which legal corpora are being integrated into the study of material culture is a symptom of the complexity of these sources and the fundamentally interdisciplinary and collaborative nature of such an enterprise.[3]

This article focuses on a set of legal questions about *ṣīnī* vessels (literally, "Chinese" vessels) sent from the Jewish community in Aden to Fustat (Old Cairo) in the mid-1130s CE. These questions survive in a memorandum subsequently deposited in the so-called Cairo Geniza, a document which eventually made its way to Cambridge University Library (see **Figure 5**).[4]

---

1 Finbarr Barry Flood's forthcoming transhistorical exploration of the "prohibition of images" (*Bilderverbot*) as a perceived characteristic of Islamic cultures also innovatively integrates legal sources into this debate (the study's working title is *Islam and Image: Polemics, Theology, and Modernity*). *Ḥisba* manuals (compilations of marketplace rules) are exceptionally rich, if complex to interpret.

2 Davis, "Toward a History of Documents," 169–70.

3 Ghabin's *Ḥisba: Arts and Craft in Islam* illustrates the problems of interpreting terms and technologies described in *ḥisba* texts without a very sharply defined geographical, historical, and material context.

4 Goitein and Friedman, *India Traders*, 387, lines 5–12. In Goitein's classification, the letter is designated as document II, 33–34, and is composed of two surviving fragments, T-S 8J37.1

While *ṣīnī* vessels are listed in various Geniza inventories and wills, this is the only known discussion of the materiality of *ṣīnī* to occur in any Geniza document, and also the earliest dated and localized query about these vessels' status with respect to Jewish law of vessels used for food consumption.[5] Although opaque at first reading, our analysis of these queries will suggest that their phrasing and timing can be linked to the contemporaneous appearance, in the Yemen, of a new type of Chinese ceramic material: in effect, an early true "porcelain."[6] Although various types of Chinese ceramic had been entering the Middle East since the first half of the ninth century, sometimes in huge quantities, this particular ceramic fabric presented Jewish scholars and householders at the port of Aden with a perplexing problem, since its properties confounded their expectations of how a ceramic fabric should look, feel, and behave. In particular, the notable translucency of these early porcelains raised issues of purity (*ṭahora*) and uncleanness (*ṭuma*) that were fundamental to proper Jewish ritual observance: concepts that were structured by complex material taxonomies. By confounding and destabilizing these taxonomies,

---

and T-S Ar. 5.2; for the English translation of the full letter with footnotes and commentary, see Ibid., 377–89. The Hebrew edition of the letter includes the full transcription of the Judaeo-Arabic original and can be found in Goitein and Friedman, *Maḍmūn ha-Nagid*, 234–48 (for the Judaeo-Arabic transcription of this passage see page 239, lines 5–12). The document is also reproduced, with the text of the Judaeo-Arabic original and a Hebrew translation, in Goitein and Friedman, *Ḥalfon ha-soḥer*, 119–25.

5 See various references to *ṣīnī* in Goitein's *Mediterranean Society* (given in the cumulative indexes in volume 6 under "porcelain" and "*ṣīnī*"). To date, we have only been able to identify possible evidence for one earlier discussion of *ṣīnī* vessels: see below, n. 7.

6 A European invention of the fourteenth century, the term "porcelain" bears no relationship to emic Chinese ceramic categories; however, it is commonly used even by specialists of Chinese ceramics to refer to high-fired ceramics with exceptionally hard, vitreous bodies: this is the sense of the term employed here. Regina Krahl notes that "in the West, the term 'porcelain' is reserved for ceramics that are white, translucent and resonant and are fired at temperatures above 1,300 degrees Celsius," whereas in China there was no distinction made between these fabrics and so-called stonewares, ceramics that can lack these characteristics and are only fired above 1,200 degrees Celsius. As she observes, "in practice there is no distinct dividing line between the two but a smooth transition, and the difference is not necessarily apparent to the naked eye" (Krahl, "White Wares of Northern China," 202). The term "porcellaneous" is often used to reflect this complexity. Technically speaking, the earliest porcelains were produced in China in Henan, at the Gongxian kilns, in the seventh century; while Jingdezhen in the south began producing early porcelains in the late Tang/Five Dynasties period (907–60 CE): see Needham, Kerr, and Wood, *Science and Civilization in China*, 151–53 and 216–19; see also Pierson, "Industrial Ceramics in China," 62. In the Middle East, Chinese ceramics quickly became known simply as *ṣīnī*, a term that translates more accurately as "chinaware," since it came to designate any Far Eastern ceramic, or indeed any of its Middle Eastern imitations.

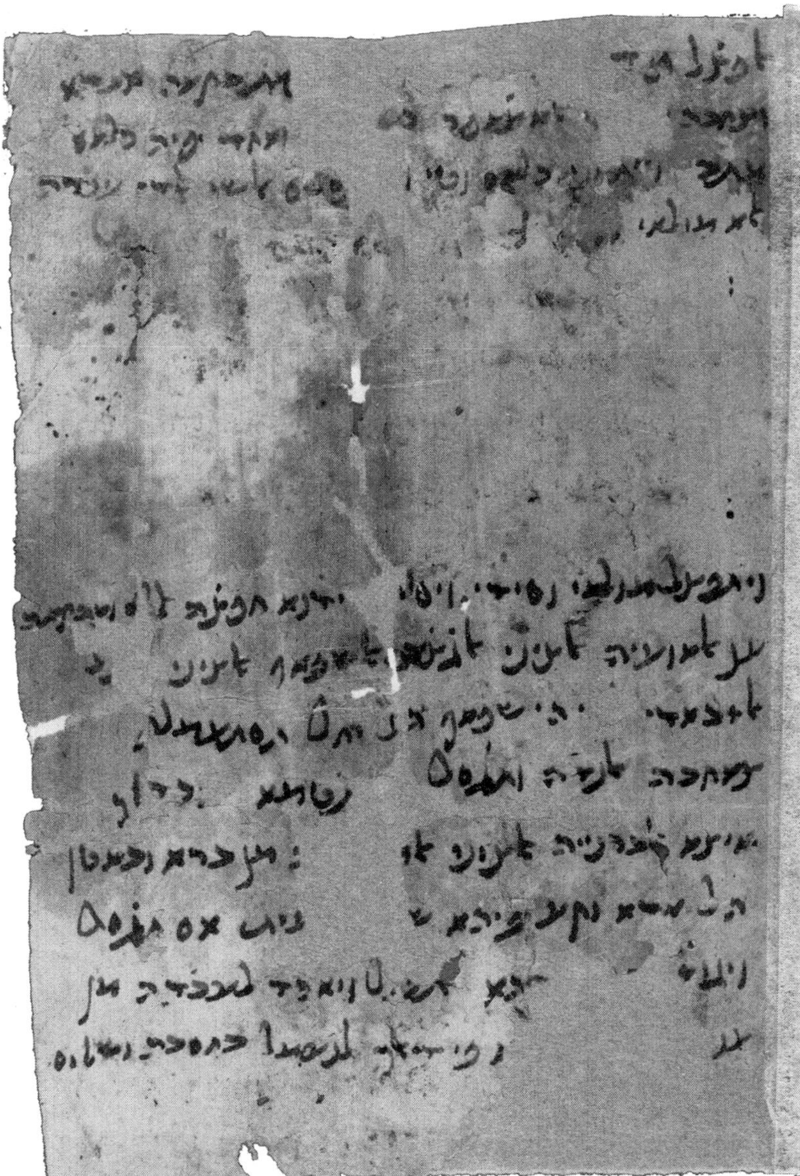

Figure 5. Page from the memorandum written by Maḍmūn b. Ḥasan Japheth (Aden, ca. 1135), showing the postscriptum query about *ṣīnī* vessels.
Cambridge University Library, T-S 8J37.1, fol. 2r.
Reproduced with permission of the Syndics of Cambridge University Library.

Chinese porcelain became a disruptive substance. Marshalling evidence from contemporary Jewish legal compendia and other writings produced in this milieu, our discussion substantially advances some interpretive angles first suggested by S. D. Goitein and Mordechai A. Friedman. We examine the efforts of Adeni Jews to place this Chinese ceramic fabric among already legislated substances, notably the "neighboring" substances of glass and earthenware, in order to derive clear rules for the proper use and purification of vessels manufactured from it. Indeed, the pattern of encounter and negotiation revealed here is characteristic of rabbinic Judaism's approach to new materials and the technologies behind them, and has a long history running from the popularization of glass vessels in the early first millennium CE through to the modern-day entry of plastics into the kosher home. And yet the specific material culture of Judaism has received comparatively little attention from scholars, so one of the aims of this article is to highlight the unique and rich potential of this field.

Only eight lines long, the query on which we focus amounts to an aside in a much longer memorandum; it might even be described as an afterthought, a postscriptum, since it occupies the last lines of this eighty-eight-line document. Nevertheless, this passage is arguably one of the longest and most complex meditations on the material culture of the region. It yields important new data on the reception of Chinese ceramics in the Middle East, and it adds to a painfully small corpus of texts documenting the early discursive history of this reception, opening new perspectives on their taxonomic integration with the varied material cultures of the region. Even the timing of this query—posed in the 1130s, three centuries after the largescale importation of Chinese ceramics began in the region—contributes new textual evidence for the chronology of exchanges between the Middle East and China. Moreover, this passage is also a significant new source for Jewish legal history. While Tziona Grossmark's innovative work on glass is beginning to sketch out the wider processes through which rabbinic Judaism accommodated new materials, the history of the encounters that produced these new materials is largely unwritten. The questions examined here represent the earliest evidence for the debate within Judaism about the ritual implications of Chinese ceramic fabrics, and thus the beginning of a process of encounter and accommodation. Hitherto, the debate about porcelain has been traced to the much later rulings about Chinese porcelain given by rabbis from the sixteenth century onwards, filtered through the lens of subsequent Jewish jurists the world over. The survival of these questions in a letter, rather than in a legal text, suggests that they should be seen as fresh evidence for the newly contested status of Chinese ceramics in a ritually observant Jewish environment rather than the remnant of a long-standing debate within Jewish law. Addressing the interdisciplinary challenges involved in the analysis of this document, this article is co-authored by a specialist in material culture (Lambourn) in collaboration with a specialist in Jewish law (Lieberman).

Decoding Two Questions about *Ṣīnī* Vessels

Sometime around 1135, a prominent Jewish merchant in Aden sent a set of very precise questions about *ṣīnī* ("Chinese") vessels to Maṣliaḥ Gaon, the head of the Palestinian yeshiva in Fustat (Old Cairo) who held the post between 1127 and 1139.[7] The merchant was Maḍmūn b. Ḥasan Japheth, the head of the Jewish community in Aden and also a shipowner and armorer.[8] The queries were not addressed directly to the Gaon but were to be asked of him, in person, by Abū Sa'īd Ḥalfon ha-Levi b. Nethanel al-Dimyāṭī, a business partner of Maḍmūn's who was returning to Egypt. Maḍmūn's questions are preserved at the end of a lengthy memorandum (*tadhkira*) he wrote to Ḥalfon ha-Levi. As is typical of Geniza documents, the memorandum is written in Judaeo-Arabic, contemporary colloquial Arabic written in Hebrew characters. Maḍmūn writes to Ḥalfon:[9]

> Please be so kind, my lord and master, to ask our lord [Maṣliaḥ Gaon]—may God protect him and keep him alive—about the *ṣīnī* vessels (*'an al-aw'īya al-ṣīnī*), the translucent pottery vessels (*al-aw'īya al-ghaḍār al-shaffāf),* and all the *ṣīnī* tablewares [which are] translucent (*wa-kull al-zibādī [al-ṣīn]ī hiyya shaffāf*): whether it is permissible for a menstruating woman (*ṣāḥibat al-nida*) to use them and wash them [or] whether they will then be ritually unclean (*im tiṭame* [Hebrew]). Furthermore, [ask about] a *ṣīnī* jar (*al-barnīya al-ṣīnī*) which is [glazed][10] outside and inside (*al-mu*[*kallas*]*a min barra wa bāṭin*): if something should fall into it (*idhā waqa'a fī-hā shayy*), [whether] that will render it unfit ([*hal ya*] *ᶜīthu*)[11] or if it is permissible to wash it and it will be fit for use. Please be

7 Dates of office given in Goitein and Friedman, *India Traders*, 379. Goitein bases his dating of the memorandum on the fact that Ḥalfon ha-Levi is known to have been in Aden in 1134; however, Friedman adds a more cautious comment, suggesting tentatively that it be dated around 1135 (see 379).

8 For Maḍmūn's biography, see Goitein and Friedman, *India Traders*, 37–47.

9 English translation from Goitein and Friedman, *India Traders*, 387, lines 5–12; for the full Judaeo-Arabic transcription and Hebrew translation, see Goitein and Friedman, *Maḍmūn ha-Nagid*, 239, lines 5–12.

10 As Goitein and Friedman indicate in their footnote (*India Traders*, 387 n. 54) the reading *mukallasa* or "glazed" is suggested on the basis of the surviving initial letter *mem* and the final *he*, and was suggested by Paul Kahle in correspondence with Goitein back in the 1950s.

11 This section of the memorandum is heavily damaged and the restitution of the missing

> so kind as to obtain for me from [our lord an answer] in this matter, so that we may act accordingly."

It is no accident that these very particular queries were sent with Ḥalfon ha-Levi on this particular journey: the memorandum makes it clear that he was transporting a substantial load of presents for family members of Maḍmūn's in Fustat, as well as for various members of the Palestinian yeshiva there. In particular, he had been charged with delivering a rather generous batch of presents to the Gaon, Maṣliaḥ ha-Kohen, alone. Ḥalfon carried six satchels containing over five kilograms of Southeast Asian aromatic woods and spices, one hundred *k'b sh't ṣīnī* (an as yet unidentified Chinese commodity), two South Indian *mandīl*s or kerchiefs, together with a small basket containing "a *dast* [set] of *ṣīnī* bowls (*aqdāḥ*),[12] numbering six bowls."[13] The dispatch of these presents belongs within a complex and long-drawn out competition between centers of Jewish learning in Iraq and Egypt—the so-called Babylonian and Palestinian academies or yeshivas—for the loyalty of Yemeni Jews, and more practically for their donations. Ḥalfon played a major part in supporting Maṣliaḥ's authority in Yemen, and these gifts are evidently connected to this religio-political struggle. Since the authority of an academy was instantiated first and foremost through its role in answering legal queries and resolving community matters, the act of asking these questions can be seen as a further expression of loyalty to the Gaon.[14] The legal questions and the gift assemblage they accompanied suggest that Maṣliaḥ was going to be able to examine the very sort of *ṣīnī* vessel about which he was being asked to give his opinion. This was not an abstract discussion of legal theory but a real-world question about the application of rabbinic law in lived practice. As Maḍmūn himself emphasized, he wanted answers so that he could "act accordingly."

---

text is still open to interpretation. Friedman was not able to make out the interrogative *hal* transcribed by Goitein but agrees with the interpretation that the verb is most probably *ʿyth*: an uncommon verb with the meaning (Form I) to spoil, ruin (s.th.), which Goitein translated as "render it unfit" (Friedman, personal communication of October 29, 2015). Friedman suggests the literal translation "spoil [it]."

12 The term *qadaḥ* (pl. *aqdāḥ*) is frequently translated "goblet." However, the surviving Chinese vessels are more frequently bowls of various sizes, without stems, the smallest of which might be used for drinking. We therefore prefer the broader translation "bowl," although one might also consider "drinking cup" as an alternative.

13 Goitein and Friedman, *India Traders*, 383, lines 6–7; for the full list of presents see 382–83, lines 13–17 and 1–7.

14 For a discussion of Maḍmūn's place in the struggle between the academies of Babylonia and the Land of Israel, see Friedman, *Ḥalfon ve-Yehuda ha-Levi*, 114–57.

Maḍmūn's two questions may seem obscure and even strange to those unfamiliar with Jewish practices of purity. But as the following analysis will show, each word was carefully chosen and the pair of questions logically constructed. Before exploring them, it is useful to give a short summary of the principles that structured Jewish ritual practice and generated a unique material taxonomy.

A foundational concern within Judaism centred on issues of purity (*ṭahora*) and its corollary, impurity (*ṭuma*): the contamination of the pure through exposure to any substance which has itself contracted impurity, and the transmission of that impurity through a variety of modes of contact. Where food and drink are concerned, not only contact with contaminated food and drink but also contact with blood or other bodily fluids can present a problem. The *Pentateuch* contains commandments for the avoidance of certain sources of contamination when eating, procreating, and worshiping God in the Temple. While a principal source of ritual impurity is contact with a human corpse, several verses in Leviticus introduce other such sources: clean and unclean foods, childbirth, menstruation and other bodily excretions, and skin ailments. Verses in the Book of Numbers also establish the principle that a utensil can be purified by being exposed to the same medium through which it was rendered unclean. Thus, vessels rendered unclean from cooking on a fire would be purified with fire, others rendered unclean through having unclean food boiled in them should themselves be boiled (Numbers 21–23). Early rabbinic sages (*tannaim*) maintained the importance of the system of purity and even extend its prohibitions to a constituency well beyond the Temple priesthood. By the early third century CE, a considerable volume of oral tradition and legal precedent had developed around this issue, in effect amplifying "the definition of what is affected by uncleanness, how uncleanness is transmitted, and the way in which uncleanness is removed."[15]

In fact, the rabbinic system of purity views liquids as more powerful than solids in communicating impurity and identifies seven liquids specifically: water, dew, oil, wine, milk, blood, and honey. Therefore, vessels or objects that may hold liquids play a particularly prominent role in Jewish considerations of ritual purity, since any utensil capable of containing a liquid may be particularly vulnerable. However, a corollary to the principles governing the transmission of impurity is the binary notion that various materials are more or less resistant to contamination. Once absorbed, impurity may be impossible to remove. Jewish authorities of the Talmudic period (that is, ca. 200–500 CE) centered their discussions of contamination around the porousness of material substances. By the medieval period, Judaism had developed a complex body of knowledge and set of practices relating

15 *Encyclopedia Judaica*, "Purity and Impurity, Ritual."

to ritual purity founded on a unique taxonomy that took into account the nature of various material substances as well as their formal qualities.

Each of Maḍmūn's questions thus sets up a subtly different scenario involving the contamination of a certain sort of *ṣīnī* vessel, first bowls, and then jars. First, Maḍmūn asks whether, if a menstruating woman touched these vessels and rendered them unclean, the vessels might be washed to repurify them. The term used here is "wash" (trilitteral root GH-S-L), suggesting a simple act of rinsing the polluted vessels in water, as opposed to the more formal process of immersion in a *mikveh*, a ritual bath. In either case, water performs a cleansing role, returning the object to purity. However, would the touch of a menstruating woman render these vessels permanently impure? If so, they could no longer be used and might even need to be broken. In his comments on this letter, the great Geniza scholar S. D. Goitein emphasizes the excessively stringent application of Jewish law which this question assumes, noting that it was only in the Land of Israel that "attempts were still made to observe the laws of purity and impurity as in the time of the Temple, when menstruating women forbidden to touch household utensils."[16] "According to normative Jewish law," he further explains, "as formulated in the Babylonian Talmud and later halakhic literature, there is no place for such a question, since no utensil is rendered unclean by a menstruating woman's touch," although menstrual blood itself was polluting.[17] Goitein notes, however, that similarly stringent practices were observable amongst Jewish communities in both Iraq and Egypt and, on the basis of this query, Yemen too.[18] Furthermore, as noted by Mordechai A. Friedman, the rank-and-file of the Jewish community might not have been able to determine whether the more restrictive practice was a matter of black-letter law or whether it was simply a pious custom.[19] In the latter case, given the significant financial loss incurred by breaking a precious *ṣīnī* vessel, it is possible that this stringency might be relaxed.[20] And yet the query does not engage with the

16 Goitein and Friedman, *India Traders*, 389. Also discussed in Friedman, "Harḥaqat ha-nida" (Distancing from Menstrual Impurity).

17 Goitein and Friedman, *India Traders*, 389. See also Friedman, *Ḥalfon ve-Yehuda ha-Levi*, 156.

18 Goitein, "Stern Religion." Maḍmūn's note and additional evidence from the Geniza for these stringencies are discussed in Friedman, "Harḥaqat ha-nida," 20; Friedman notes that the more stringent practice of the Land of Israel was known in Yemen.

19 Friedman, "Harḥaqat ha-nida," 13.

20 The Austrian authority Jacob Reischer (1661–1733) records that a group of Venetian rabbis had permitted polluted earthenware vessels to be used after remaining unused for only twenty-four hours, but argued that such a leniency should only be allowed in the event of significant monetary loss: Minḥat Yaʿaqov, 85:64; cited in Walter, "Can Porcelain Be *Kashered*?," 118 n. 21. In present-day debates about the repurification of china or

question of what should become of an unusable vessel—whether it needed to be broken or, alternatively and far more probably, whether it could be sold outside the Jewish community with no loss of value in the eyes of other consumers. Maḍmūn's question belongs within a wider discussion among Middle Eastern Jewry of the question of impurity imparted to vessels by menstruant women and recorded in contemporary responsa from Egypt and elsewhere.[21] However, Maḍmūn is the only one to frame this question with specific regard to *ṣīnī* vessels, and Aden's dominant position in the trade of the Indian Ocean no doubt played a part in this.

Maḍmūn's second question asks how to repurify a *ṣīnī* jar (*barnīya*) after some "thing" has fallen into it. The halakhic literature is rife with such questions—"Rabbi, a drop of milk fell into my chicken soup!"[22] Where the first question uses the Hebrew term *tiṭma*, "rendered impure," here the vessel is described as potentially "unfit for use," literally "spoiled" even "ruined." As we have seen, all vessels and their contents can contract impurity through contact with impure substances or people in a state of ritual impurity. But Jewish legal material also places considerable focus on the material from which the vessel is made, whether the external or internal surface of the vessel is concerned, whether the vessel itself is finished or not, the intent of the agents involved, the relative quantities of the various contaminating substances, and whether the act of contamination occurs deliberately. Maḍmūn's second question carefully engages these parameters by shifting the discussion from tablewares to kitchenwares, from vessels used for eating or drinking to vessels used for storage or cooking. Where the first question repeatedly mentions the translucency of the vessel type discussed, this question focuses instead on the fact that the vessel is glazed externally and internally (*al-mu*[*kallas*]*a min barra wa bāṭin*);[23] and where the first question emphasizes the human source of contamination, the menstruating woman, the agent of contamination here is a generic non-human "thing" (*shayy*).

Both of Maḍmūn's questions indicate that contemporary Jews discussed and reflected on the materiality of the objects in their households and did so specifically in terms of the ritual implications of their material properties. In

porcelain dinner services, the issue of financial loss plays an important part in determining a more lenient interpretation. In this vein, contemporary authorities such as Ovadya Yosef (1920–2013, Israel) apply the principle of "significant monetary loss" to permit the use of porcelain dishes on which non-kosher meat has been served (Yabia' Omer, Yoreh De'a I:6, nos. 16, 17, cited in Walter, "Can Porcelain be Kashered?," 118, n. 23).

21 See the extensive discussion of these sources in Friedman, "Harḥaqat ha-nida."

22 See, for example, *Talmud Bavli*, Pesaḥim 75b–76a, concerning permitted matter falling into prohibited, or vice versa.

23 Note that the word *al-mu*[*kallas*]*a* has been restored by Goitein and Friedman.

this instance, they were particularly interested in the materiality of *ṣīnī* vessels, whether translucent bowls or glazed jars, and were concerned enough to forward a query about this to the religious authorities in Fustat. Was this ceramic fabric so glass-like—in its translucency, perhaps its smoothness and thinness too—that it should in fact be categorized as glass within the rabbinic system? The intense observation and handling of different vessels and utensils implicit in these two questions underlines rabbinic Judaism's unique epistemology, a relationship with the material world forged around complex taxonomies of substances, pollutants, purifiers, forms, and modes of contact. Mary Douglas's now famous anthropological study of systems of ritual purity, *Purity and Danger*, emphasizes the important role of such taxonomies in controlling pollutants, which were seen as "anomalous" and disruptive to the symbolic system.[24] But Maḍmūn's questions helpfully underline that it is not only pollutants that threaten this order but any change to one of its constituent material categories. By the twelfth century many elements of this system—polluting substances, modes of contact—were already clearly and comprehensively identified; however, any new material from which utensils were fashioned represented a challenge. New materials, and the technologies that allowed their manufacture, were also anomalous and disruptive of the system. Grossmark's examination of the processes through which glass vessels entered rabbinic taxonomies is an important milestone in the study of this world view and ultimately the creation of specifically Jewish materialities. Glass's disruption of rabbinic taxonomies is evidenced by the multiple, often contradictory categorizations of this new material—variously likened to metal, earthenware, or even wood, leather, and bone—issued by rabbis well into the twelfth century.[25] In the present article, it is porcelain's highly vitrified body and glaze that was "anomalous," and which threatened to destabilize established ceramic categories.

What Was Maḍmūn's *Ṣīnī*?

The date of Maḍmūn's questions, penned in Aden around 1135, will immediately seem strange to historians of material culture. Chinese ceramics had been imported to the Middle East since the first half of the ninth century,[26] and Aden

---

24 Douglas, *Purity and Danger*.

25 Grossmark, "And He Decreed."

26 There is a vast bibliography on the early history of Chinese ceramic imports to the Middle East; for more recent publications including archaeological material, see Rougeulle, "Les importations de céramiques chinoises," and Hallet, "Pearl Cups." While the majority of early Chinese ceramic imports would still have been recognizably ceramic (if novel in their durability, decoration, and form), a smaller number of porcellaneous or porcelain-like wares

was a key node in the Fatimid Indian Ocean trade, a port that the geographer al-Muqaddasī had described, two centuries earlier, as "the vestibule of China" (*dihlīz al-Ṣīn*).[27] Although medieval Aden has never been formally excavated, a wide variety of Chinese ceramic types have been reported as surface finds at nearby sites[28] and have been excavated from Fatimid levels at the port of Aqaba on the very northern coast of the Red Sea where they are dated to the second half of the tenth and eleventh centuries.[29] They have also been found in large quantities at Fatimid Fustat from the later tenth century onwards.[30] Why then did Maḍmūn need to ask these questions? Were there not earlier rulings about the ritual status of *ṣīnī* vessels to turn to for guidance?

There is suggestive evidence that questions about the ritual status of *ṣīnī* vessels were asked almost as soon as early porcelains began to enter the Middle East in the later tenth and early eleventh centuries. A sixteenth-century discussion by Rabbi David b. Zimra (known as Radbaz) alludes to an earlier ruling which stated that, during Passover, *ṣīnī* vessels were to be treated like earthenware vessels: that is, considered incapable of repurification. The opinion is neither dated nor attributed to a specific authority, however Radbaz acknowledged its great age and that it was recorded in the midst of a collection of responsa which included some from Hai Gaon (939–1038) and other contemporary figures active in the Jewish academies of Abbasid Iraq.[31] Nevertheless, such discussions appear to

---

did reach the Middle East at this early period: see Guy, "Rare and Strange Goods," who notes that alongside the 55,000 Changsha bowls in the cargo of the Belitung wreck (an Arabian vessel *en route* to China from Africa around 830 CE) were smaller consignments of two or three hundred high-end whitewares and green-splashed whitewares from northern Chinese kilns (20).

27 al-Muqaddasī, *Best Divisions for Knowledge*, 83.

28 Islamic-period Yemen is poorly surveyed while Aden, as a major port, poses numerous archaeological challenges making it impossible to present well stratified evidence. For the abundance of imported Chinese wares in the twelfth century, see Lane and Serjeant, "Pottery and Glass"; King and Tonghini, *Survey of the Islamic Sites*; as well as broad introductions to the archaeology of the Aden area by Hardy-Guilbert and Rougeulle, "Archaeological Research" and "Al-Shihr."

29 Whitcomb, "Fatimid Residence at Aqaba," 211. For an overview of ceramic circulation in both the Gulf and Red Sea at this period, see Rougeulle, "Golfe persique et Mer Rouge." Zhao's work on Sharma provides excellent distribution maps for Chinese ceramics all along the Red Sea coast: "La céramique chinoise."

30 For a concise and clear summary of the sometimes confusing publications from the Fustat excavations, with full bibliography, see Bongianino, "'And Their Figures.'"

31 This early reference was first noted by Goitein and Friedman (*India Traders*, 387n54), who deemed the source too vague to allow any conclusions to be drawn. Further perusal

be extremely rare, and we have been unable to identify any other references to *ṣīnī* earlier than Maḍmūn's queries. The paucity of discursive evidence may well reflect the comparative rarity of *ṣīnī* and runs parallel to similar patterns in the halakhic discussion of glass. As Grossmark has shown, a delay of several centuries can be discerned between the first expansion in the production of glasswares in the Middle East, in the first century CE, and the discussion of the ritual status of glass in the fifth century. These are precisely the centuries during which glass became more popularly available in the region and when issues of its use began to affect Jewish households on a regular basis, finally triggering a formal scholarly response.[32] Against this background, Maḍmūn's queries might be read as an early sign of the popularization of Chinese ceramics in Jewish households in Aden, and perhaps in the wider Middle East; indeed, this was the conclusion reached by Goitein and Friedman in their edition of the memorandum.[33] Unfortunately, the absence of archaeological data for medieval Aden makes it impossible to corroborate this hypothesis. However, the substantial contemporary evidence for the importation of Chinese ceramics to Egypt via the Red Sea suggests that Chinese ceramics *were* in widespread use. One might also point to *The Book of Gifts and Rarities* (*Kitāb al-Hadāyā wa-l-Tuḥaf*), a Fatimid compilation by Qadi Ibn al-Zubayr (1053–71), in which *ṣīnī* vessels are rarely mentioned—and then only because of some outstanding feature, such as immense size or unusual color or precious contents, indicating that more common vessels were both ubiquitous and beneath notice.[34] The overall impression is that while Chinese wares were not everyday objects, they had nonetheless been widely available beyond the Fatimid elite for some time before the 1130s.[35] The timing of this question therefore remains puzzling: why the need to ask about *ṣīnī* now?

---

of the commentary shows, however, that Radbaz cites part of the earlier Judaeo-Arabic responsum verbatim, although the text is corrupt in the printed edition. It is clear that the geonic responsum is not answering Maḍmūn's question but deals specifically with the use of *ṣīnī* vessels during Passover.

32 Grossmark, "'And He Decreed,'" 191–212.

33 Goitein and Friedman, *India Traders*, 389.

34 Ibn al-Zubayr, *Kitāb al-Hadāyā wa-l-Tuḥaf*, 384–85 (for example).

35 The contemporary market for, and circulation of, Chinese ceramics beyond the Middle East is the subject of considerable debate. While Whitehouse ("Chinese Porcelain in Medieval Europe") points to the scarcity of finds, and François ("La porcelaine de Chine") argues that their absence from Byzantium and the Christian east is evidence for a fundamentally different taste in ceramics, Milwright (in "Modest Luxuries," 86 n. 16) notes that "stonepaste jars were often the containers for expensive commodities such as spices, medicines, or preserved fruit. It is clear, however, that the vessels themselves were subjects of admiration

We propose that the timing and particular angles of Maḍmūn's inquiry can only be explained by the presence in Aden of significant quantities of a substantially new type of Chinese ceramic ware, a fabric that was substantially different from previous imports and one that thus challenged established material taxonomies and elicited new questions from its Jewish consumers. One aspect of this document's significance is therefore its contribution to our understanding of the chronology of Chinese ceramic imports to the Middle East, testifying to the arrival of a type now known as *qingbai* 青白, "bluish-white," because of the light blue tinge of its glaze: a porcellaneous ware of a new translucency and thinness.[36] *Qingbai* was, as Rose Kerr states, "the material from which most later white porcelain bodies developed. It was a white and translucent material that could be thinly potted to create forms of extraordinary delicacy."[37] *Qingbai*'s exceptional qualities were due to its china stone (petuntse) body, which was almost 50 percent quartz and high in calcia and mica. China stone also contained kaolin "so that it produced a more plastic body" according to Stacey Pierson.[38] For export to the Middle East, *qingbai* was frequently decorated with combed or incised floral designs. Finally, the *qingbai* vessel was glazed with a mixture of china stone mixed with crushed, burnt limestone that produced a hard, vitrified transparent glaze. As Pierson explains, "not surprisingly, tableware was the most important aspect of *qingbai* production, and much of it was destined for frequent use. The porcelain body is ideal for making durable but light and attractive tablewares."[39]

Porcelain stone was abundantly available in the Jingdezhen area of southeastern China, and it is here, during the later tenth century, that *qingbai* proper was first developed.[40] Bing Zhao notes that *qingbai* begins to appear regularly in Chinese tombs from the year 1000 onwards, and this no doubts marks the beginnings of its wider popularity in China, even if comparatively little is understood about

in medieval European courts."

36 Kessler (*Song Blue and White Porcelain*, 348–54) has argued that the term actually refers to blue and white underglaze porcelains; however, this interpretation has not been widely accepted.

37 Kerr, *Song Dynasty Ceramics*, 96. The technology itself was comparatively simple by Chinese standards, involving low firing temperatures (1170–1260 degrees Celsius) with the body made from porcelain stone and glazes that used the same porcelain stone together with a limestone flux. The ceramics were reduction-fired in wood fired kilns.

38 Pierson, *Qingbai Ware*, 15.

39 Pierson, *Qingbai Ware*, 18.

40 Pierson, *Qingbai Ware*, 15; and eadem, "Industrial Ceramics," 62–63. See also Zhao, "L'importation de la céramique chinoise," 257 n. 5.

Figure 6. *Qingbai* bowl with combed decoration, twelfth century.
British Museum, accession number 1991.1028.5. Height: 8.00 cm. Diameter: 21.20 cm. Weight: 400g.

the Chinese consumers of this ware.[41] From Jingdezhen, the technology of *qingbai* manufacture spread during the eleventh century to northern and southern China: between the tenth and thirteenth centuries, several dozen *qingbai* production centers have been identified.[42] One should note, however, that Chinese ceramic specialists generally reserve the term *qingbai* for wares produced at Jingdezhen itself or in Jiangxi Province, reserving local names for "*qingbai*-type" wares manufactured at these other locations, which range over forty-four counties and nine Chinese provinces to the north and south of the Yangzi river.[43] *Qingbai* and *qingbai*-type tablewares were not only extremely popular in China but found a large export market and were exported to more than twenty different countries in Asia, Africa, and Europe.[44] That wide distribution has been confirmed and refined through subsequent archaeology, on land and at sea.[45]

41 The oldest tomb from which *qingbai* wares were excavated is dated to 983 CE; see Zhao, "L'importation de la céramique chinoise," 263 n. 22.

42 Zhao, "L'importation de la céramique chinoise," 258. We are grateful to the author for clarifying that the French *fours* refers to production centres rather than to single kilns.

43 Once Yuan period production centers are included, the number rises significantly to over 136 sites producing *qingbai* wares in the area of Jingdezhen alone for the Song and Yuan dynasties: see Peng, *Song Yuan*, 30–36. We are grateful to Rosemary E. Scott for this reference.

44 Li, "Chinese Export Porcelain," 103. Of interest for the maritime export trade to the Middle East is the fact that production centers for *qingbai*-type wares are found in Guangdong and northern Fujian, as well as the area of Minnan, the hinterland of the great maritime port of Quanzhou, in the mid- to late eleventh century: see Pierson, *Qingbai Ware*, 17. For developments around Quanzhou, see especially Ho, "Ceramic Boom in Minnan," 258–60.

45 The most recent distribution map for *qingbai* wares in the western Indian Ocean and Middle East is in Zhao, "La céramique chinoise," fig. 222;" see also her "Global Trade," fig. 9. For shipwreck archaeology see, for example, Dupoizat, "Ceramic Cargo."

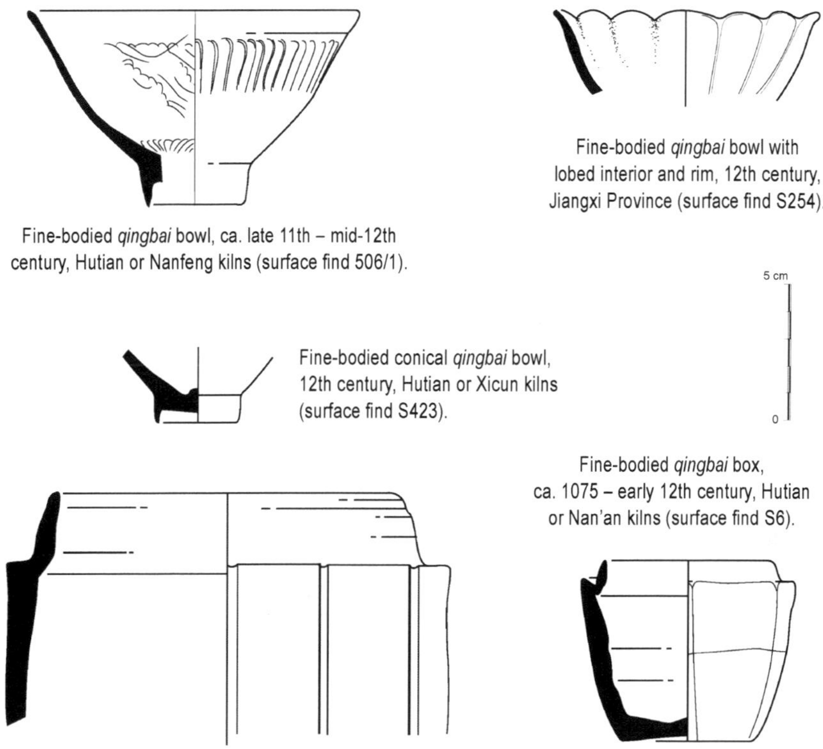

Fine-bodied *qingbai* bowl, ca. late 11th – mid-12th century, Hutian or Nanfeng kilns (surface find 506/1).

Fine-bodied *qingbai* bowl with lobed interior and rim, 12th century, Jiangxi Province (surface find S254).

Fine-bodied conical *qingbai* bowl, 12th century, Hutian or Xicun kilns (surface find S423).

Fine-bodied *qingbai* box, ca. 1075 – early 12th century, Hutian or Nan'an kilns (surface find S6).

Medium-bodied *qingbai* box, ca. 1050–1100, Xicun kilns (surface find S172).

Figure 7. Shard fragments of fine porcelain *qingbai* bowls and lidded boxes from the entrepôt of Sharma, Yemen, spanning the mid-eleventh to twelfth century. The largest, most complete sherds are often surface finds. *Attributions and dates from Zhao, 'La céramique chinoise à Sharma,' Figs. 203–4, 204–1, 206–4, 208–4, 208–5; drawings by Vincent Bernard and Hélène Renel, reproduced by kind permission of Axelle Rougeulle.*

Although we cannot prove which ceramic wares Maḍmūn handled, we wish to suggest that there is a strong likelihood that they were *qingbai*. The translucency of these pieces would have been in marked contrast to the majority of earlier Chinese imports and would have elicited exactly the puzzled reaction recorded in the memorandum. It is impossible to represent through one example the diversity of *qingbai* tablewares produced for consumers inside and outside China; nevertheless, by way of general illustration, we include here a photograph of a twelfth-century *qingbai* bowl with combed decoration from the collections of the British Museum (**Figure 6**). To the best of our knowledge, no complete *qingbai* pieces survive from the Middle East—largely because Islam and Judaism alike prohibited burial goods, whereas ceramics from Chinese tombs provide some of the best datable pieces. But **Figure 7** shows sherds from a range of *qingbai* bowls and lidded boxes excavated at the entrepôt of Sharma in the Yemen and spanning the mid-eleventh to twelfth centuries. The delicate bowls of various shapes and design, usually with a diameter of around five centimeters, may well correspond to the *aqdāḥ*—"small bowls" or "drinking cups"—sent to the Gaon in Fustat for inspection. The lidded boxes found at Sharma, some of which had a diameter of over ten centimetres, may correspond to the *barnīya* jar described in our legal query.

Goitein urged caution when translating the term *ṣīnī* in the Fatimid period, since it was by then applied to wide range of Far Eastern ceramics as well as to their Middle Eastern imitations.[46] In many contexts, the term is best translated simply as "chinaware," in the inclusive (modern) sense, rather than as "Chinese porcelain" strictly defined.[47] In this particular instance, however, Maḍmūn was certainly referring to some form of high-fired, porcellaneous Far Eastern ceramic. No contemporary local (Yemeni) ceramics are known to have attempted to imitate Chinese prototypes and thus merit the appellation *ṣīnī*.[48] It would be nonsensical to send comparatively coarse Yemeni glazed wares, even if they existed at this period, to such an eminent figure as Maṣliaḥ ha-Kohen; an exchange in the other direction would have been more likely, as Geniza documents indicate that Aden's Jewish elite brought in better quality ceramics from Egypt and Syria.[49] The batch

46 Goitein, *Mediterranean Society*, 4:145–46.

47 Goitein advocated using the term "fine earthenware," since the low prices indicated for some *sīnī*, and the fact that some pieces were owned by the poorer members of Cairo's Jewish community, would indicate that this was not a high-end ware. In fact, it is more likely that lower-end wares were locally manufactured vessels with a new fritware (also known as stonepaste) body developed in direct response to Chinese porcellaneous bodies. See n. 61, below.

48 Although local Adeni ceramics have not been studied, there is no firm evidence for production of glazed ceramics in the Yemen until the late eleventh and mainly twelfth centuries, and these have been identified at the site of Sharma in the Hadhramaut. In the opinion of the site's excavators, these wares may be predecessors of the much better known Yemeni "mustard ware" so called because of its yellow glaze, which can be dated more securely to ca. 1250 to 1350 and was produced either around Zabid in the Tihama or Aden (Axelle Rougeulle, personal communication of September 17, 2015). For more on this ware, see Rougeulle, "Les céramiques à glaçure," 250–51. So far, the only known contemporary parallels for this ceramic ware are an assemblage of bowls excavated at the port of Ghulayfiqa in the Tihama and dateable to the twelfth century.

49 See, for example, a list of items requested from Fustat for dispatch to Aden, likely on the occasion of a wedding, which included "a basket of good earthenware made in Amid or Fustat": Goitein and Friedman, *India Traders*, 422, line 17 ("India Book," document II, 44, Westminster Misc. 9).

of gifts among which this *ṣīnī* travelled to Egypt—Chinese *k'b sh't* (whatever this unidentified commodity was); Southeast Asian cloves, nutmeg, and mace; a variety of aromatic woods; as well as silks from the port of Kollam in southern Malabar—also support the hypothesis of the vessels' Chinese provenance, since it is clear that the entire cache of presents destined for Maṣliaḥ ha-Kohen had been assembled through the maritime networks of the eastern Indian Ocean and the South China Sea, with the spices and woods originating in eastern Indonesia, the *k'b sh't* and *ṣīnī* in China.

Maḍmūn's questions may accordingly contribute to a still imprecise understanding of the chronology and routes of *qingbai* imports into the Middle East. Chinese ceramics specialists date the start of large scale exports of *qingbai* to the late eleventh and early twelfth centuries and some scholars have picked out 1127 as a key date in the development of *qingbai* as an export product, since it is the date at which the northern Song territories were conquered and the southern Song polity reoriented itself and its exports towards southern China and the south China Sea.[50] Pierson has suggested, instead, that it was the opening of a maritime administration at Quanzhou forty years earlier, in 1087, which marked the turning point in the development of this ware for export.[51] For Chuimei Ho, too, there is little doubt that the forty-seven large kilns producing *qingbai*-type wares that appear *ex nihilo* in Minnan, the hinterland of Quanzhou, in the later eleventh century, should be dated to around 1087.[52] A rise in exports in the latter half of the eleventh century finds corroboration in contemporary textual sources and the Song dynasty text 萍洲可談 *Pingzhou Ketan* (Discourse of the Floating Islands) published in 1119, which discusses the maritime trade in Guangzhou during the period 1086–94 and notes that "the greater part of the cargo consists of pottery, the small pieces packed in the larger, till there is not a crevice left."[53]

New archaeological data from the Middle East and East Africa is refining this periodization. *Qingbai* bowl bases excavated at Fustat have been dated by Bongionino to the Five Dynasties or northern Song, and thus to the late tenth or eleventh centuries.[54] *Qingbai* sherds excavated in a Fatimid residence at Ayla on the

50 For example, Kerr, *Song Dynasty Ceramics*, 103; Teo, "Qingbai Ware for Export," 250.

51 Pierson, *Qingbai Ware*, 17.

52 Ho, "Ceramic Boom in Minnan," 258.

53 Cited in Miksic, *Southeast Asian Ceramics*, 73. The text of the *Pingzhou Ketan* has not been translated into English, and this well-known passage exists in a number of English translations, paraphrases, and summaries of the Chinese original. We are grateful to Rosemary E. Scott for pointing us to this source.

54 Bongionino, "'And their Figures,'" 38 and fig. 11. By contrast, Tadanori Yuba's discussion

northern Red Sea coast have similarly been dated to the tenth or eleventh centuries.[55] Such early dates—largely coeval with the earliest finds of *qingbai* in Chinese dated tombs—indicate that some of the very first *qingbai* productions, believed by most Chinese ceramic historians to be manufactured at this period primarily for the Chinese market, were reaching consumers in the Middle East with little delay.[56] This is not as surprising as it may seem: the Middle East's enthrallment with Chinese ceramic technology, growing since the ninth century, may have made it a target market for new ceramic types.[57] Islamic ceramic historians have certainly accepted the idea of an early contact with *qingbai*. As Oliver Watson has shown, it is likely these Chinese ceramic fabrics that effected a substantial revolution in Egyptian ceramic technology during the earlier eleventh century. In reaction to such imports, Egyptian potters are believed to have developed a new white ceramic body composed substantially of ground quartz particles that produced a vitrified and sometimes translucent finish: the stonepaste or fritware vessels noted above.[58] The early and apparently positive reception of *qingbai* in the Middle East ensured a firm demand in later centuries.[59] Zhao has even stated that *qin-*

---

of similar, if not identical, shards assigns them a twelfth to thirteenth century date: "Chinese Ceramics Found at al-Fustat."

55 Whitcomb, "Fatimid Residence at Aqaba," 222. The site is believed to have been abandoned in the early twelfth century, perhaps around 1116, and these ceramics must predate that event.

56 The same is true of East African markets: see discussion and distribution maps in Zhao, "Global Trade," 53, 68, and fig. 9. *Qingbai* shards are also identifiable at the entrepôt site of Mantai in northern Sri Lanka, believed to have been abandoned in the early eleventh century. The shards are reproduced in the CD accompanying Carswell, Deraniyagala, and Graham, *Mantai*. We are grateful to Melanie Gibson for pointing out this reference.

57 It should not be forgotten that Chinese ceramics could remain in circulation for lengthy periods precisely because of their perceived value, causing "historic" pieces to be discovered in substantially later archaeological layers. For example, Zhao notes that "at Mahilaka in Madagascar, tenth- and eleventh-century *qingbai* wares have been discovered from the 'occupation IIa' phase of settlement (which is dated to the thirteenth and fourteenth centuries). This shows that Chinese ceramics might have been kept for centuries as markers of wealth." See "Global Trade," 62.

58 According to Watson ("Chinese-Iranian Relations"), *qingbai* "could not be adequately copied in earthenwares, which were of necessity thick-bodied and whose opaque glazes did not allow for subtle underglaze decoration. As a solution the Near Eastern potters developed a new fabric based on an ancient Egyptian technology: fritware, compounded of ground quartz with small quantities of clay and glaze. When fired it yielded a pure-white body; if sufficiently thin, it could be translucent. It matched the Chinese ware in all but hardness." See also Watson, "Fritware."

59 Pirazzoli-t'Serstevens, "Une denrée recherchée," 73–74.

gbai wares "may have been the main category of Chinese ceramics imported into the western Indian Ocean from the late tenth to the mid thirteenth century."[60] *Qingbai* may also have been among the Chinese ceramics that, in the twelfth and early thirteenth centuries, inspired Persian potters at the city of Kashan to work with stonepaste and to experiment with substantially new ceramic forms.[61]

Beyond this broad picture, however, details about the phases and routes of *qingbai*'s arrival in the Middle East remain patchily mapped. The general lack of focus on this ware in the Middle East reflects a comparable neglect in Chinese ceramic studies, as Catherine Teo has remarked: "when compared to the longer production periods and popularity of other ceramic types, e.g. blue and white, and celadons, it is not difficult to understand why so little is known of qingbai wares."[62] One important site that offers data for a better understanding of *qingbai* imports to the Middle East is the entrepôt of Sharma on the northern Hadrami coast, excavated between 2000 and 2001. The commercial nature of the site has yielded a fine-grained phasing of Chinese ceramic imports over the lifetime of the entrepôt between ca. 980 and ca. 1150. Analysis of the these ceramics by Zhao has demonstrated that the *qingbai* wares from Jingdezhen, along with *qingbai*-type wares from other kiln sites in China, together represent 41.5 percent of the Chinese ceramic imports found throughout the lifetime of the site, with a peak in importation between 1050 and 1120 CE.[63] During this period, at least twenty-four different groups of ceramics were imported from at least eleven different ceramic production centres, principally in Jiangxi and Guangdong provinces; of these, the greatest variety of types, fifteen or 62.5 percent, was seen in *qingbai* wares from

60 Zhao, "Global Trade," 74.

61 Research is currently underway in this area, led by Melanie Gibson and presented by her at two recent conferences: "The Impact of Song Period 'Chīnī' in Iran" (panel, "Things and Their Ideas: Exchanges in the Visual and Material Cultures of Islamicate Asia," convened by Sussan Babaie and Elizabeth Lambourn at the Association of Art Historians 41st Annual Conference and Bookfair, University of East Anglia, April 11, 2015) and "The Impact of Southern Song *Chīnī* in the Production of Twelfth-Century Kashan" (British Museum Study Day, "Chinese *Qingbai* Ceramics and their Contexts," May 15, 2015).

62 Teo, "Qingbai Ware for Export," 250.

63 The site chronology for Sharma changes subtly between Zhao's first publication of the *qingbai* shards in 2004 as "L'importation de la céramique chinoise," and the final chapter in the site publication published in 2015 as "La céramique chinoise." In 2004, Phase III was dated to ca. 1050–1120 and Phase IV to ca. 1120–50; in the final publication, Phase III terminates around 1060, Phase IV spans ca. 1060–1120, while Phase V now marks the period 1120–1220.

Jingdezhen and in *qingbai*-type wares from other Chinese kilns.[64] In sum, the data from Sharma demonstrate the existence of intense commercial networks connecting the Arabian coast to kilns across China and exhibiting a high preference for the importation of *qingbai* tablewares from Jingdezhen or *qingbai*-type wares from other manufacturing centres, particularly between 1050 and 1120 but continuing well into the mid-twelfth century.

Sharma is, of course, only one entrepôt site, and it was also a redistribution centre; we do not know where its Chinese imports moved on to, or by whom they were moved. Axelle Rougeulle, Sharma's principal excavator, has suggested that Aden might have been one of these destinations and this part of the coast was certainly an important crossroads for ships crossing the western Indian Ocean, either north to the Gulf or south to the Red Sea. Whether or not Sharma supplied Aden in *qingbai* wares and other Chinese ceramics at this period, the site offers a template that might be applied to other sites in the Arabian Peninsula. It further suggests that Maḍmūn's que stions were posed after almost eighty-five years of substantial *qingbai* imports to the region, time enough for merchant elites to accumulate a substantial number of such vessels in their homes, and to begin questioning the material properties of these items. Maḍmūn's question implies that his own household contained large quantities of translucent Chinese wares: he asks "about the *ṣīnī* vessels (*'an al-aw'iya al-ṣīnī*), the translucent pottery vessels (*al-ghaḍār al-shaffāf*), and all the *ṣīnī* tablewares [which are] translucent ([*wa*]-*kull al-zibād,* [*al-ṣīn*]*ī hiyya shaffāf*)." The accumulation of large quantities of fine *qingbai* wares in Aden suggested by this document may thus represent some of the earliest textual evidence for their large scale commercial trade in the western Indian Ocean, corroborating the archaeological evidence from Sharma and evidence emerging from other sites in the western Indian Ocean.

The site of Sharma also preserves exported Chinese ceramics previously believed to be unique to the Southeast Asian market. Research on *qingbai* imports in Southeast Asia has noted that Chinese *qingbai* kilns manufactured a type of small lidded box specifically for Philippine and Indonesian consumers; the form is never found in China itself.[65] Their size suggests that they were used to hold preserved fruits, sauces, spices, and, above all, medicines and ointments. Yet in her analysis of the *qingbai* found at Sharma, Zhao identified exactly this box type:[66] perhaps a clue that the *qingbai* wares reaching Sharma were not purchased

64 Zhao, "L'importation de la céramique chinoise," 263–64.

65 Teo, "Qingbai Ware for Export," 249. These small boxes came in various forms notably globular or square with two to three lugs on their shoulders.

66 Zhao, "L'importation de la céramique chinoise," 275, figs. 3–12 and 3–13.

directly from China but had made their way from Indonesia or the Philippines. Such boxes in particular might have reached the Yemen, not as commodities in their own right, but as containers for other exotic products from those regions.[67]

The evidence from Sharma encourages us to look at commercial networks of ceramic supply, but we should not dismiss the possibility that some Chinese wares were obtained via noncommercial modes of exchange. New research on provisioning and supply in the Indian Ocean is demonstrating the importance of private transportation networks among Jewish India traders, particularly for household items, and it is possible that some of the Chinese ceramics in Maḍmūn's household reached him through such networks.[68] As far as we know, Jewish merchants from the Middle East were not established in Chinese ports, and much skepticism has been cast on Benjamin of Tudela's twelfth-century description of China;[69] nevertheless, Geniza documents do record that Jewish merchants at this period traded in Southeast Asia, where *qingbai* vessels were actively imported.[70] Nor should we disregard the other, non-Jewish networks that Maḍmūn's close association with Bilāl b. Jarīr, the governor of Aden, likely opened for him, and which may well have extended directly to China. The contemporary historian 'Umāra al-Ḥakamī noted that, when Bilāl b. Jarīr died in 1151 or 1152, his chattels included "Indian rarities and Chinese fineries (*tuḥaf al-Hind wa alṭāf al-Ṣīn*)."[71] There is ample evidence from Chinese sources that many other Middle Eastern communities were permanently represented in Chinese ports at this period and maintained exchanges with the Middle East.[72] There were also regular exchanges of embassies between the Middle East and China. Indeed, the sixty-five years between 1071 and 1136 saw some thirteen merchant-led tribute missions from Arab lands (the *Ta-Shi*) to the Song court. While Chinese sources do not distinguish between Fatimid-sponsored embassies, which traveled the Red Sea route, and those from the Sunni Abbasid Caliphs in Baghdad, which very likely travelled via the Gulf, certain gift assemblages point clearly to embassies travelling via the Red Sea route and thus likely to

---

67 The Philippine and Indonesian export markets for *qingbai* are especially well researched: see Teo, "Qingbai Ware for Export."

68 See Elizabeth Lambourn's forthcoming monograph *Abraham's Luggage: A Social Life of Things in the Medieval Indian Ocean World.*

69 See *Encyclopedia Judaica*, "Benjamin (ben Jonah) of Tudela."

70 See letters from merchants departing for Southeast Asia in Goitein, *Letters of Medieval Jewish Traders*, letters 46 and 47, 227–29.

71 From the *Ta'rīkh* of 'Umāra al-Ḥakamī (d. 1174) cited by Kay, *Yaman,* 80 (and, for the Arabic, 59). Al-Ḥakamī was a Yemeni and a contemporary of Bilāl's.

72 For a good overview of sources, see Chaffee, "Diasporic Identities"; and Heng, "Shipping."

have come from the Fatimids or their local allies in the Yemen.[73] Envoys were often merchants, and they were always recompensed for their tribute, and not infrequently with ceramics; it is not impossible, then, that returning merchant envoys brought *qingbai* back with them. Whatever their route to Aden, the six *ṣīnī* cups dispatched to Fustat in the satchel of gifts afforded the perfect opportunity for Maḍmūn to clarify the status of *qingbai* within Jewish material taxonomies.

Taming a Disruptive Substance

Maḍmūn's eight-line query represents the earliest securely dated and localized evidence for a debate about the material status of porcellaneous Chinese ceramic fabrics within Judaism. The translucency and vitrified body of these wares disrupted established material taxonomies, confounding expectations of how a ceramic fabric should "look," "feel" and "behave"; it was a disruptive substance. Since earlier *ṣīnī* fabrics scarcely appear to have been the object of rabbinic legislation, Maḍmūn had no existing rulings to turn to, and, in the absence of these, he began to formulate his own ideas based on empirical observation of the vessels and by analogical reasoning from known materials. As Goitein briefly indicates in his commentary on the document, Maḍmūn's two questions are carefully crafted to frame *ṣīnī* vessels between the much better known materials of glass and earthenware.[74] As we have seen, the new material (and technologies) of glass had already been incorporated into rabbinic Judaism during the first half of the first millennium CE. Maḍmūn and the Gaon would have been able to turn to an abundant body of legislation about earthenware, glazed earthenware, and glass which were all well legislated by the twelfth century—even if contradictory opinions persisted. In this section of our article we unpack the reasoning and precedents both men might have applied to this problem.

Maḍmūn's first question, about a menstruating woman's contact with *ṣīnī* tablewares, is notable for its repeated emphasis on the translucency of the vessels under discussion. As we have seen, Maḍmūn refers to "the translucent pottery vessels" and "all the *ṣīnī* tablewares [which are] translucent." Goitein remarks that this chosen vocabulary points to an understanding of *ṣīnī* as a glass-like substance. Translucency is indeed a quality more often associated with glass than with

73 See Bielenstein, *Diplomacy and Trade*. For example, in 1131 an Arab embassy fronted by a certain P'u-ya-li (likely Abu 'Ali) brought thirty-five large rhinoceros horns and 209 large elephant tusks, products of East Africa; another in 1136 offered frankincense, a product of the Arabian coast north of Aden, valued by the Maritime Trade Bureau at Quan-zhou at 300,000 strings of 1,000 cash: a huge sum (362).

74 Goitein and Friedman, *India Traders*, 378.

ceramics, which are generally opaque, and the use of the term *shaffāf* in Maḍmūn's question points clearly towards this other material. The translucency and glass-like properties of certain Chinese ceramic bodies had already been noted by Middle Eastern merchants as early as the ninth century; the author of the *Akhbār al-Ṣin wa-l-Hind*, a mid-ninth century Arabic language manual on trade with India and China, reports that the Chinese "have excellent quality pottery (*ghaḍār)* from which are made bowls (*aqdāḥ*)[75] as fine as [glass] flasks (*al-qarāwīr*): one can see the gleam of the water through them, even though they are made of pottery."[76] This material similarity continued to be recorded by later Middle Eastern authors. The Iranian polymath al-Bīrūnī (d. 1048) is perhaps most explicit in his comparison of Chinese ceramic fabrics with glass. In *The Sum of Knowledge about Precious Stones* (*Kitāb al-Jamāhir fī Ma'rifat al-Jawāhir*) al-Bīrūnī includes bowls made from *ṣīnīyya* (*al-qiṣa' al-ṣīnīyya*), that is from "China stone," a separate category of "precious stone," and places them directly after his discussions of glass (*zajjāj*) and glass enamel (*minā'*). Al-Bīrūnī was most concerned with documenting how *ṣīnīyya* was used in the manufacture of Chinese ceramics, and as part of this he reported (erroneously) that the best bowls were like glass, for "if they break, they are molten and recast." According to one of al-Bīrūnī's informants, the best bowls were "thin of body, sheer" (*al-raqīqa al-jirm al-ṣāfiya*).[77] Al-Tha'ālibī (d. 1038), writing in Iran around the same period, also included Chinese porcelain among the specialities of the country in his *Book of Curious and Entertaining Information* (*Kitāb Laṭā'if al-Ma'ārif*). He describes how the Chinese "have fine, translucent pottery (*al-ghaḍā'ir al-mustashaffa*) which they cook food in and one piece of this may be [used as] a pot on one occasion, a frying pan another or a serving dish another": that is, it could be used for boiling, frying, and serving.[78] *Mustashaffa* derives from the same Arabic trilitteral root (SH-F-F) as the term *shaffāf* later used by Maḍmūn, signifying transparent, diaphanous, or translucent. On occasion, Chinese writers also pondered the material similarities between glass and ceramic

75 For the translation of the term *qadaḥ* (pl. *aqdāḥ*), see discussion in note 12, above.

76 "Wa la-hum al-ghaḍār al-jayyid wa yaʿmal minhu aqdāḥ fī riqqa al-qawārir yarā ḍau' al-mā' fīhi wa huwwa min ghaḍār": *Akhbār al-Sīn wa-l-Hind*, 16. Although the author does not explicitly compare these ceramics to glass, the fabric's glass-like qualities are implied and were highlighted by the translator Jean Sauvaget in his French translation of this text.

77 Al-Bīrūnī, *Kitāb al-Jamāhir fī Ma'rifat al-Jawāhir*, 195.

78 "Wa la-hum al-ghaḍā'ir al-mustashaffa yuṭbakh fī-hā al-ṭabīkh fa-yakūn al-wāḥid minhā qidr marra wa miqla tāra wa qaṣ'a ukhrā": al-Tha'ālibī, *Kitāb Laṭā'if al-Ma'ārif* (ed. Abyari and Sayrafi), 221. Bosworth's translation (*Book of Curious and Entertaining Information*, 141) explicitly associates the *qidr* with boiling and the *miqla* with frying. A different translation again is given in Kahle, "Chinese Porcelain," 338.

fabrics. Although in China itself the highest quality ceramics aspired to be jade or silver-like, at least one Tang writer, Wei Zheng (580–643), noted that "greenware [celadon] was no different from glassware."[79] Maḍmūn would obviously not have been aware of Chinese material taxonomies, and there is no suggestion that he even knew these two Islamic sources; nevertheless, we suggest that all three passages perfectly illustrate the complex technological position of porcellaneous ceramics whose ingredients do indeed produce a vitrification of the body and glaze, rendering them glass-like. It is therefore with glass, porcelain's most recent material ancestor, that we begin our discussion.

Glass was not one of the materials originally legislated in the *Pentateuch*, as noted above. However, as it became more common in the Middle East over the course of the first two millennia BCE, it was finally declared subject to ritual impurity by the mid-second century BCE. Thereafter, glass was considered a substance capable of contracting impurity and entered Jewish legal debate. The central and more complex problem that ensued, as later with *ṣīnī*, was whether, and if so how, glass vessels could be returned to a state of purity. To determine that, as Grossmark's work has shown, the new substance needed to be framed by existing material categories. The distinction between the new glass vessels and the much older tradition of earthenware utensils is outlined in the Babylonian Talmud,[80] a central text of rabbinic Judaism composed in Mesopotamia between ca. 200 and 550 CE. The timing of this integration coincides with the popularization of glass vessels across the Middle East as a result of the invention of glass-blowing in Syro-Palestine in the first century CE.

Yet opinions were contradictory, and glass refused to be tamed. The most comprehensive discussion of the ritual purity laws relating to glass vessels is found in Tractate *Kelim* of the Mishna (itself generally held to have been redacted around 220 CE). There, glass vessels are grouped with wood, leather, and bone utensils: "in order to purify the contaminated item, its existence as a vessel must cease, which is usually done by breaking it."[81] Broken glass can be melted and remade relatively easily, but the vessel is nevertheless destroyed. However, rabbinic Judaism gave ample space for alternative analysis and categorizations, and the Talmudic sage Rav Ashi (fl. 375–427 CE) argued that "utensils of glass, since they may be repaired when broken, are like utensils of metal."[82] By "repaired," Rav Ashi clearly refers to the fact that, like scrap metal, broken glass (i.e., glass cullet) may be

79 Cited in Hsueh-Man, "Luxury or Necessity," 73 n. 7.

80 *Talmud Bavli*, ʿAvoda Zara 75b.

81 Grossmark, "'And He Decreed,'" 203.

82 See *Talmud Bavli*, ʿAvoda Zara 75b.

melted and reworked; accordingly, glass utensils could be treated like metal ones. And yet glass was arguably not tamed for another seven hundred years when Moses Maimonides's highly influential *Mishneh Torah*, an encyclopedic systematization and restatement of Jewish law written at the end of the twelfth century, grouped glass vessels with earthenware based on the fact that glass was made from earth, specifically sand. Based on this reasoning, Maimonides declared glass to be incapable of repurification in a *mikveh*, a ritual bath.[83]

We do not know which opinion about the status of glass was current in Egypt and the Yemen in the 1130s; Maimonides's influential ruling postdates Maḍmūn's question by half a century, and more liberal interpretations of glass's potential for repurification continued to circulate. The early medieval *Avot of Rabbi Nathan*, a discourse centered around the mishnaic tractate Avot (which was likely composed in Mesopotamia in the wake of the redaction of the Babylonian Talmud, between the sixth and ninth centuries) approached the issue through the question of porousness rather than repair. It rules that a glass vessel is not considered absorptive or porous like earthenware and could thus be used for both dairy and meat, and restored to a state of purity simply by washing: "three things are said of a glass vessel. It does not absorb, it does not discharge, and it shows everything that is inside it. In a hot place it is hot; in a cool place it is cool."[84] The material proof of glass's neutral absorptive qualities was that it did not preserve heat or cold; furthermore, being transparent, it was possible to see that no substances had been absorbed into the fabric. The *Avot of Rabbi Nathan* became a widely influential text and its ruling on glass vessels can be found repeated in the late twelfth/early thirteenth century by the German Rabbi Eliezer b. Joel ha-Levi ("Raviya"). Discussing the same issue—namely, the separation of meat from dairy in Jewish cooking—the latter added the proviso that Jews could even use glass vessels purchased from a gentile which might have served in ritually impure or idolatrous contexts.

> Old glass vessels [belonging to a gentile][85] that have been used for leaven [or by a gentile] or for wine libations are permissible, since they do not absorb. So it is said in a Baraita of *Avot de-R. Nathan*: three things are said about an earthenware vessel and three about a glass vessel. An earthenware vessel absorbs, discharges, and preserves what is inside it, which is

83 Maimonides, *Mishneh Torah,* Laws of Utensils (*Hilkhot Kelim*) 1:5. For an introduction to the Mishneh Torah, see Twersky's *Introduction to the Code of Maimonides.*

84 *Avot de-Rabbi Natan*, (a), ch. 42. We are grateful to Zvi Stampfer for suggesting this reference.

85 These words are bracketed in the Hebrew text, indicating the editor's suggestion that they be deleted.

> not true of a glass vessel. The reason is that it is smooth, as we say about the heart: (*Talmud Bavli*, Pesaḥim 74b), "The heart is different because it is smooth," and it does not absorb (for if so it would be like the old ones)[86] and does not discharge.[87]

If the more liberal rulings of Rav Ashi and the *Avot of Rabbi Nathan* were applied, Maḍmūn's alignment of this new *ṣīnī* fabric with glass, implied by his emphasis on its translucence, would open the way to a variety of non-destructive methods of repurification. Whether by analogy with metals or contrast with porous earthenware, *ṣīnī* could be repurified by washing in cold water, boiling, or heating directly in a fire.

Ṣīnī's high heat resistance would have been especially valuable in this context, since repurification also took into account the temperature of the polluting substance, often non-kosher food, with which vessels had come into contact. The operative principle, canonized in the Talmud,[88] is "as it absorbs, so it expels" (*ke-bol'o, kakh polṭo*): that is, a vessel which was used for cold food may be repurified and made usable through washing in water, while a vessel used for boiling or directly cooking non-kosher food on the fire required more robust processes (immersion in boiling water or immersion in fire until the vessel itself becomes burning hot, respectively). Although the thermal resistance of Chinese ceramics is mainly mentioned in Islamic sources and in relation to their use for cooking—as al-Tha'ālibī noted, translucent Chinese pottery could be used in cooking as a pot, a pan, and a serving dish—it is clear that in the Jewish context these same properties made Chinese ceramic fabrics extremely versatile in terms of the variety of repurification methods that vessels could sustain without cracking.

Maḍmūn's second question shifts to considering *ṣīnī* storage vessels and the pollution of the interior of such vessels by non-human agents. These *ṣīnī* vessels are not specifically described as translucent because this quality was irrelevant to the particular angle of reasoning this question explored. Instead, Maḍmūn focuses on the fact that both the exteriors and interiors of these vessels are glazed. In framing this question, he appears to be testing *ṣīnī* against earthenware and glazed earthenware vessels, perhaps the most obvious categories of comparison

---

86 Note that the modern editor of this classical text, Avigdor Aptowitzer, read the parenthetical phrase as incomprehensible in their present location and placed them after the word "and does not discharge"; cf. *Sefer Raviya*, 91 n. 23.

87 "...וכלי זכוכית ישנים (של גוי) שנשתמשו בהן חמץ או [של גוי או של] יין נסך שרי, דלא בלעי. והכי אמרינן בברייתא דאבות דרבי נתן שלשה דברים נאמרו בכלי חרס ושלשה בכלי זכוכית כלי חרס בולע ומפליט ומשמר מה שבתוכו מה שאין כן בכלי זכוכית. וטעמא משום דשיעי, כדאמרינן גבי לב שני לב דשיע, ולא בל (דאם כן היה ליה כישנים) ולא פליט..." *Sefer Raviya*, Part 2, Section 464, 91. We are grateful to Zvi Stampfer for suggesting this reference.

88 *Talmud Bavli*, Pesaḥim 30b.

for Chinese ceramics and ones for which an abundant halakhic literature already existed. Guidance on the treatment of earthenware vessels is given in the *Pentateuch* and provides the basis for subsequent rulings on this material. As Leviticus 11:33 instructs, "any earthenware container into whose inner space one of these [dead creatures] will fall, whatever is inside it shall become unclean, and you shall break [the container] itself."[89] From Leviticus onwards, earthenware vessels were understood to behave in a distinctive manner, contracting impurity only via their inner spaces, and to be particularly intransigent in terms of repurification. Because earthenware is understood to be less durable than glass or metal, it may not be purified through immersion in boiling water or in fire, and therefore if it has come into contact with non-kosher food that is hot it may not be purified at all.[90]

This passage from Leviticus clearly provides the starting point for Maḍmūn's query about the ritual status of a *ṣīnī* jar should some polluting "thing"—a maggot or polluting substance—fall into it, the caveat being that this jar is glazed inside and out; it is not unglazed earthenware. Does glaze substantially alter the properties of the interior of a ceramic jar and thus the processes through which it can be rendered pure again? This specific question points to a smaller body of opinions which developed as glazed ceramics became more common in the Middle East during the first half of the first millennium CE. While one authority, Ravina (d. 499), likened glazed earthenware to glass, which (like metal) might be repurified by washing or immersion in boiling water or fire, his near contemporary Rav Aḥai (late fifth/early sixth century) viewed glazed ceramics as behaving like unglazed earthenware; as instructed in Leviticus, therefore, glazed ceramics could only be rendered pure again by being broken and effectively rendered useless in the process. These opposing conclusions depended on whether glazed vessels were judged according to their original or their final states: the clay body of a glazed vessel arguably made it taxonomically close to earthenware; however, its final glaze, which in the Middle East incorporated lead, brought it close to metals and by association to glass.[91] According to the Babylonian Talmud, it was the latter opinion that prevailed and established that glazed ceramics should be judged

89 Cf. Maimonides, *Mishneh Torah*, Chapter 13, Halacha 1.

90 For further detail, see the sources in Newman, *ha-Maʿasim li-vene Ereṣ Yisrael*, 52 and following; Margulies, *Hilkhot Ereṣ Yisrael*, 93; and Friedman, "Shne qeṭʿaim mi-sefer," 14–36.

91 "Concerning glazed utensils Rav Aḥai and Ravina differ; one maintains [that it must be treated] according to its original state, while the other maintains [that it must be treated] according to its final state. The ultimate decision is [that it must be treated] according to its final state," "קוניא - פליגי בה רב אחא ורבינא, חד אמר: כתחלתו, וחד אמר: כסופו. והלכתא: כסופו...". *Talmud Bavli*, *ʿAvoda Zara* 75b. Note that Marcus Jastrow (*Dictionary of the Targumim*, 1335) translates this word as indicating a powdered lime glaze.

according to their final state. The glazing of the entire vessel appears to have been particularly important in allowing this conclusion: in a fourteenth-century Catalan commentary on Isaac Alfasi's eleventh-century Talmudic digest, the jurist Rabbenu Nissim of Gerona explained that the lenient treatment of earthenware items covered in a glaze applies only when these items are glazed both on their exterior and interior surfaces.[92]

While Talmudic literature had considered glass, earthenware, and items glazed on both sides in a manner that made their absorptive properties (or, perhaps more correctly, their lack of absorption) like glass, the Talmud had not been able to consider porcellanous, vitrified ceramic bodies. The second question therefore frames this hypothetical *barnīya* between earthenware and glazed vessels. We cannot be certain that the opinion of Ravina and his successors was also followed in twelfth-century Egypt and Yemen. However, Maḍmūn's emphasis on the finished state of the vessel, on the fact that his *ṣīnī* jar was glazed both inside and out, appears designed to point towards this ruling, distancing his glazed *ṣīnī* jar from earthenware and allowing it to be repurified according to the far more flexible methods prescribed for metals and glass, and sparing him the financial loss of destroying it or having to sell it.

Conclusions

We do not know what reply Maḍmūn received from the Gaon; few of the letters sent from Egypt to the Yemen ever made their way back into the Cairo Geniza. Nor is it possible to judge the contemporary currency of such questions and the answers tendered, since only one trace of this debate has been identified: Maḍmūn's memorandum. And yet porcelain clearly remained a disruptive substance within Jewish material taxonomies. As Chinese ceramic imports grew in volume from the later sixteenth century, and as Europe developed its own approximations of chinaware, questions about *ṣīnī*'s material status became more common and leave more significant textual traces. Although there is currently no comprehensive compilation and focused study of later debates about its purification, one might point to the record of the experiments carried out in the sixteenth century by the Egyptian and Palestinian authority Radbaz, who tested *ṣīnī*'s porosity. In one experiment, a piece of china was weighed before and after having been soaked in food, and was found to have taken on additional weight after having been soaked.[93] In the sec-

92 Rabbenu Nissim on Alfasi, ʻAvoda Zara 39b-40a, s.v. "ve-hilkheta ke-sofo".

93 Shut ha-Radbaz, 3:401; discussed but incorrectly cited in Walter's "Can Porcelain be *Kashered*?"

ond experiment, a dish was heated and Radbaz noticed "a flame emerge from the dish, [so] he concluded that there must have been residue in the china which was the source of the combustion."[94] From the two experiments, Radbaz concluded that china was porous like earthenware and therefore impossible to render clean again. Nevertheless, his opinion did not settle the question and Chinese porcelain continued—and continues—to disrupt rabbinic taxonomies.

Even with the advent of modern materials science in the nineteenth and twentieth centuries, which finally provided incontrovertible evidence for the vitreous nature of porcelain, porcelain continues to be evaluated in Judaism within material taxonomies established in late antiquity; in that context, porcelain can only ever be problematical and "Other." The modern prevalence of porcelain or bone china dinner services and the proliferation of porcelain for sinks and other kitchen fittings has engendered a veritable flood of queries about the status of these materials, traceable through the numerous questions and answers exchanged online between observant householders and rabbis.[95] There is, however, some suggestion that rabbinic authorities in North America and Europe are increasingly reaching the consensus that porcelain is not "kosherable." The subtle premodern calibrations of porcelain between earthenware, glazed ceramics, and glass examined in this article are increasingly giving way to its inclusion among a bulk group of ceramic technologies to which one rule applies: as Wayne Allen wrote in 1994, "the standard halakhic rule is that earthenware, enamel, porcelain, and glazed china cannot be 'koshered.'"[96] Instead, it is the principle of "great loss" (*hefsed merubeh*)[97] on which a leniency might be hinged, should an heirloom dinner service (for example) have been exposed to non-kosher food items.[98] Maḍmūn's queries show that these modern questions must be understood in a deeper historical context: the disruptive potential of ceramic materials within Jewish material taxonomies has been debated for well over two millennia. Indeed, the introduction of new technologies for the production and storage of food continue to challenge the existing typologies established within Jewish law. The mass production

---

94 Cited in Walter, "Can Porcelain be *Kashered*?" 113 n. 9. In the words of Ibn Abi Zimra, "...וזה דרך הנסיון כי לקחתי ממנו חתיכה והכנסתי אותה באש ויצא ממנה שלהבת כדרך הכלים הבלועים..." (This was my experiment: I took a piece [of porcelain] and put it in the fire, and a flame came out of it just like those utensils which absorb [. . .]).

95 See, for example, "China Dishes, Porcelain" <http://www.aish.com/atr/China-Dishes-Porcelain.html> [accessed April 8, 2015].

96 Allen, "Kashering China," 147.

97 Jewish law overrides certain prohibitions ascribed to rabbinic (as opposed to Torahitic) law in the case of a significant financial loss; cf. *Encyclopedia Talmudit*, "hefsed merubeh."

98 Allen, "Kashering China," 149–50.

of plastic from the 1940s onward has challenged rabbinic authorities to consider whether plastic should be considered akin to stone (considering its petrochemical source) and therefore not subject to the absorption of impure foods, or like wood and therefore porous.[99] The contemporary responsa call to mind the question Maḍmūn posed to Maṣliaḥ Gaon in the twelfth century.

Maḍmūn's queries open unique new perspectives on the reception of Chinese ceramics in the wider Middle East. They add nuance to a story that has tended to focus on technological and formal responses and to treat the region's inhabitants as a monolithic, apparently areligious, group. They remind us that a significant religious minority within the largely Muslim population might have a radically different history of reception compared to other faith communities. Muslim, Christian, even Zoroastrian ritual purity systems operated within very different material taxonomies, and there is no evidence that any of these faiths ever questioned the place and propriety of Chinese ceramics. Instead, for most Middle Eastern consumers, the glass-like qualities of certain Chinese ceramic vessels would have been a matter of wonder rather than concern. Al-Tha'ālibī's short description of Chinese ceramics occurs in a chapter on the special crafts practiced by different peoples, presented alongside Chinese statues, paintings, patterned silks, felts, and other manufactured things as evidence for "the skill of their hands and for their expertise in fashioning rare and beautiful objects."[100]

Maḍmūn's questions also represent an important addition to the small corpus of textual references to *ṣīnī* in sources from the medieval Middle East. As work on the much later European reception of Chinese ceramics has demonstrated, what people thought and wrote about chinaware, and how they did so, offers an essential complementary perspective to surviving material evidence.[101] Physical and visual analysis grounded in material culture studies, now supplemented by an array of advanced scientific techniques, have provided insights into the most microscopic details of design and manufacture, information unlikely to have entered contemporary written records. On a macro scale, as analysis of the Chinese ceramics from the site of Sharma has shown, shard percentages can give us a good idea of the proportion of Chinese ceramics within the larger ceramic

99 See, for example, Responsa Minḥat Yiṣḥaq (Isaac Jacob Weiss, twentieth-century Poland, Palestine and Israel), 8:92; Responsa Ṣiṣ Eliʿezer (Eliezer Yehuda Waldenberg, twentieth-century Palestine and Israel), 7:37.

100 "Makhṣuṣūn bi-ṣinaʿa al-yad wa-l-ḥidhq fī ʿamal al-ṭuraf wa-l-mulaḥ": al-Tha'ālibī, *Kitāb Laṭā'if al-Ma'ārif*, 220 (for Bosworth's English translation, see *Book of Curious and Entertaining Information*, 141).

101 See a good overview of this literature and new work on the sixteenth century in Hwang Degenhardt, "Cracking the Mysteries of 'China.'"

assemblage of any given site in the Middle East at a given period. Yet these material sources privilege economic, technological, and design perspectives and cannot tell the whole story of reception. In the 1950s, the German scholar Paul Kahle initiated the important task of combing Islamic texts for references to Chinese ceramics, but this enterprise has hardly progressed since,[102] and this type of discursive historiography remains absent from current surveys of the topic.[103] Legal queries and halakhic opinions, such as those discussed here, constitute an important addition to this corpus and open new avenues for writing a history of the reception of Chinese ceramics that does not begin in 1500, nor center on Europe.

---

102 See Kahle's seminal "Chinese Porcelain in the Lands of Islam" and "Chinese Porcelain in the Lands of Islam –Supplement." Milwright's "Pottery in the Written Sources" is a rare exception among later scholarship; while not specifically focused on Chinese imports, he demonstrates the wealth of textual references awaiting scholarly attention.

103 For broad panoramas of the global impact of Chinese ceramics. see Pierson, *Transfer*; and (with caution, since the author is a historian rather than a ceramic specialist) Finlay's *Pilgrim Art*. A recent thematic issue on Chinese ceramics also provides a useful overview of recent scholarship: *Journal of World History* 23.1 (2012).

Bibliography

Primary Sources

Akhbār al-Ṣīn wa-l-Hind. Edited and translated by Jean Sauvaget as *Relation de la Chine et de l'Inde. Redigée en 851*. Paris: Société d'Édition "Les Belles Lettres," 1948.

Avot de-Rabbi Natan. Edited by Solomon Schechter. Vienna, 1887; repr. New York: Feldheim, 1967.

al-Bīrūnī, Muḥammad ibn Aḥmad. *Kitāb al-Jamāhir fī Ma'rifat al-Jawāhir*. Edited by Yusuf al-Hadi. Teheran: Sharika al-Nashr al-'Alami wa al-Thaqafi, 1995.

——. *Kitāb al-Jamāhir fī Ma'rifat al-Jawāhir*. Translated by Hakim Mohammad said as *Al-Beruni's Book on Mineralogy. The Book Most Comprehensive in Knowledge on Precious Stones*. Islamabad: Pakistan Hijra Council, 1989.

al-Fasi, Isaac b. Jacob. *Halakhot Rabati*. Published in facsimile with an English introduction by Shamma Friedman. 2 vols. Jerusalem: Makor, 1974.

Ha-Levi of Bonn, Eliezer b. Joel. *Sefer Ra'avyah*. Edited by Avigdor Aptowitzer. 2 vols. Jerusalem: Mekize Nirdamim, 1964.

Ibn Abi Zimra. *She'elot u-teshuvot ha-Radbaz*. Edited by David b. Solomon. New York: A.Y. Friedman, 1990.

Ibn al-Zubayr. *Kitāb al-Hadāyā wa-l-Tuḥaf*. Transated by Ghada Hijjawi Qaddumi as *Book of Gifts and Rarities*. Cambridge, MA: Harvard University Press, 1996.

Maimonides, Moses. *Mishneh Torah*. Edited by Shabse Frankel et al. 15 vols. Bene Barak: Hotzaat Shabse Frankel, 1975–2001.

al-Muqaddasī, Muḥammad ibn Aḥmad. *Kitāb Aḥsan al-Taqāsim fī Ma'rifat al-Aqalīm*. Translated by Basil Anthony Collins as *The Best Divisions for Knowledge of the Regions*. Reading: Garnet, 1994.

——. *Kitāb Aḥsan al-Taqāsim fī Ma'rifat al-Aqalīm*. Edited by M. J. de Goeje as *Descriptio Imperii Moslemici*. Leiden: Brill, 1906.

Talmud Bavli. Jerusalem: Tal-Man, 1981.

al-Tha'ālibī, 'Abd al-Malik ibn Muḥammad. *Kitāb Laṭā'if al-Ma'ārif*. Edited by Ibrahim Abyari and Hasan Kamil Sayrafi. Cairo: Dar Ihya' al-Kutub al-'Arabiya, 1960.

——. *Kitāb Laṭā'if al-Ma'ārif*. Translated by C. E. Bosworth as *The Book of Curious and Entertaining Information*. Edinburgh: Edinburgh University Press, 1968.

Weiss, Isaac Jacob. *Liquṭey Teshuvot Minḥat Yiṣḥaq*. Jerusalem: Minḥat Yiṣḥaq, 1995.

Waldenberg, Eliezer Yehuda. *She'elot u-Teshuvot Ṣiṣ Eli'ezer*. Jerusalem: A.Y. Waldenberg, 1984.

Secondary Sources

Allen, Wayne. "Kashering China." In *Perspectives on Jewish Law and Contemporary Issues*, 147–51. Bloomington, IN: Trafford Publishing, 2011.

Bielenstein, Hans. *Diplomacy and Trade in the Chinese World, 589–1276*. Leiden: Brill, 2005.

Bongianino, Umberto. "'And their Figures and Colours Should Be Different.' Incised and Carved Glazed Wares from Fustāt (9th–12th century) in the Martin Collection (International Museum of Ceramics in Faenza)–Part I." *Faenza* 2 (2014): 28–48.

Botticini, Maristella, and Zvi Eckstein. *The Chosen Few: How Education Shaped Jewish History, 70–1492*. Princeton: Princeton University Press, 2012.

Bramoullé, David. "The Fatimids and the Red Sea (969–1171)." In *Navigated Spaces, Connected Places, Proceedings of Red Sea Project V Held at the University of Exeter, 16–19 September 2010*, edited by Dionisius A. Agius, John P. Cooper, Athena Trakadas and Chiara Zazzaro, 127–36. Oxford: Archaeopress, 2012.

Burke, Katherine Strange. *Archaeological Texts and Contexts on the Red Sea: The Sheikh's House at Quseir Al-Qadim*. PhD diss., University of Chicago, 2007.

Carswell, John, Siran Deraniyagala, and Alan Graham. *Mantai: City by the Sea*. Aichwald: Linden Soft, 2013.

Chaffee, John. "Diasporic Identities in the Historical Development of the Maritime Muslim Communities of Song-Yuan China." *Journal of the Economic and Social History of the Orient*, 49 (2006): 395–420.

Douglas, Mary. *Purity and Danger: An Analysis of Concepts of Pollution and Taboo.* London: Routledge, 2002.

Dupoizat, Marie-France. "The Ceramic Cargo of a Song Dynasty Junk Found in the Philippines and its Significance in the China-South East Asia Trade." In *South East Asia & China: Art, Interaction & Commerce – Colloquies on Art & Archaeology in Asia No. 17*, edited by Rosemary Scott and John Guy, 205–24. London: Percival David Foundation, 1995.

Encyclopedia Judaica. 2nd ed. Detroit: Macmillan Reference, 2007.

Encyclopedia Talmudit. Jerusalem: Yad ha-Rav Herzog, 1996.

Finlay, Robert. *The Pilgrim Art. Cultures of Porcelain in World History*. Los Angeles: University of California Press, 2010.

Flood, Finbar Barry. *Islam and Image: Polemics, Theology, and Modernity*. Forthcoming.

François, Veronique. "La porcelaine de Chine à Byzance et dans l'Orient chrétien: une absence remarquable." *Taoci* 4 (2005): 67–73.

Freidenreich, David M. *Foreigners and Their Food: Constructing Otherness in Jewish, Christian, and Islamic Law*. Berkeley: University of California Press, 2011.

Friedman, Mordechai A. *Ḥalfon ve-Yehuda ha-Levi. Le-qorotehem shel soḥer maskil u-meshorrer dagul ʿal pi teʿudot Genizat Qahir: Sefer Hodu IV/A.* (Halfon and Judah Ha-Levi. The Lives of a Merchant Scholar and a Poet Laureate According to the Cairo Geniza Documents, India Book IV/A). Jerusalem: Ben-Zvi Institute and The Rabbi David Moshe and Amalia Rosen Foundation, 2013.

——. "Harḥaqat ha-nida ve-ha-minut eṣel ha-geʾonim, ha-Rambam, u-veno Avraham ʿal pi kitvei Genizat Qahir," (Menstrual Impurity and Sectarianism in the Writings of the Geonim and of Moses and Abraham Maimonides.) *Maimonidean Studies* 1 (1990): 1–20.

——. "Shne qeṭʿaim mi-sefer ha-maʿasim li-vene Ereṣ Yisrael." (Two Sections from the *Book of Acts* of the People of the Land of Israel.) *Sinai* 74 (1973): 14–36.

Ghabin, Ahmad. *Ḥisba: Arts and Craft in Islam*. Wiesbaden: Otto Harrasowitz, 2009.

Goitein, S. D. *Letters of Medieval Jewish Traders. Translated from the Arabic with Introductions and Notes.* Princeton: Princeton University Press, 1973.

——. *A Mediterranean Society; the Jewish Communities of the Arab World as Portrayed in the Documents of the Cairo Geniza*. 6 vols. Gustave E. Von Grunebaum Center for Near Eastern Studies. Berkeley: University of California Press, 1967–93.

——. "The Stern Religion." In *Sefer Dinaburg*, edited by Y. Baer, J. Gutmann, and M. Schwabe, 151–64. Jerusalem: Qiryat Sefer, 1949.

Goitein, S. D., and Mordechai A. Friedman. *Avraham ben Yiju: Soḥer ve-yaṣran be-Hodu: Sefer Hodu III*. (Abraham Ben Yiju: India Trader and Manufacturer. India Book III). Jerusalem: Ben-Zvi Institute and The Rabbi David Moshe and Amalia Rosen Foundation, 2010.

——. *Ḥalfon ha-soḥer ha-maskil ve-ha-noseʿa ha-gadol: Sefer Hodu IV/B.* (Halfon the Traveling Merchant Scholar: Cairo Geniza Documents: India Book IV/B). 2 vols. Jerusalem: Ben-Zvi Institute and the Rabbi David Moshe and Amalia Rosen Foundation, 2013.

——. *India Traders of the Middle Ages: Documents from the Cairo Geniza ("India Book")*. Leiden: Brill, 2008.

——. *Maḍmun ha-Nagid Ereṣ Teiman ve-soḥer Hodu: Sefer Hodu II*. (Maḍmūn Nagid of Yemen and the India Trade: India Book II). Cairo Geniza Documents. Jerusalem: Ben-Zvi Institute and the Rabbi David Moshe and Amalia Rosen Foundation, 2010.

Gray, Basil. "The Export of Chinese Porcelains to the Islamic World. Some Reflections on its Significance for Islamic Art, before 1400." *Transactions of the Oriental Ceramic Society* 41 (1975–77): 231–61.

Grossmark, Tziona. "'And He Decreed that Glassware is Susceptible to Becoming Unclean': The Application of the Laws of Ritual Purity to Glassware Reconsidered." *Jewish Studies Quarterly* 17 (2010): 191–212.

Guy, John. "Rare and Strange Goods: International Trade in Ninth-Century Asia." In *Shipwrecked: Tang Treasures and Monsoon Winds*, edited by Regina Krahl et al., 19–34. Washington, DC: Smithsonian Institution, 2010.

Gyllensvard, B. "Recent Finds of Chinese Ceramics at Fostat." *Bulletin of the Museum of Far Eastern Antiquities* 45 (1973): 99–119; 47 (1975): 93–117.

Halevi, Leor. *Muhammad's Grave: Death Rites and the Making of Islamic Society*. New York: Columbia University Press, 2007.

Hallet, Jessica. "Pearl Cups Like the Moon: The Abbasid Reception of Chinese Ceramics." In *Shipwrecked: Tang Treasures and Monsoon Winds*, edited by Regina Krahl, John Guy, Julian Raby and J. Keith Wilson, 75–81. Washington, DC: Smithsonian Institution, 2010.

Hardy-Guilbert, Claire, and Axelle Rougeulle. "Al-Shihr and the Southern Coast of the Yemen: Preliminary Notes on the French Archaeological Expedition, 1995." *Proceedings of the Seminar for Arabian Studies* 27 (1997): 129–40.

——. "Archaeological Research into the Islamic Period in Yemen: Preliminary Notes on the French Expedition, 1993." *Proceedings of the Seminar for Arabian Studies* 25 (1995): 29–44.

Heng, Derek. "Shipping, Customs Procedures, and the Foreign Community: The 'Pingzhou ketan' on Aspects of Guangzhou's Maritime Economy in the Late Eleventh Century." *Journal of Song-Yuan Studies* 38 (2008): 1–38.

Ho, Chuimei. "The Ceramic Boom in Minnan." In *The Emporium of the World: Maritime Quanzhou, 1000–1400*, edited by A. Schottenhammer, 237–81. Leiden: Brill, 2001.

Hsueh-Man, Shen. "Luxury or Necessity: Glassware in Sarīra Relic Pagodas of the Tang and Northern Song Periods." In *Chinese Glass: Archaeological Studies on the Uses and Social Context of Glass Artefacts from the Warring States to the Northern Song Period (Fifth Century B.C. to Twelfth Century A.D.)*, edited by Cecilia Braghin, 71–110. Florence: Olschki, 2002.

Hwang Degenhardt, Jane. "Cracking the Mysteries of 'China': China(ware) in the Early Modern Imagination." *Studies in Philology* 110 (2013): 133–68.

Jastrow, Marcus. *A Dictionary of the Targumim, the Talmud Babli and Yerushalmi, and the Midrashic Literature*. New York: Judaica Press, 1992.

Kahle, P. "Chinese Porcelain in the Lands of Islam." In *Opera Minora von Paul Kahle*, 326–50. Leiden: Brill, 1956.

——. "Chinese Porcelain in the Lands of Islam – Supplement." In *Opera Minora von Paul Kahle*, 351–61. Leiden: Brill, 1956.

Kana'an, Ruba. "The *de Jure* 'Artist' of the Bobrinski Bucket: Production and Patronage of Metalwork in pre-Mongol Khurasan and Transoxiana." *Islamic Law and Society* 16, no. 2 (2009): 175–201.

——. "Patron and Craftsman of the Freer Mosul Ewer of 1232: A Historical and Legal Interpretation of the Roles of Tilmidh and Ghulam in Islamic Metalwork." *Ars Orientalis* 42 (2012): 67–78.

Kay, H. C., ed. *Yaman: Its Early Medieval History*. Mansfield Center, CT: Martino, 2005.

Kerr, Rose. *Song Dynasty Ceramics*. London: Victoria and Albert Museum, 2004.

Kessler, Adam T. *Song Blue and White Porcelain on the Silk Road*. Leiden: Brill, 2012.

King, Geoffrey, and Christina Tonghini. *A Survey of the Islamic Sites near Aden and in the Abyan District of Yemen*. London: School of Oriental and African Studies, 1996.

Krahl, Regina. "Chinese Ceramics in the Late Tang Dynasty." In *Shipwrecked: Tang Treasures and Monsoon Winds*, edited by Regina Krahl, John Guy, Julian Raby and J. Keith Wilson, 45–74. Washington, DC: Smithsonian Institution, 2010.

——. "White Wares of Northern China." In *Shipwrecked: Tang Treasures and Monsoon Winds*, edited by Regina Krahl, John Guy, Julian Raby and J. Keith Wilson, 200–207. Washington, DC: Smithsonian Institution, 2010.

Krahl, Regina, John Guy, Julian Raby and J. Keith Wilson, eds. *Shipwrecked: Tang Treasures and Monsoon Winds*. Washington, DC: Smithsonian Institution, 2010.

Lambourn, Elizabeth. *Abraham's Luggage: A Social Life of Things in the Medieval Indian Ocean World*. Cambridge: Cambridge University Press. Forthcoming.

Lane, Arthur. *Early Islamic Pottery: Mesopotamia, Egypt and Persia*. London: Faber and Faber, 1947.

——. "Sung Wares and the Saljuq Pottery of Persia." *Transactions of the Oriental Ceramic Society* 22 (1946–47): 19–30.

Lane, Arthur, and R. B. Serjeant. "Pottery and Glass Fragments from the Aden Littoral, with Historical Notes." *Journal of the Royal Asiatic Society of Great Britain and Ireland* 2 (1948): 108–33.

Li, De-Jin. "Chinese Export Porcelain in the VIII–XIV Centuries." In *UNESCO Maritime Route of Silk Roads – Nara Symposium '91 – Report*, 102–4. Nara: Nara International Foundation, 1993.

Margariti, Roxani E. *Aden and the Indian Ocean Trade: 150 Years in the Life of a Medieval Arabian Port*. Chapel Hill: University of North Carolina Press, 2007.

Margulies, Mordecai. *Hilkhot Ereṣ Yisrael min ha-Geniza*. (Laws of the Land of Israel from the Geniza). Mosad ha-Rav Quq, 1973.

Mason, R. B. "Medieval Egyptian Lustre-painted and Associated Wares: Typology in a Multidisciplinary Study." *Journal of the American Research Center in Egypt* 34 (1997): 201–42.

——. *Shine Like the Sun: Lustre-Painted and Associated Pottery from the Medieval Middle East*. Costa Mesa, CA: Mazda, 2004.

Miksic, John N., ed. *Southeast Asian Ceramics: New Light on Old Pottery*. Singapore: Southeast Asian Ceramic Society, 2009.

Mikami, T. "China and Egypt: Fustat." *Transactions of the Oriental Ceramic Society* 45 (1980–81): 67–87.

Milwright, Marcus. "Modest Luxuries: Decorated Lead-Glazed Pottery in the South of Bilad al-Sham (Thirteenth and Fourteenth Centuries)." *Muqarnas* 20 (2003): 85–111.

——. "Pottery in the Written Sources of the Ayyubid-Mamluk Period (*c.* 567–923/1171–1517)." *Bulletin of the School of Oriental and African Studies* 62 (1999): 504–18.

Needham, Joseph, Rose Kerr, and Nigel Wood. *Science and Civilization in China*. Vol. 5, *Chemistry and Chemical Technology*; Part 12, *Ceramic Technology*. Cambridge: Cambridge University Press, 2004.

Neusner, J. "Purity and Impurity in Judaism." In *The Encyclopaedia of Judaism*, edited by Jacob Neusner, Alan J. Avery-Peck, and William Scott Green, 3:1109–23. Leiden: Brill, 2000.

Newman, Hillel I. *Ha-Maʿasim li-vene Ereṣ Yisrael*. ("Acts" of the People of the Land of Israel). Jerusalem: Yad Ben-Ṣevi, 2011.

Peng, Shifan ed. *Song yuan jinian qingbai ci*. (Dated Qingbai Wares of the Song and Yuan Dynasties). Hong Kong: Cheng Leng Foundation, 1998.

Pierson, Stacey. "Industrial Ceramics in China: Ceramic Production at Jingdezhen from the 10th to the 16th Century." In *Lost at Sea: The Strange Route of the Lena Shoal Junk*, edited by Franck Goddio and Gabriel Casal, 59–69. Periplus: London, 2002.

———, ed. *Qingbai Ware: Chinese Porcelain of the Song and Yuan Dynasties*. London: Percival David Foundation, 2002.

———, ed. *Transfer: The Influence of China on World Ceramics*. London: Percival David Foundation, 2009.

Pirazzoli-t'Serstevens, Michèle. "Une denrée recherchée: la céramique chinoise importée dans le golfe arabo-persique, IXᵉ–XIVᵉ siècles." *Mirabilia Asiatica* 12 (2005): 69–88.

Rackman, Emmanuel, Michael Broyde, and Amy Lynne Fishkin. "Halakhah, Law in Judaism," *Encyclopaedia of Judaism* (Brill Online, 2012). [accessed August 17, 2012].

Rougeulle, Axelle. "Les céramiques à glaçure." In *Sharma: un entrepôt de commerce médiéval sur la côte du Hadramawt (Yémen, ca. 980–1180)*, edited by Axelle Rougeulle, 237–75. Oxford: Archaeopress, 2015.

——. "Golfe persique et Mer Rouge: notes sur les routes de la céramique aux X–XII siècles." *Taoci* 4 (2005): 41–51.

——. "Les importations de céramiques chinoises dans le golfe arabo-persique (VIIIe–IXe siècles)." *Archéologie Islamique* (1991): 5–46.

Schottenhammer, Angela. *The Emporium of the World: Maritime Quanzhou, 1000–1400*. Leiden: Brill, 2001.

Teo, Catherine. "Qingbai Ware for Export." In *Qingbai Ware: Chinese Porcelain of the Song and Yuan Dynasties*, edited by Stacey Pierson, 244–51. London: Percival David Foundation, 2002.

Twersky, Isadore. *Introduction to the Code of Maimonides (Mishneh Torah)*. New Haven: Yale University Press, 1980.

Walter, Moshe. "Can Porcelain be *Kashered*?" *Journal of Halacha and Contemporary Society* 52 (2006): 110–23.

Watson, Oliver. "Chinese-Iranian Relations XI. Mutual Influence of Chinese and Persian Ceramics," Encyclopedia Iranica 5 (1991) <http://www.iranicaonline.org/articles/chinese-iranian-xi [accessed April 9, 2015].

——. "Fritware: Fatimid Egypt or Seljuq Iran?" In *L'Egypte Fatimide son art et son histoire*, edited by M. Barrucand, 299–307. Paris: Presses de l'Université de Paris-Sorbonne, 1999.

Whitcomb, Donald. "A Fatimid Residence at Aqaba, Jordan." *Annual of the Department of Antiquities of Jordan* 32 (1988): 207–24.

Whitehouse, David. "Chinese Porcelain in Medieval Europe." *Medieval Archaeology* 16 (1973): 78–63.

Yuba, Tadanori. "Chinese Ceramics Found at al-Fustat, Cairo, 9th to 16th Century." *Taoci* 4 (2005), 87–95.

——. "Chinese Porcelain from Fustat based on Research from 1998–2001." *Transactions of The Oriental Ceramic Society* 76 (2011–12): 1–18.

Zhao, Bing. "La céramique chinoise à Sharma: pour un essai d'étude d'approche typo-chronologique et spatiale." In *Sharma: un entrepôt de commerce médiéval sur la côte du Hadramawt (Yémen, ca. 980–1180)*, edited by Axelle Rougeulle, 277–321. Oxford: Archaeopress, 2015.

——. "Global Trade and Swahili Cosmopolitan Material Culture: Chinese-style Ceramic Shards from Sanje ya Kati and Songo Mnara (Kilwa, Tanzania)." *Journal of World History* 23 (2012): 41–85.

——. "L'importation de la céramique chinoise à Sharma (Hadramaout) au Yémen." In *Ports et commerce en Islam médiéval, entre Asie, Afrique et Arabie*, special issue, *Annales Islamologiques* 38 (2004): 255–84.

Acknowledgments

Elizabeth Lambourn thanks the Leverhulme Trust for funding her Major Research Fellowship during 2011–13; the present article is a direct outcome of research conducted during that period as part of her project on *West Asia in the Indian Ocean, 500–1500 CE*. She is also extremely grateful to Jessica Harrison-Hall (Curator of Chinese Ceramics and the Sir Percival David Collection at the British Museum) for including her in the British Museum Study Day on *Chinese* Qingbai *Ceramics and Their Contexts* (May 15, 2015). The handling session was invaluable and discussions with the specialists in Chinese ceramics present at this event have been highly influential on the writing of the final draft of this article. Special thanks go to Rosemary E. Scott (International Academic Director of Asian Art at Christie's), who generously shared a large number of references from Chinese and other specialist sources; her contributions are acknowledged in the footnotes. Thanks, too, to Li Baoping (Senior International Researcher at Sotheby's) for his engagement with the ideas presented here and for sharing some of his recent publications and suggesting additional bibliographic material. In Paris, Zhao Bing of the Collège de France has been more than generous in reading and commenting on the final draft as well as sharing the final proofs of her article "La céramique chinoise à Sharma." Axelle Rougeulle also shared her piece on "Les céramiques à glaçure" and kindly answered my queries about the rather late development of glazed ceramic production in the Yemen. Melanie Gibson generously commented on an early draft of this article, shared some of the less accessible articles found in the bibliography, and generally helped demystify the scholarship on the Middle East's response to Chinese ceramics.

Phil Lieberman would also like to thank the Leverhulme Trust, as well as Rabbi Joshua Barton of Nashville, Tennessee, for his assistance in translating difficult passages in the rabbinic literature related to the subject matter of this article.

Both authors wish to thank the anonymous peer reviewers for their generous and perceptive comments. Any errors are, of course, the authors' own.

Phillip Ackerman-Lieberman (phil.lieberman@vanderbilt.edu) is Associate Professor of Jewish Studies and Law, Associate Professor of Religious Studies, and Affiliated Associate Professor of Islamic Studies and History, at Vanderbilt University in Nashville, Tennessee. He is a social, economic, and legal historian of the medieval Islamic world. His current project examines Jewish urbanization under the early Abbasids and subsequent Jewish migration to the emerging communities of the Islamic Mediterranean. His 2014 book, *The Business of Identity* (Stanford University Press) was a finalist for the National Jewish Book Award. He also served as one of the editors of *The Encyclopedia of Jews in the Islamic World* (Brill, 2010).

Elizabeth Lambourn (elambourn@dmu.ac.uk) is Reader in South Asian and Indian Ocean Studies at De Montfort University in the United Kingdom, where she works on diverse aspects of mobility in the precolonial Indian Ocean world. Coming to history from a background in the study of material culture, her research is particularly focused on Indian Ocean materialities and the identification and study of new material archives. Her monograph, *Abraham's Luggage: A Social Life of Things in the Medieval Indian Ocean World*, will be published with Cambridge University Press in 2017.

Abstract This article focuses on a set of legal questions about *ṣīnī* vessels (literally, "Chinese" vessels) sent from the Jewish community in Aden to Fustat (Old Cairo) in the mid-1130s CE and now preserved among the Cairo Geniza holdings in Cambridge University Library. This is the earliest dated and localized query about the status of *ṣīnī* vessels with respect to the Jewish law of vessels used for food consumption. Our analysis of these queries suggests that their phrasing and timing can be linked to the contemporaneous appearance in the Yemen of a new type of Chinese ceramic ware, *qingbai*, which confounded and destabilized the material taxonomies underpinning rabbinic Judaism. Marshalling evidence from contemporary Jewish legal compendia and other writings produced in this milieu, our discussion substantially advances interpretive angles first suggested by S. D. Goitein and Mordechai A. Friedman to examine the efforts of Adeni Jews to place this Chinese ceramic fabric among already legislated substances, notably the "neighboring" substances of glass and earthenware, in order to derive clear rules for the proper use and purification of vessels manufactured from it.

Keywords Aden, Yemen, China, Indian Ocean, 'India Book', Cairo Geniza, Judaism, medieval, Middle Ages, ceramic, porcelain, *qingbai*, glass, earthenware, halakha, purity, purification, pollution, kosher, koshering, menstruation, material taxonomies, material culture.

INDEX